PART-1
SEPTEMBER

# AZU MANGA DAIOH

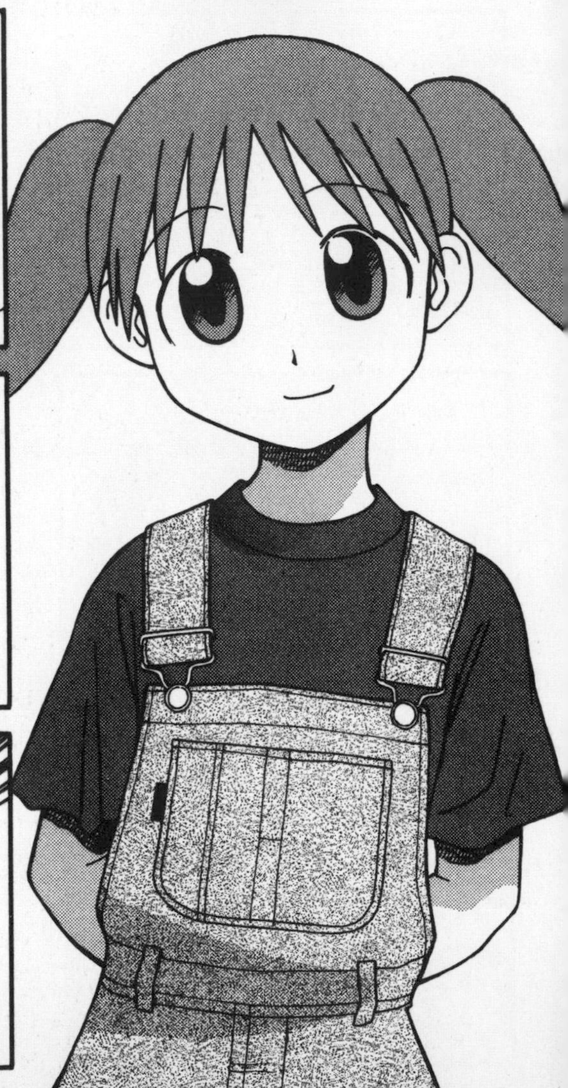

HEY, HEY, YO!

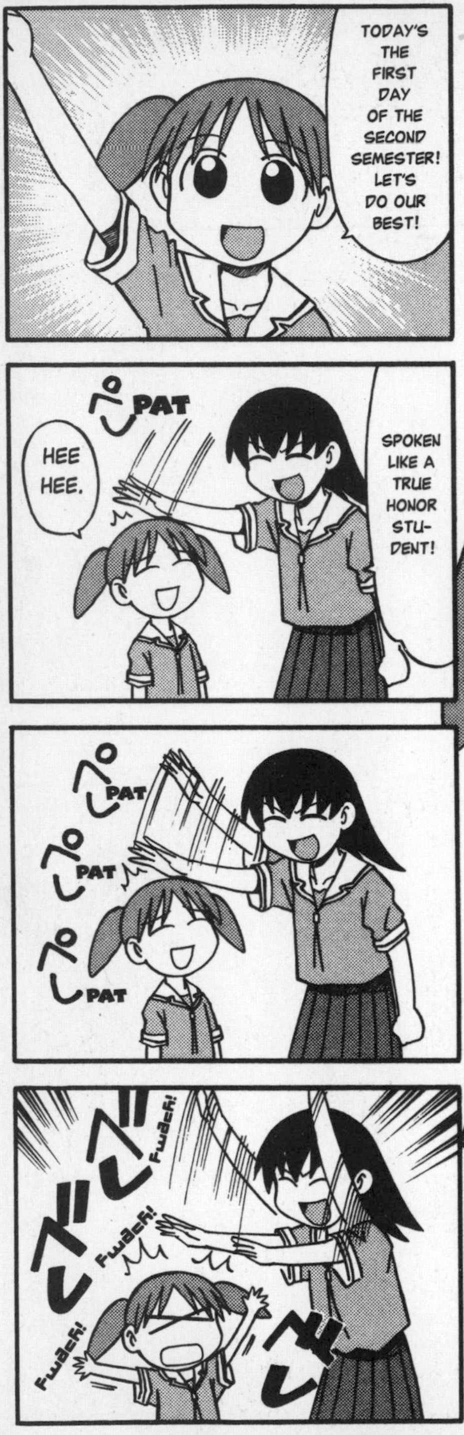
TODAY'S THE FIRST DAY OF THE SECOND SEMESTER! LET'S DO OUR BEST!
SPOKEN LIKE A TRUE HONOR STU- DENT!
PAT
HEE HEE.
PAT
PAT
PAT
FWACK!
FWACK!
FWACK!
FWACK!

S

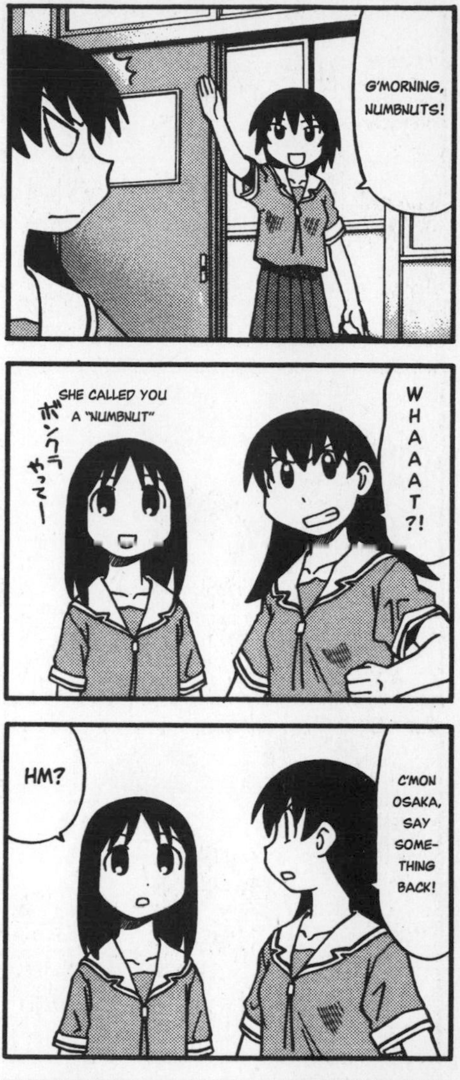
G'MORNING, NUMBNUTS!
WHAAAT?!
SHE CALLED YOU A "NUMBNUT"
C'MON OSAKA, SAY SOMETHING BACK!
HM?
SHE SAID "NUMBNUTS." PLURAL!
HEY, WHAT?!

AUTUMN

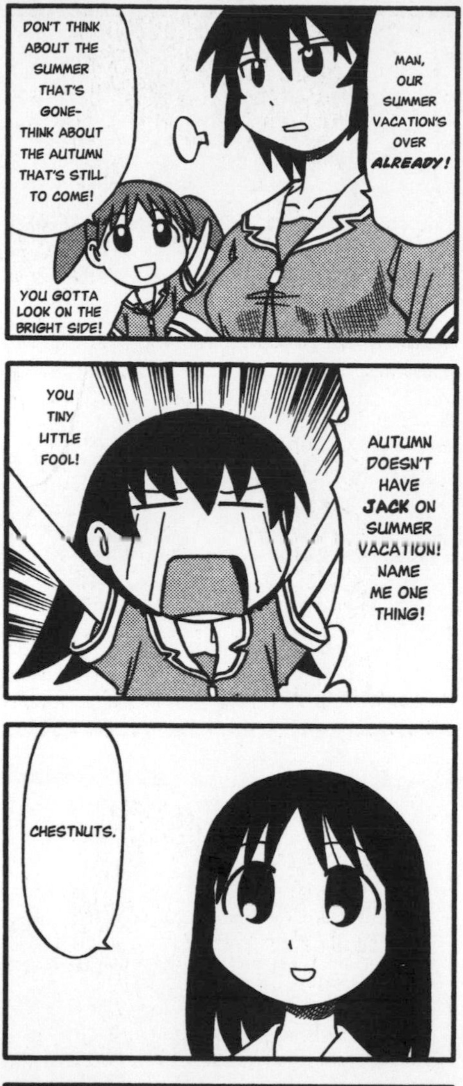
MAN, OUR SUMMER VACATION'S OVER ALREADY!
DON'T THINK ABOUT THE SUMMER THAT'S GONE- THINK ABOUT THE AUTUMN THAT'S STILL TO COME!
YOU GOTTA LOOK ON THE BRIGHT SIDE!
AUTUMN DOESN'T HAVE JACK ON SUMMER VACATION! NAME ME ONE THING!
YOU TINY LITTLE FOOL!
CHESTNUTS.
CHESTNUTS COME OUT IN AUTUMN.
YEAH. I CAN TASTE 'EM NOW...

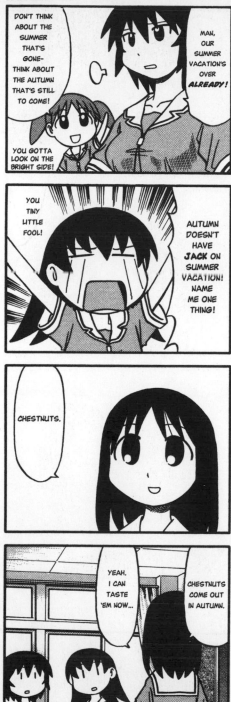

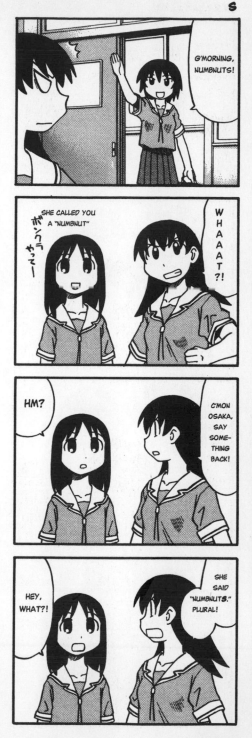

CHESTNUTS

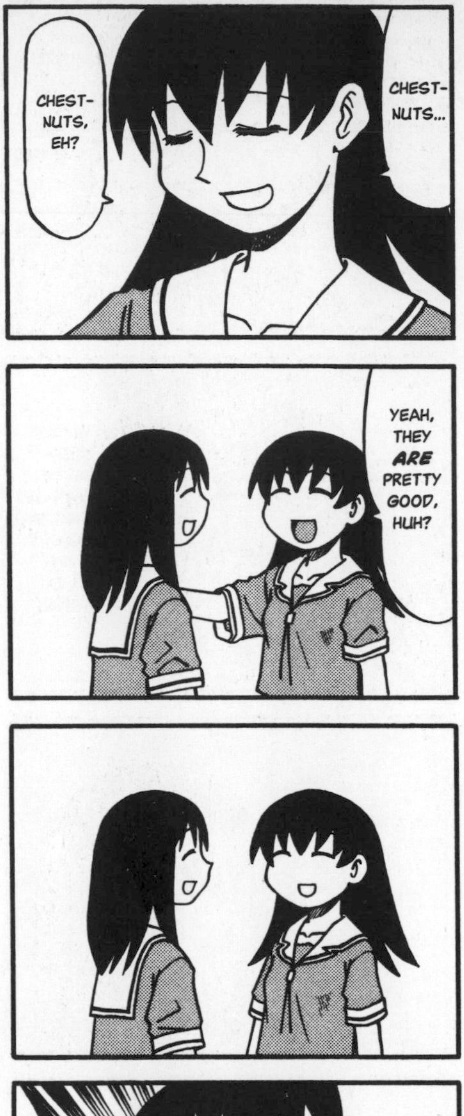

CHEST-NUTS...
CHEST-NUTS, EH?
YEAH, THEY *ARE* PRETTY GOOD, HUH?
COME BACK, SUMMER VACATION! ALL IS FORGIVEN!
?


ULTRA-OSAKA

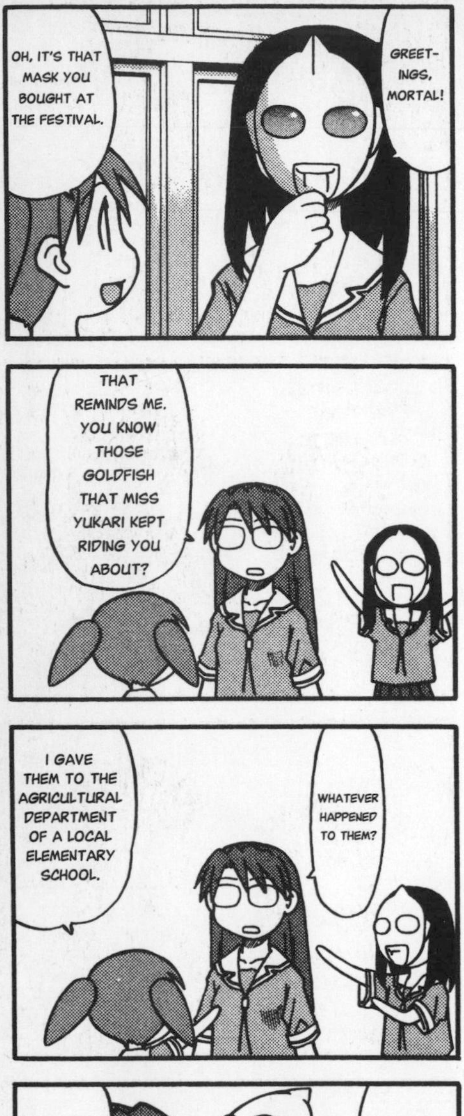

GREET-INGS, MORTAL!
OH, IT'S THAT MASK YOU BOUGHT AT THE FESTIVAL.
THAT REMINDS ME. YOU KNOW THOSE GOLDFISH THAT MISS YUKARI KEPT RIDING YOU ABOUT?
WHATEVER HAPPENED TO THEM?
I GAVE THEM TO THE AGRICULTURAL DEPARTMENT OF A LOCAL ELEMENTARY SCHOOL.
TA-DAA! IT WAS ME ALL ALONG!
UM, I'M NOT EXACTLY SURPRISED...

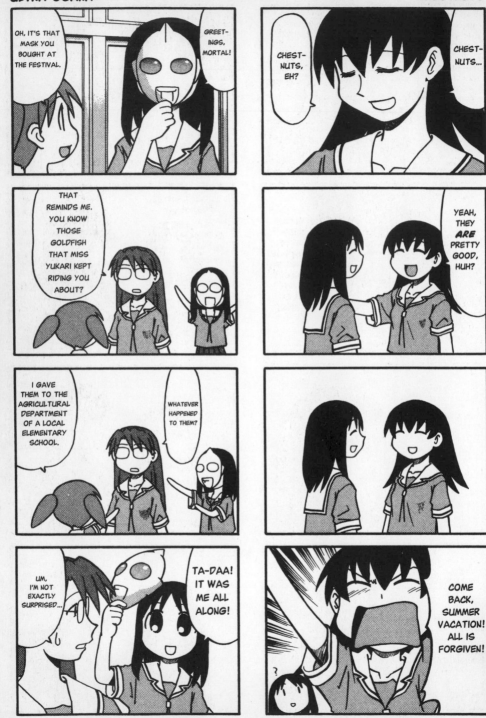

H IS FOR HONESTY

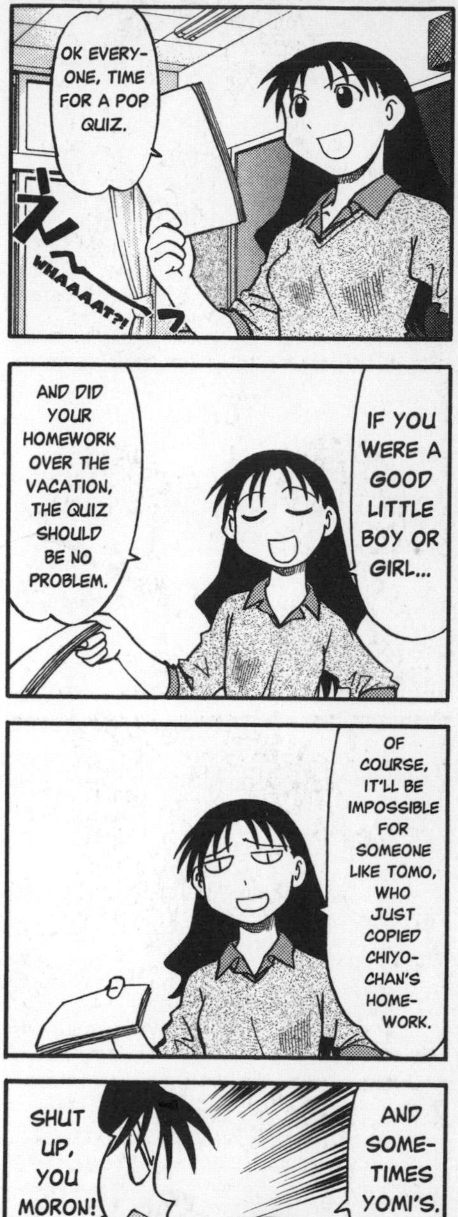
OK EVERY-ONE, TIME FOR A POP QUIZ.
WHAAAAAT?!
IF YOU WERE A GOOD LITTLE BOY OR GIRL...
AND DID YOUR HOMEWORK OVER THE VACATION, THE QUIZ SHOULD BE NO PROBLEM.
OF COURSE, IT'LL BE IMPOSSIBLE FOR SOMEONE LIKE TOMO, WHO JUST COPIED CHIYO-CHAN'S HOME-WORK.
AND SOME-TIMES YOMI'S.
SHUT UP, YOU MORON!

SUMMER VACATION IS...

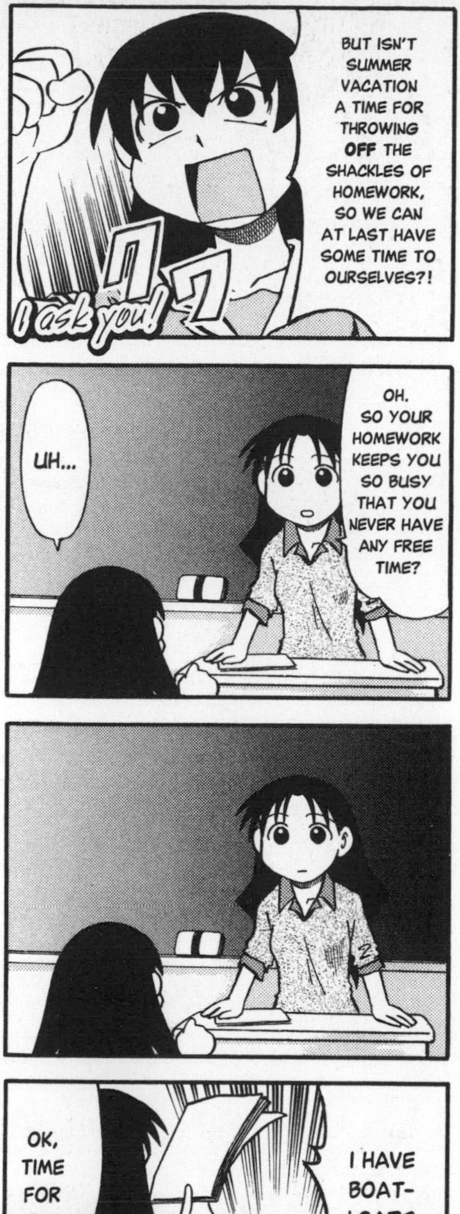
BUT ISN'T SUMMER VACATION A TIME FOR THROWING **OFF** THE SHACKLES OF HOMEWORK, SO WE CAN AT LAST HAVE SOME TIME TO OURSELVES?!
I ask you!
OH. SO YOUR HOMEWORK KEEPS YOU SO BUSY THAT YOU NEVER HAVE ANY FREE TIME?
UH...
I HAVE BOAT-LOADS OF TIME!
OK, TIME FOR THE TEST!

TERRIBLE

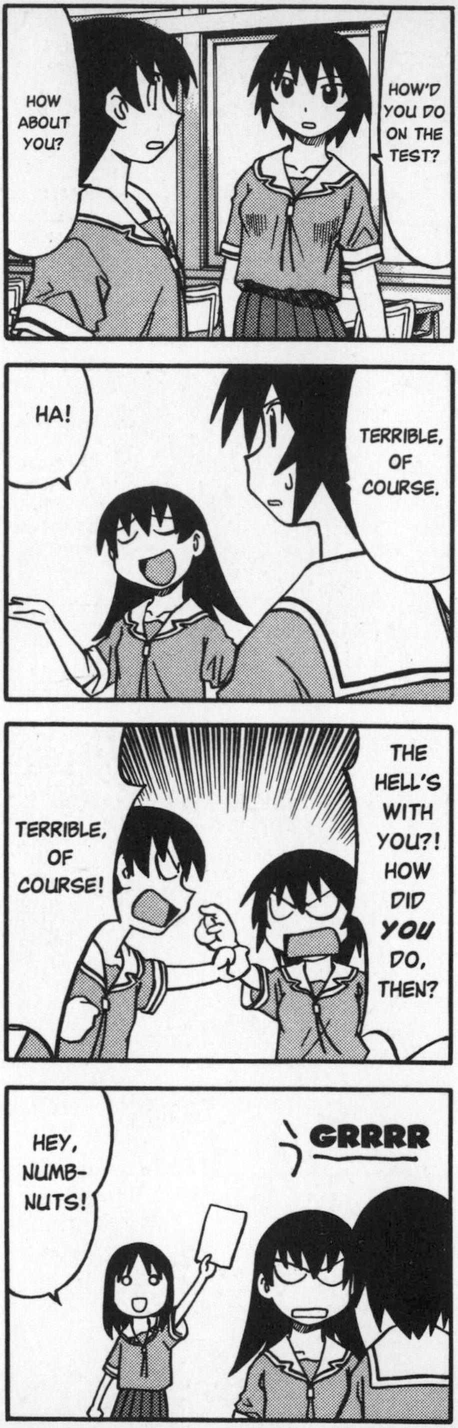
HOW'D YOU DO ON THE TEST?
HOW ABOUT YOU?
TERRIBLE, OF COURSE.
HA!
THE HELL'S WITH YOU?! HOW DID YOU DO, THEN?
TERRIBLE, OF COURSE!
GRRRR
HEY, NUMB-NUTS!

ROTTEN

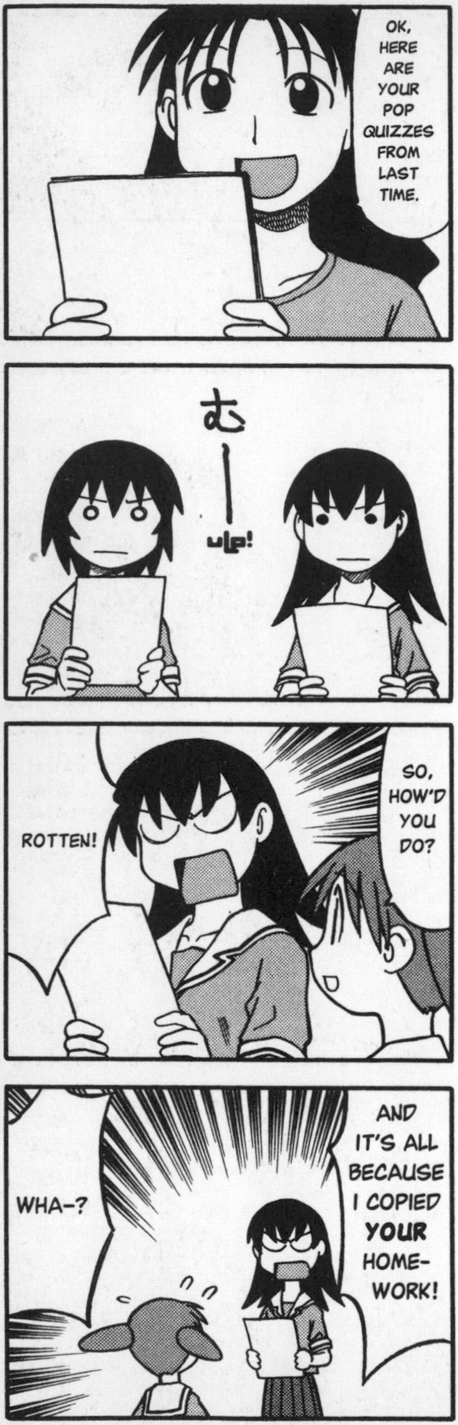
OK, HERE ARE YOUR POP QUIZZES FROM LAST TIME.
むー
ulp!
SO, HOW'D YOU DO?
ROTTEN!
AND IT'S ALL BECAUSE I COPIED YOUR HOMEWORK!
WHA-?

## THE ORGANIZATION

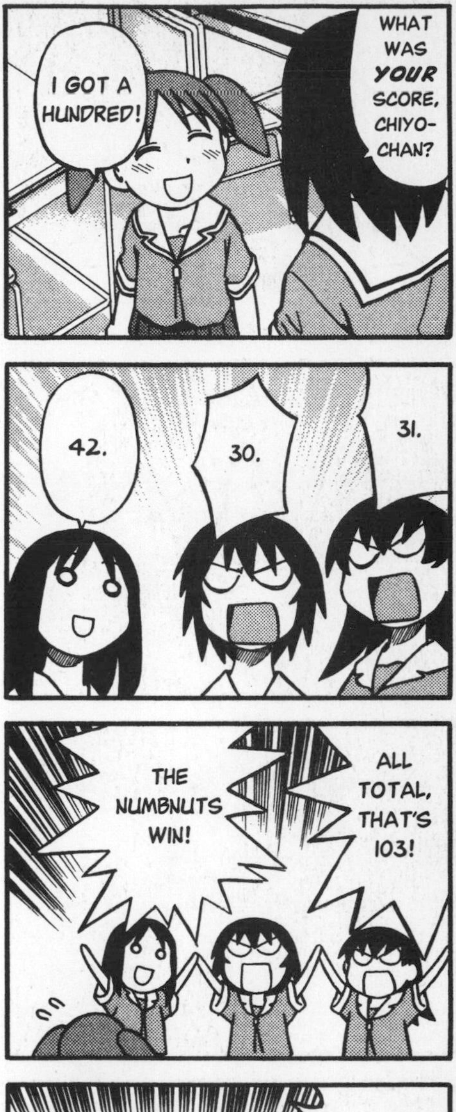
WHAT WAS *YOUR* SCORE, CHIYO-CHAN?
I GOT A HUNDRED!
31.
30.
42.
ALL TOTAL, THAT'S 103!
THE NUMBNUTS WIN!
DON'T CALL US NUMB-NUTS, OSAKA!

## IF YOU CAN'T TOUCH 'EM...

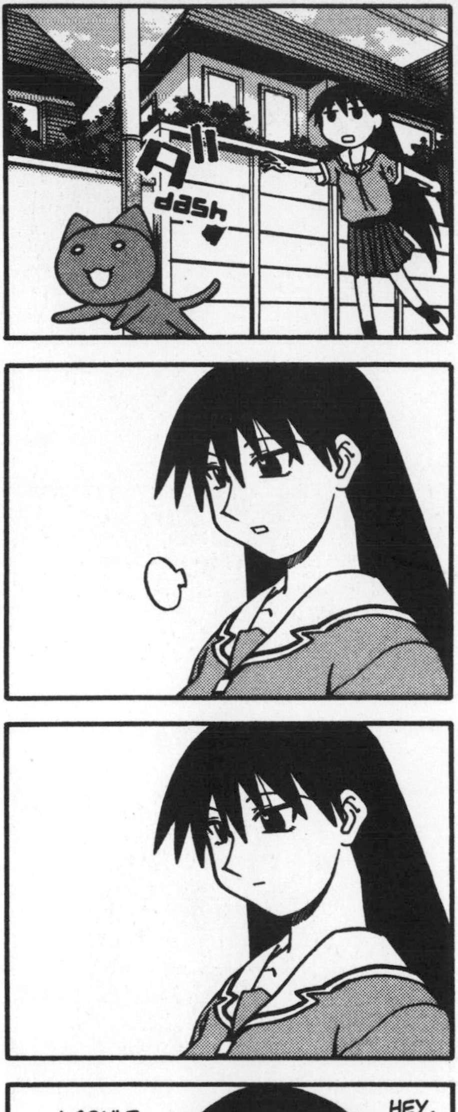
dash
HEY, YEAH!
I COULD TAKE A PICTURE!

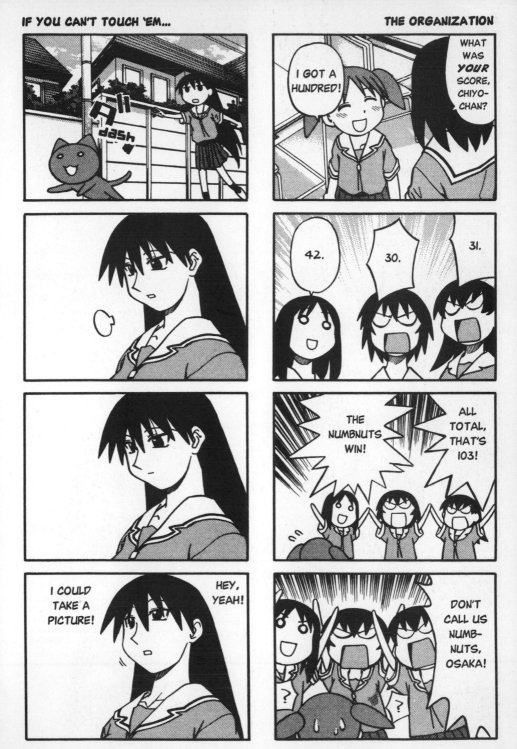

**CAT PICS**

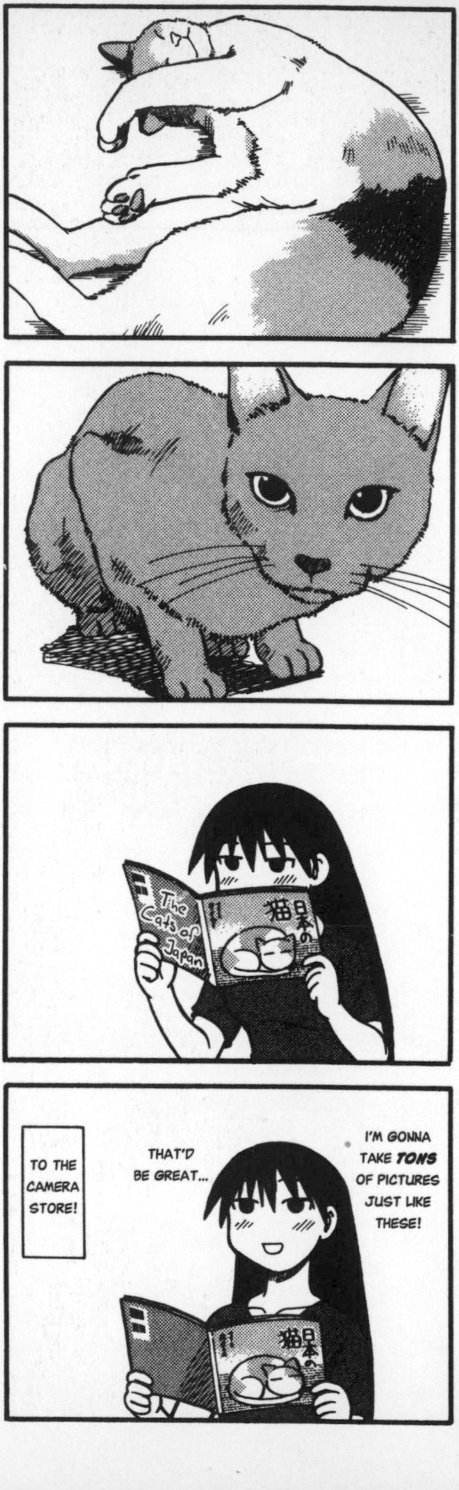
The Cats of Japan
日本の猫
I'M GONNA TAKE TONS OF PICTURES JUST LIKE THESE!
THAT'D BE GREAT...
TO THE CAMERA STORE!

**AND THE WINNER IS...**

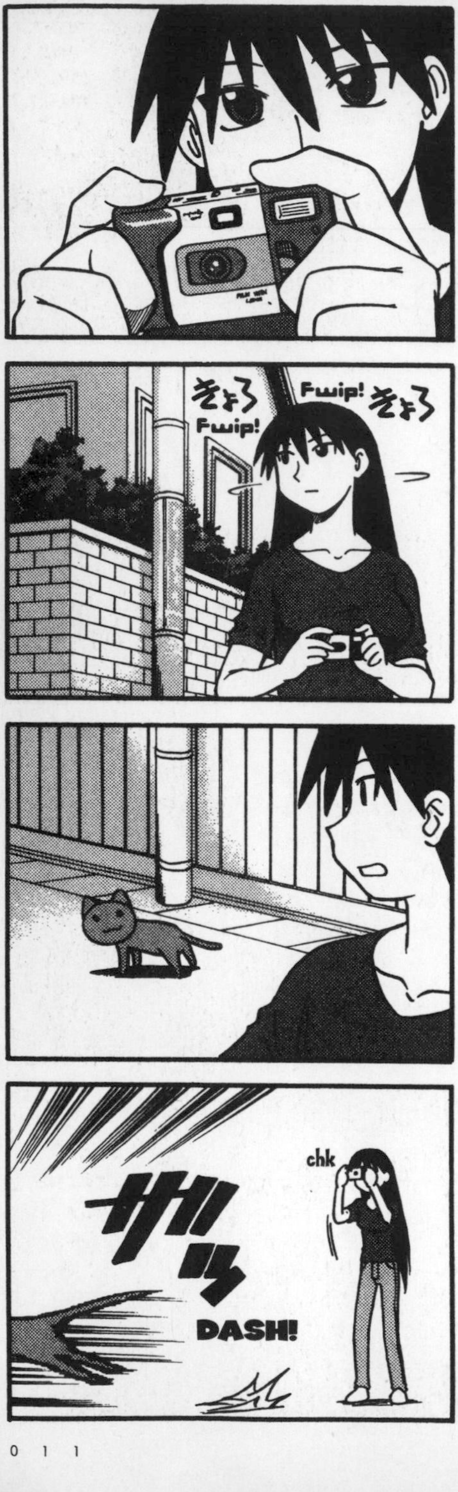
Fwip! きょろ
きょろ Fwip!
chk
DASH!

THE RACE TO PHOTOGRAPH THE BITING CAT

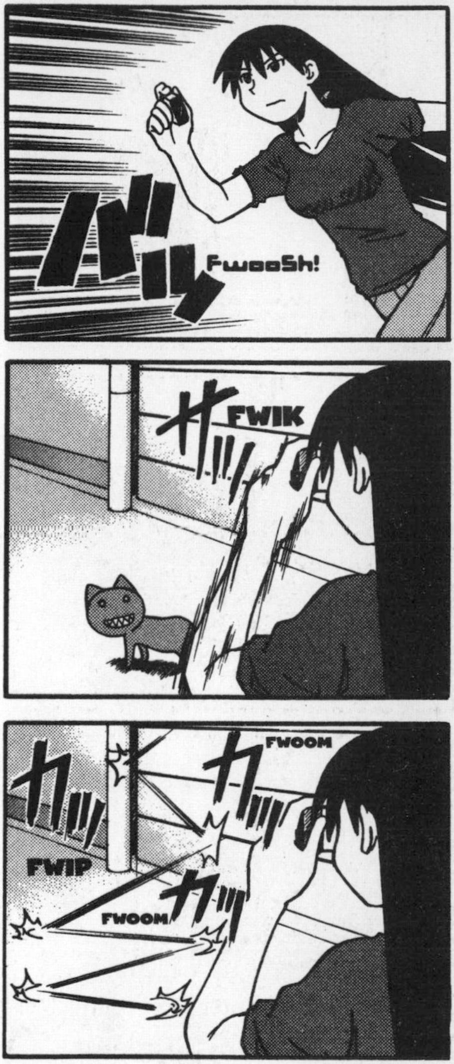
FwooSh!
FWIK
FWOOM
FWIP
FWOOM

AND THE WINNER IS...

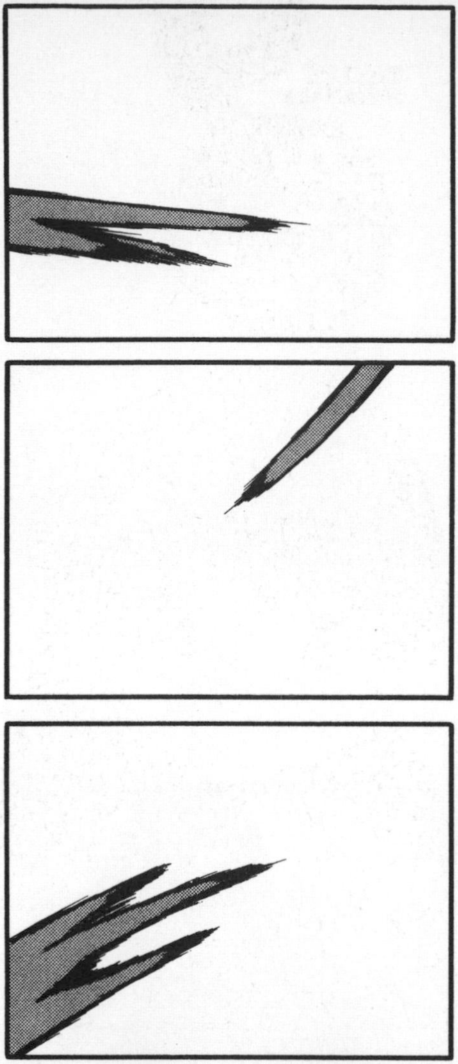
YOU'LL BE TAKING THESE PRINTS, THEN?
...YES.

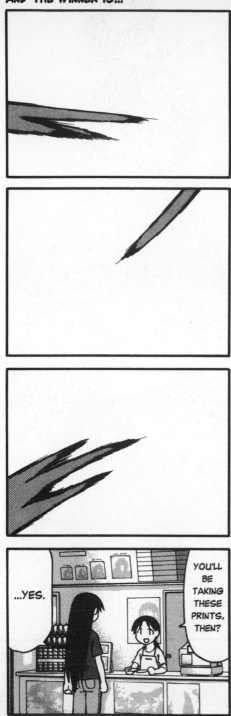

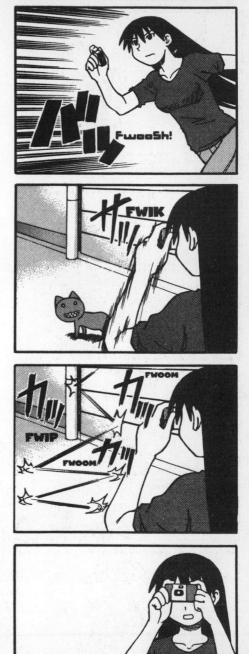

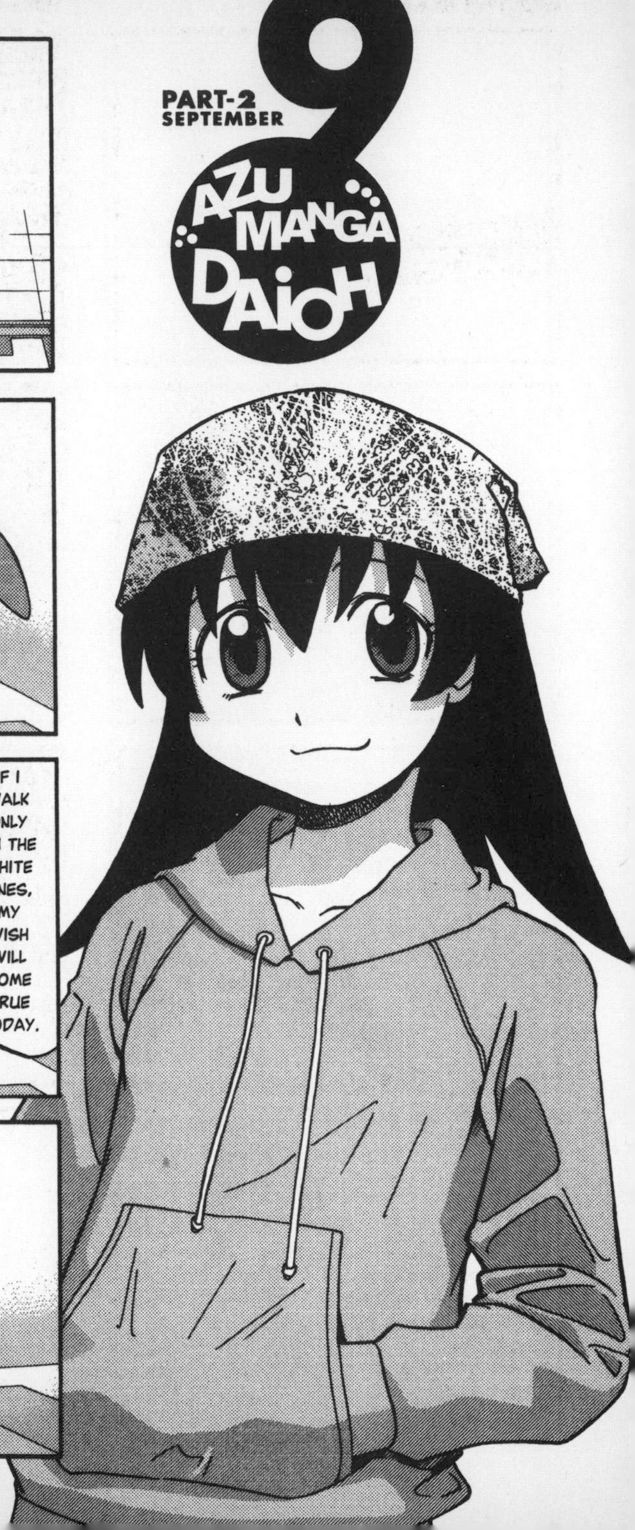
PART-2
SEPTEMBER
AZU MANGA DAIOH

LET'S GO, CHIYO-CHAN!

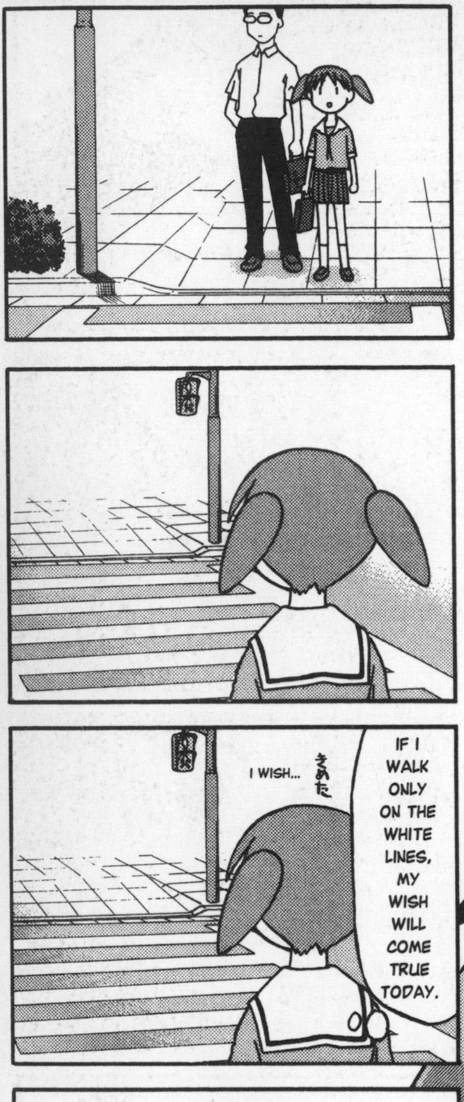
IF I WALK ONLY ON THE WHITE LINES, MY WISH WILL COME TRUE TODAY.
きめた
I WISH...

AND TODAY'S FORTUNE IS...

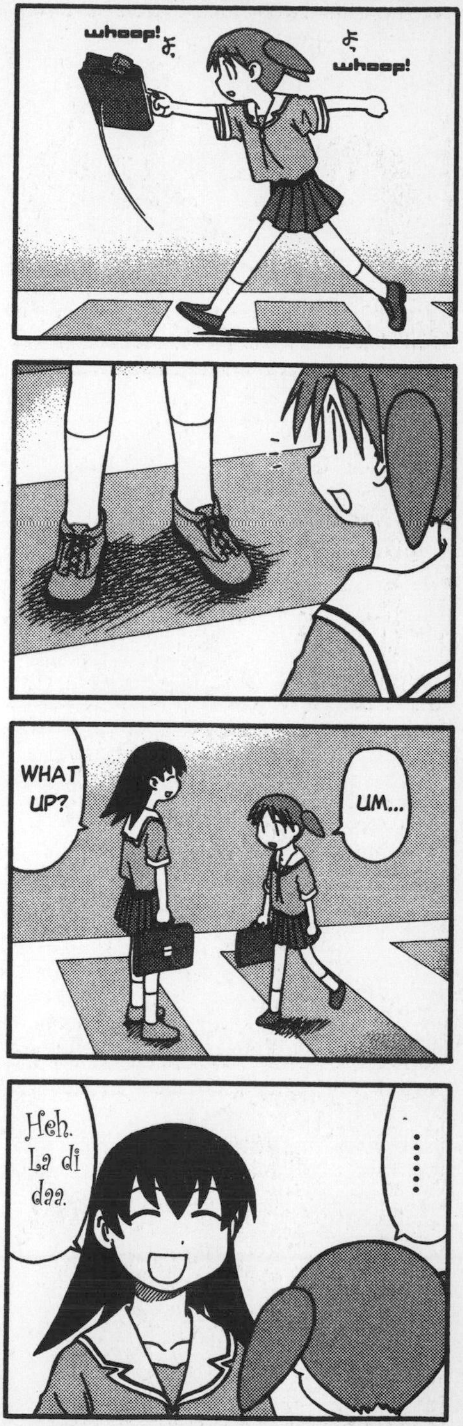
whoop! よ、
よ、 whoop!
!
WHAT UP?
UM...
......
Heh. La di daa.

GUILTY!

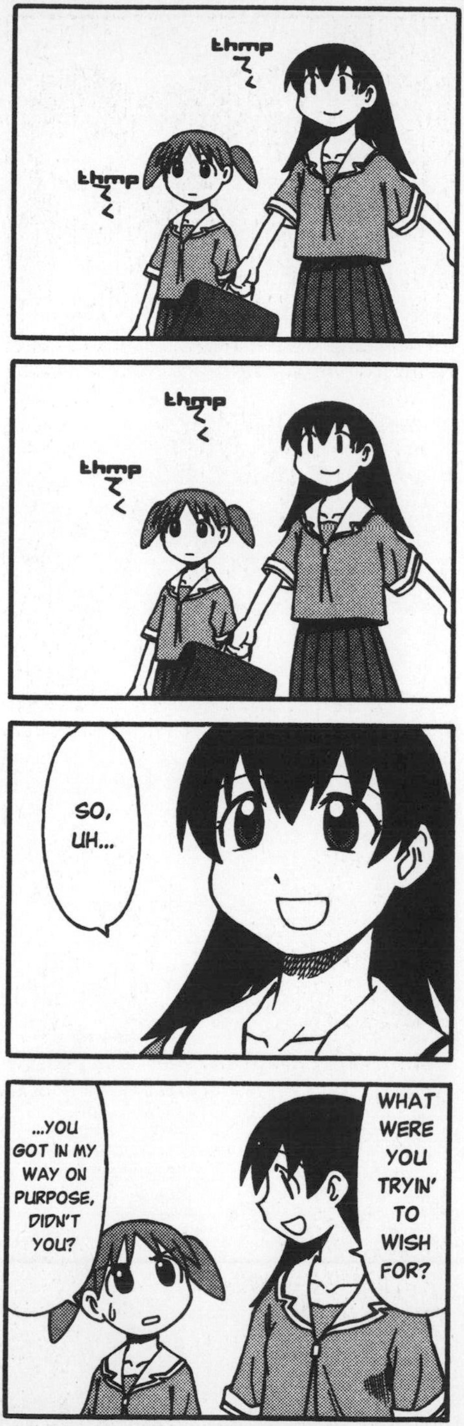
thmp
thmp
thmp
thmp
SO, UH...
WHAT WERE YOU TRYIN' TO WISH FOR?
...YOU GOT IN MY WAY ON PURPOSE, DIDN'T YOU?

## EARLY WARNING SYSTEM

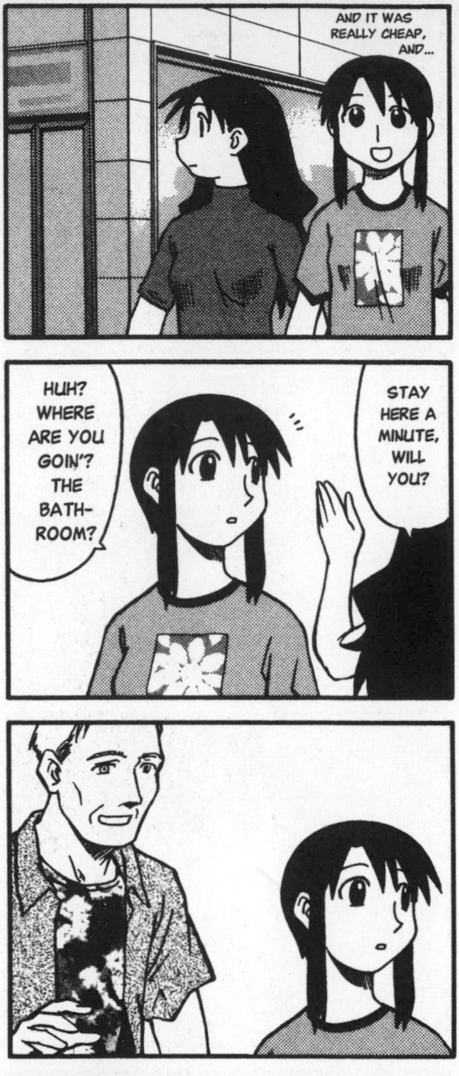
AND IT WAS REALLY CHEAP, AND...
STAY HERE A MINUTE, WILL YOU?
HUH? WHERE ARE YOU GOIN'? THE BATH-ROOM?
excuse me
WAUGH!

## A COMPLICATED QUESTION

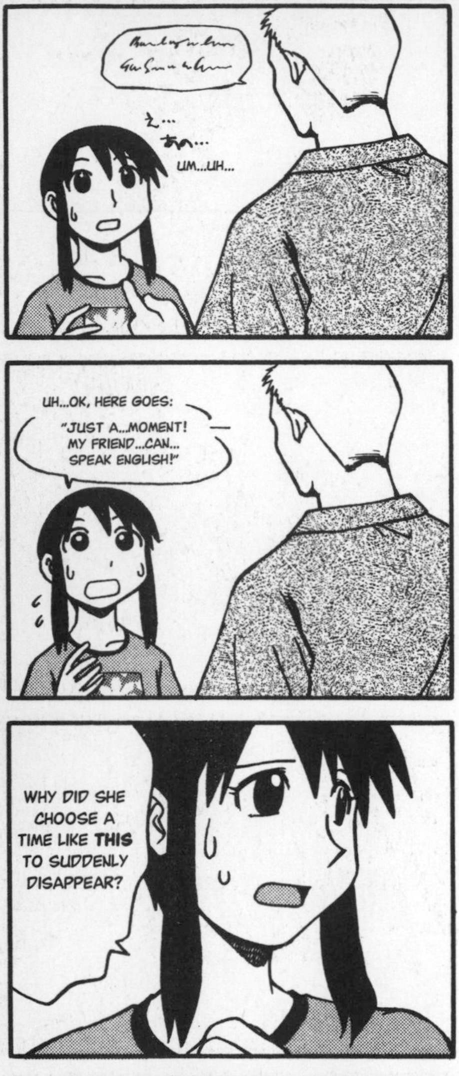
え…
あの…
UM...UH...
UH...OK, HERE GOES:
"JUST A...MOMENT! MY FRIEND...CAN... SPEAK ENGLISH!"
WHY DID SHE CHOOSE A TIME LIKE **THIS** TO SUDDENLY DISAPPEAR?

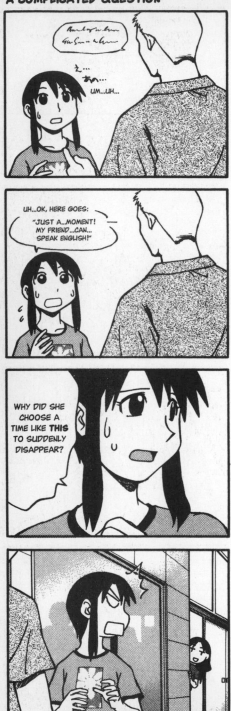

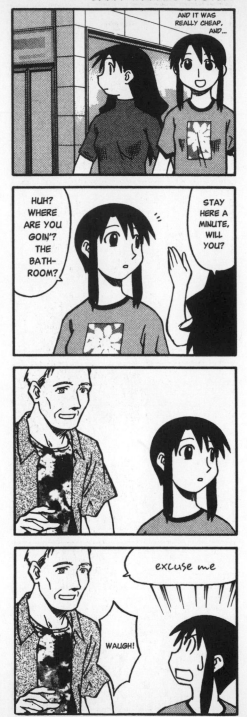

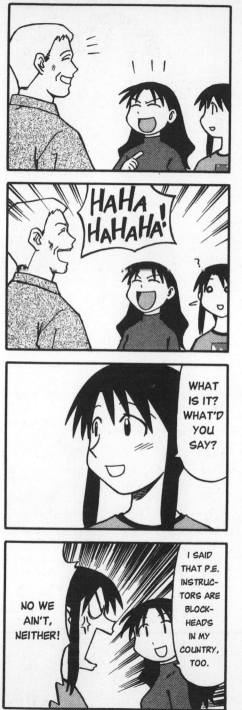

I AM A TEACHER, YOU KNOW

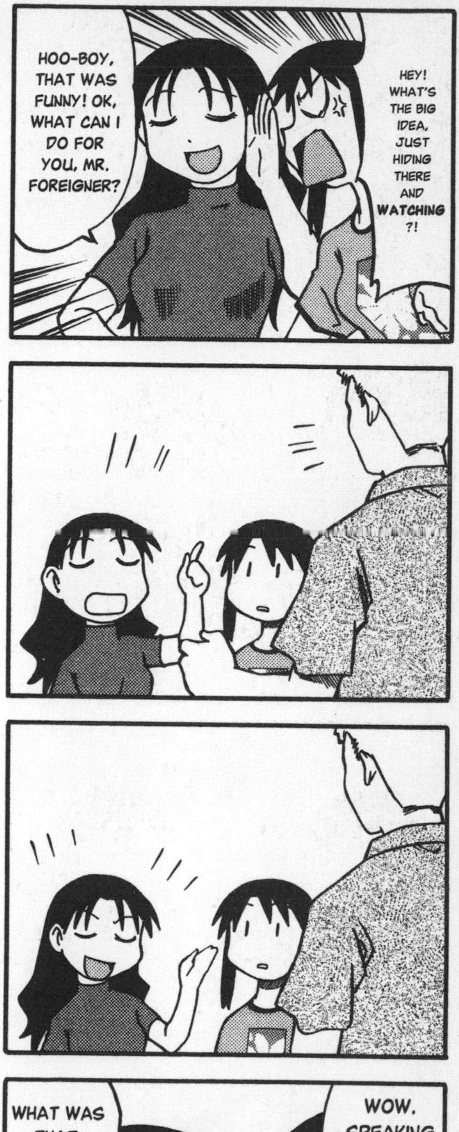
HEY! WHAT'S THE BIG IDEA, JUST HIDING THERE AND **WATCHING**?!
HOO-BOY, THAT WAS FUNNY! OK, WHAT CAN I DO FOR YOU, MR. FOREIGNER?
WOW. SPEAKING ENGLISH MAKES YOU ACTUALLY ***NOT*** LOOK LIKE AN IDIOT.
WHAT WAS THAT, MISS P.E. TEACHER?!

THAT'S NOT SO BAD

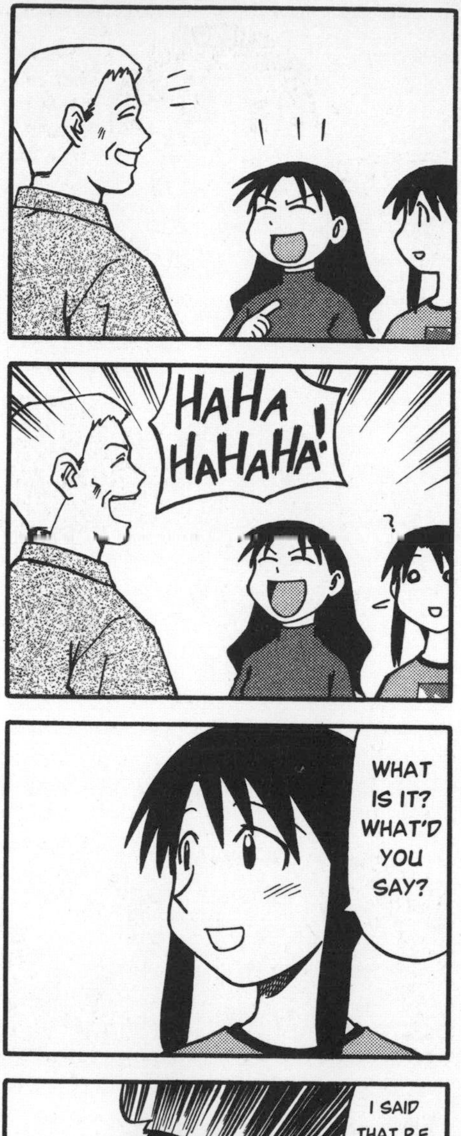
HAHA HAHAHA!
WHAT IS IT? WHAT'D YOU SAY?
I SAID THAT P.E. INSTRUC-TORS ARE BLOCK-HEADS IN MY COUNTRY, TOO.
NO WE AIN'T, NEITHER!

AN UNFAMILIAR MENU

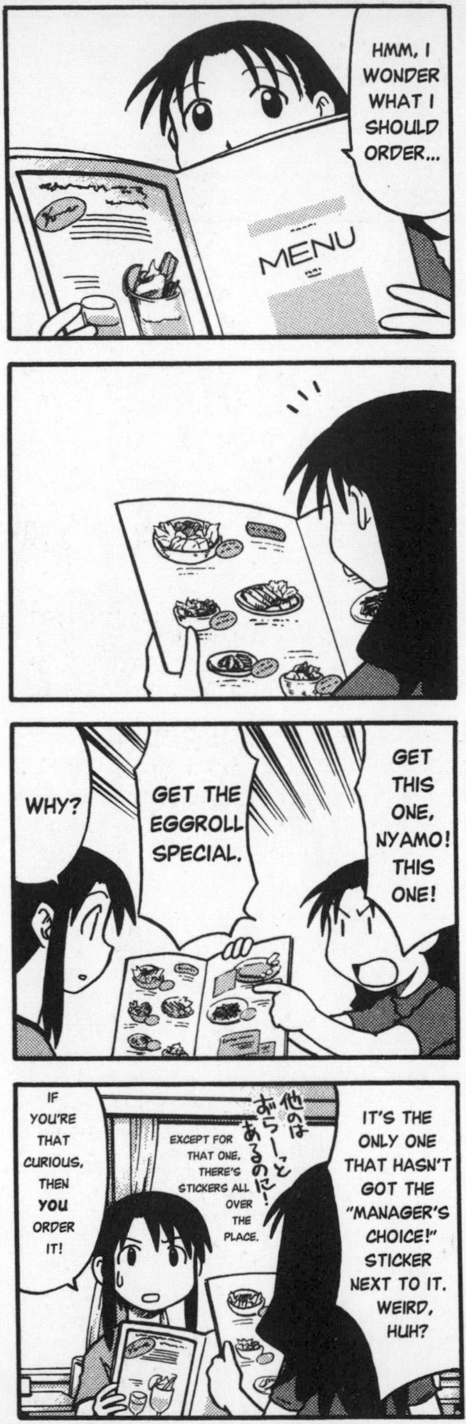
HMM, I WONDER WHAT I SHOULD ORDER...
MENU
GET THIS ONE, NYAMO! THIS ONE!
GET THE EGGROLL SPECIAL.
WHY?
IT'S THE ONLY ONE THAT HASN'T GOT THE "MANAGER'S CHOICE!" STICKER NEXT TO IT. WEIRD, HUH?
他のはずらーっとあるのに！
EXCEPT FOR THAT ONE, THERE'S STICKERS ALL OVER THE PLACE.
IF YOU'RE THAT CURIOUS, THEN YOU ORDER IT!

THE BILL

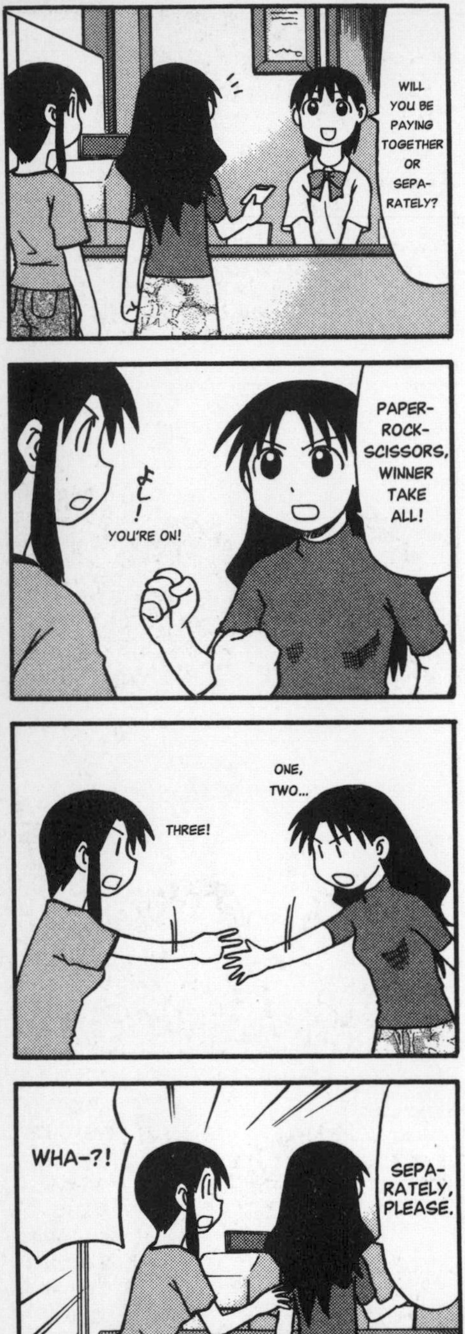
WILL YOU BE PAYING TOGETHER OR SEPA-RATELY?
PAPER-ROCK-SCISSORS, WINNER TAKE ALL!
よし！
YOU'RE ON!
ONE, TWO...
THREE!
SEPA-RATELY, PLEASE.
WHA-?!

THE ATTACK

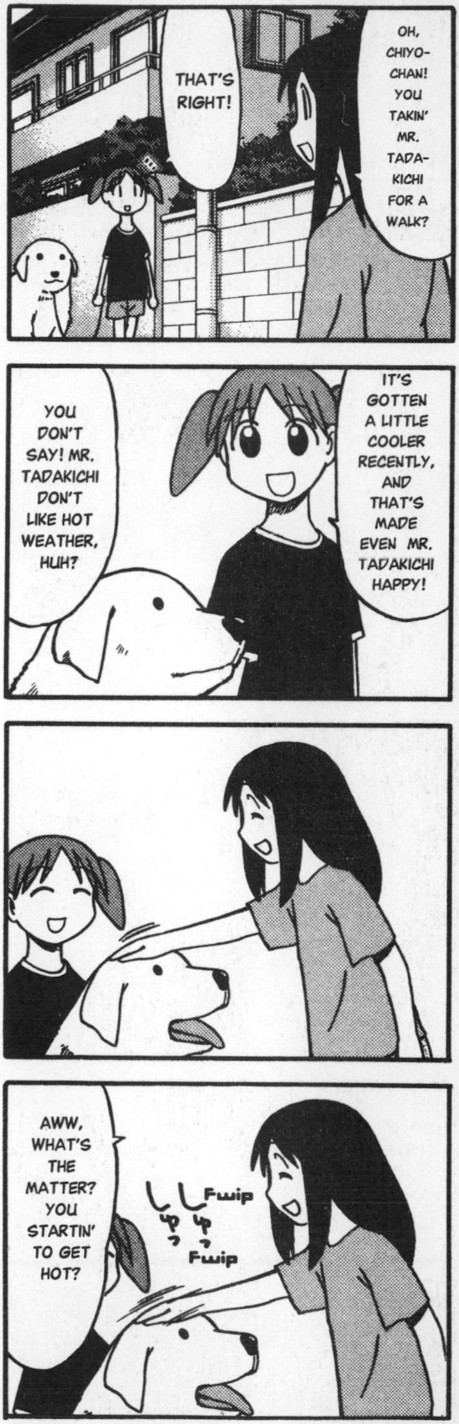
OH, CHIYO-CHAN! YOU TAKIN' MR. TADA-KICHI FOR A WALK?
THAT'S RIGHT!
IT'S GOTTEN A LITTLE COOLER RECENTLY, AND THAT'S MADE EVEN MR. TADAKICHI HAPPY!
YOU DON'T SAY! MR. TADAKICHI DON'T LIKE HOT WEATHER, HUH?
AWW, WHAT'S THE MATTER? YOU STARTIN' TO GET HOT?
Fwip
Fwip

GREAT

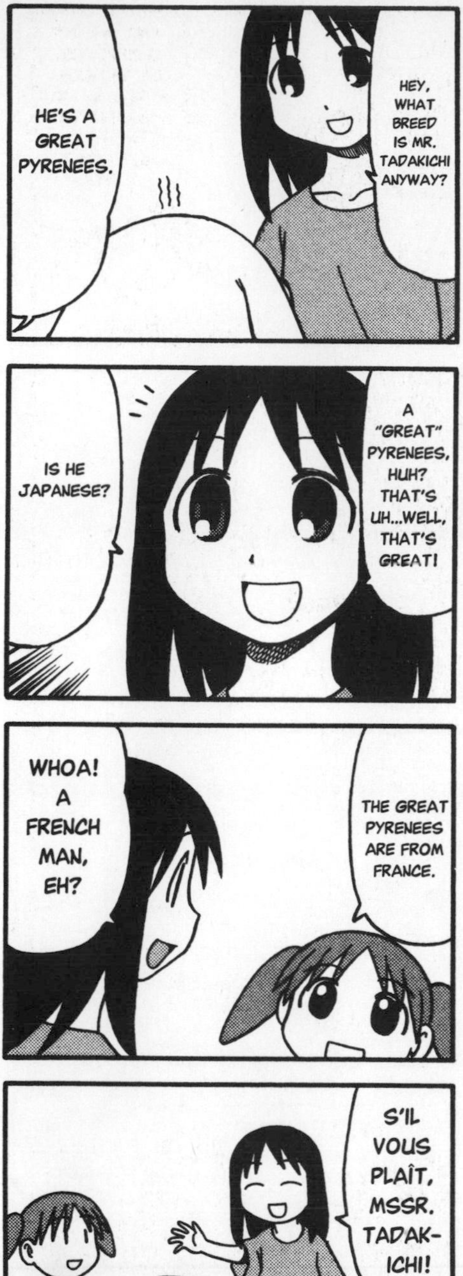
HEY, WHAT BREED IS MR. TADAKICHI ANYWAY?
HE'S A GREAT PYRENEES.
A "GREAT" PYRENEES, HUH? THAT'S UH...WELL, THAT'S GREAT!
IS HE JAPANESE?
THE GREAT PYRENEES ARE FROM FRANCE.
WHOA! A FRENCH MAN, EH?
S'IL VOUS PLAÎT, MSSR. TADAK-ICHI!

THE EYES HAVE IT

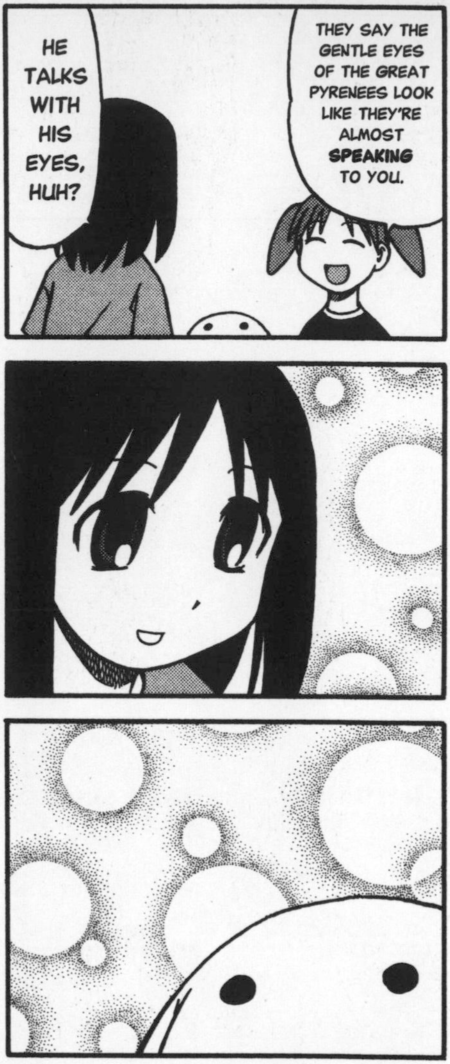
THEY SAY THE GENTLE EYES OF THE GREAT PYRENEES LOOK LIKE THEY'RE ALMOST **SPEAKING** TO YOU.
HE TALKS WITH HIS EYES, HUH?
NAAH, I DON'T THINK HE UNDER-STANDS FRENCH.

HAPPY

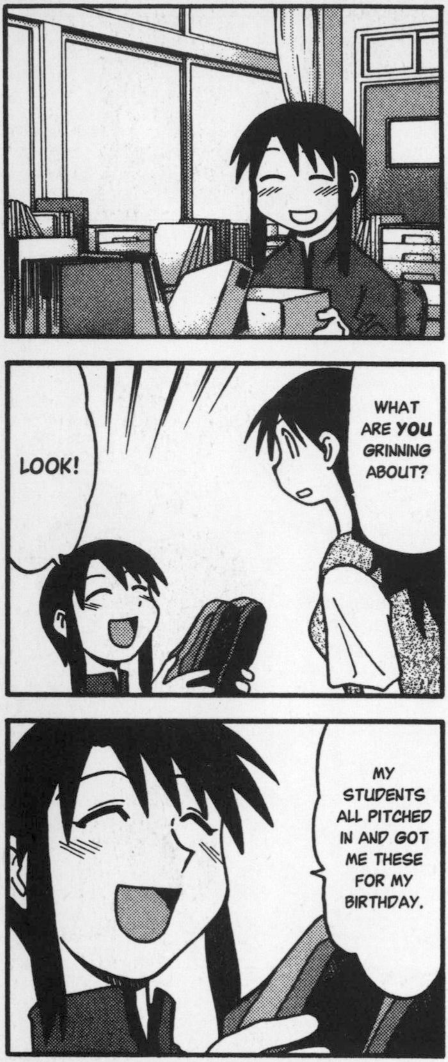
WHAT ARE **YOU** GRINNING ABOUT?
LOOK!
MY STUDENTS ALL PITCHED IN AND GOT ME THESE FOR MY BIRTHDAY.
WENCH! WHAT ARE YOU, THE WASHED-UP TEACHER FROM SOME B-GRADE TEEN DRAMA?
WHY ARE YOU SO ANGRY?

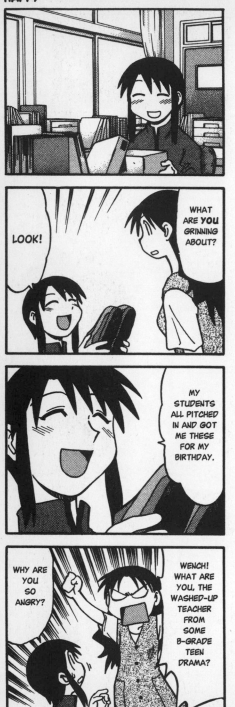

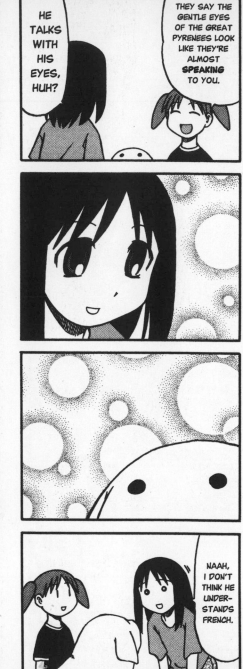

IT'S NO BIG DEAL, REALLY

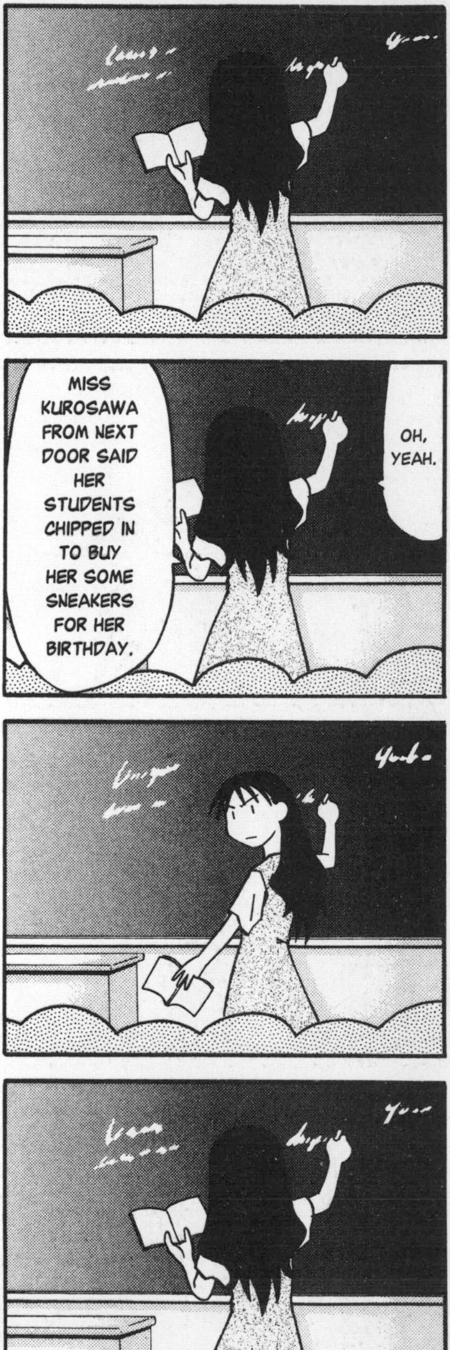
OH, YEAH.
MISS KUROSAWA FROM NEXT DOOR SAID HER STUDENTS CHIPPED IN TO BUY HER SOME SNEAKERS FOR HER BIRTHDAY.

THE BIRTHDAY

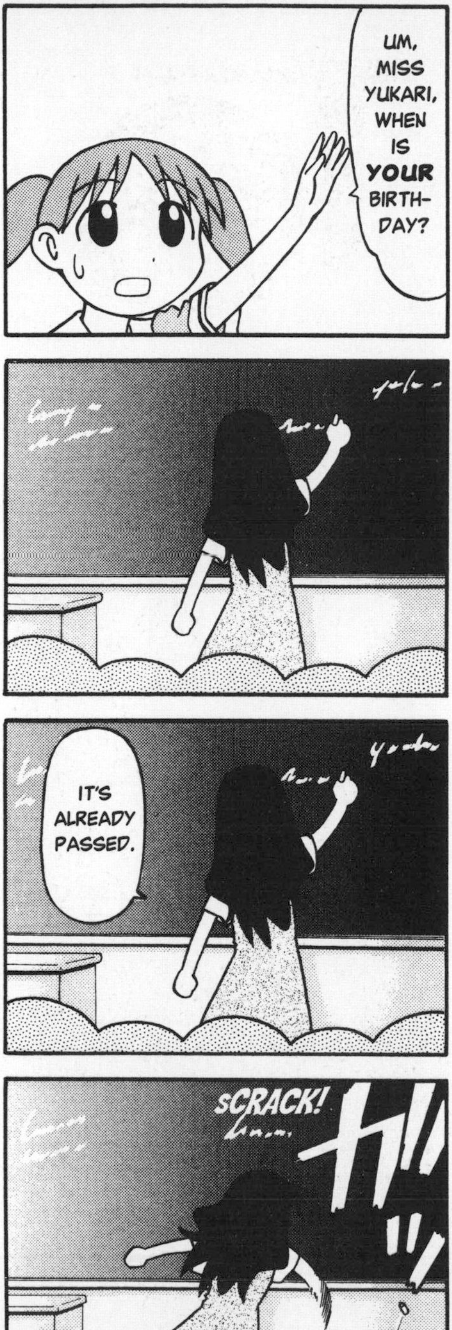
UM, MISS YUKARI, WHEN IS **YOUR** BIRTHDAY?
IT'S ALREADY PASSED.
SCRACK!

# 10 OCTOBER PART-1

AZU MANGA DAIOH

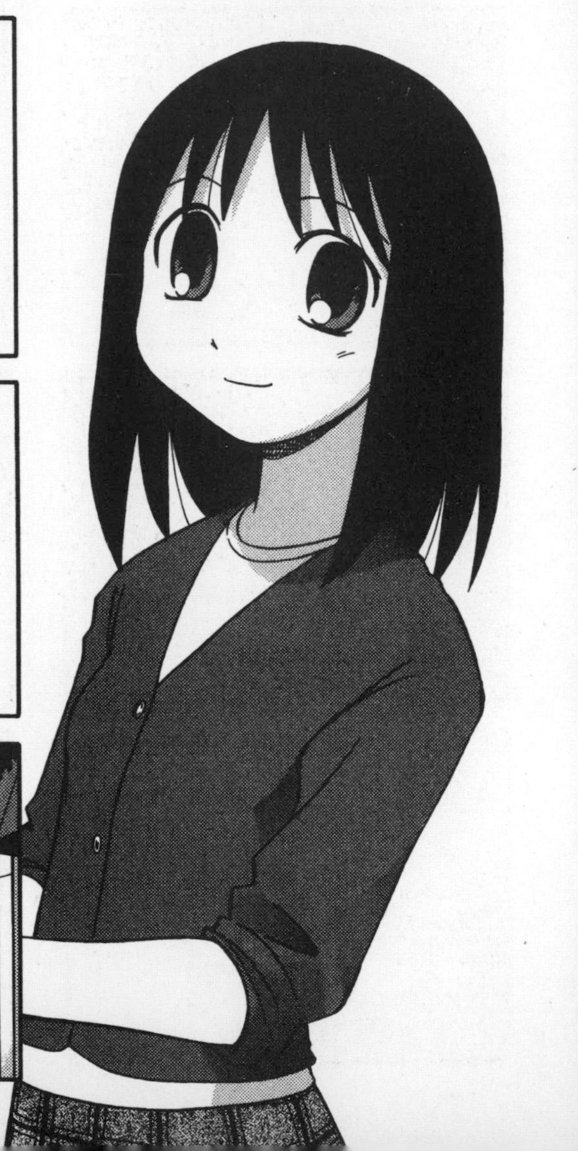

THE AUTUMN SKY

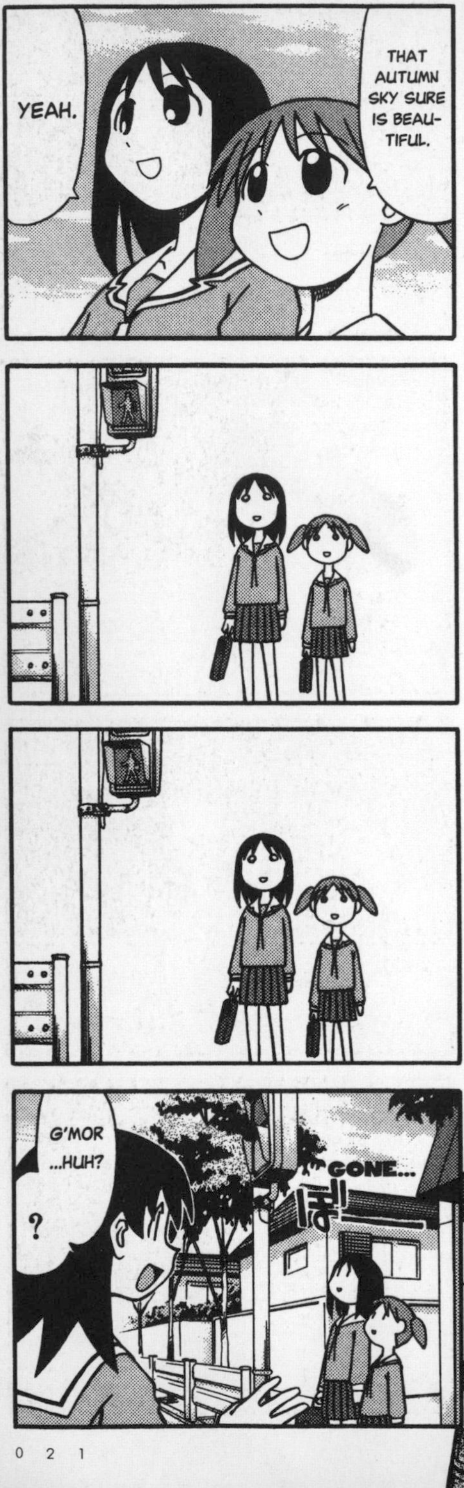
THAT AUTUMN SKY SURE IS BEAU-TIFUL.
YEAH.
GONE...
G'MOR ...HUH?
?

THE OSAKA RANKING

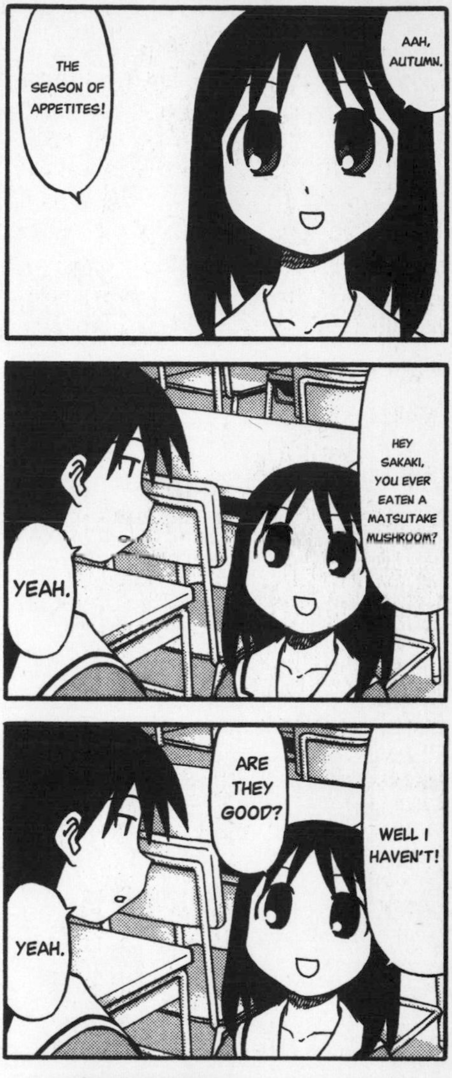
AAH, AUTUMN.
THE SEASON OF APPETITES!
HEY SAKAKI, YOU EVER EATEN A MATSUTAKE MUSHROOM?
YEAH.
WELL I HAVEN'T!
ARE THEY GOOD?
YEAH.
WHAT IF SOME-ONE WAS ALL, "THIS HAS GOT MATSUTAKE IN IT" BUT IT WAS TOTALLY SHIITAKE-COULD YOU TELL THE DIFFER-ENCE?!
UH... YEAH.

MATSUTAKE OF DREAMS

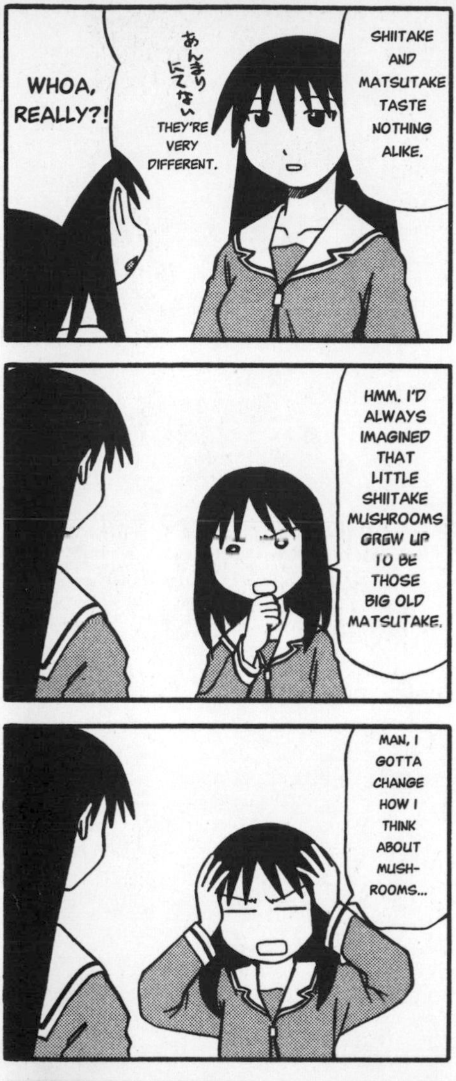
SHIITAKE AND MATSUTAKE TASTE NOTHING ALIKE.
あんまりにてない
THEY'RE VERY DIFFERENT.
WHOA, REALLY?!
HMM. I'D ALWAYS IMAGINED THAT LITTLE SHIITAKE MUSHROOMS GREW UP TO BE THOSE BIG OLD MATSUTAKE.
MAN, I GOTTA CHANGE HOW I THINK ABOUT MUSH-ROOMS...
OK. SO THEY TASTE AS DIFFERENT AS, LIKE, HAM AND BACON?
UM...

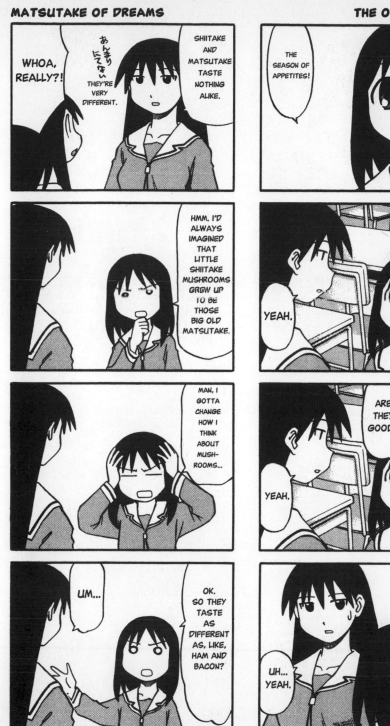

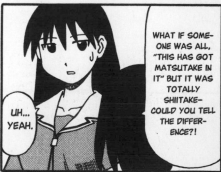

## GROWTH SPURT

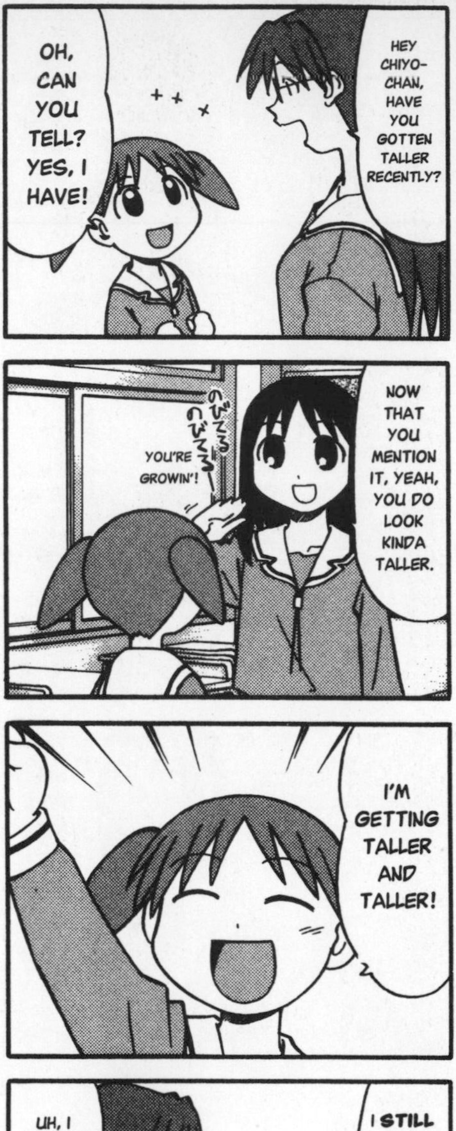
HEY CHIYO-CHAN, HAVE YOU GOTTEN TALLER RECENTLY?
OH, CAN YOU TELL? YES, I HAVE!
NOW THAT YOU MENTION IT, YEAH, YOU DO LOOK KINDA TALLER.
YOU'RE GROWIN'!
I'M GETTING TALLER AND TALLER!
I STILL GET CON-FUSED FOR AN ELEMEN-TARY SCHOOL KID, THOUGH.
UH, I DON'T THINK THERE'S ANY-THING YOU CAN DO ABOUT THAT...

## I WANNA BE...BIG!

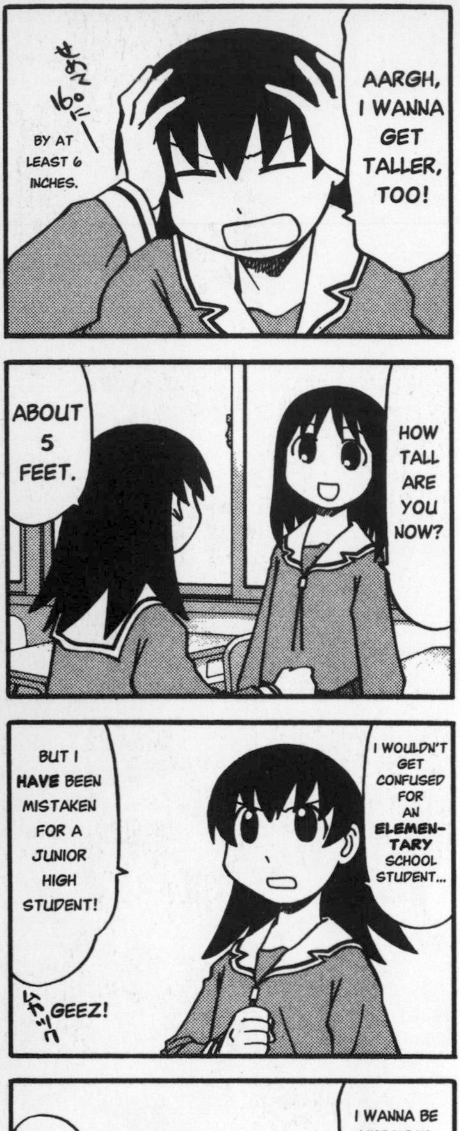
AARGH, I WANNA GET TALLER, TOO!
BY AT LEAST 6 INCHES.
HOW TALL ARE YOU NOW?
ABOUT 5 FEET.
I WOULDN'T GET CONFUSED FOR AN ELEMEN-TARY SCHOOL STUDENT...
BUT I HAVE BEEN MISTAKEN FOR A JUNIOR HIGH STUDENT!
GEEZ!
I WANNA BE LIKE YOMI, AND GET MISTAKEN FOR A COLLEGE STUDENT! OR A SECRETARY!
SHUT YOUR TRAP!

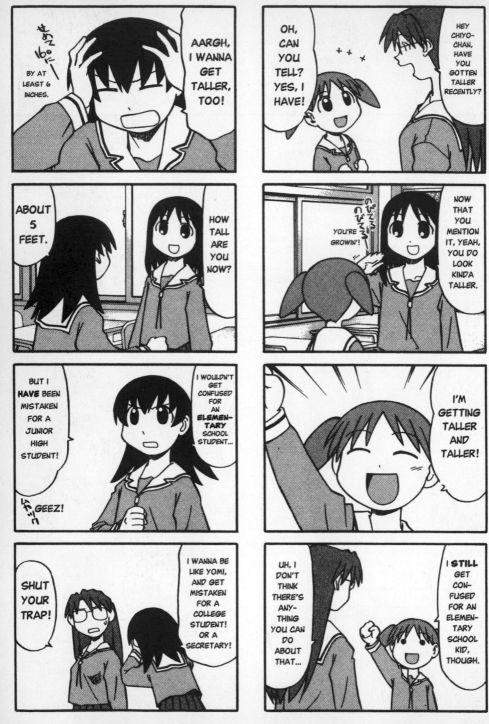

## BIRDS OF A FEATHER

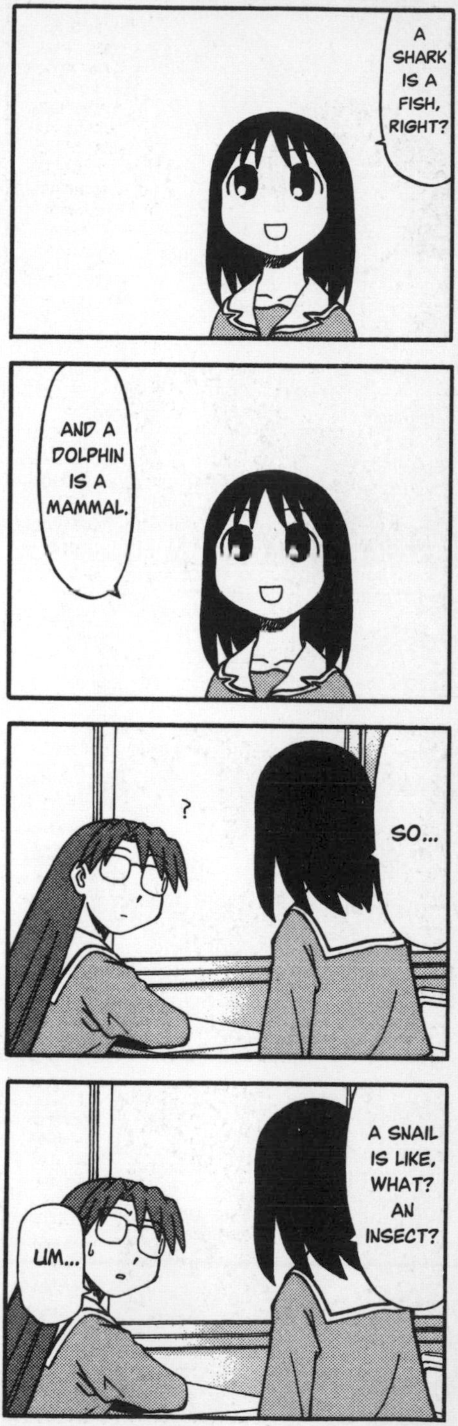
A SHARK IS A FISH, RIGHT?
AND A DOLPHIN IS A MAMMAL.
SO...
?
A SNAIL IS LIKE, WHAT? AN INSECT?
UM...

## IS THAT AN INSECT IN MY GARDEN?

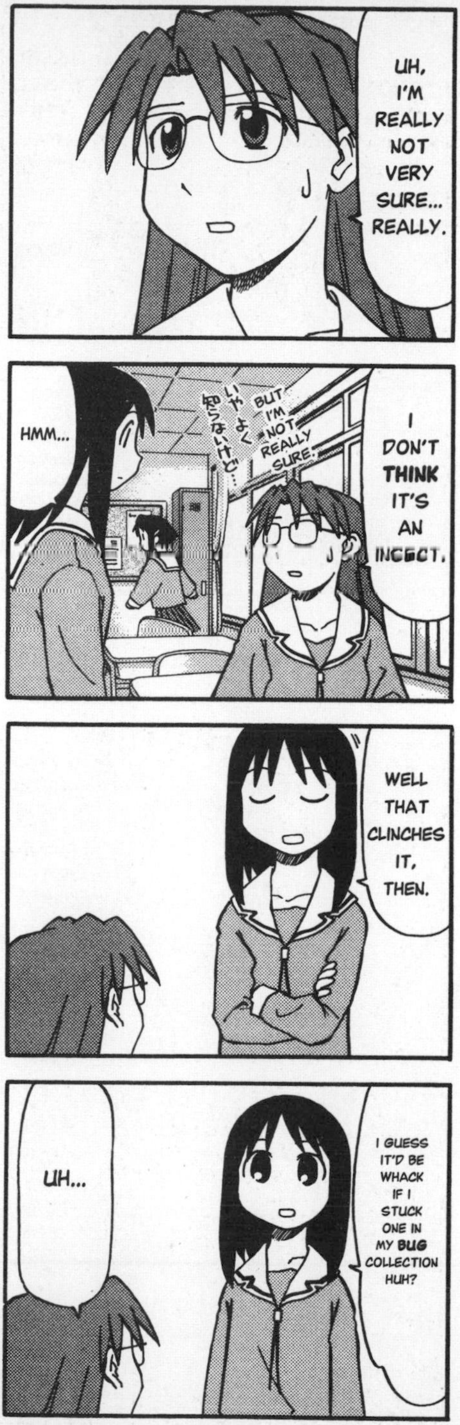
UH, I'M REALLY NOT VERY SURE... REALLY.
I DON'T **THINK** IT'S AN INSECT.
BUT I'M NOT REALLY SURE.
いやよく知らないけど…
HMM...
WELL THAT CLINCHES IT, THEN.
I GUESS IT'D BE WHACK IF I STUCK ONE IN MY **BUG** COLLECTION HUH?
UH...

## TO PUT A PRICE TAG ON IT...

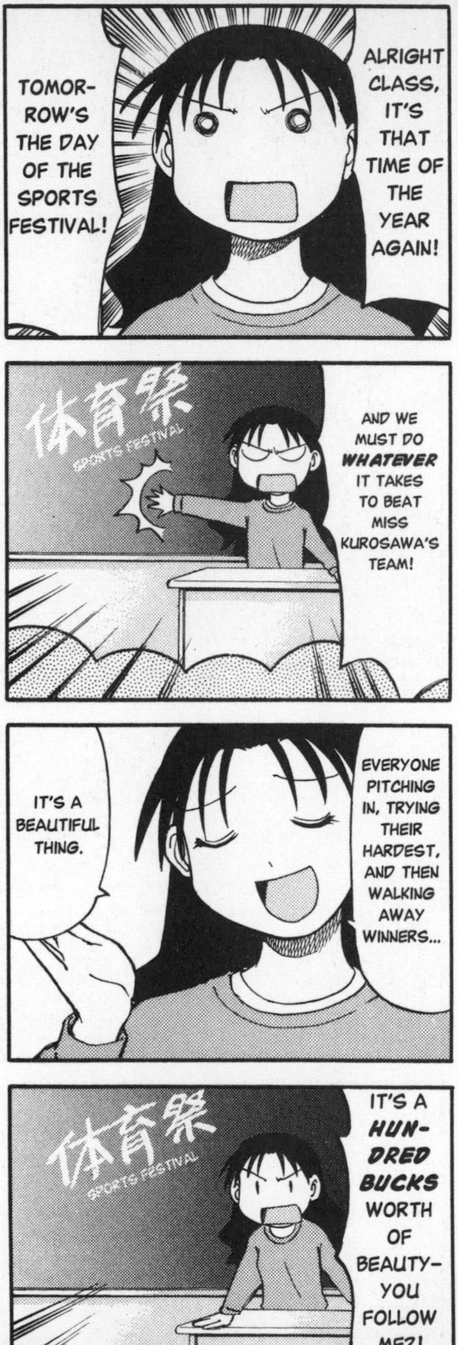
ALRIGHT CLASS, IT'S THAT TIME OF THE YEAR AGAIN!
TOMOR-ROW'S THE DAY OF THE SPORTS FESTIVAL!
体育祭
SPORTS FESTIVAL
AND WE MUST DO **WHATEVER** IT TAKES TO BEAT MISS KUROSAWA'S TEAM!
EVERYONE PITCHING IN, TRYING THEIR HARDEST, AND THEN WALKING AWAY WINNERS...
IT'S A BEAUTIFUL THING.
体育祭
SPORTS FESTIVAL
IT'S A **HUN-DRED BUCKS** WORTH OF BEAUTY— YOU FOLLOW ME?!

## SWEETENING THE DEAL

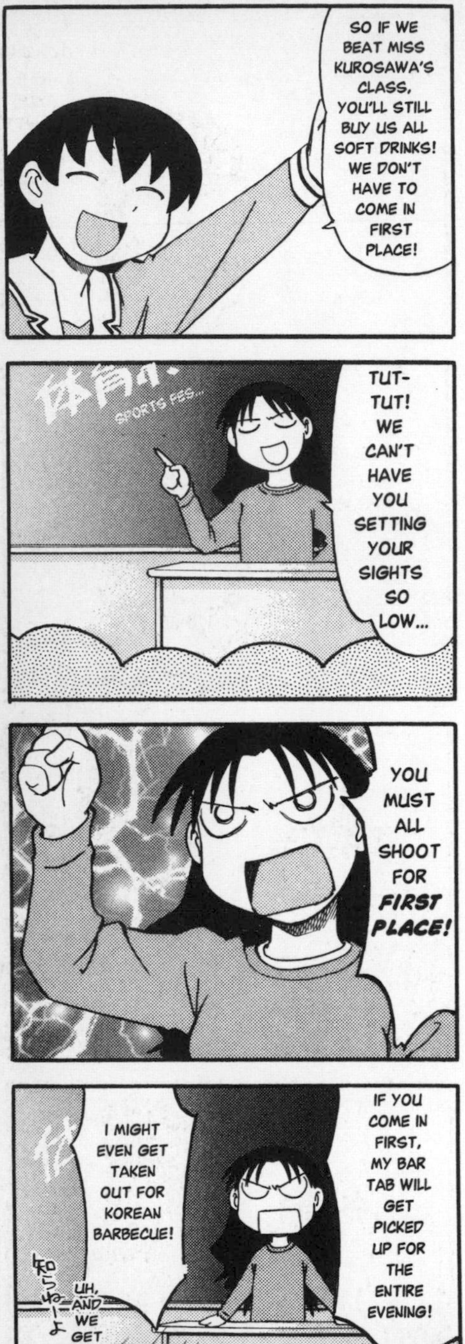
SO IF WE BEAT MISS KUROSAWA'S CLASS, YOU'LL STILL BUY US ALL SOFT DRINKS! WE DON'T HAVE TO COME IN FIRST PLACE!
SPORTS FES...
TUT-TUT! WE CAN'T HAVE YOU SETTING YOUR SIGHTS SO LOW...
YOU MUST ALL SHOOT FOR **FIRST PLACE!**
IF YOU COME IN FIRST, MY BAR TAB WILL GET PICKED UP FOR THE ENTIRE EVENING!
I MIGHT EVEN GET TAKEN OUT FOR KOREAN BARBECUE!
知らねーよ
UH, AND WE GET **NOTHING...**

MOVE, KAGURA!

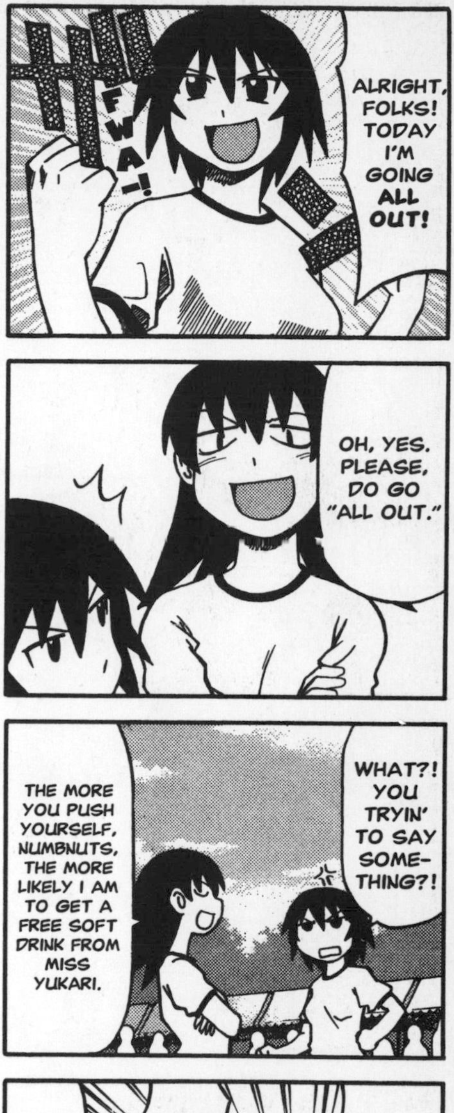
ALRIGHT, FOLKS! TODAY I'M GOING ALL OUT!
FWA-!
OH, YES. PLEASE, DO GO "ALL OUT."
WHAT?! YOU TRYIN' TO SAY SOME-THING?!
THE MORE YOU PUSH YOURSELF, NUMBNUTS, THE MORE LIKELY I AM TO GET A FREE SOFT DRINK FROM MISS YUKARI.
DANCE! DANCE FOR ME, MY PUPPET!
DAMN YOU!
IT'S LIKE WATCHING B-GRADE ACTORS DUKE IT OUT.

SCAVENGE

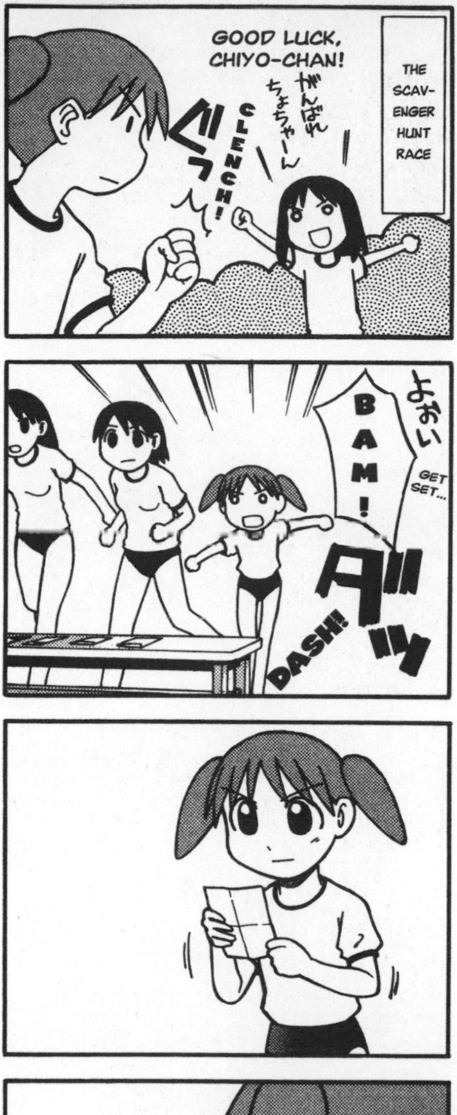
THE SCAV-ENGER HUNT RACE
がんばれちよちゃーん
GOOD LUCK, CHIYO-CHAN!
ぐっ
CLENCH!
よおい
GET SET...
BAM!
ダッ
DASH!
FIND AN IDIOT

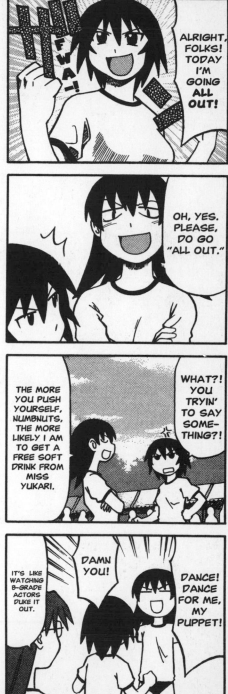

## FOUND ONE!

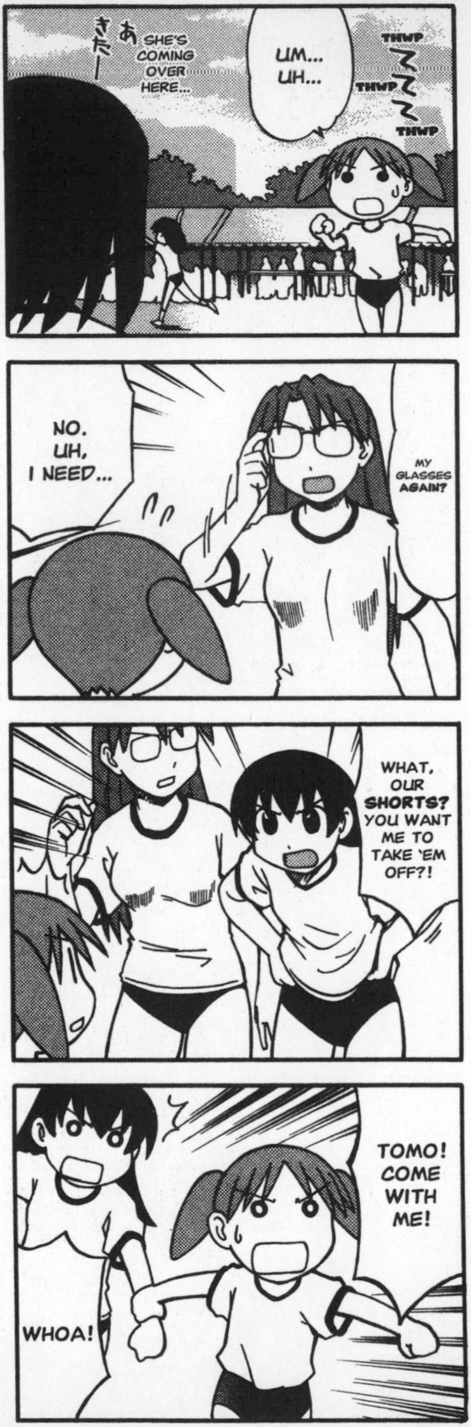
UM... UH...
THWP
THWP
THWP
あきたー
SHE'S COMING OVER HERE...
MY GLASSES AGAIN?
NO. UH, I NEED...
WHAT, OUR SHORTS? YOU WANT ME TO TAKE 'EM OFF?!
TOMO! COME WITH ME!
WHOA!

## SO WHAT WAS IT?

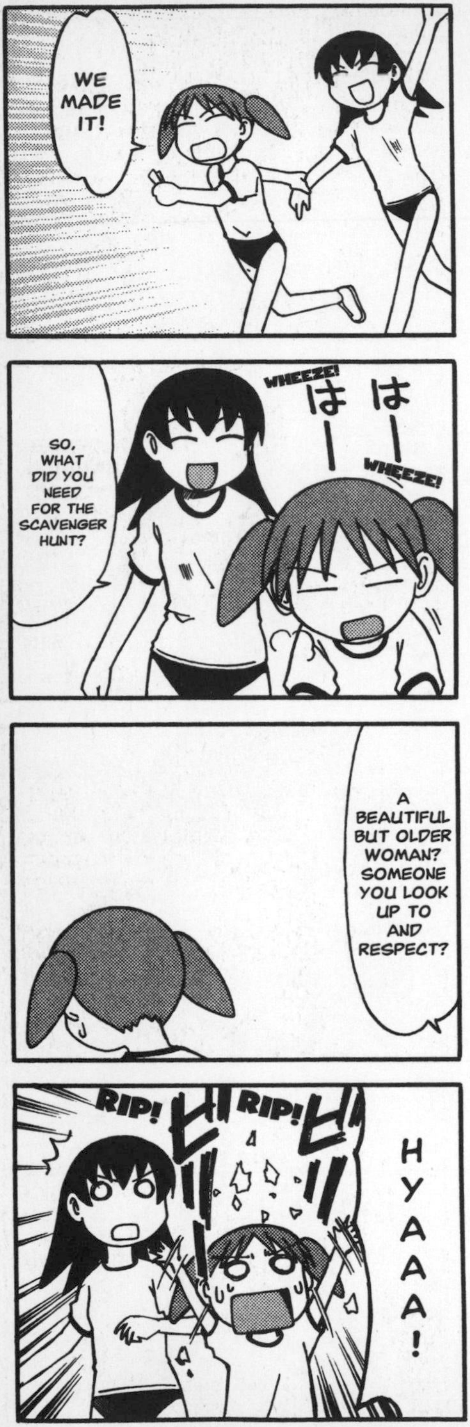
WE MADE IT!
WHEEZE!
はー
はー
WHEEZE!
SO, WHAT DID YOU NEED FOR THE SCAVENGER HUNT?
A BEAUTIFUL BUT OLDER WOMAN? SOMEONE YOU LOOK UP TO AND RESPECT?
HYAAA!
RIP!
RIP!

NOWHERE FAST

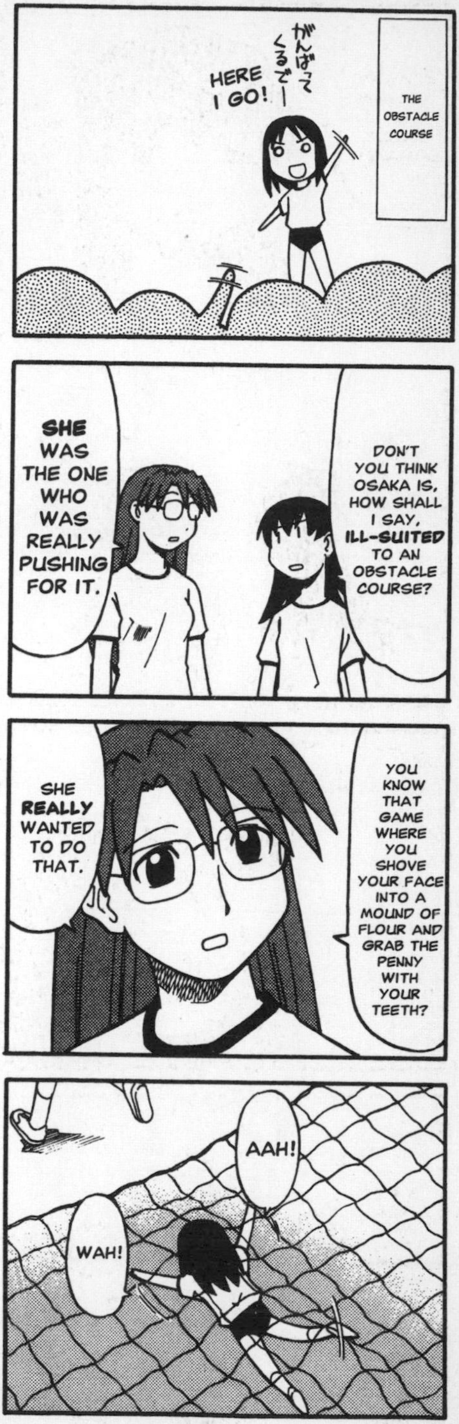
THE OBSTACLE COURSE
がんばってくるでー
HERE I GO!
DON'T YOU THINK OSAKA IS, HOW SHALL I SAY, ILL-SUITED TO AN OBSTACLE COURSE?
SHE WAS THE ONE WHO WAS REALLY PUSHING FOR IT.
YOU KNOW THAT GAME WHERE YOU SHOVE YOUR FACE INTO A MOUND OF FLOUR AND GRAB THE PENNY WITH YOUR TEETH?
SHE REALLY WANTED TO DO THAT.
AAH!
WAH!

WHERE IS IT?

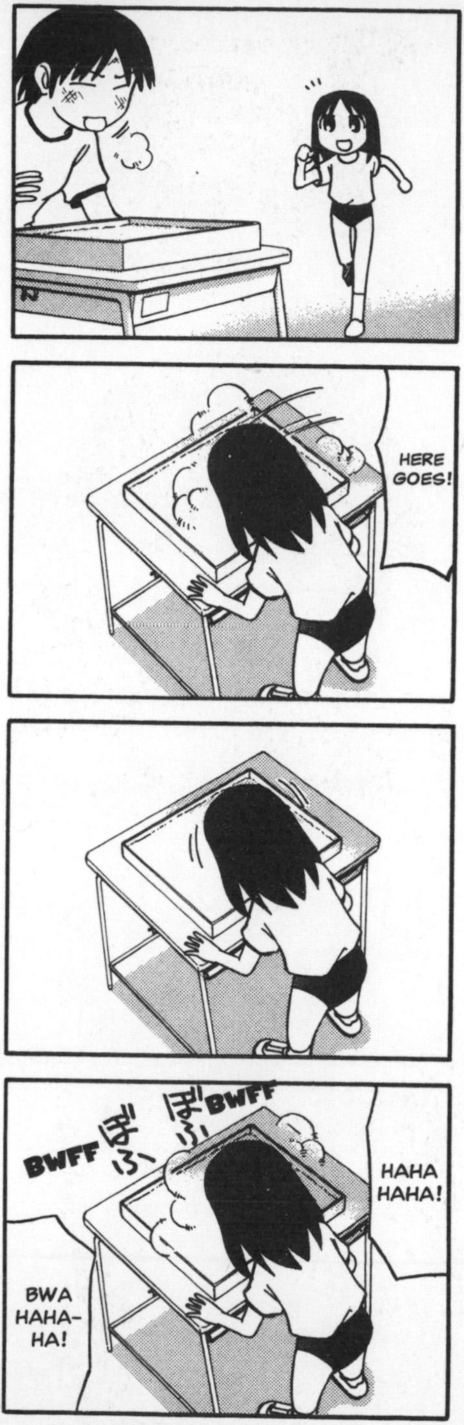
HERE GOES!
ぼふ BWFF
BWFF ぼふ
HAHA HAHA!
BWA HAHA-HA!

BREAD

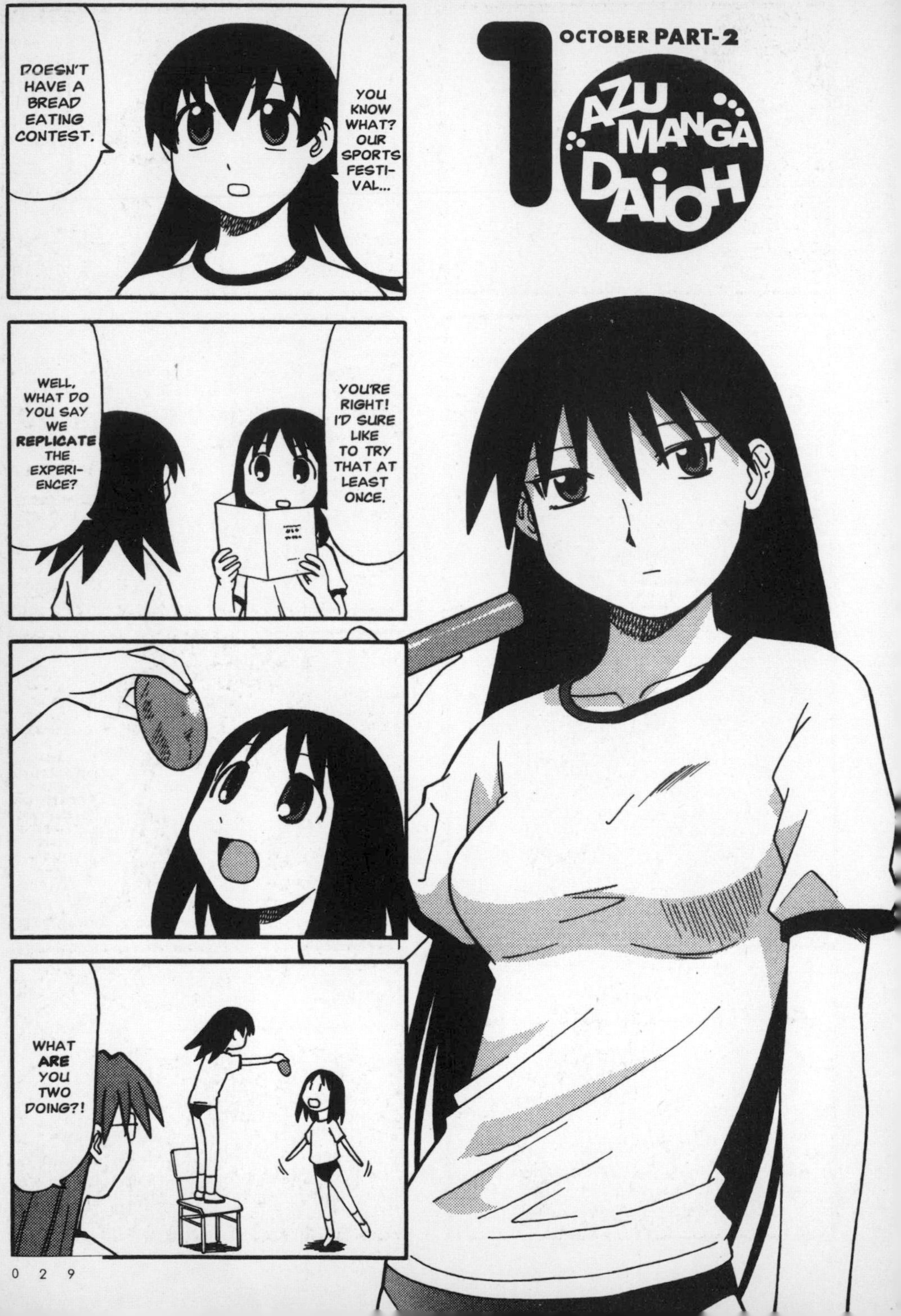
10 OCTOBER PART-2
AZU MANGA DAIOH
YOU KNOW WHAT? OUR SPORTS FESTIVAL...
DOESN'T HAVE A BREAD EATING CONTEST.
YOU'RE RIGHT! I'D SURE LIKE TO TRY THAT AT LEAST ONCE.
WELL, WHAT DO YOU SAY WE **REPLICATE** THE EXPERIENCE?
WHAT **ARE** YOU TWO DOING?!

## SHE'S GONE!

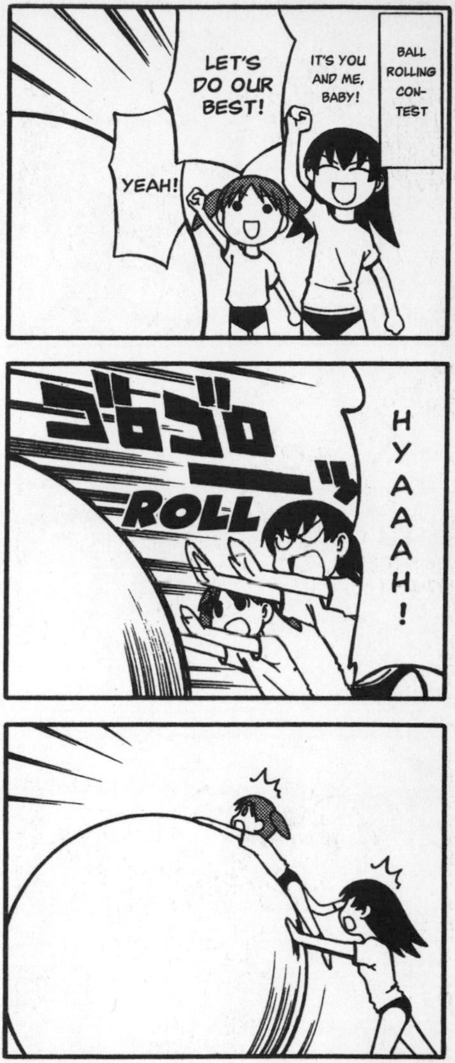
BALL ROLLING CON-TEST
IT'S YOU AND ME, BABY!
LET'S DO OUR BEST!
YEAH!
HYAAAH!
ゴロゴロ
ROLL
CHIYO-CHAN?!

## DOUBLE WHAMMY

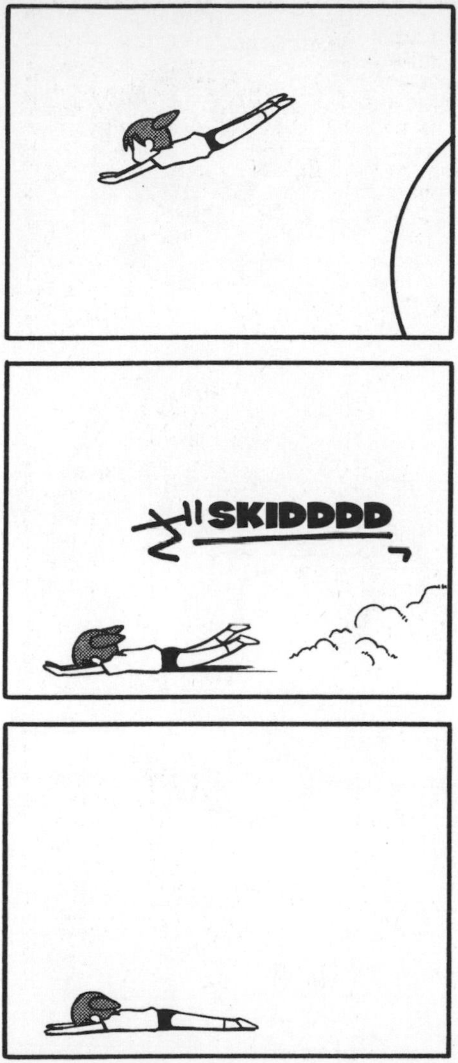
SKIDDDD
BWOMP!
ぐしゃ

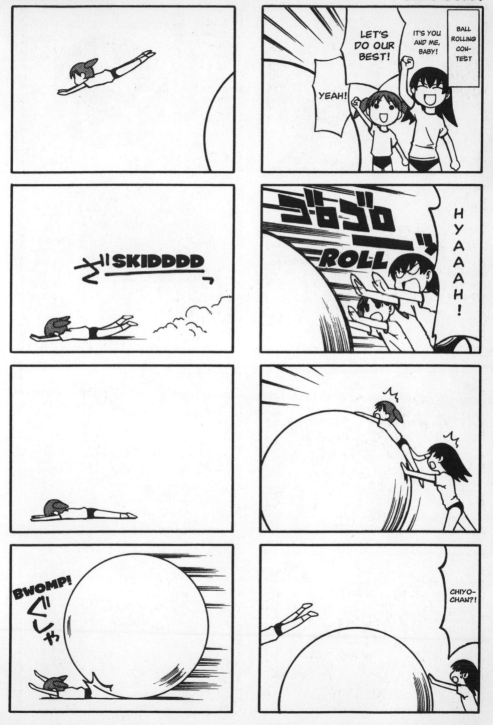

DETERMINATION

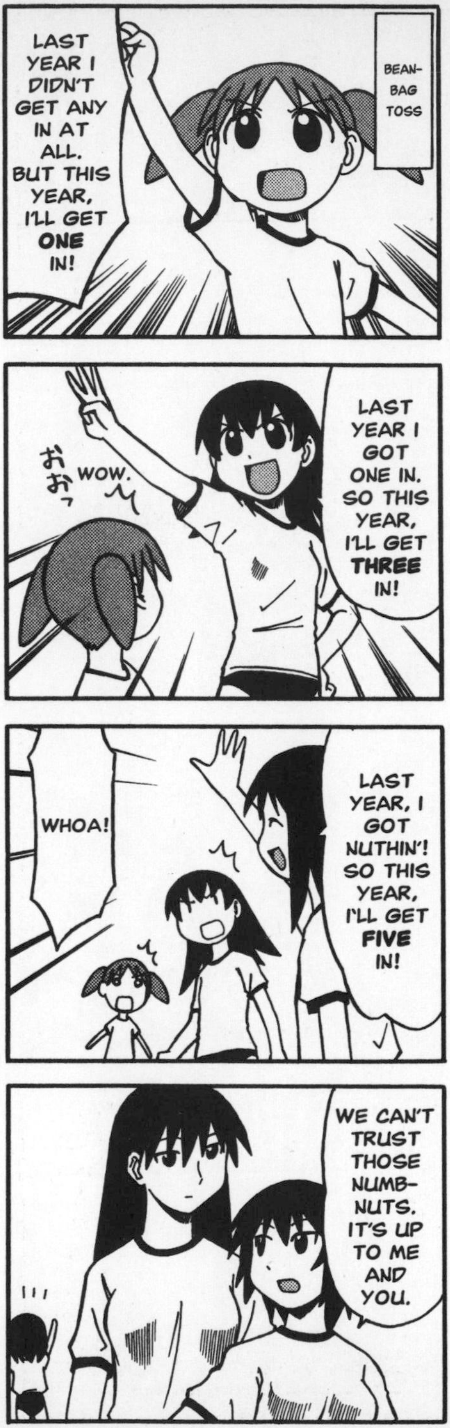
BEAN-BAG TOSS
LAST YEAR I DIDN'T GET ANY IN AT ALL. BUT THIS YEAR, I'LL GET **ONE** IN!
LAST YEAR I GOT ONE IN. SO THIS YEAR, I'LL GET **THREE** IN!
おおっ
WOW.
LAST YEAR, I GOT NUTHIN'! SO THIS YEAR, I'LL GET **FIVE** IN!
WHOA!
WE CAN'T TRUST THOSE NUMB-NUTS. IT'S UP TO ME AND YOU.

DID YOU SEE THAT? DID YOU?

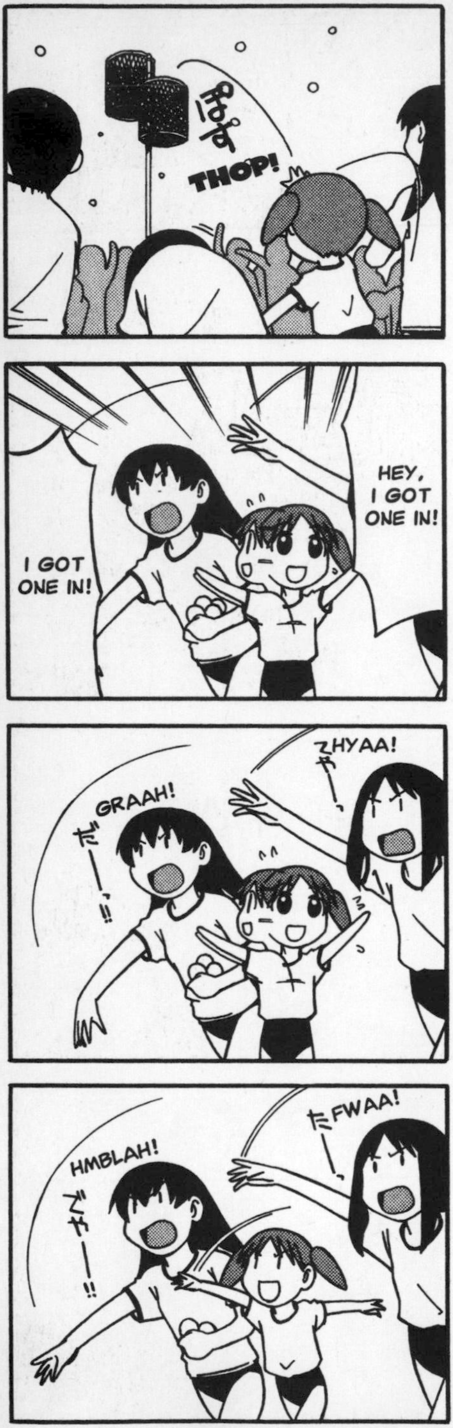
ぽす
THOP!
HEY, I GOT ONE IN!
I GOT ONE IN!
ZHYAA!
やー、
GRAAH!
だー!!
FWAA!
たー
HMBLAH!
でやー!!

NO!!

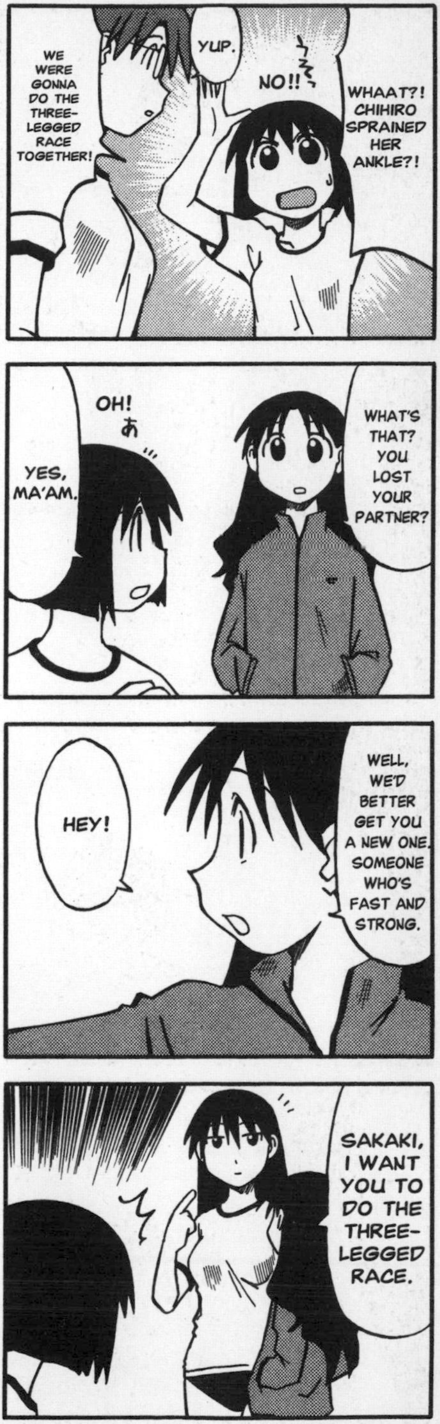
WHAAT?! CHIHIRO SPRAINED HER ANKLE?!
YUP.
NO!!
WE WERE GONNA DO THE THREE-LEGGED RACE TOGETHER!
WHAT'S THAT? YOU LOST YOUR PARTNER?
OH! あ
YES, MA'AM.
WELL, WE'D BETTER GET YOU A NEW ONE. SOMEONE WHO'S FAST AND STRONG.
HEY!
SAKAKI, I WANT YOU TO DO THE THREE-LEGGED RACE.

DON'T PUSH YOURSELF. I MEAN IT.

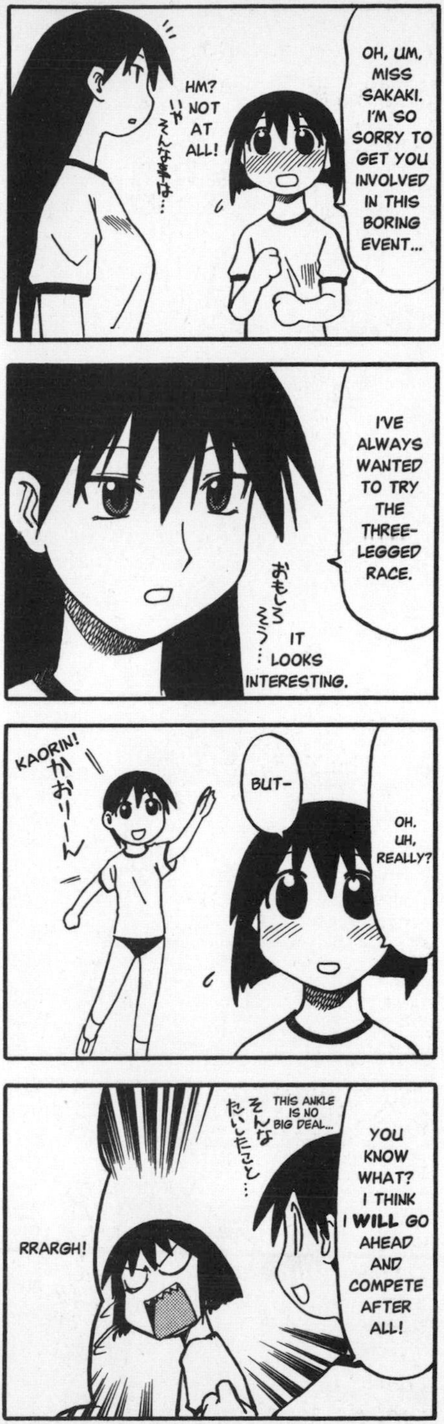
OH, UM, MISS SAKAKI. I'M SO SORRY TO GET YOU INVOLVED IN THIS BORING EVENT...
HM? NOT AT ALL!
いや そんな事は…
I'VE ALWAYS WANTED TO TRY THE THREE-LEGGED RACE.
おもしろそう…
IT LOOKS INTERESTING.
OH. UH, REALLY?
BUT-
KAORIN!
かおりーん
YOU KNOW WHAT? I THINK I WILL GO AHEAD AND COMPETE AFTER ALL!
THIS ANKLE IS NO BIG DEAL...
そんなたいしたこと…
RRARGH!

## EVERYTHING I'VE GOT

I...I'M GONNA TRY MY HARDEST, OK?
'K.
I MEAN IT! I'M GONNA RUN LIKE MY LIFE DEPENDS ON IT! MY VERY LIFE!!
UM... 'K.
'CUZ I'M SO HAPPY I COULD JUST DIE!

## THE SOUVENIR

WE DID IT!!
WE DID IT, MISS SAKAKI!
WE'RE NUMBER ONE!
NUMBER ONE!!
WAAA!
AH! COULD I AT LEAST OFFER YOU THIS FLAG AS A TOKEN OF MY SINCEREST THANKS?!
UM, THAT'S ALRIGHT.

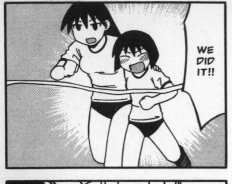

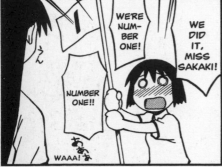

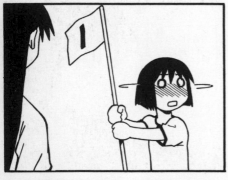

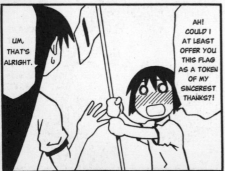

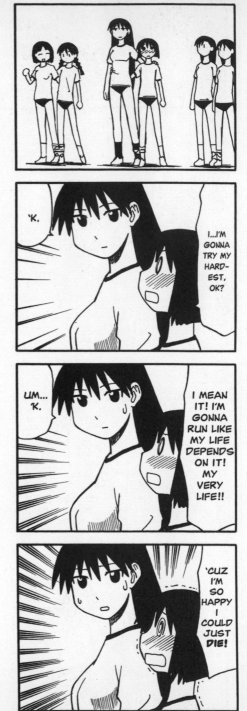

## THE WISH

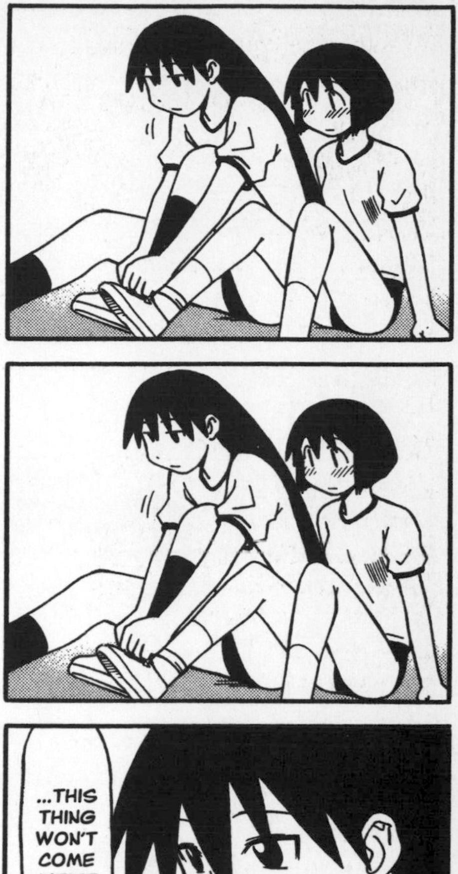
...THIS THING WON'T COME UNTIED.
OH. WELL, MAYBE WE SHOULD JUST LEAVE IT ON...
UH...

## THE BIG BOSS

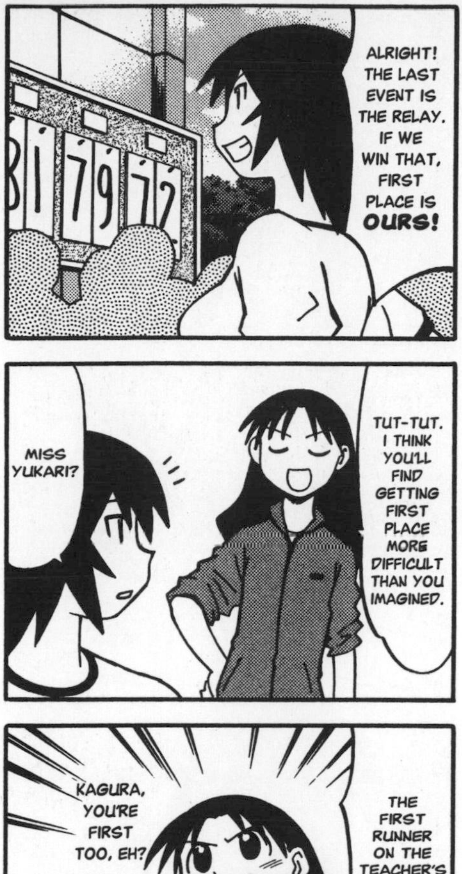
ALRIGHT! THE LAST EVENT IS THE RELAY. IF WE WIN THAT, FIRST PLACE IS **OURS!**
TUT-TUT. I THINK YOU'LL FIND GETTING FIRST PLACE MORE DIFFICULT THAN YOU IMAGINED.
MISS YUKARI?
THE FIRST RUNNER ON THE TEACHER'S RELAY TEAM IS **YOURS TRULY!**
KAGURA, YOU'RE FIRST TOO, EH?
I'VE GOT A HUNDRED BUCKS AND KOREAN BARBECUE RIDING ON THIS— THE GLOVES ARE **OFF!**
私負けるのは大嫌いだからね
AND I HATE LOSING!
UM, OK...

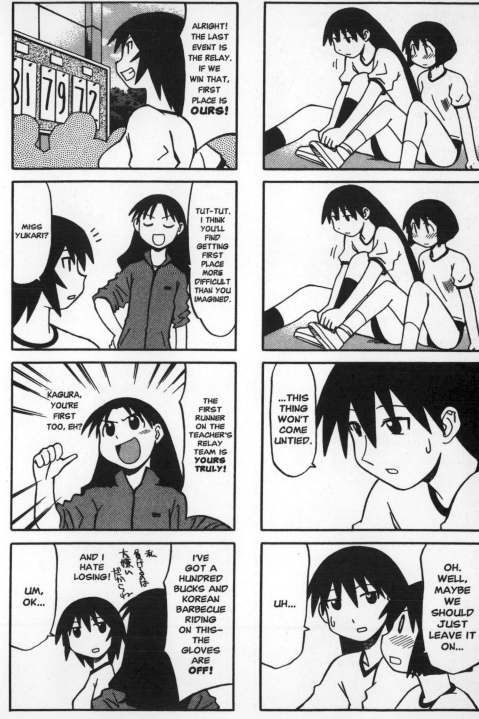

HUH?!

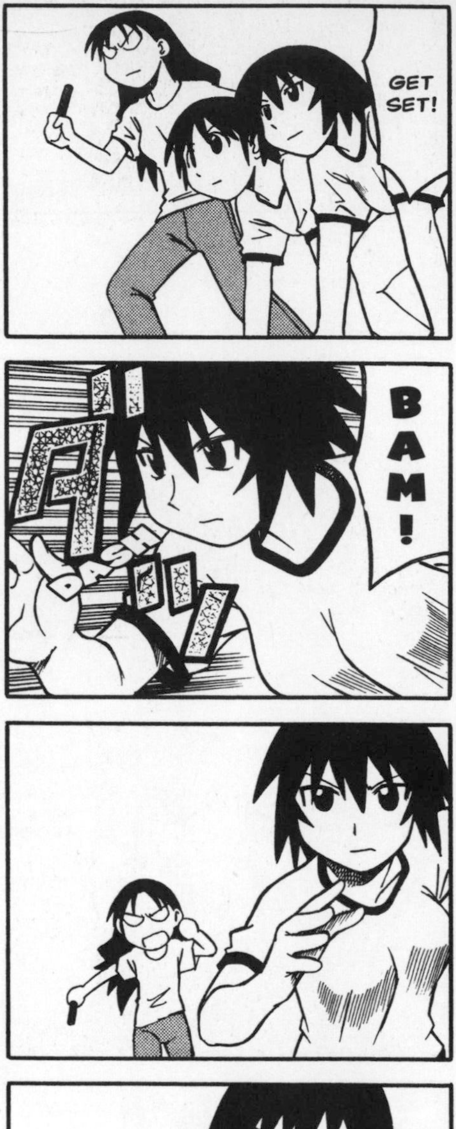
GET SET!
BAM!
ダッ
DASH

YOU SONOFA-!

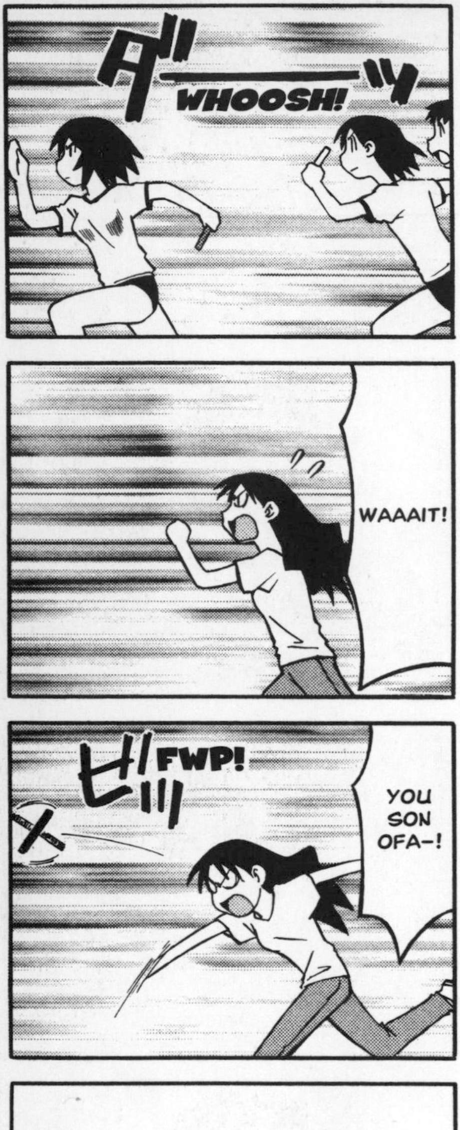
ダーッ
WHOOSH!
WAAAIT!
ビッ
FWP!
YOU SON OFA-!
ああー
ARGH!
CLANG CLANG
ころころ

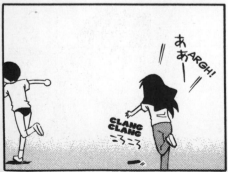

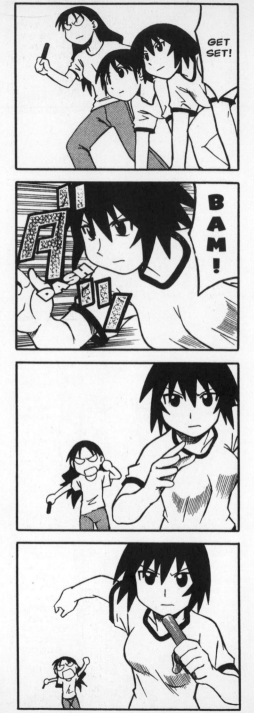

VICTORY!

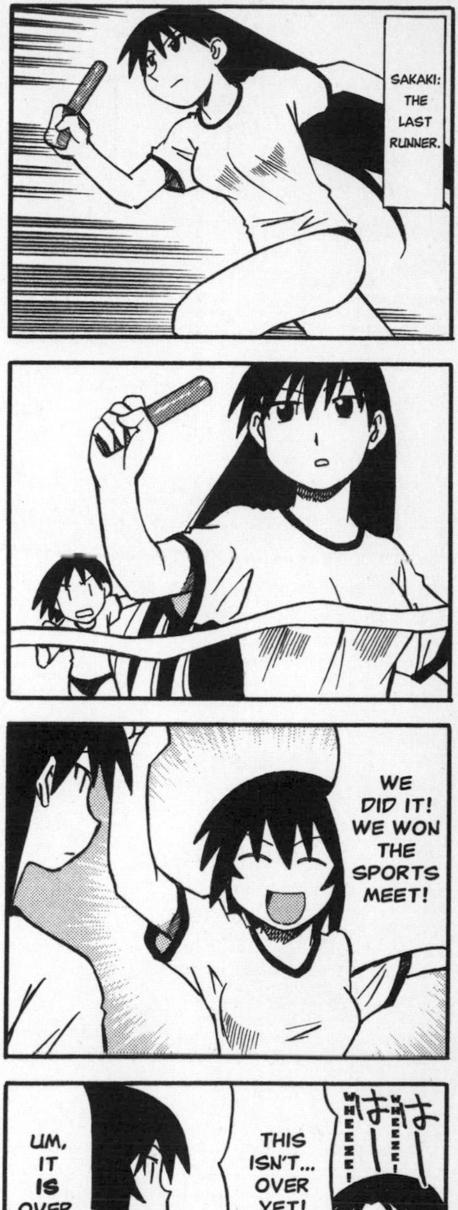
SAKAKI: THE LAST RUNNER.
WE DID IT! WE WON THE SPORTS MEET!
はーはー
WHEEZE! WHEEZE!
THIS ISN'T... OVER YET!
UM, IT IS OVER. WE WON.
はーはー
WHEEZE! WHEEZE!

BE MORE OF A LOSER, WILL YA?!

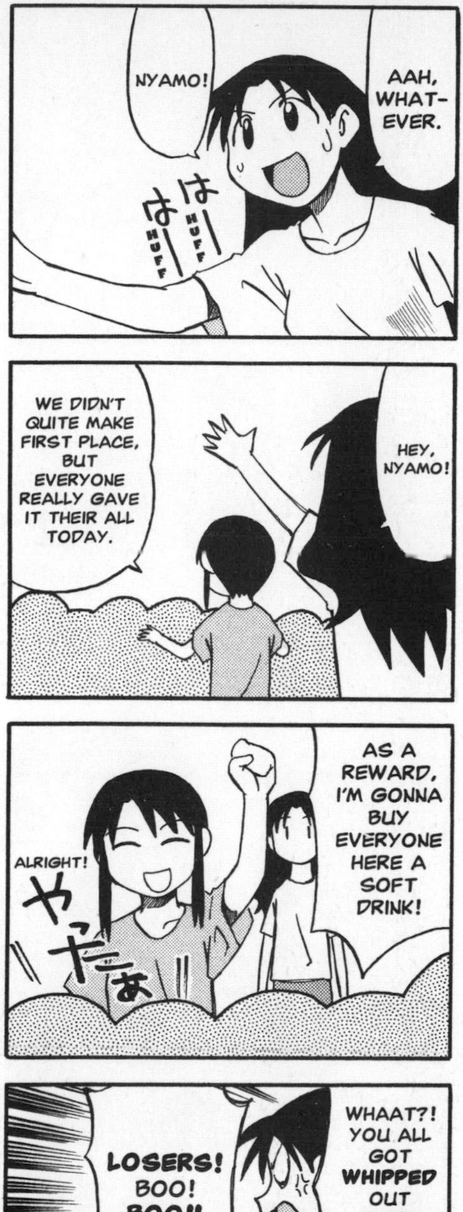
AAH, WHAT-EVER.
NYAMO!
はーはー
HUFF HUFF
HEY, NYAMO!
WE DIDN'T QUITE MAKE FIRST PLACE, BUT EVERYONE REALLY GAVE IT THEIR ALL TODAY.
AS A REWARD, I'M GONNA BUY EVERYONE HERE A SOFT DRINK!
ALRIGHT!
やったーぁ
WHAAT?! YOU ALL GOT WHIPPED OUT THERE TODAY! YOU GOT WHIPPED GOOD!
LOSERS! BOO! BOO!!

**AZUMANGA-DAIOH**

# 037

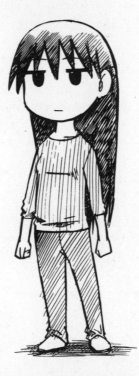

*You belong*

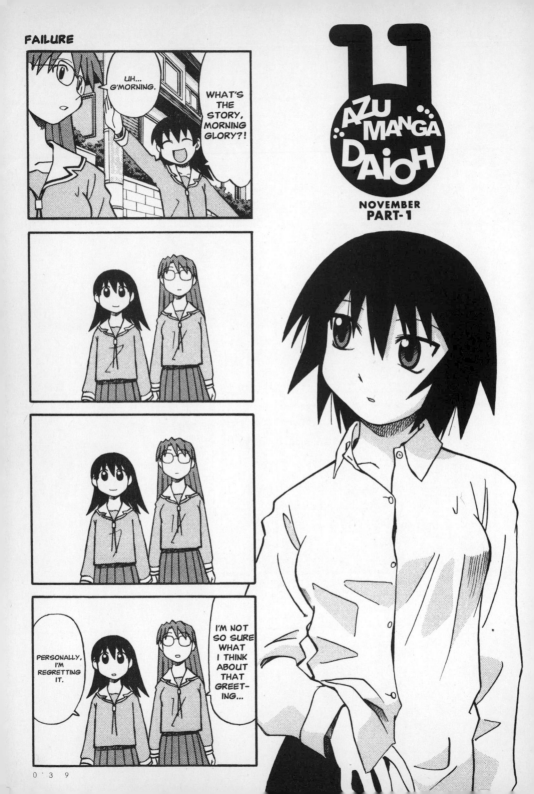

## 11
## AZUMANGA DAIOH
### NOVEMBER PART-1

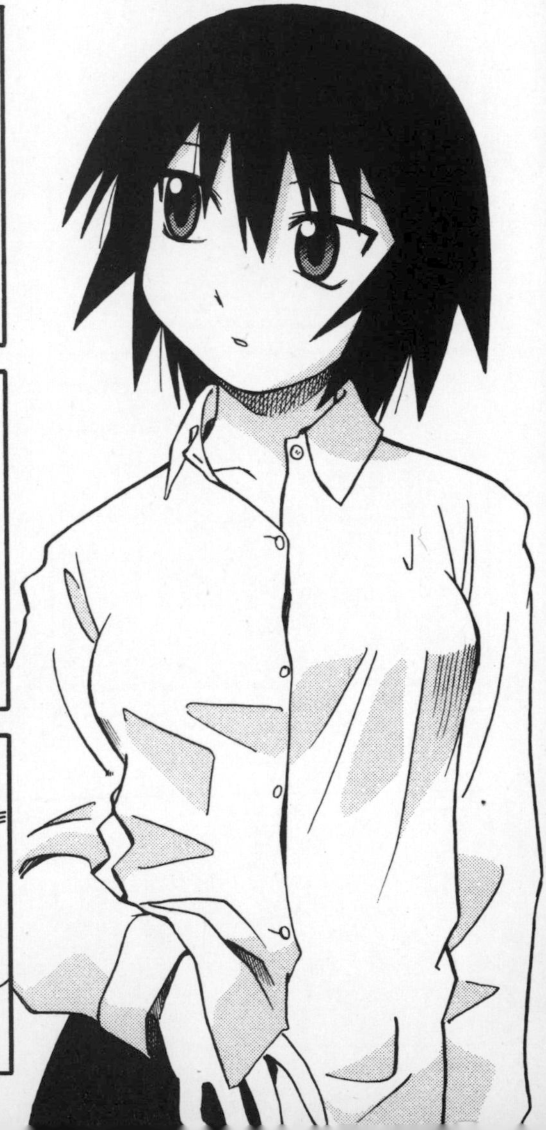

**FAILURE**

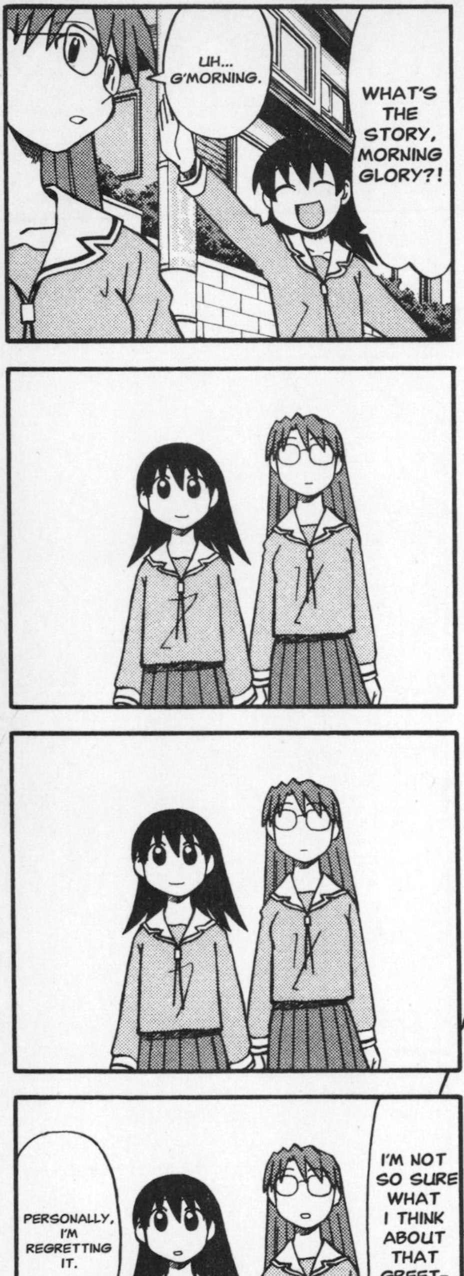
WHAT'S THE STORY, MORNING GLORY?!
UH... G'MORNING.
I'M NOT SO SURE WHAT I THINK ABOUT THAT GREET-ING...
PERSONALLY, I'M REGRETTING IT.

## LAISSEZ-FAIRE

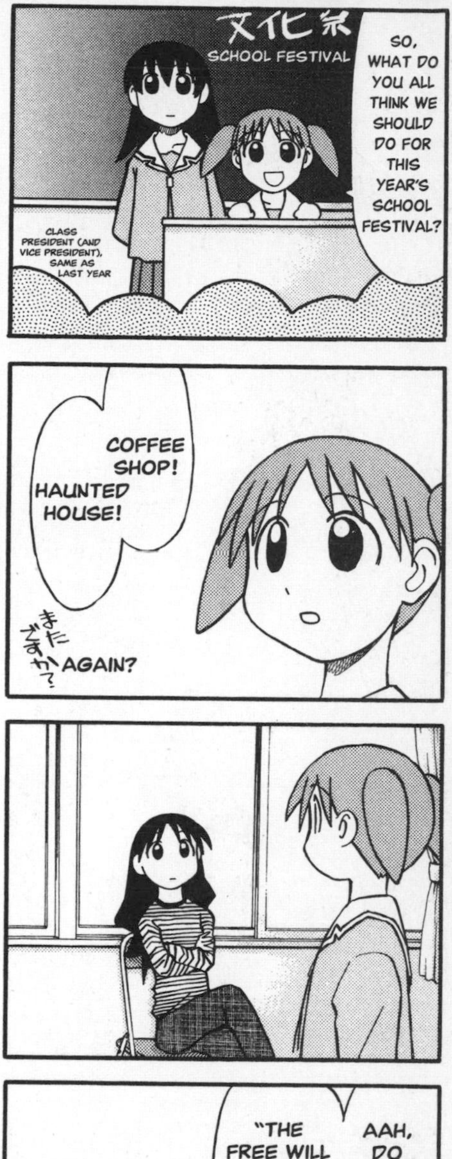
SO, WHAT DO YOU ALL THINK WE SHOULD DO FOR THIS YEAR'S SCHOOL FESTIVAL?
文化祭
SCHOOL FESTIVAL
CLASS PRESIDENT (AND VICE PRESIDENT), SAME AS LAST YEAR
COFFEE SHOP!
HAUNTED HOUSE!
またですか？
AGAIN?
AAH, DO WHAT-EVER YOU WANT.
"THE FREE WILL OF THE STUDENTS" AND ALL THAT CRAP.

## MILK THROUGH THE NOSE

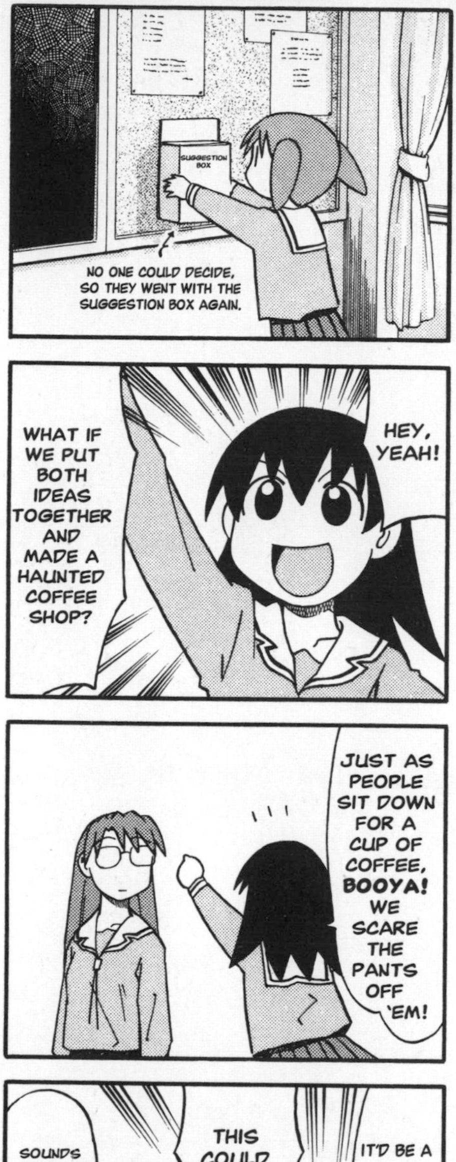
SUGGESTION BOX
NO ONE COULD DECIDE, SO THEY WENT WITH THE SUGGESTION BOX AGAIN.
HEY, YEAH!
WHAT IF WE PUT BOTH IDEAS TOGETHER AND MADE A HAUNTED COFFEE SHOP?
JUST AS PEOPLE SIT DOWN FOR A CUP OF COFFEE, **BOOYA!** WE SCARE THE PANTS OFF 'EM!
IT'D BE A COFFEE SHOP... WHERE YOU COULDN'T DRINK ANYTHING AT ALL!
THIS COULD REALLY WORK!
SOUNDS LIKE WHAT WE DID TO EACH OTHER AT LUNCH BACK IN ELEMEN-TARY SCHOOL.
THE BREAK WE'VE BEEN AFTER!

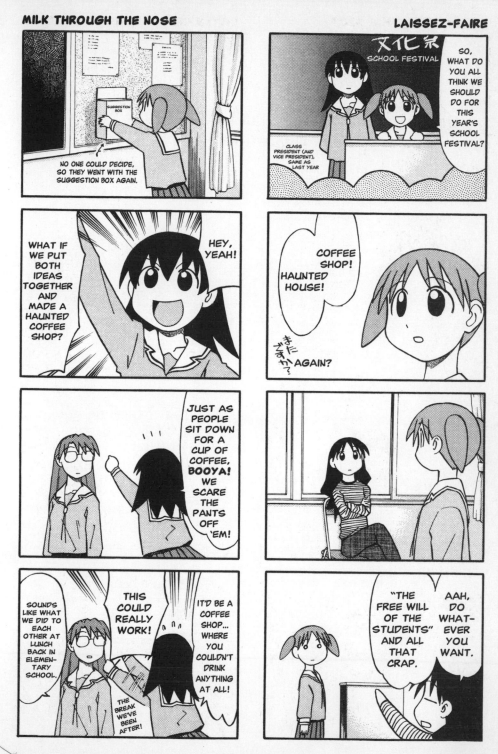

## LITTLE COFFEE SHOP OF HORRORS

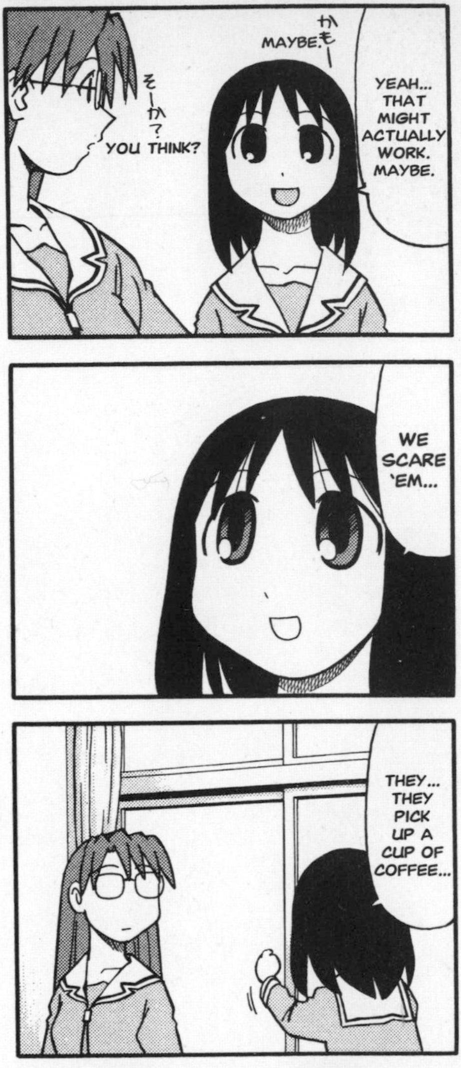

YEAH... THAT MIGHT ACTUALLY WORK. MAYBE.
かもー MAYBE.
そーか？ YOU THINK?
WE SCARE 'EM...
THEY... THEY PICK UP A CUP OF COFFEE...
AND THERE'S A BIG FREAKIN' COCKROACH FLOATING IN IT!
THEY'LL BE LIKE, "YO, WHAT'S UP WITH THIS? GIMME ANOTHER COFFEE!"
THAT DOESN'T SOUND MUCH LIKE A HAUNTED HOUSE...


## A HAUNTED COFFEE SHOP

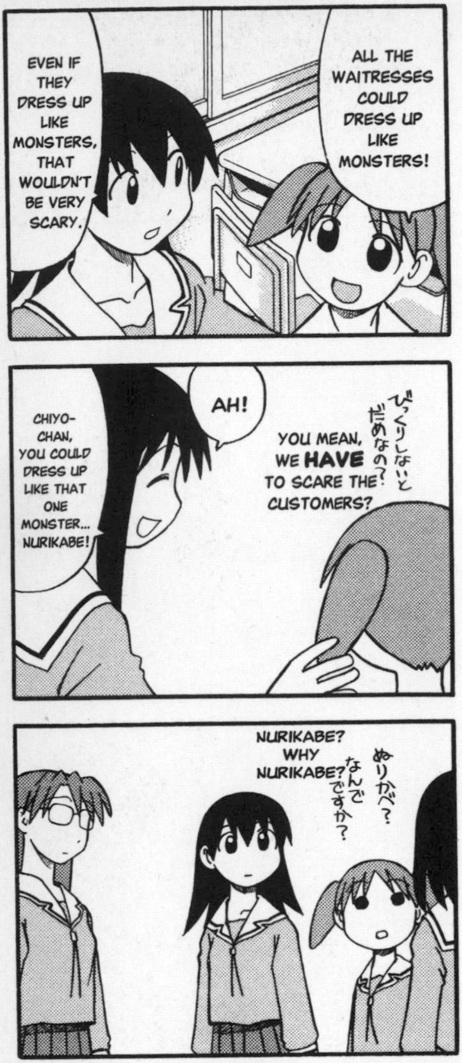

ALL THE WAITRESSES COULD DRESS UP LIKE MONSTERS!
EVEN IF THEY DRESS UP LIKE MONSTERS, THAT WOULDN'T BE VERY SCARY.
びっくりしないとだめなの？ YOU MEAN, WE HAVE TO SCARE THE CUSTOMERS?
AH!
CHIYO-CHAN, YOU COULD DRESS UP LIKE THAT ONE MONSTER... NURIKABE!
ぬりかべ？なんでですか？ NURIKABE? WHY NURIKABE?
IT'D PROBABLY BE PRETTY CUTE.

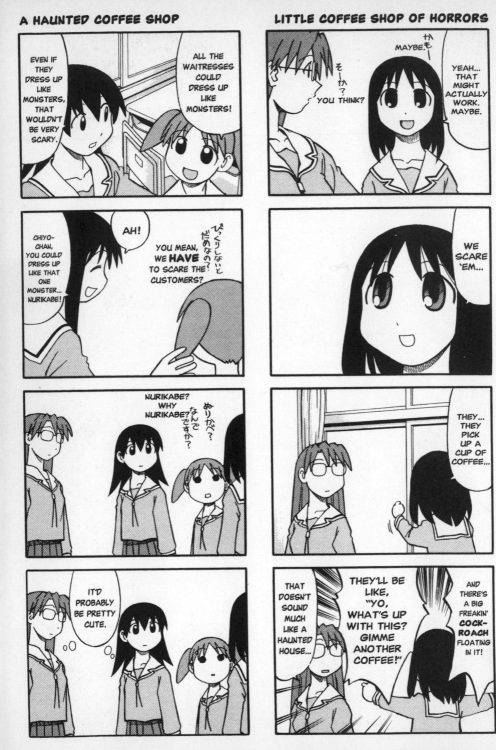

## NURIKABE-CHIYO

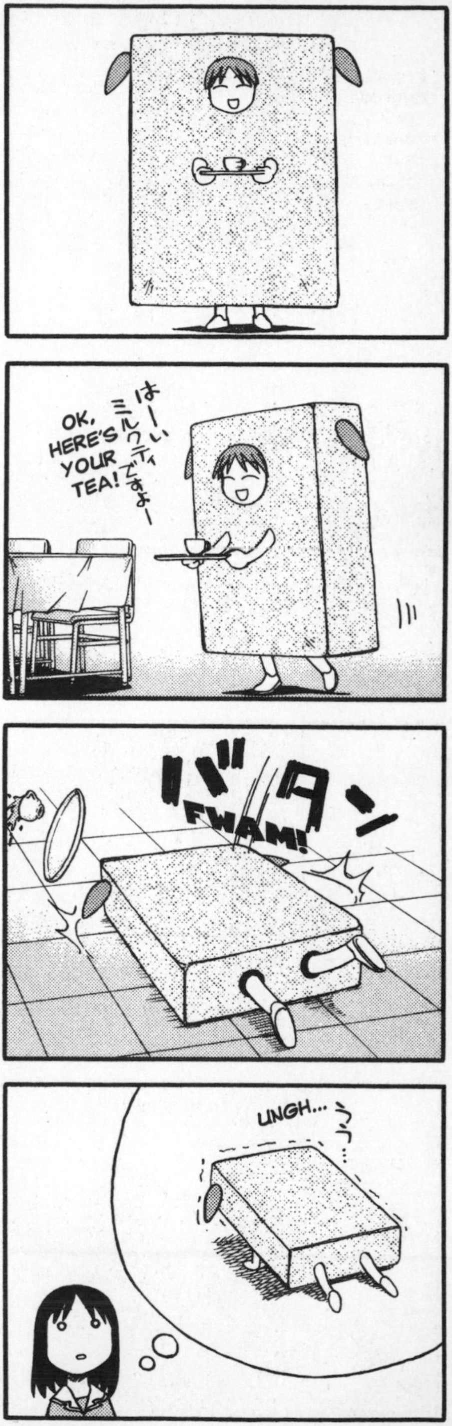

OK, HERE'S YOUR TEA!
はーい ミルクティですよー
バタン
FWAM!
UNGH...
うう…


## A FLAW IN THE DESIGN

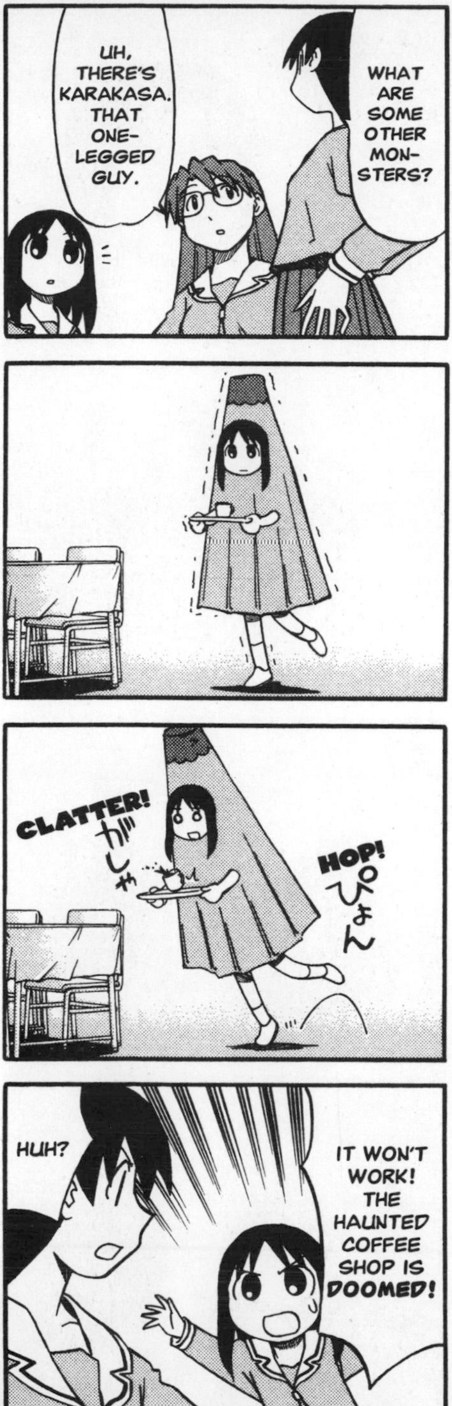

WHAT ARE SOME OTHER MONSTERS?
UH, THERE'S KARAKASA. THAT ONE-LEGGED GUY.
HOP!
ぴょん
CLATTER!
がしゃ
IT WON'T WORK! THE HAUNTED COFFEE SHOP IS **DOOMED!**
HUH?

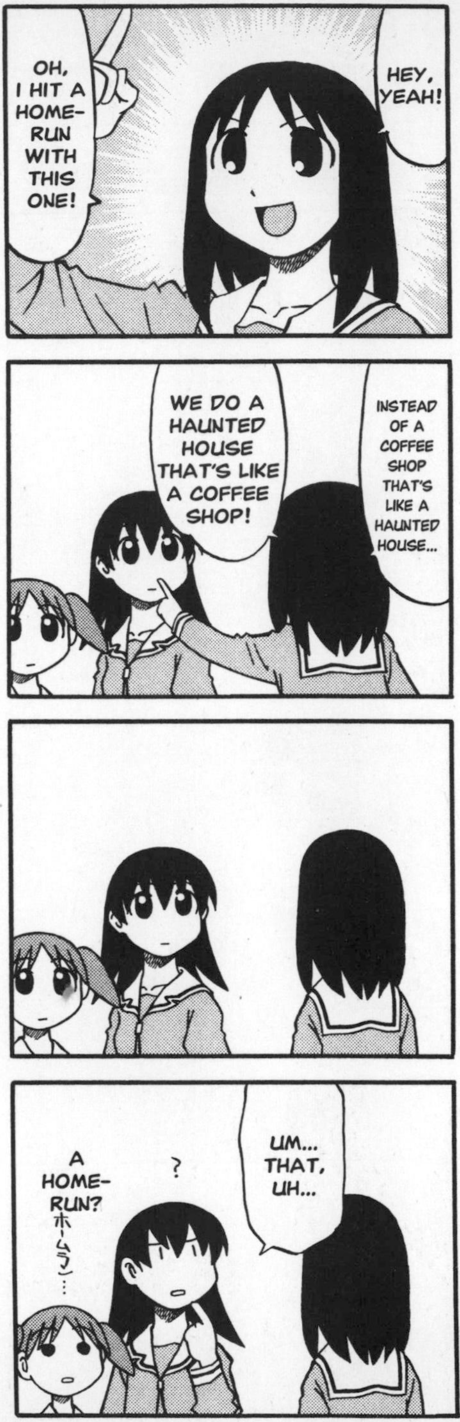
HEY, YEAH!
OH, I HIT A HOME-RUN WITH THIS ONE!
INSTEAD OF A COFFEE SHOP THAT'S LIKE A HAUNTED HOUSE...
WE DO A HAUNTED HOUSE THAT'S LIKE A COFFEE SHOP!
UM... THAT, UH...
?
A HOME-RUN?
ホームラン…



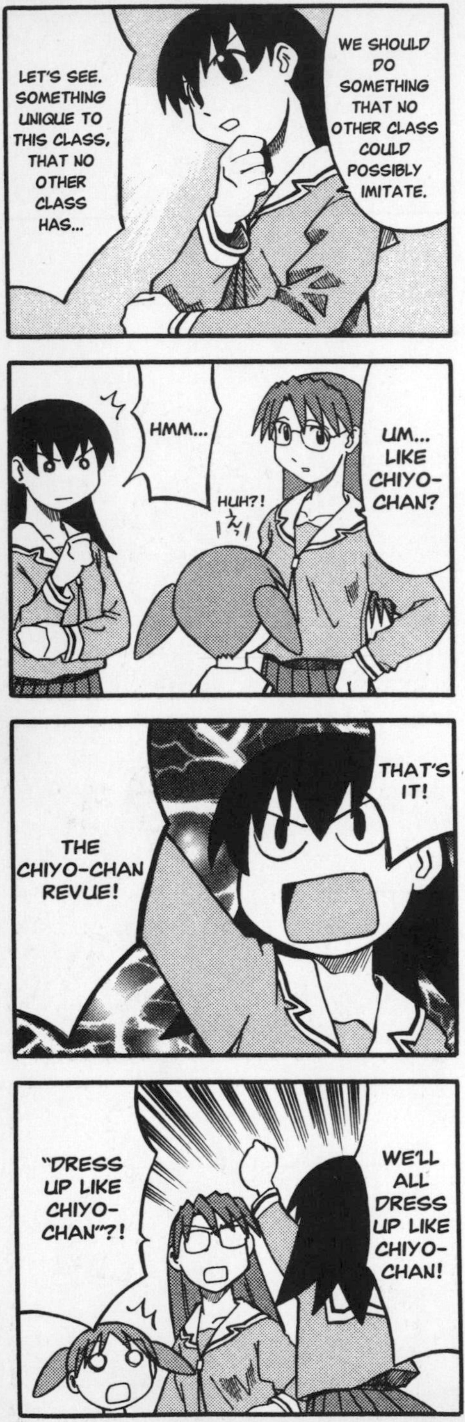
WE SHOULD DO SOMETHING THAT NO OTHER CLASS COULD POSSIBLY IMITATE.
LET'S SEE. SOMETHING UNIQUE TO THIS CLASS, THAT NO OTHER CLASS HAS...
UM... LIKE CHIYO-CHAN?
HMM...
HUH?!
えっ
THAT'S IT!
THE CHIYO-CHAN REVUE!
WE'LL ALL DRESS UP LIKE CHIYO-CHAN!
"DRESS UP LIKE CHIYO-CHAN"?!

I'M CHIYO!

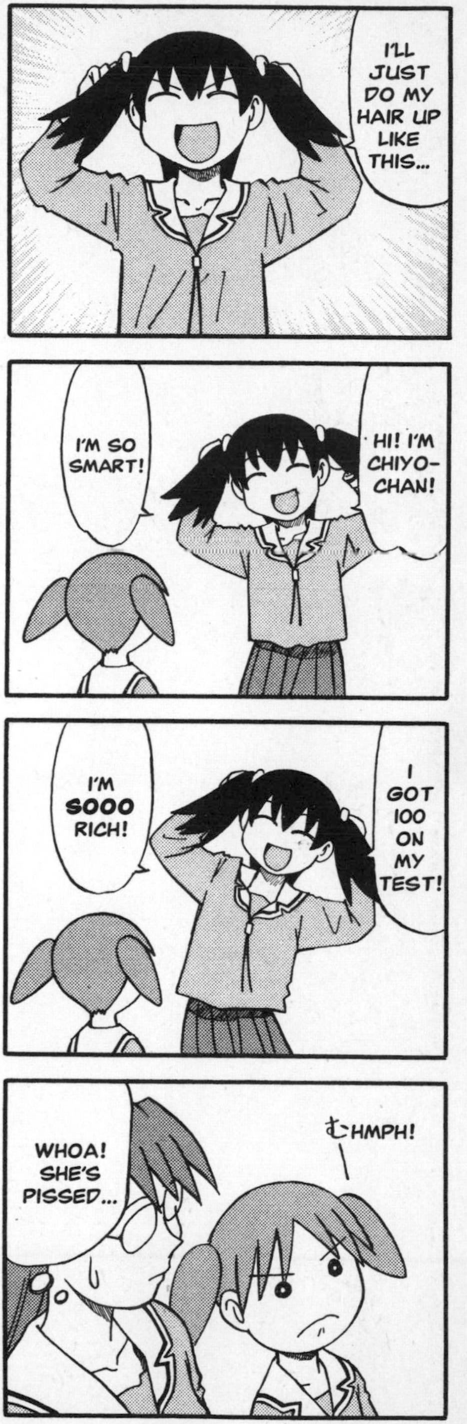

I'LL JUST DO MY HAIR UP LIKE THIS...
HI! I'M CHIYO-CHAN!
I'M SO SMART!
I GOT 100 ON MY TEST!
I'M **SOOO** RICH!
むHMPH!
WHOA! SHE'S PISSED...


CHIYO VER. 2

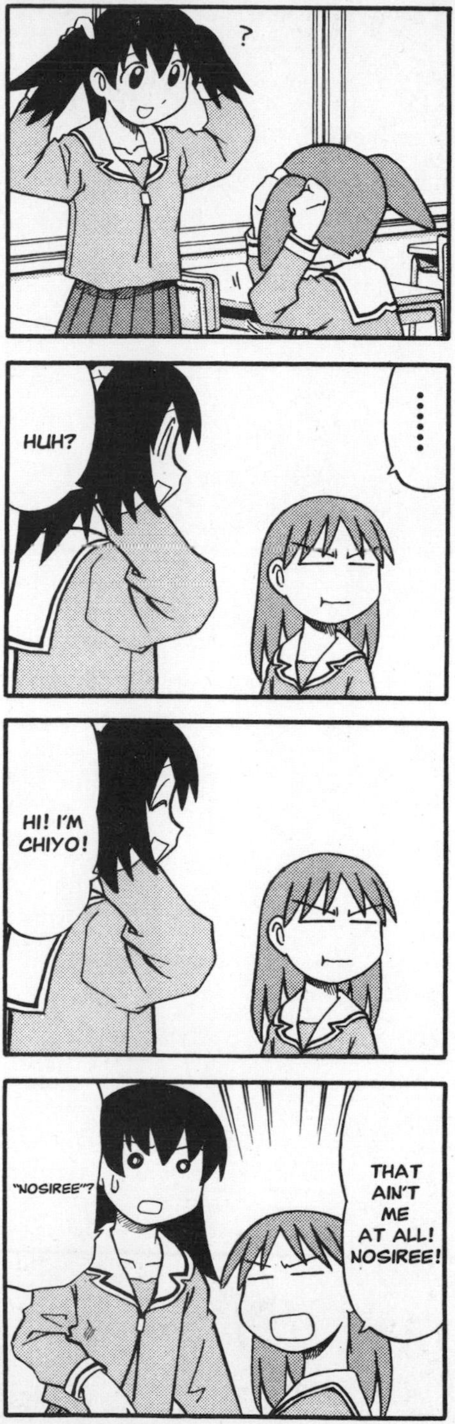

?
......
HUH?
HI! I'M CHIYO!
THAT AIN'T ME AT ALL! NOSIREE!
"NOSIREE"?

PEAS OF THE SAME POD

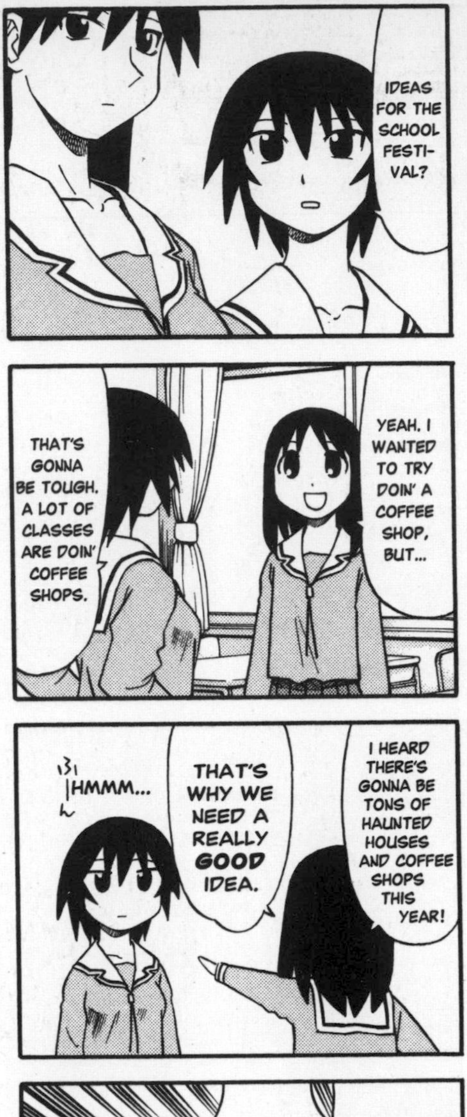
IDEAS FOR THE SCHOOL FESTIVAL?
YEAH. I WANTED TO TRY DOIN' A COFFEE SHOP, BUT...
THAT'S GONNA BE TOUGH. A LOT OF CLASSES ARE DOIN' COFFEE SHOPS.
I HEARD THERE'S GONNA BE TONS OF HAUNTED HOUSES AND COFFEE SHOPS THIS YEAR!
THAT'S WHY WE NEED A REALLY GOOD IDEA.
ふーん HMMM...
I'VE GOT IT! YOU COULD PUT 'EM BOTH TOGETHER TO MAKE A HAUNTED COFFEE SHOP!
IT'S A GREAT IDEA!
HEY! WE'RE ON THE SAME WAVELENGTH!
GRRR...
むう

THE COMBINATION

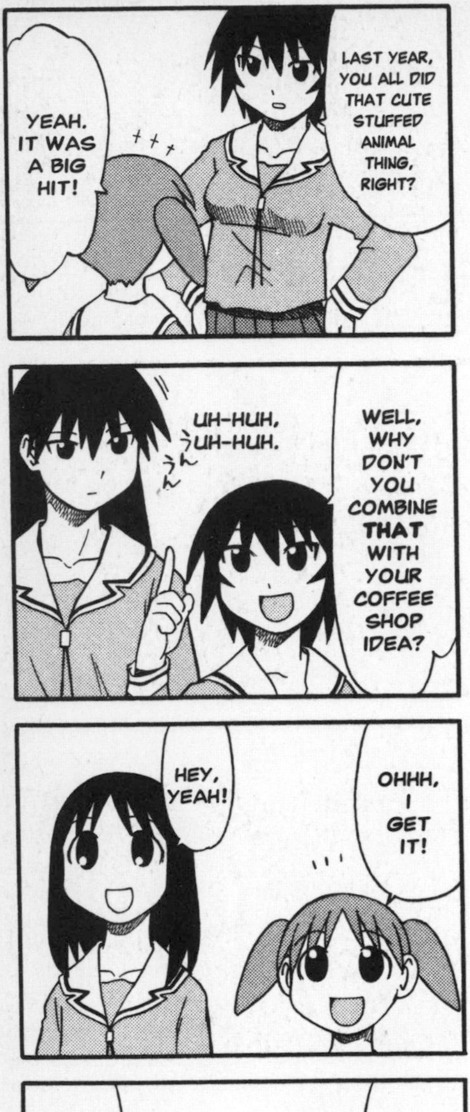
LAST YEAR, YOU ALL DID THAT CUTE STUFFED ANIMAL THING, RIGHT?
YEAH. IT WAS A BIG HIT!
WELL, WHY DON'T YOU COMBINE THAT WITH YOUR COFFEE SHOP IDEA?
うんうん UH-HUH, UH-HUH.
OHHH, I GET IT!
HEY, YEAH!
A CUTE HAUNTED COFFEE SHOP!
NO, NO!

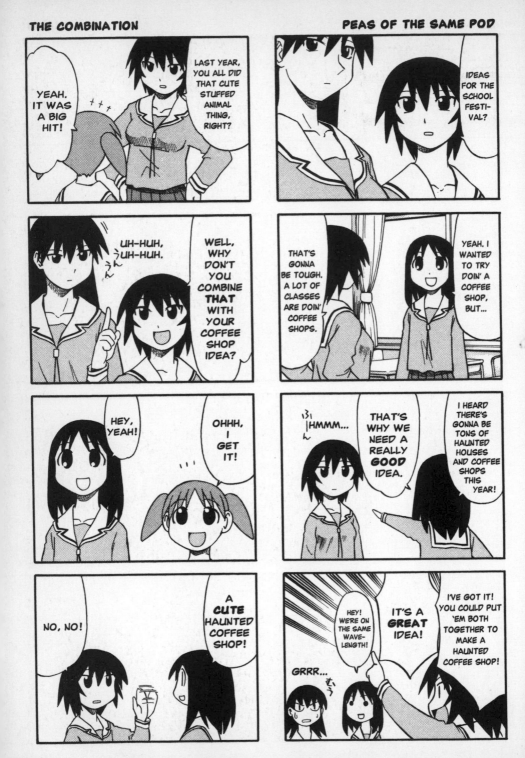

## ALL MIXED UP

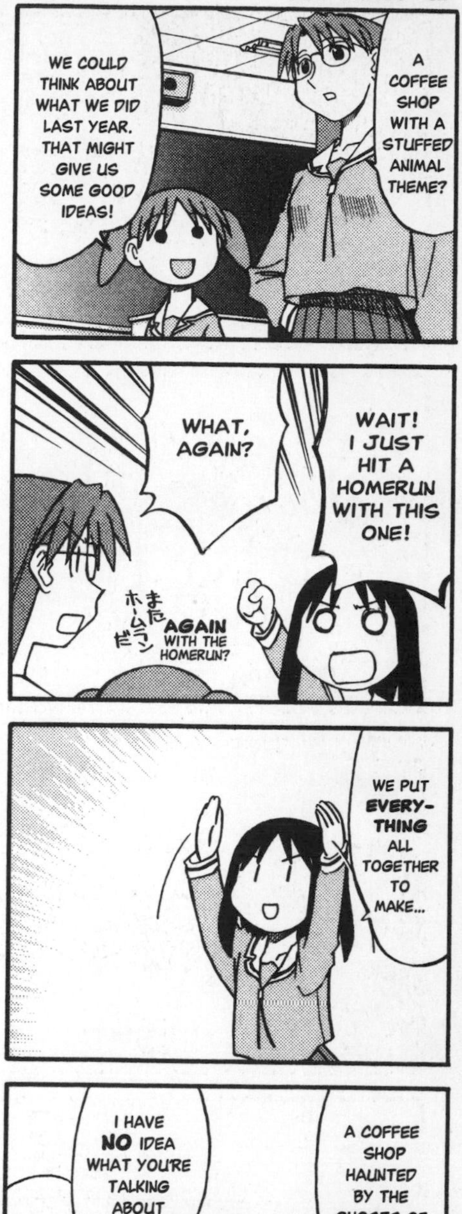
A COFFEE SHOP WITH A STUFFED ANIMAL THEME?
WE COULD THINK ABOUT WHAT WE DID LAST YEAR. THAT MIGHT GIVE US SOME GOOD IDEAS!
WAIT! I JUST HIT A HOMERUN WITH THIS ONE!
WHAT, AGAIN?
またホームランだ
AGAIN WITH THE HOMERUN?
WE PUT EVERYTHING ALL TOGETHER TO MAKE...
A COFFEE SHOP HAUNTED BY THE GHOSTS OF CUDDLY LITTLE ANIMALS!
I HAVE NO IDEA WHAT YOU'RE TALKING ABOUT ANYMORE!
THAT'S MORE OF A FOUL BALL THAN A HOMERUN.

## OH, MY

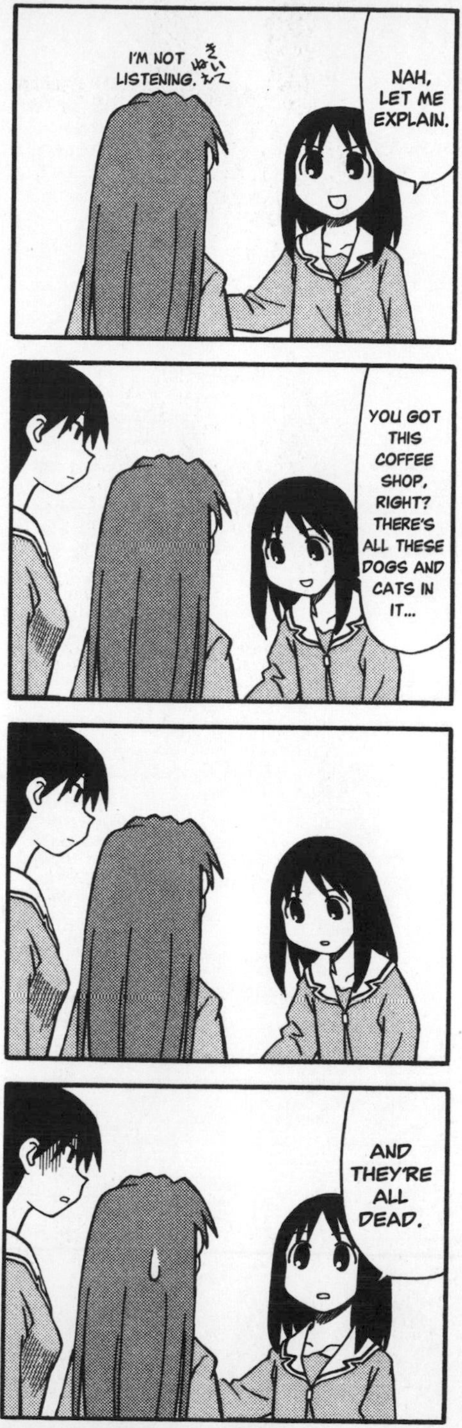
NAH, LET ME EXPLAIN.
I'M NOT LISTENING.
YOU GOT THIS COFFEE SHOP, RIGHT? THERE'S ALL THESE DOGS AND CATS IN IT...
AND THEY'RE ALL DEAD.

# 11 NOVEMBER PART-2

AZU MANGA DAIOH

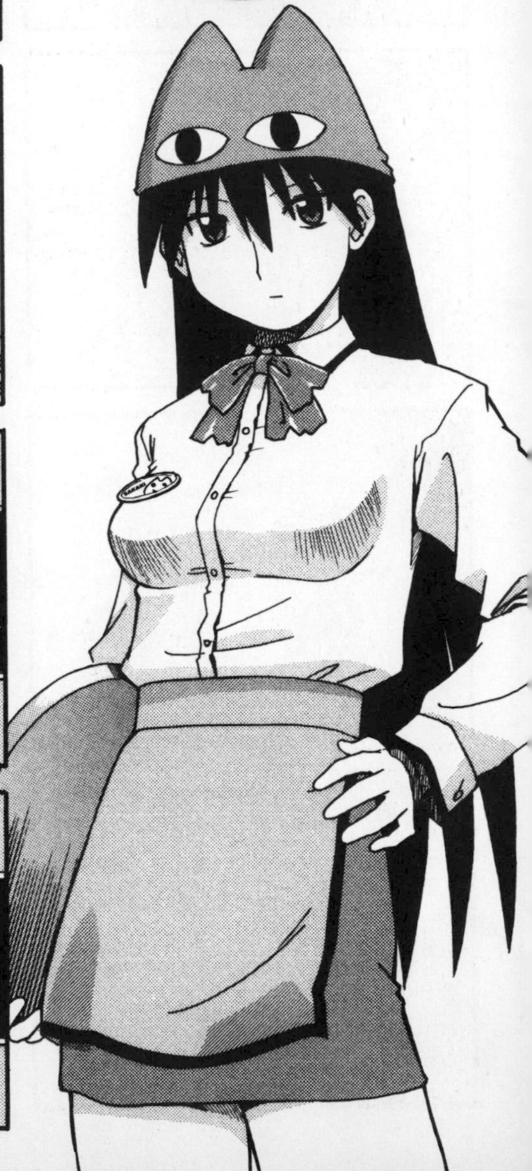

FERVENT

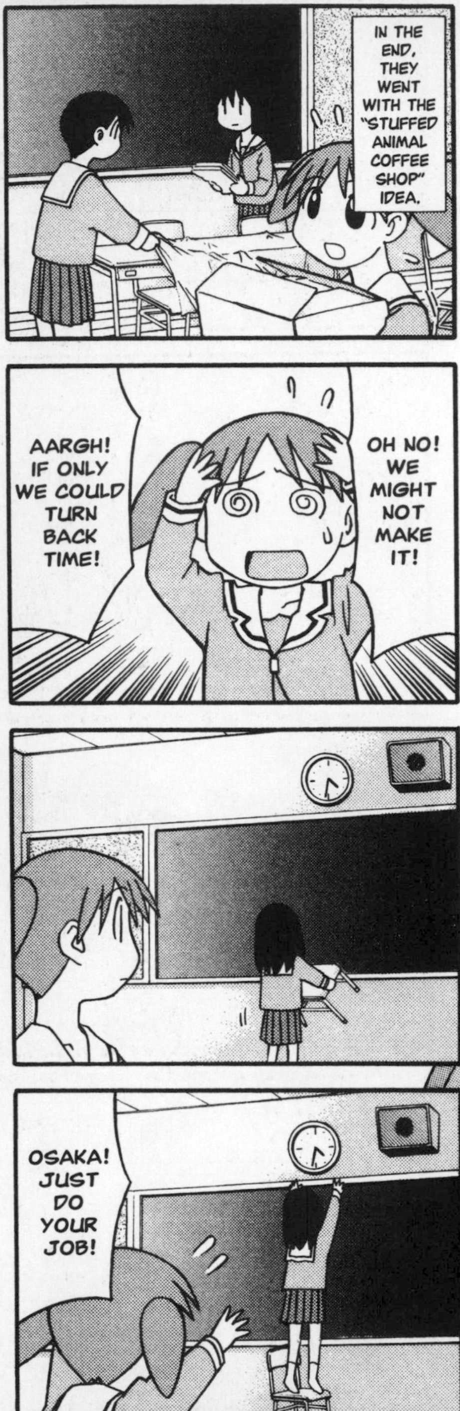
IN THE END, THEY WENT WITH THE "STUFFED ANIMAL COFFEE SHOP" IDEA.
OH NO! WE MIGHT NOT MAKE IT!
AARGH! IF ONLY WE COULD TURN BACK TIME!
OSAKA! JUST DO YOUR JOB!

THE SHOWDOWN

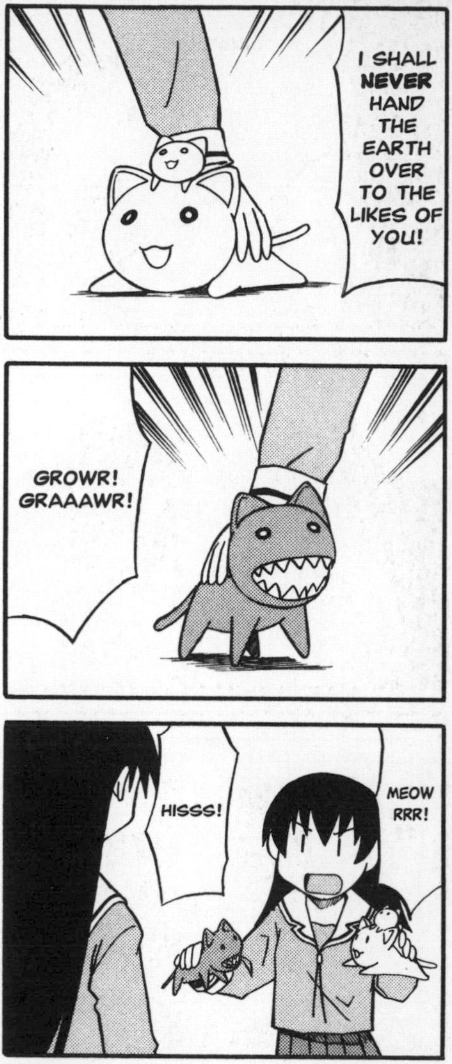
I SHALL NEVER HAND THE EARTH OVER TO THE LIKES OF YOU!
GROWR! GRAAAWR!
MEOW RRR!
HISSS!
VERY WELL! TO THE DEATH!
よし 勝負だー
WILL YOU PLEASE GET BACK TO WORK?!

THE ADVENT

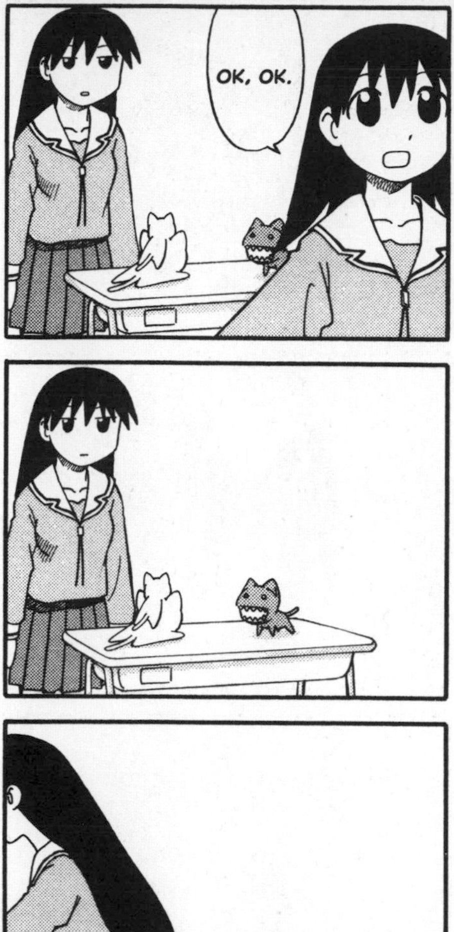
OK, OK.

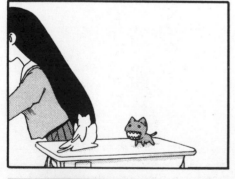

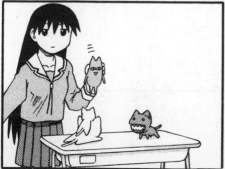

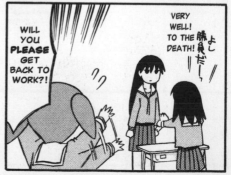

CHIYO-CHAN'S DAD

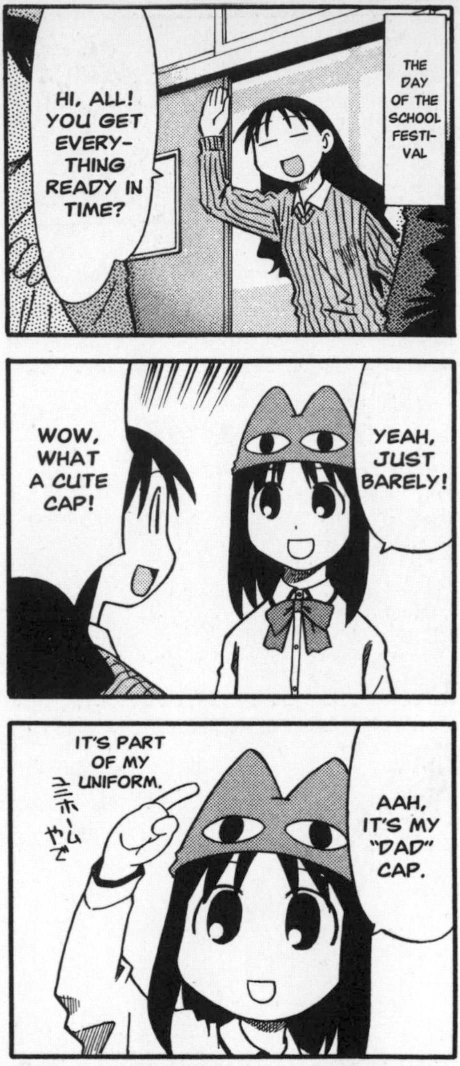
THE DAY OF THE SCHOOL FESTI-VAL
HI, ALL! YOU GET EVERY-THING READY IN TIME?
YEAH, JUST BARELY!
WOW, WHAT A CUTE CAP!
AAH, IT'S MY "DAD" CAP.
IT'S PART OF MY UNIFORM.
ユニホームやで
"DAD"?
YEAH. THAT'S WHAT SAKAKI STARTED CALLING IT.

HEADGEAR

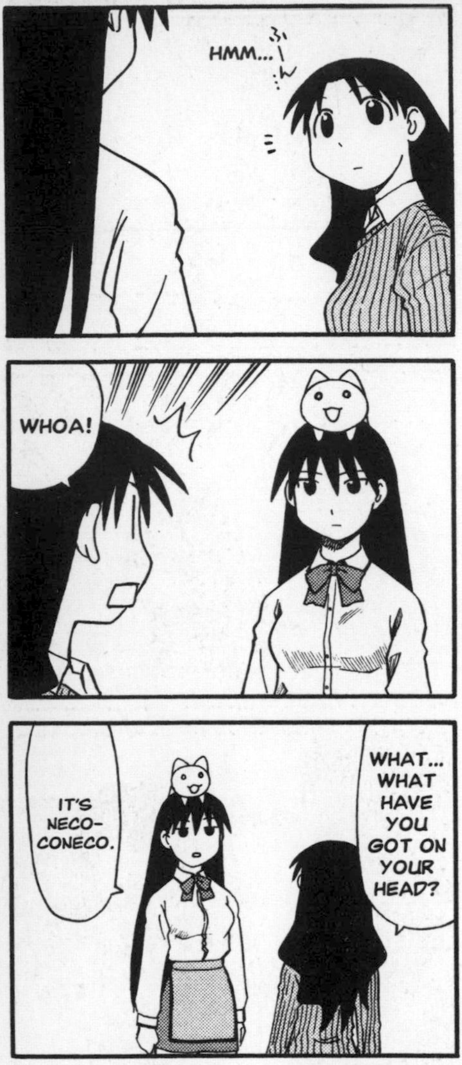
HMM...
ふーん
WHOA!
WHAT... WHAT HAVE YOU GOT ON YOUR HEAD?
IT'S NECO-CONECO.
I KNOW THAT, BUT WHAT'S IT DOING UP THERE?

## IMMENSELY SATISFIED

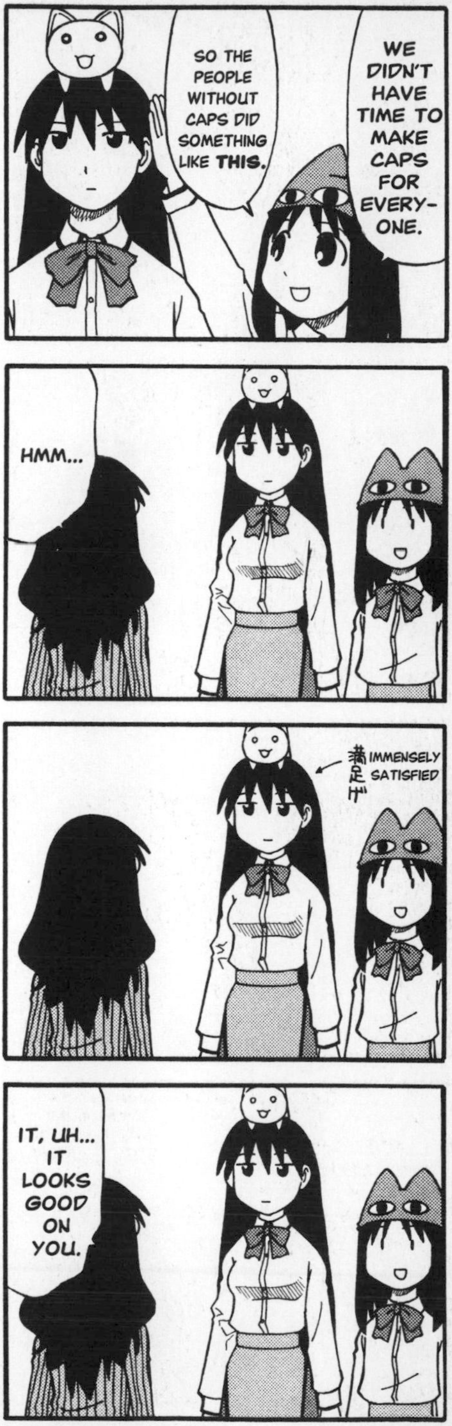
WE DIDN'T HAVE TIME TO MAKE CAPS FOR EVERY-ONE.
SO THE PEOPLE WITHOUT CAPS DID SOMETHING LIKE **THIS**.
HMM...
満足げ
IMMENSELY SATISFIED
IT, UH... IT LOOKS GOOD ON YOU.

## CAPTAIN ON THE BRIDGE!

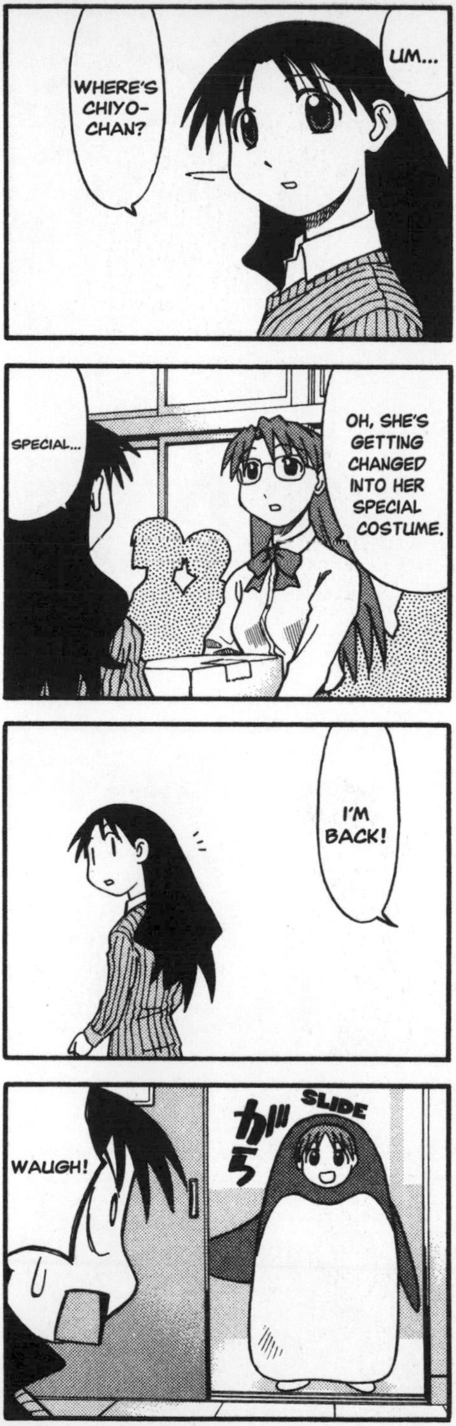
UM...
WHERE'S CHIYO-CHAN?
OH, SHE'S GETTING CHANGED INTO HER SPECIAL COSTUME.
SPECIAL...
I'M BACK!
がら
SLIDE
WAUGH!

SO CUTE!

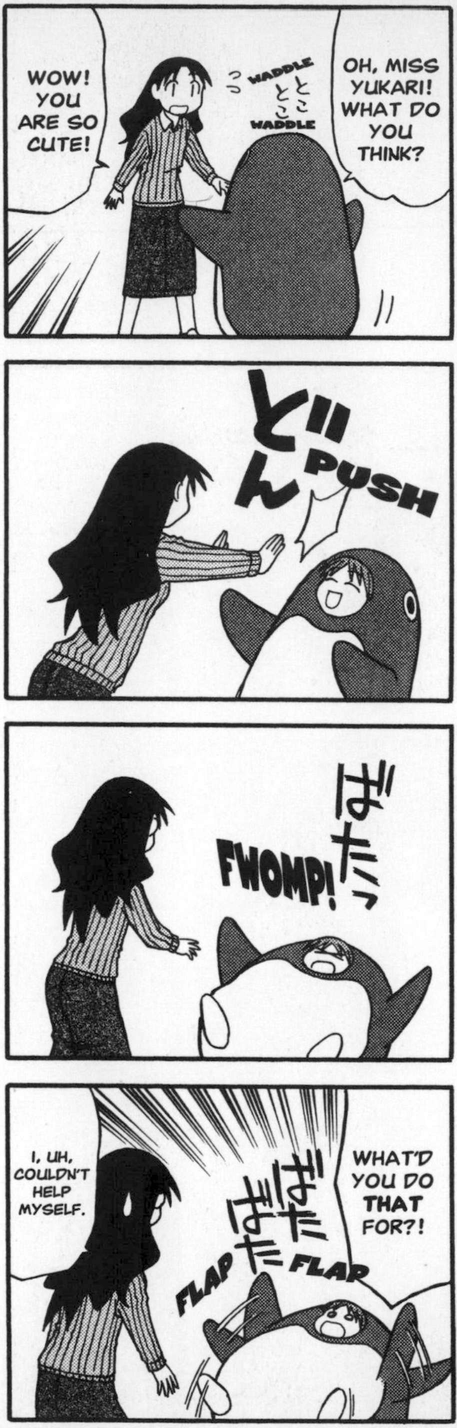

OH, MISS YUKARI! WHAT DO YOU THINK?
WADDLE とことこ WADDLE
WOW! YOU ARE SO CUTE!
とん
PUSH
ばたっ
FWOMP!
WHAT'D YOU DO THAT FOR?!
ばたばた
FLAP FLAP
I, UH, COULDN'T HELP MYSELF.


MAN!!

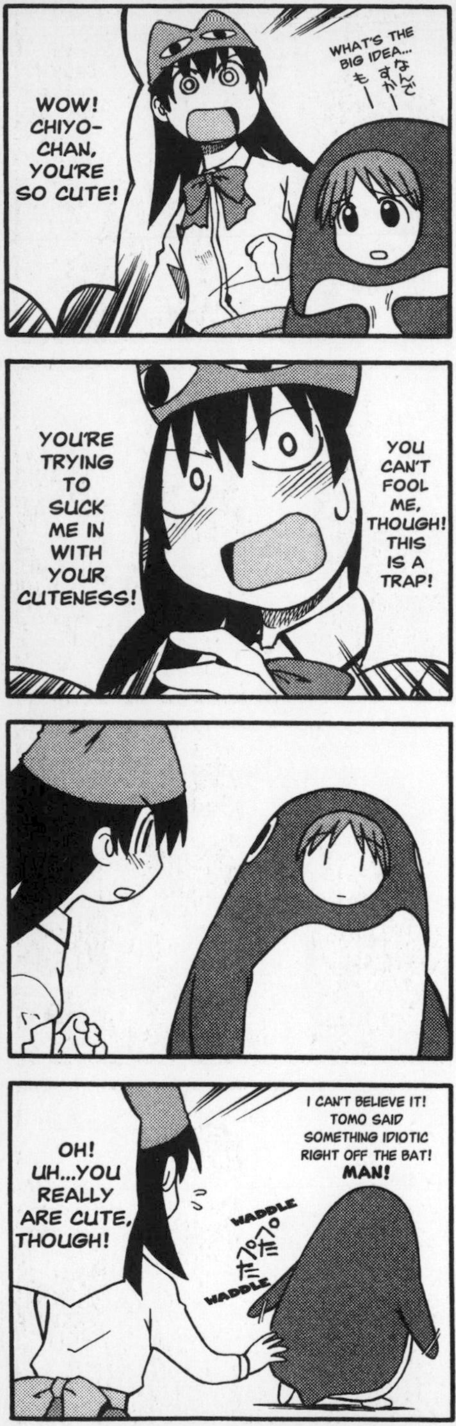

WHAT'S THE BIG IDEA... なんですかー もー
WOW! CHIYO-CHAN, YOU'RE SO CUTE!
YOU CAN'T FOOL ME, THOUGH! THIS IS A TRAP!
YOU'RE TRYING TO SUCK ME IN WITH YOUR CUTENESS!
I CAN'T BELIEVE IT! TOMO SAID SOMETHING IDIOTIC RIGHT OFF THE BAT! MAN!
WADDLE ぺたぺた WADDLE
OH! UH...YOU REALLY ARE CUTE, THOUGH!

## NOT TO WORRY

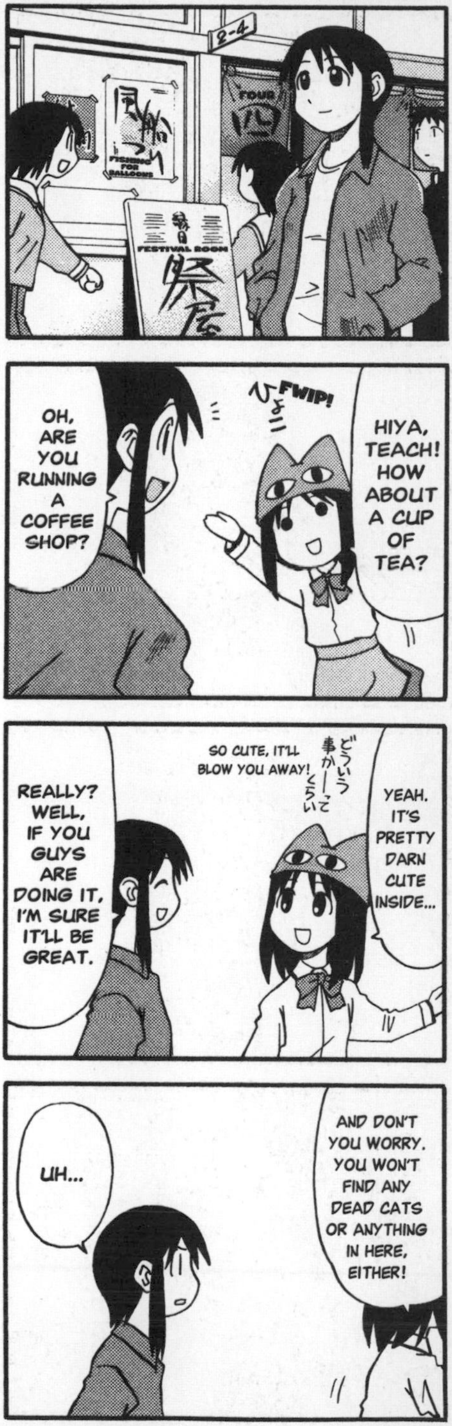
2-4
FOUR
FISHING FOR BALLOONS
FESTIVAL ROOM
祭屋
ひょこ
FWIP!
HIYA, TEACH! HOW ABOUT A CUP OF TEA?
OH, ARE YOU RUNNING A COFFEE SHOP?
YEAH. IT'S PRETTY DARN CUTE INSIDE...
どういう事かーってくらい
SO CUTE, IT'LL BLOW YOU AWAY!
REALLY? WELL, IF YOU GUYS ARE DOING IT, I'M SURE IT'LL BE GREAT.
AND DON'T YOU WORRY. YOU WON'T FIND ANY DEAD CATS OR ANYTHING IN HERE, EITHER!
UH...

## THIS IS...

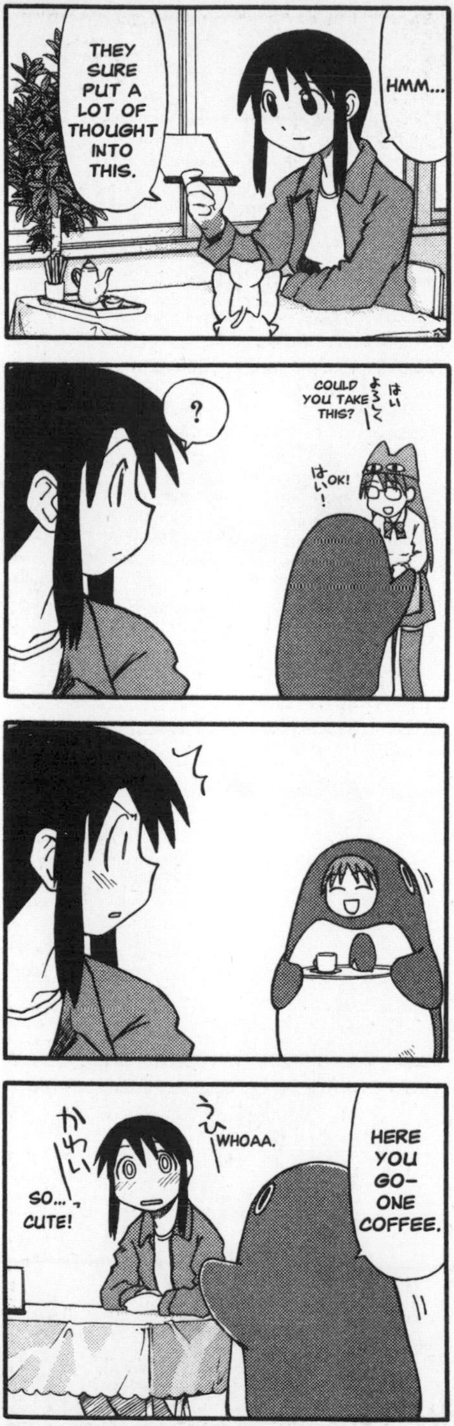
HMM...
THEY SURE PUT A LOT OF THOUGHT INTO THIS.
はい よろしくー
COULD YOU TAKE THIS?
はい！
OK!
?
HERE YOU GO— ONE COFFEE.
うひ
WHOAA.
かわいー
SO... CUTE!

## THE ORDER

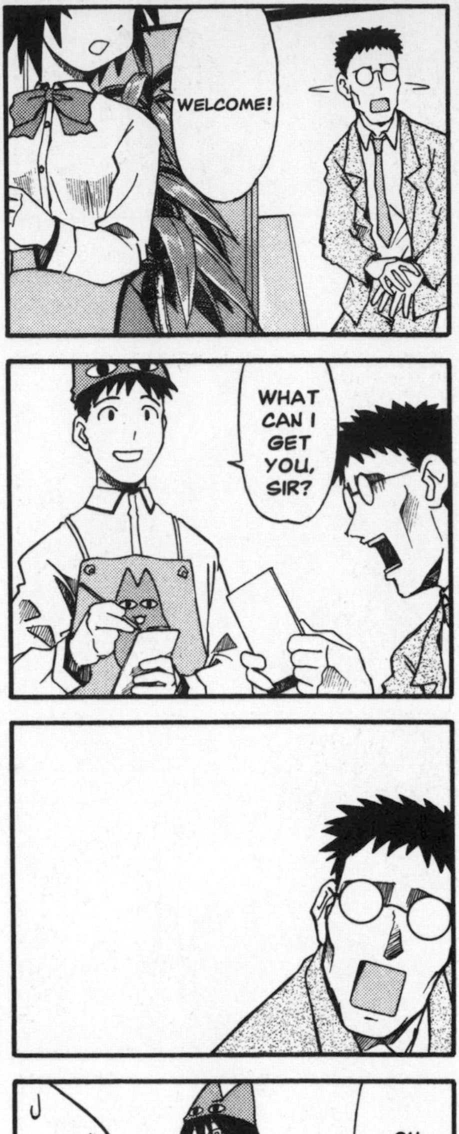
WELCOME!
WHAT CAN I GET YOU, SIR?
OH, MISS? I'M READY TO ORDER.

## I CAN HELP

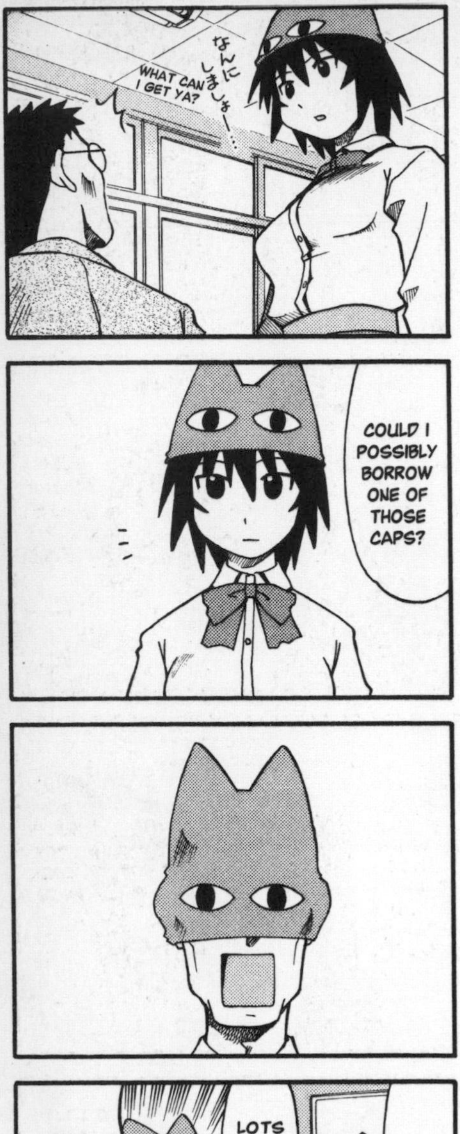
なんにしましょ…
WHAT CAN I GET YA?
COULD I POSSIBLY BORROW ONE OF THOSE CAPS?
HURRY, HURRY, STEP RIGHT UP!
LOTS OF CUTE STUFF IN HERE!
WE DON'T NEED ANY **HELP**, THANKS VERY MUCH!

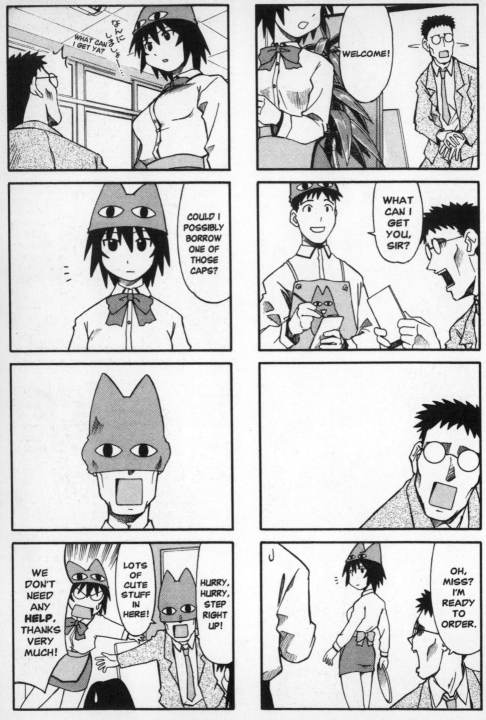

## MISSING A CERTAIN...SOMETHING

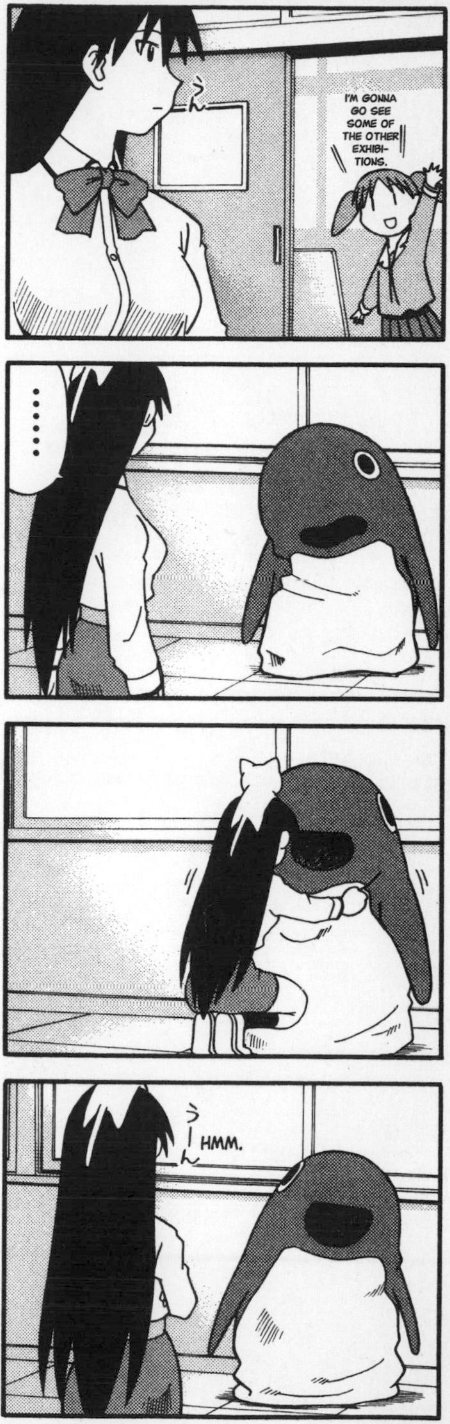
うーん
I'M GONNA GO SEE SOME OF THE OTHER EXHIBITIONS.
......
うーん
HMM.

## THE FINISHING TOUCH

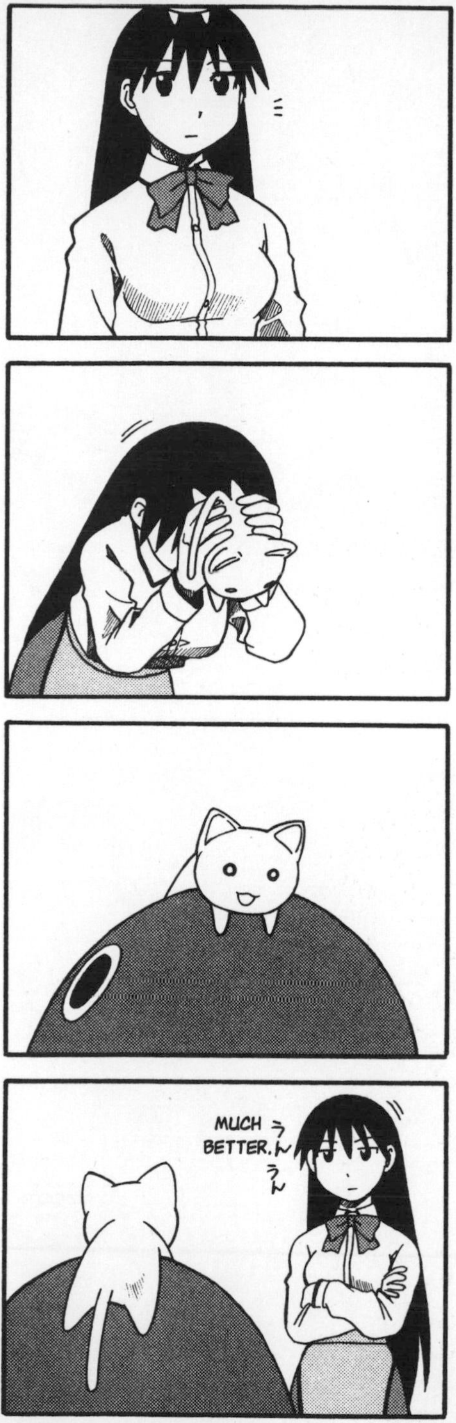
MUCH BETTER.
うん うん

# AZUMANGA-DAIOH
# 055

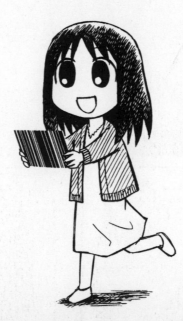

*You belong*

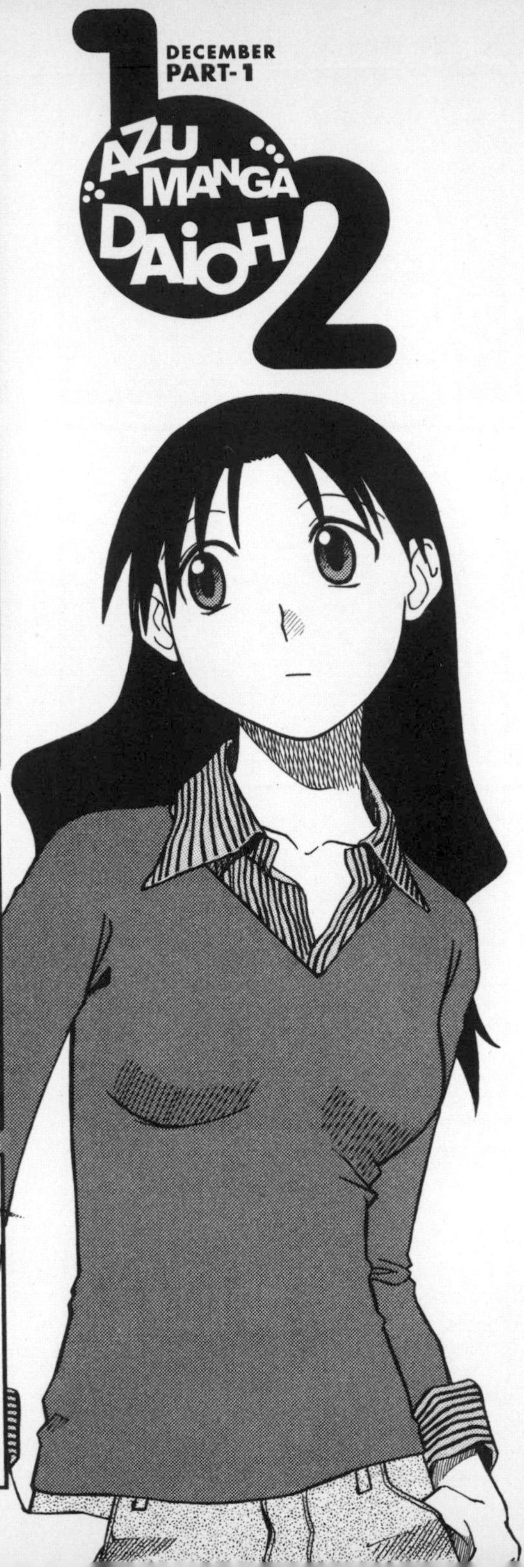
DECEMBER
PART-1
AZUMANGA DAIOH 2

ILL-PREPARED

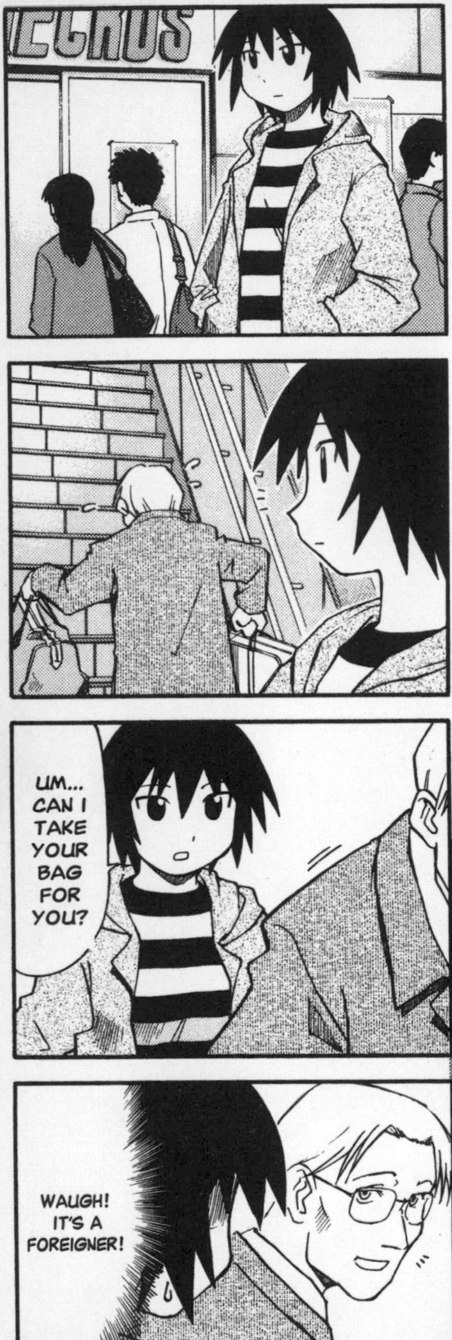
UM... CAN I TAKE YOUR BAG FOR YOU?
WAUGH! IT'S A FOREIGNER!

I...

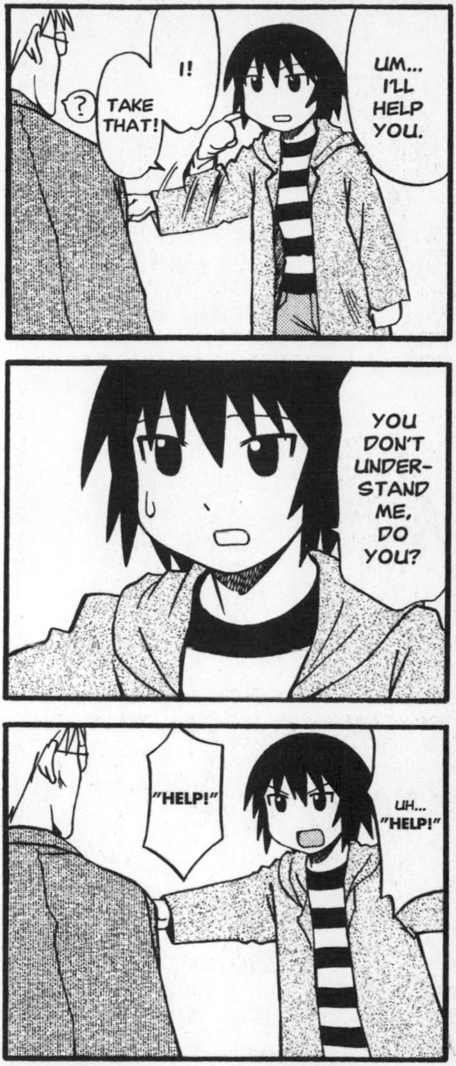
UM... I'LL HELP YOU.
!!
TAKE THAT!
?
YOU DON'T UNDER-STAND ME, DO YOU?
UH... "HELP!"
"HELP!"
"HELP ME!"

BON VOYAGE

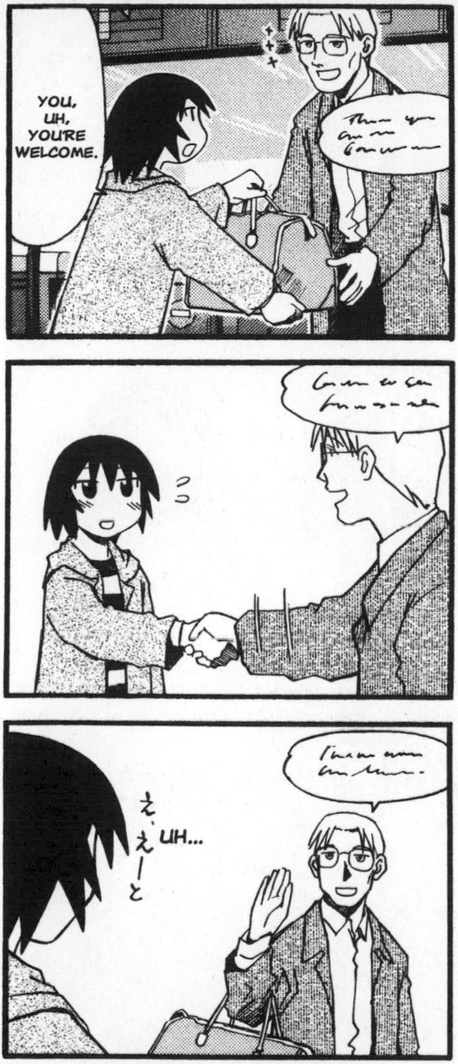
YOU, UH, YOU'RE WELCOME.
UH...
え、えーと
"YAY!"

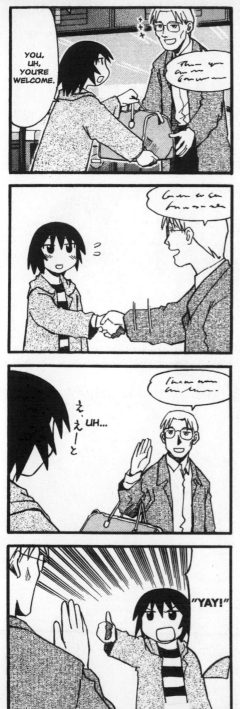

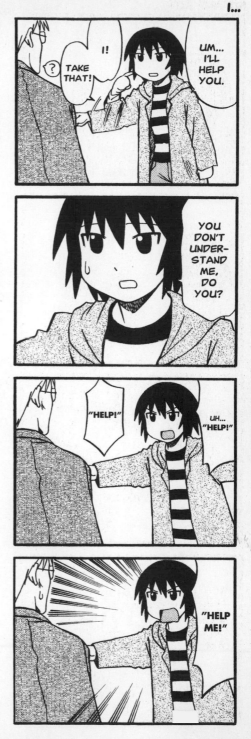

## AN INTERNATIONAL CITY

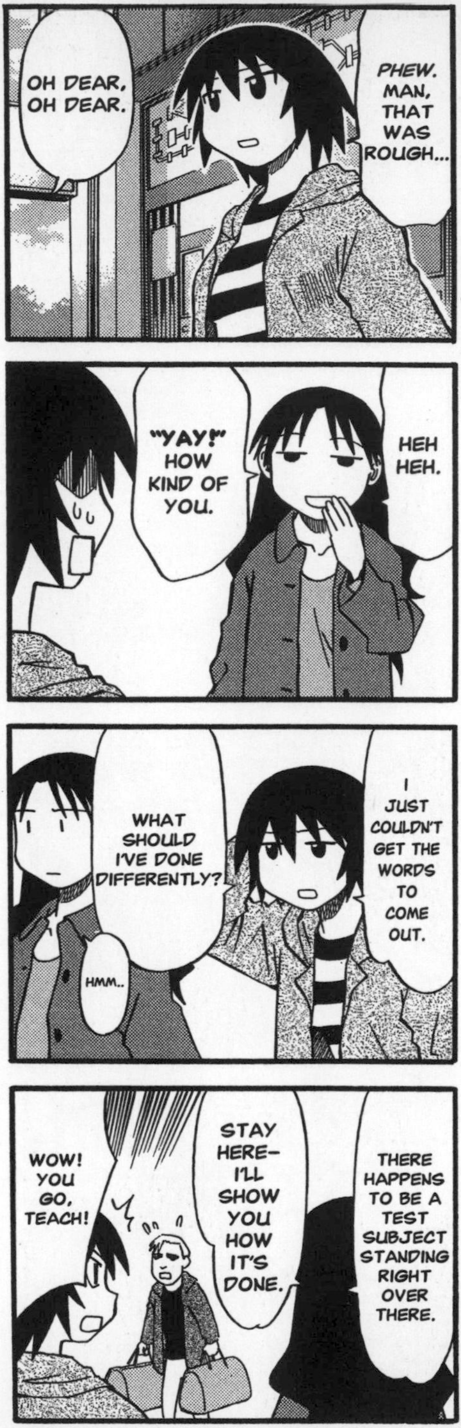
PHEW. MAN, THAT WAS ROUGH...
OH DEAR, OH DEAR.
HEH HEH.
"YAY!" HOW KIND OF YOU.
I JUST COULDN'T GET THE WORDS TO COME OUT.
WHAT SHOULD I'VE DONE DIFFERENTLY?
HMM..
THERE HAPPENS TO BE A TEST SUBJECT STANDING RIGHT OVER THERE.
STAY HERE— I'LL SHOW YOU HOW IT'S DONE.
WOW! YOU GO, TEACH!

## HIT AND RUN

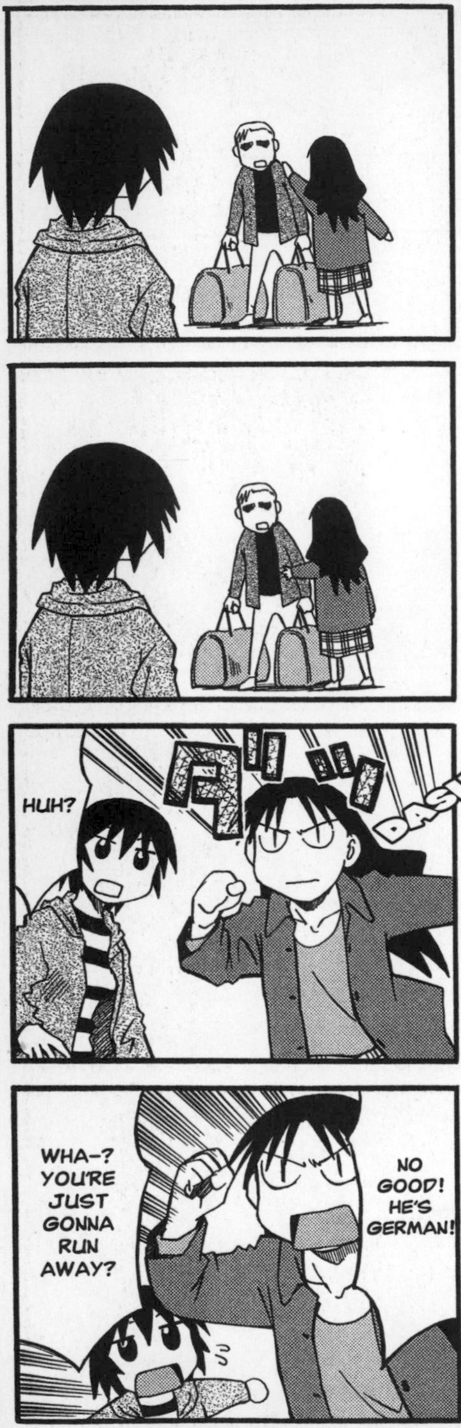
DASH
HUH?
NO GOOD! HE'S GERMAN!
WHA-? YOU'RE JUST GONNA RUN AWAY?

BULLET

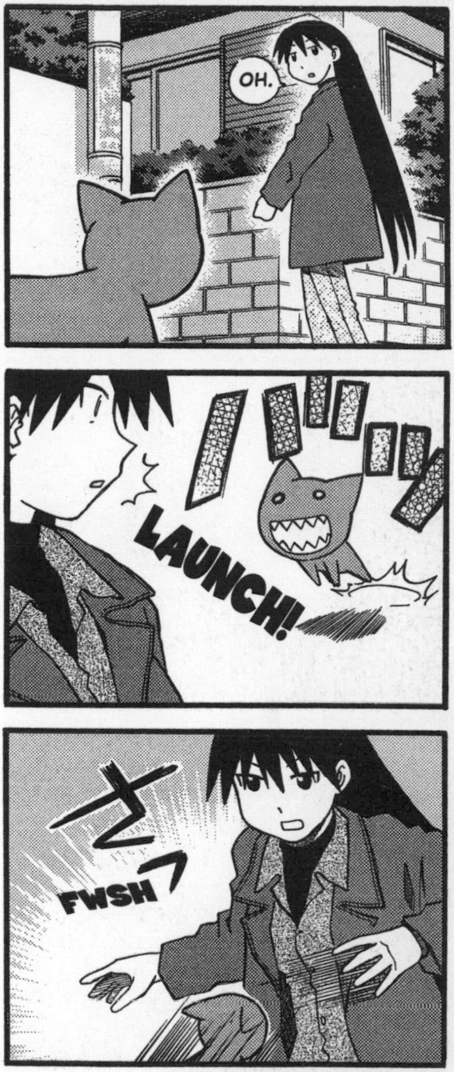
OH.
LAUNCH!
FWSH
GRARGH!
THWOMP!

TECHNIQUE

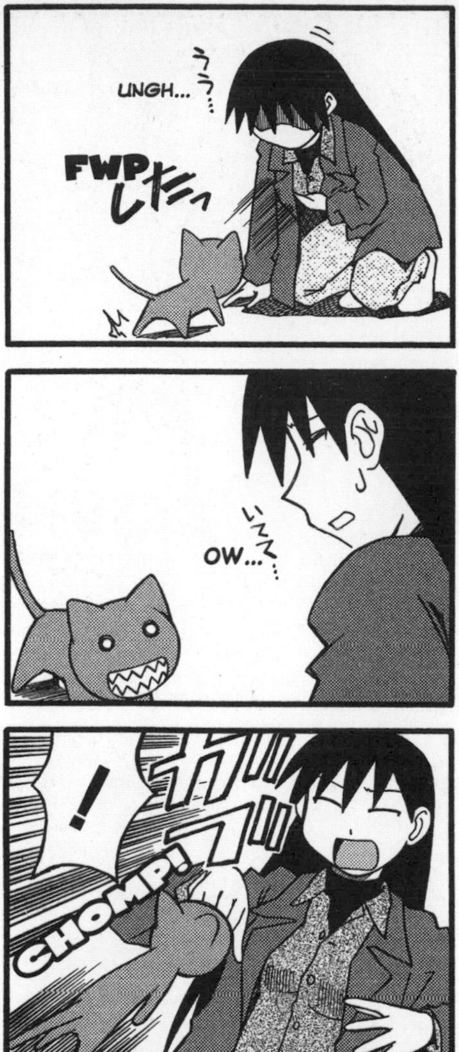
UNGH...
FWP
OW...
!
CHOMP!
?!
FWOOP
FWOOP

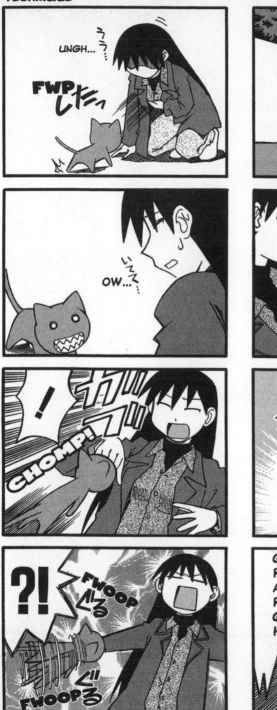

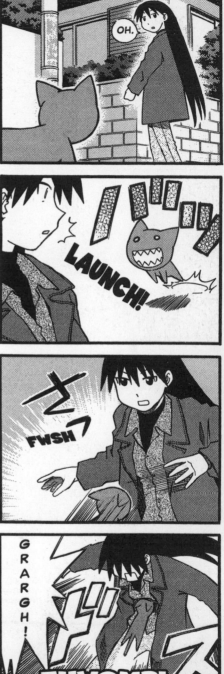

## DISCIPLINE

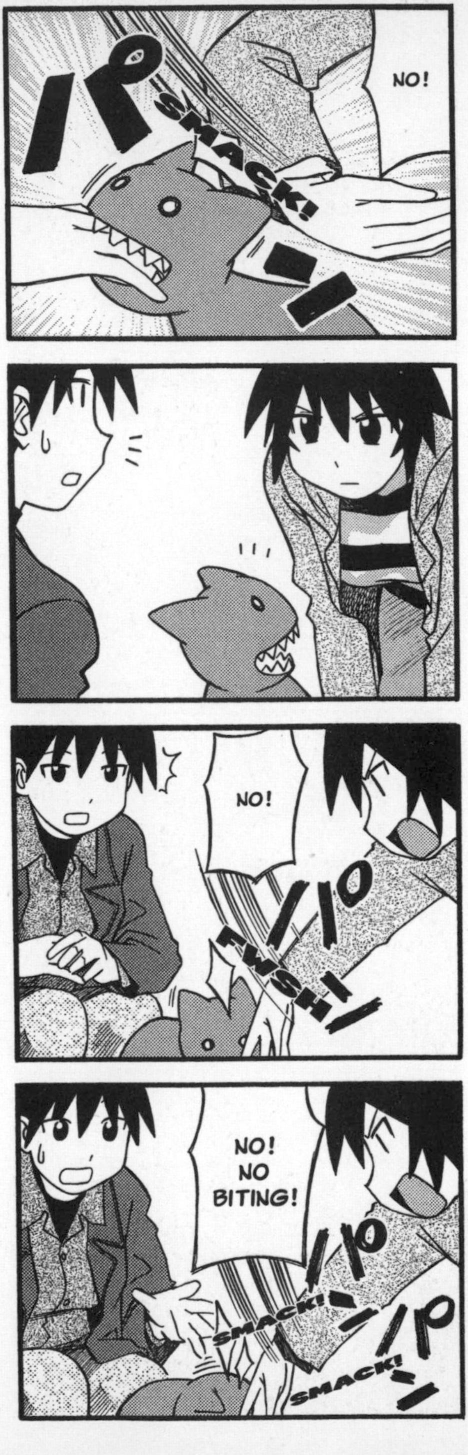
NO!
パ
SMACK!
NO!
FWSH!
NO!
NO BITING!
SMACK!
SMACK!

## YOU DIDN'T HAVE TO HIT HIM...

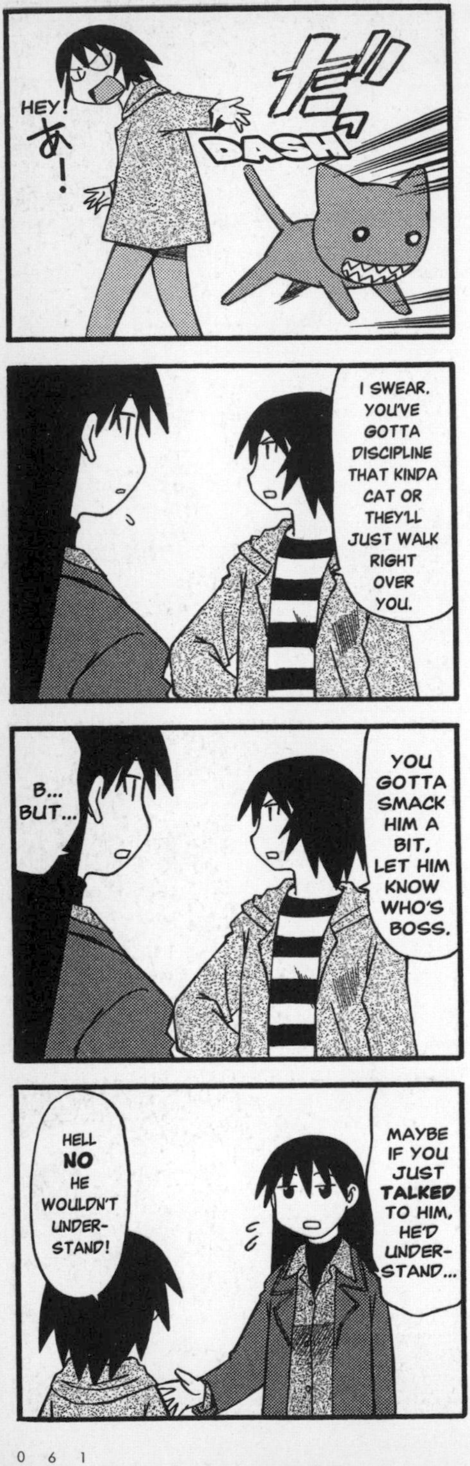
だっ
DASH
HEY!
あ!
I SWEAR. YOU'VE GOTTA DISCIPLINE THAT KINDA CAT OR THEY'LL JUST WALK RIGHT OVER YOU.
YOU GOTTA SMACK HIM A BIT, LET HIM KNOW WHO'S BOSS.
B... BUT...
MAYBE IF YOU JUST **TALKED** TO HIM, HE'D UNDER-STAND...
HELL **NO** HE WOULDN'T UNDER-STAND!

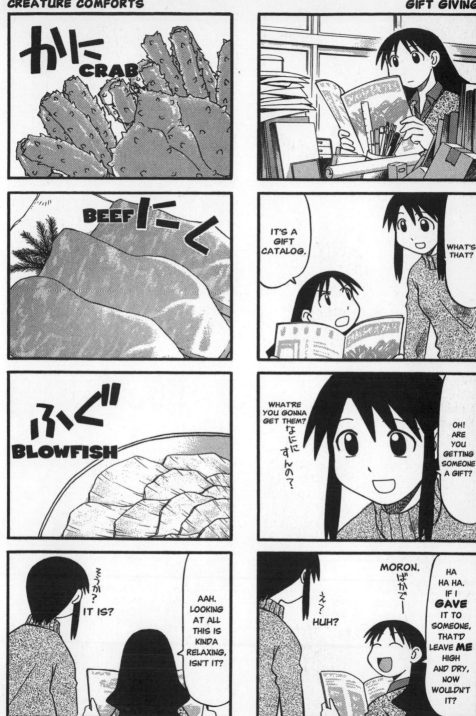

GIFT GIVING

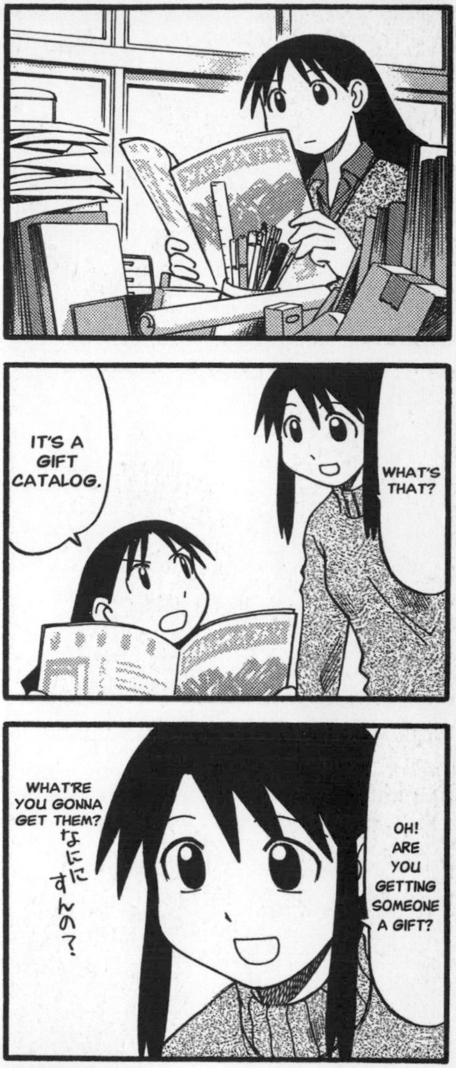
WHAT'S THAT?
IT'S A GIFT CATALOG.
OH! ARE YOU GETTING SOMEONE A GIFT?
WHAT'RE YOU GONNA GET THEM? なにすんの？
HA HA HA. IF I GAVE IT TO SOMEONE, THAT'D LEAVE ME HIGH AND DRY, NOW WOULDN'T IT?
MORON. ばかでー
え？ HUH?

CREATURE COMFORTS

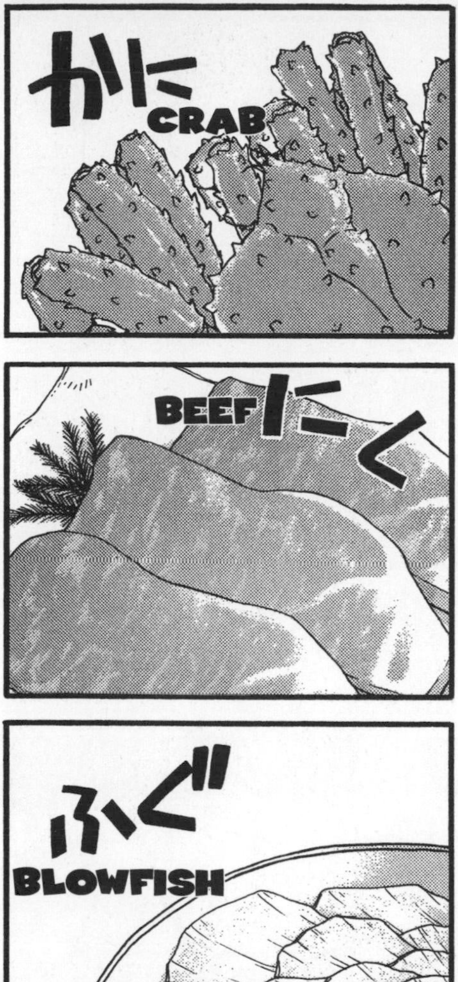
かに CRAB
BEEF にく
ふぐ BLOWFISH
AAH. LOOKING AT ALL THIS IS KINDA RELAXING, ISN'T IT?
そうか？ IT IS?

WAKE UP!

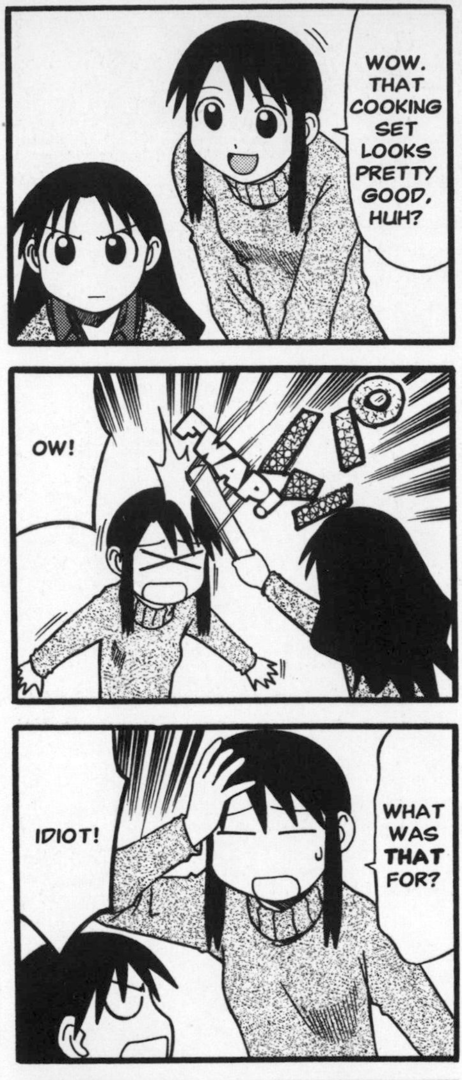
WOW. THAT COOKING SET LOOKS PRETTY GOOD, HUH?
OW!
FWAP!
WHAT WAS THAT FOR?
IDIOT!
DON'T ACT LIKE YOU'RE NOT INTERESTED IN THE FOOD!
LOOK- SNOW CRABS! SNOW CRABS!!

THE BEEF

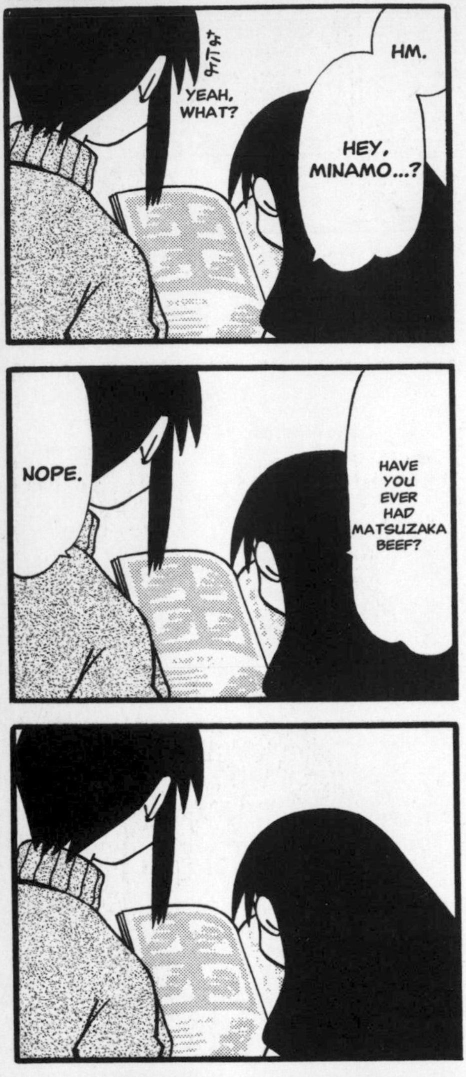
HM.
HEY, MINAMO...?
YEAH, WHAT?
HAVE YOU EVER HAD MATSUZAKA BEEF?
NOPE.
THEY SAY IT'S REALLY, REALLY GOOD...
THAT'S WHAT THEY SAY.

ANGER

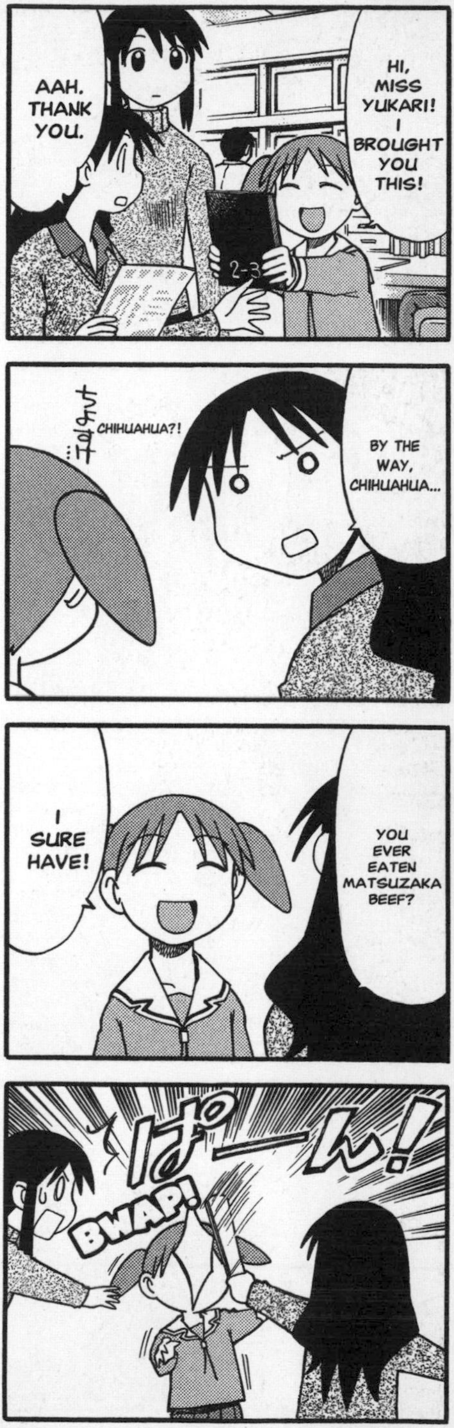
HI, MISS YUKARI! I BROUGHT YOU THIS!
AAH. THANK YOU.
BY THE WAY, CHIHUAHUA...
ちよすけ…
CHIHUAHUA?!
YOU EVER EATEN MATSUZAKA BEEF?
I SURE HAVE!
ぱーん!
BWAP!

DON'T PLAY INNOCENT WITH ME!

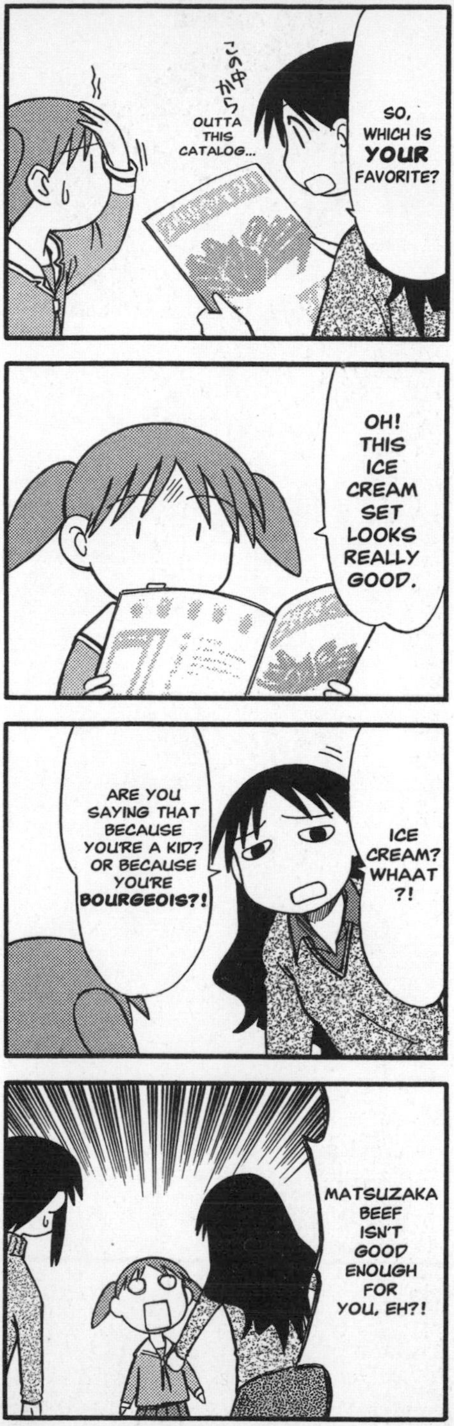
SO, WHICH IS YOUR FAVORITE?
この中から
OUTTA THIS CATALOG...
OH! THIS ICE CREAM SET LOOKS REALLY GOOD.
ICE CREAM? WHAAT?!
ARE YOU SAYING THAT BECAUSE YOU'RE A KID? OR BECAUSE YOU'RE BOURGEOIS?!
MATSUZAKA BEEF ISN'T GOOD ENOUGH FOR YOU, EH?!

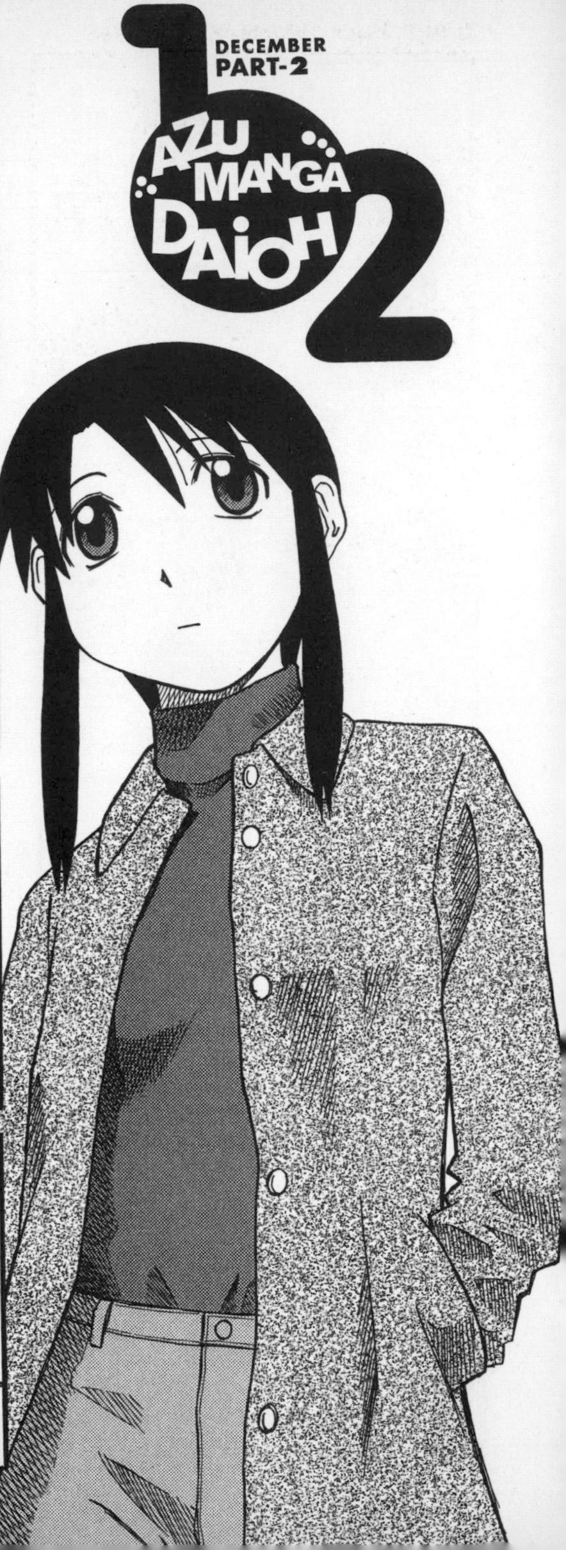

DECEMBER PART-2
AZU MANGA DAIOH 2


RUN, TEACHER, RUN

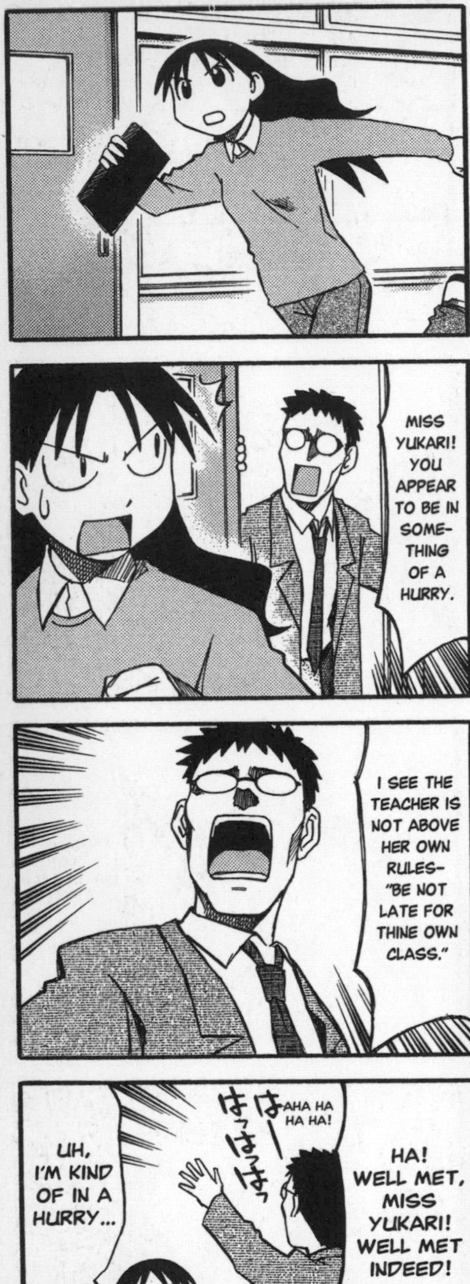

MISS YUKARI! YOU APPEAR TO BE IN SOMETHING OF A HURRY.
I SEE THE TEACHER IS NOT ABOVE HER OWN RULES– "BE NOT LATE FOR THINE OWN CLASS."
HA! WELL MET, MISS YUKARI! WELL MET INDEED!
はーはっはっ
AHA HA HA HA!
UH, I'M KIND OF IN A HURRY...

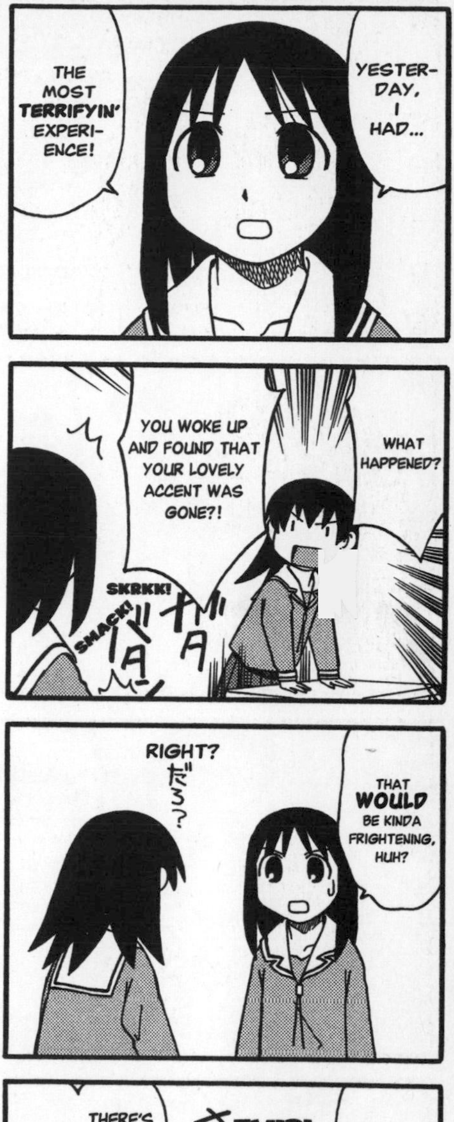
YESTER-DAY, I HAD...
THE MOST TERRIFYIN' EXPERIENCE!
WHAT HAPPENED?
YOU WOKE UP AND FOUND THAT YOUR LOVELY ACCENT WAS GONE?!
SKRKK!
SMACK!
THAT WOULD BE KINDA FRIGHTENING, HUH?
RIGHT?
だろ?
... WAZZUP ?!
FWIP!
THERE'S THAT LINGO WE KNOW AND LOVE!
NOW GO ON WITH YOUR STORY.



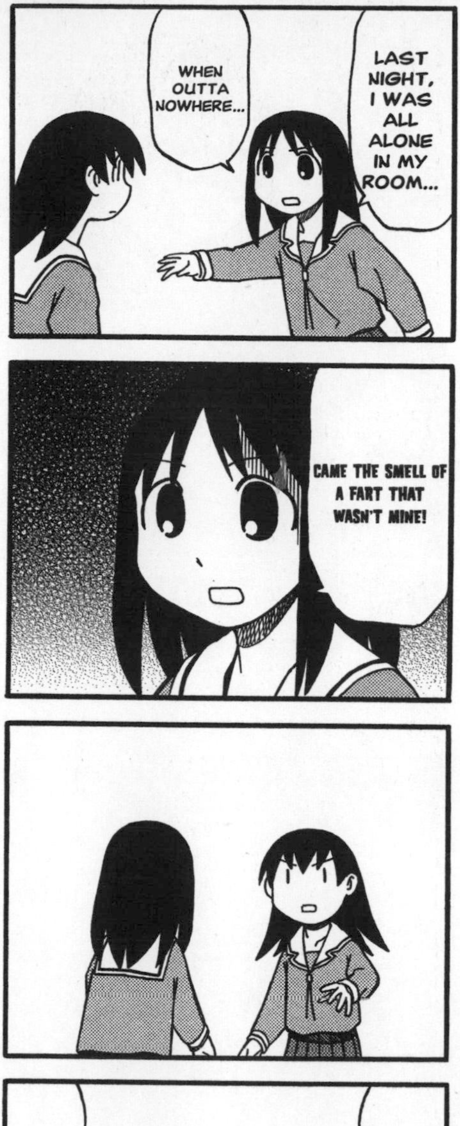
LAST NIGHT, I WAS ALL ALONE IN MY ROOM...
WHEN OUTTA NOWHERE...
CAME THE SMELL OF A FART THAT WASN'T MINE!
MAN, THAT'S SCARY!
RIGHT?

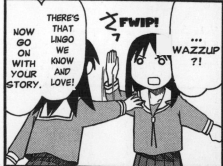

I'M DRAWING 'EM!

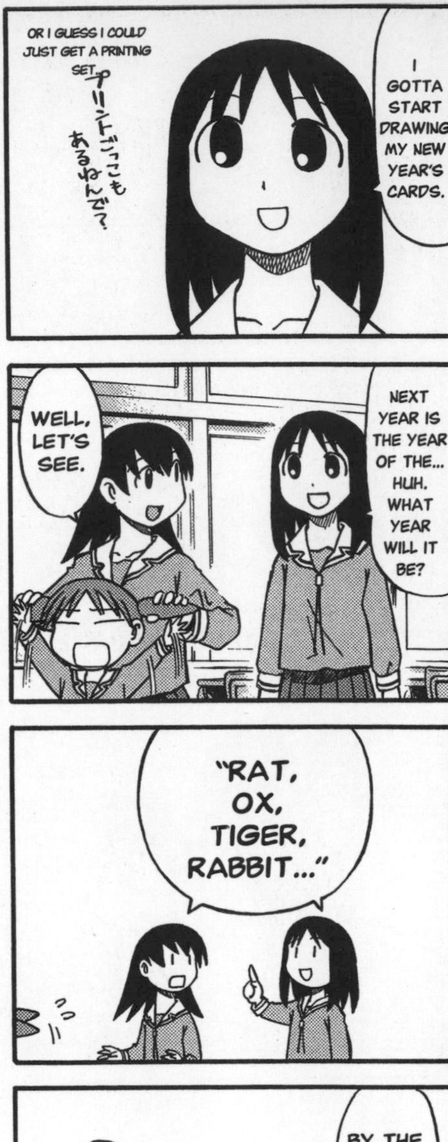
I GOTTA START DRAWING MY NEW YEAR'S CARDS.
OR I GUESS I COULD JUST GET A PRINTING SET.
プリントごっこもあるねんで?
NEXT YEAR IS THE YEAR OF THE... HUH. WHAT YEAR WILL IT BE?
WELL, LET'S SEE.
"RAT, OX, TIGER, RABBIT..."
BY THE WAY, WHAT YEAR IS IT **THIS** YEAR?
BEATS ME.

UM...

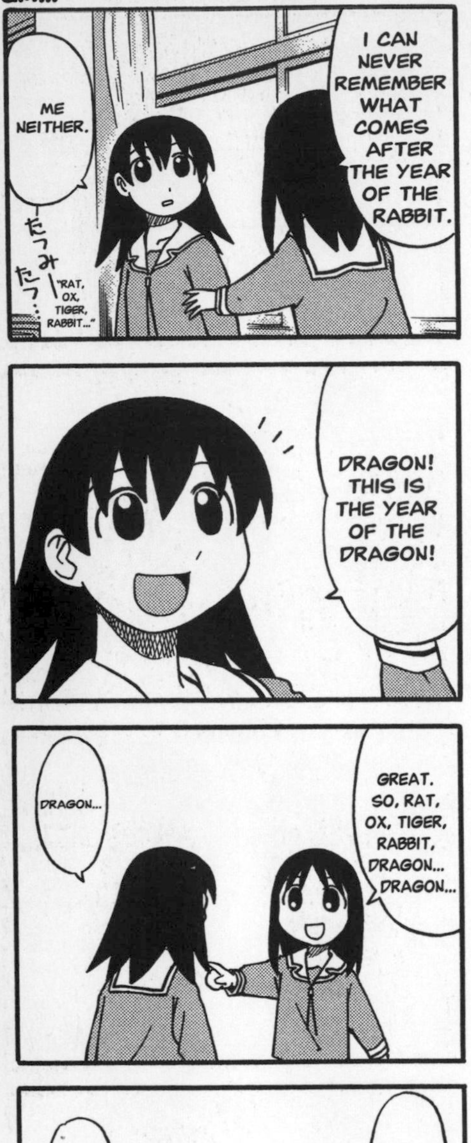
I CAN NEVER REMEMBER WHAT COMES AFTER THE YEAR OF THE RABBIT.
ME NEITHER.
たつみー たつ…
"RAT, OX, TIGER, RABBIT..."
DRAGON! THIS IS THE YEAR OF THE DRAGON!
GREAT. SO, RAT, OX, TIGER, RABBIT, DRAGON... DRAGON...
DRAGON...
...DRAGON, RIGHT?
I THINK WE'RE STUCK.

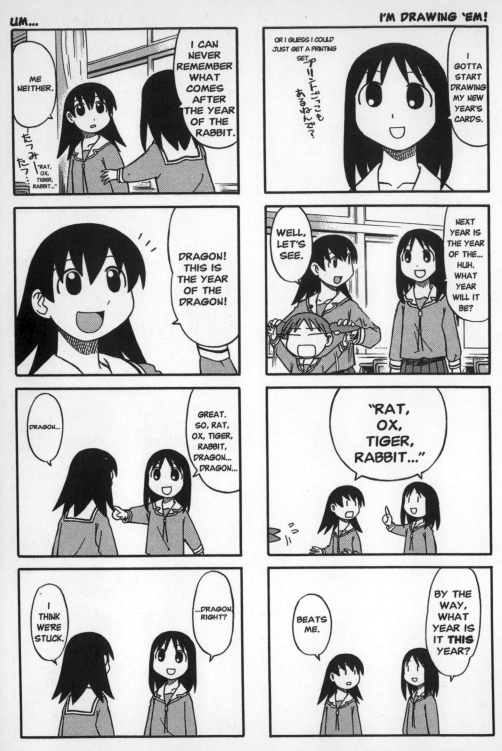

GO AHEAD AND ASK

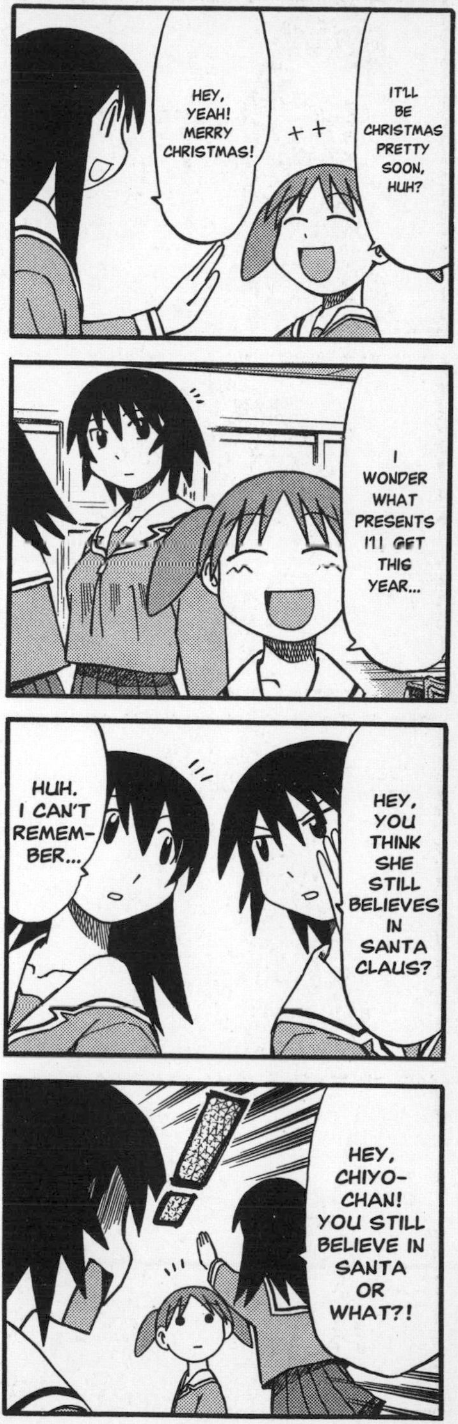
IT'LL BE CHRISTMAS PRETTY SOON, HUH?
HEY, YEAH! MERRY CHRISTMAS!
I WONDER WHAT PRESENTS I'LL GET THIS YEAR...
HEY, YOU THINK SHE STILL BELIEVES IN SANTA CLAUS?
HUH. I CAN'T REMEM-BER...
HEY, CHIYO-CHAN! YOU STILL BELIEVE IN SANTA OR WHAT?!

CHILDHOOD DREAMS

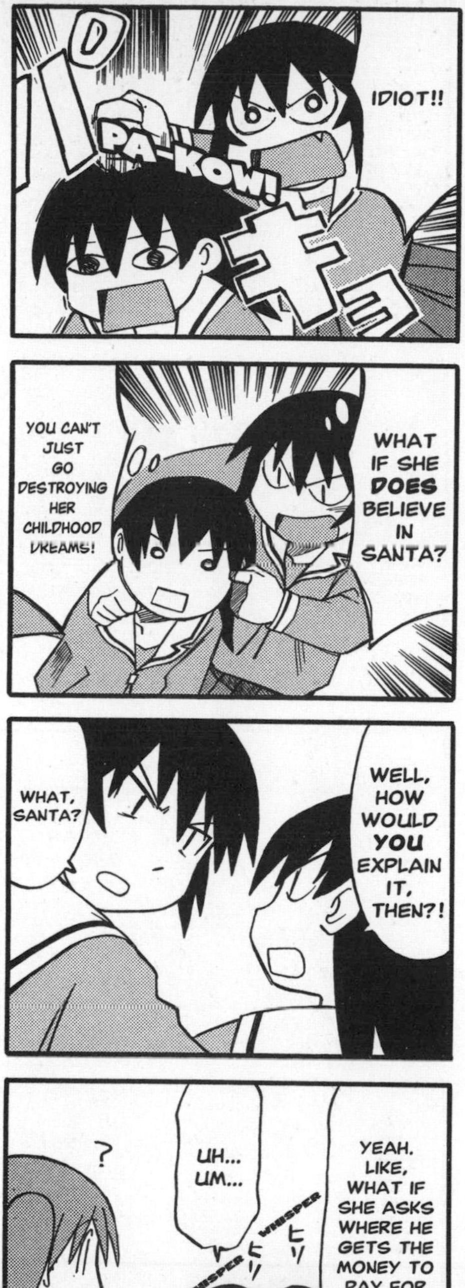
IDIOT!!
PA-KOW!
WHAT IF SHE DOES BELIEVE IN SANTA?
YOU CAN'T JUST GO DESTROYING HER CHILDHOOD DREAMS!
WELL, HOW WOULD YOU EXPLAIN IT, THEN?!
WHAT, SANTA?
YEAH. LIKE, WHAT IF SHE ASKS WHERE HE GETS THE MONEY TO PAY FOR ALL THOSE KIDS' PRESENTS?
WHISPER
UH... UM...
WHISPER
?

## SANTA

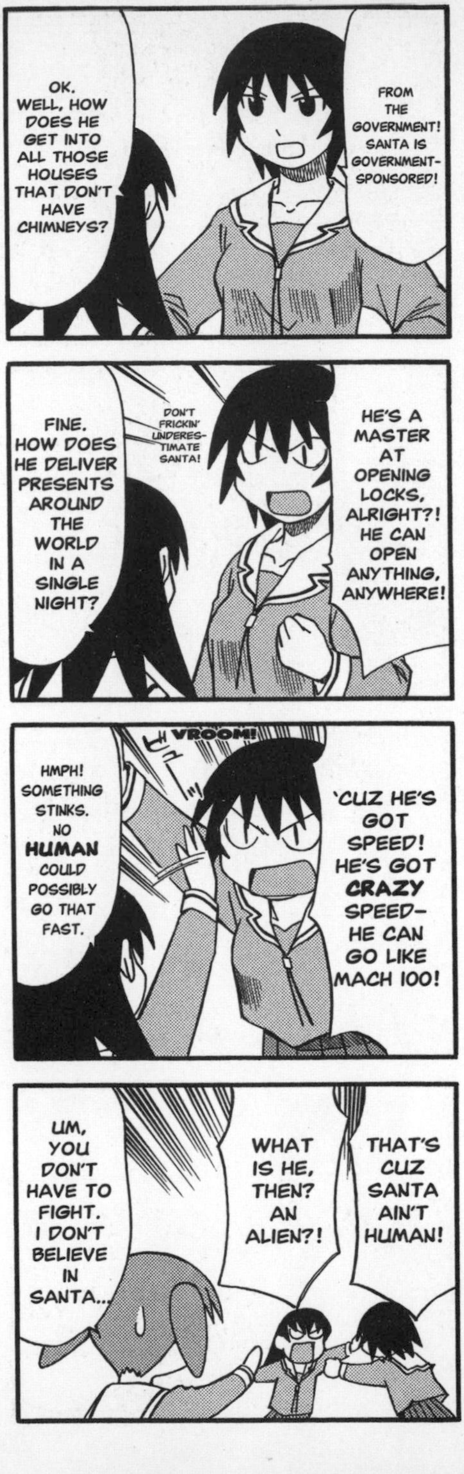
FROM THE GOVERNMENT! SANTA IS GOVERNMENT-SPONSORED!
OK. WELL, HOW DOES HE GET INTO ALL THOSE HOUSES THAT DON'T HAVE CHIMNEYS?
HE'S A MASTER AT OPENING LOCKS, ALRIGHT?! HE CAN OPEN ANYTHING, ANYWHERE!
DON'T FRICKIN' UNDERESTIMATE SANTA!
FINE. HOW DOES HE DELIVER PRESENTS AROUND THE WORLD IN A SINGLE NIGHT?
VROOM!
'CUZ HE'S GOT SPEED! HE'S GOT **CRAZY** SPEED—HE CAN GO LIKE MACH 100!
HMPH! SOMETHING STINKS. NO **HUMAN** COULD POSSIBLY GO THAT FAST.
THAT'S CUZ SANTA AIN'T HUMAN!
WHAT IS HE, THEN? AN ALIEN?!
UM, YOU DON'T HAVE TO FIGHT. I DON'T BELIEVE IN SANTA...

## TRUE IDENTITY

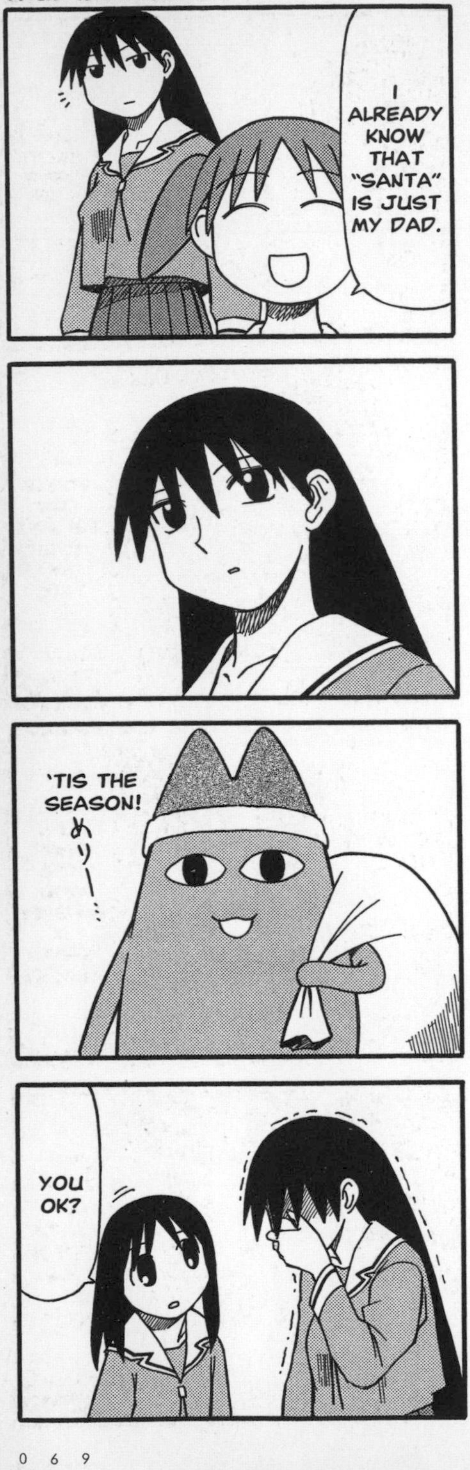
I ALREADY KNOW THAT "SANTA" IS JUST MY DAD.
'TIS THE SEASON!
めりー…
YOU OK?

## AMAZIN' SANTA

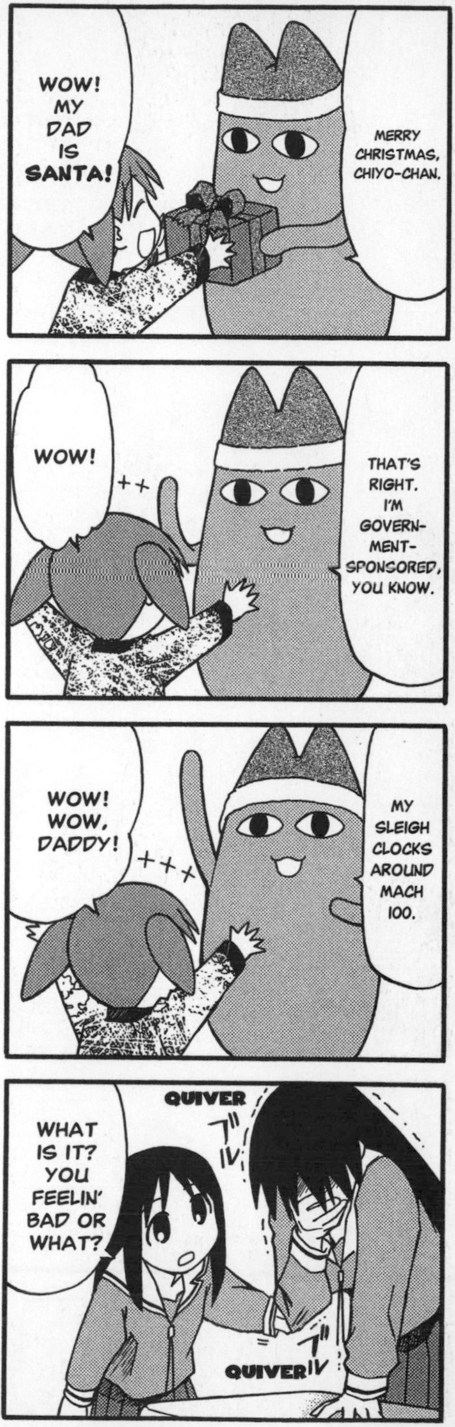
MERRY CHRISTMAS, CHIYO-CHAN.
WOW! MY DAD IS SANTA!
THAT'S RIGHT. I'M GOVERNMENT-SPONSORED, YOU KNOW.
WOW!
MY SLEIGH CLOCKS AROUND MACH 100.
WOW! WOW, DADDY!
QUIVER
WHAT IS IT? YOU FEELIN' BAD OR WHAT?
QUIVER

## THE DREAM

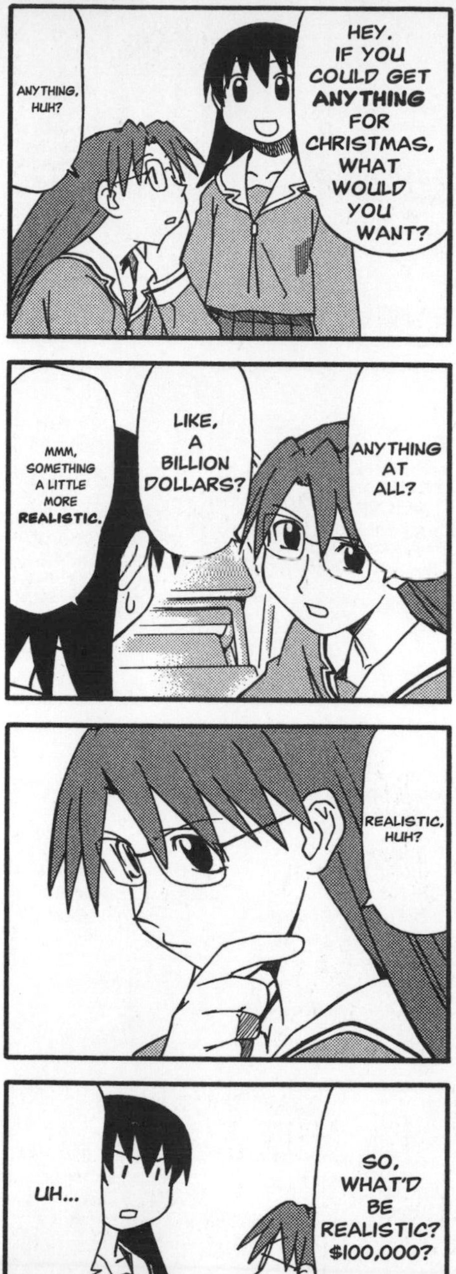
HEY. IF YOU COULD GET ANYTHING FOR CHRISTMAS, WHAT WOULD YOU WANT?
ANYTHING, HUH?
ANYTHING AT ALL?
LIKE, A BILLION DOLLARS?
MMM, SOMETHING A LITTLE MORE REALISTIC.
REALISTIC, HUH?
SO, WHAT'D BE REALISTIC? $100,000?
UH...

## GIMME

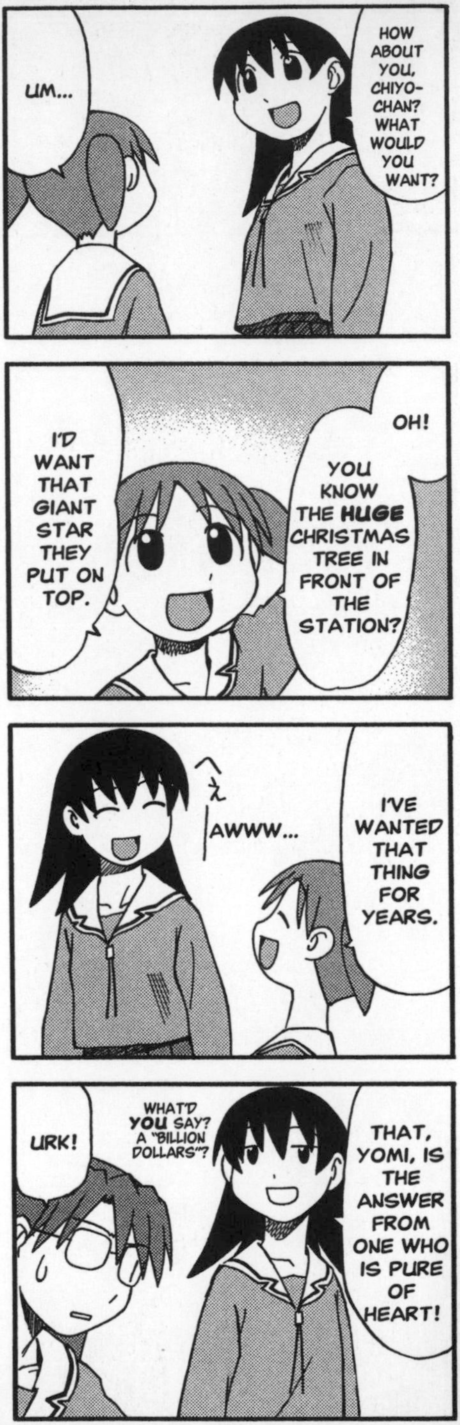
HOW ABOUT YOU, CHIYO-CHAN? WHAT WOULD YOU WANT?
UM...
OH!
YOU KNOW THE **HUGE** CHRISTMAS TREE IN FRONT OF THE STATION?
I'D WANT THAT GIANT STAR THEY PUT ON TOP.
I'VE WANTED THAT THING FOR YEARS.
へえ
AWWW...
THAT, YOMI, IS THE ANSWER FROM ONE WHO IS PURE OF HEART!
WHAT'D **YOU** SAY? A "BILLION DOLLARS"?
URK!

## ARE THEY REAL?

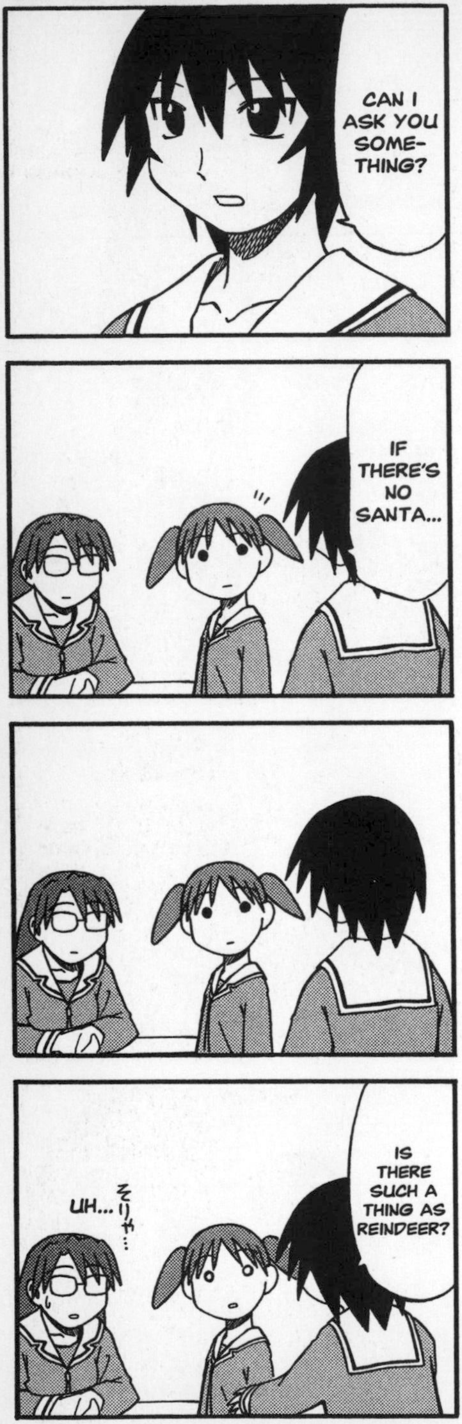
CAN I ASK YOU SOMETHING?
IF THERE'S NO SANTA...
IS THERE SUCH A THING AS REINDEER?
UH...
そりゃ...

REINDEER

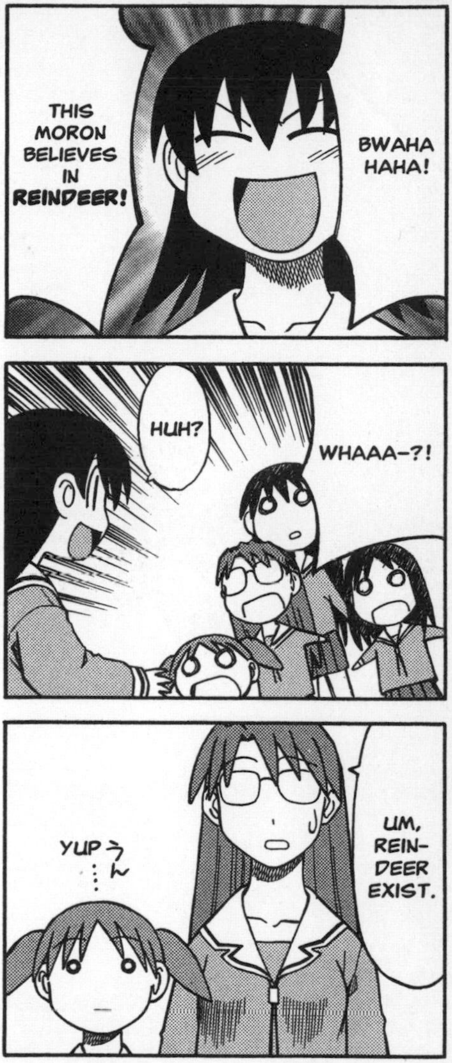
BWAHA HAHA!
THIS MORON BELIEVES IN REINDEER!
WHAAA-?!
HUH?
UM, REIN-DEER EXIST.
YUP うん……
SHUT UP! NO DEER IN THE WORLD COULD FLY THROUGH THE AIR LIKE THAT!
DON'T TRY AND PULL ONE OVER ON ME!
UM... ARE YOU FOR REAL?

DON'T LOOK!

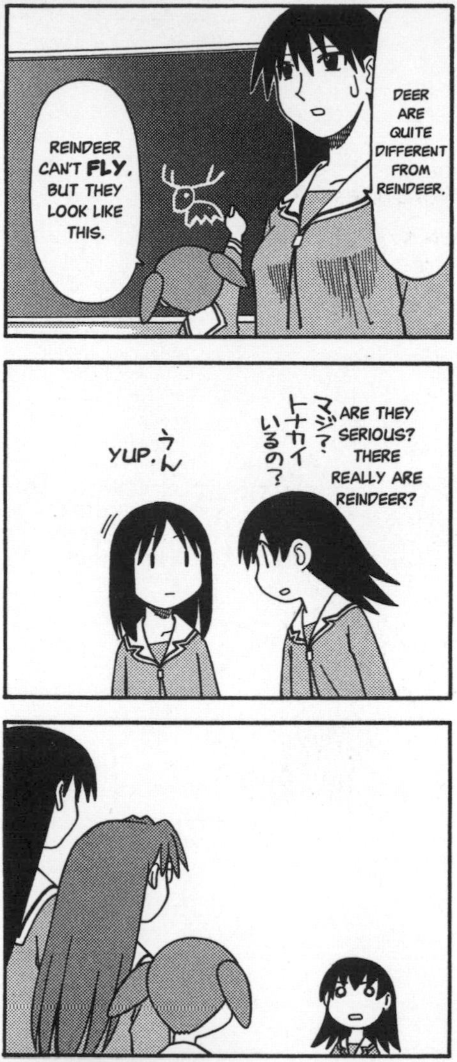
DEER ARE QUITE DIFFERENT FROM REINDEER.
REINDEER CAN'T FLY, BUT THEY LOOK LIKE THIS.
マジ？トナカイいるの？
ARE THEY SERIOUS? THERE REALLY ARE REINDEER?
うん
YUP.
WAAAUGH!! I'M NOT THE MORON! I'M NOT THE MORON!!

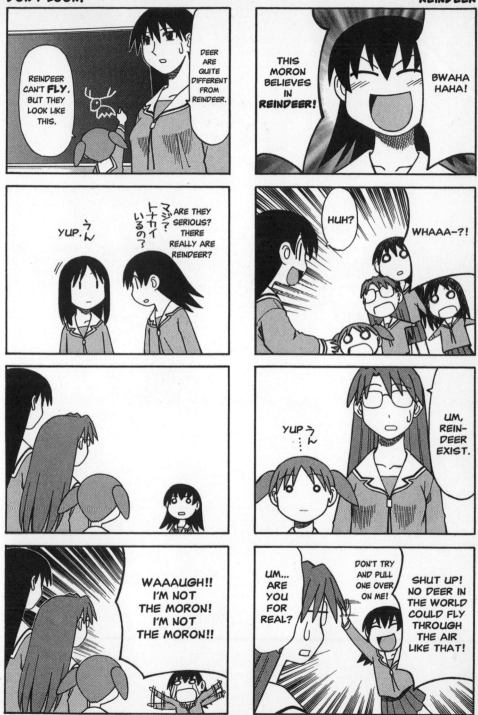

AZUMANGA-DAIOH

# 073

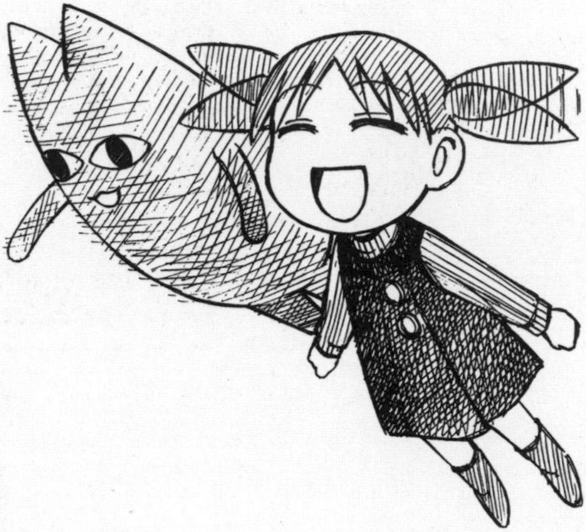

***You belong***

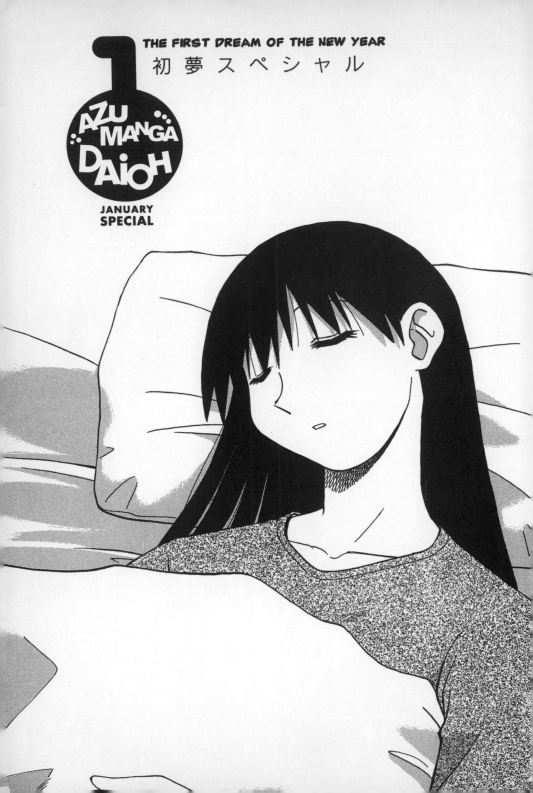

# THE FIRST DREAM OF THE NEW YEAR

初夢スペシャル

AZUMANGA DAIOH

JANUARY SPECIAL

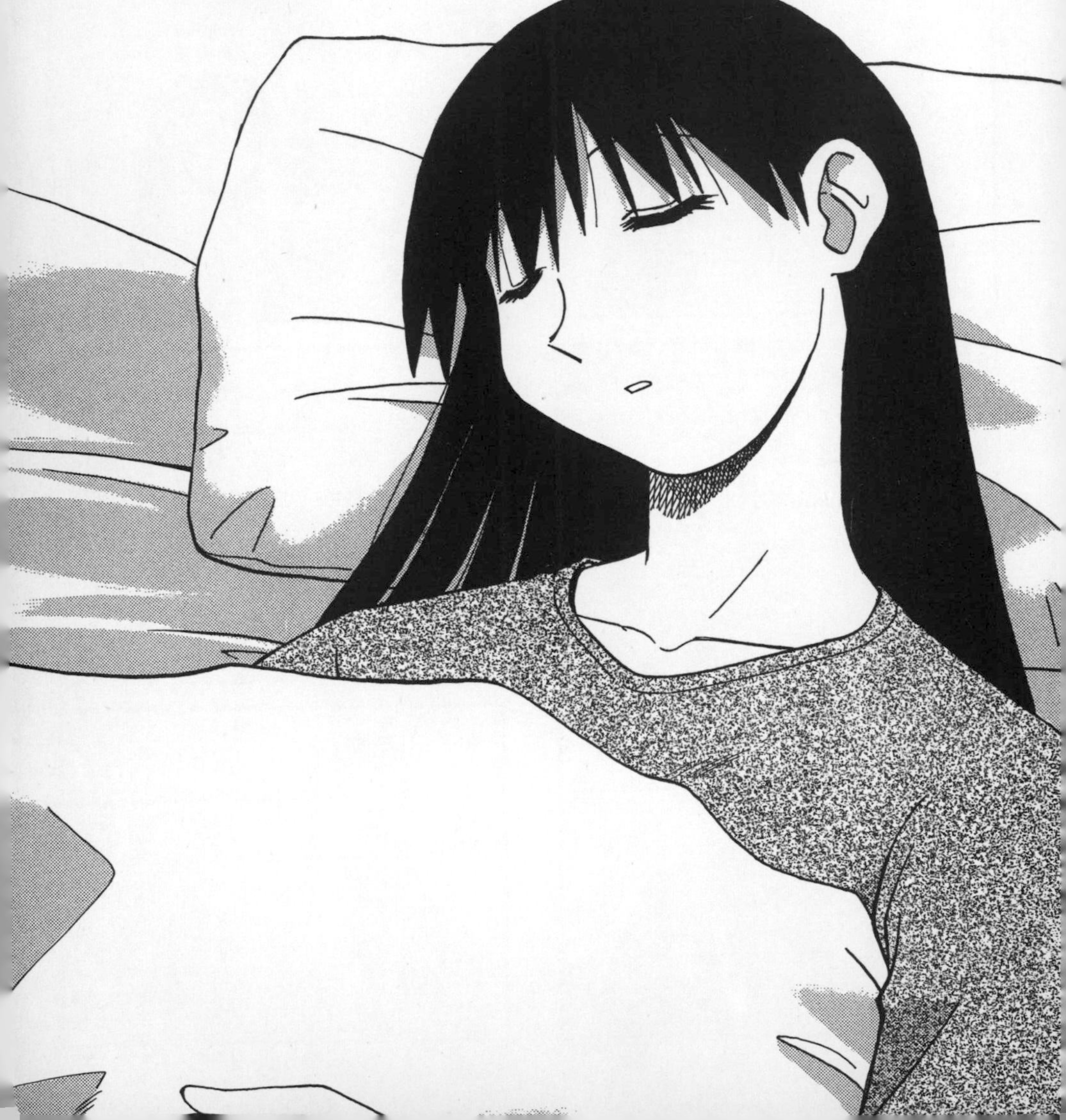

WELCOME

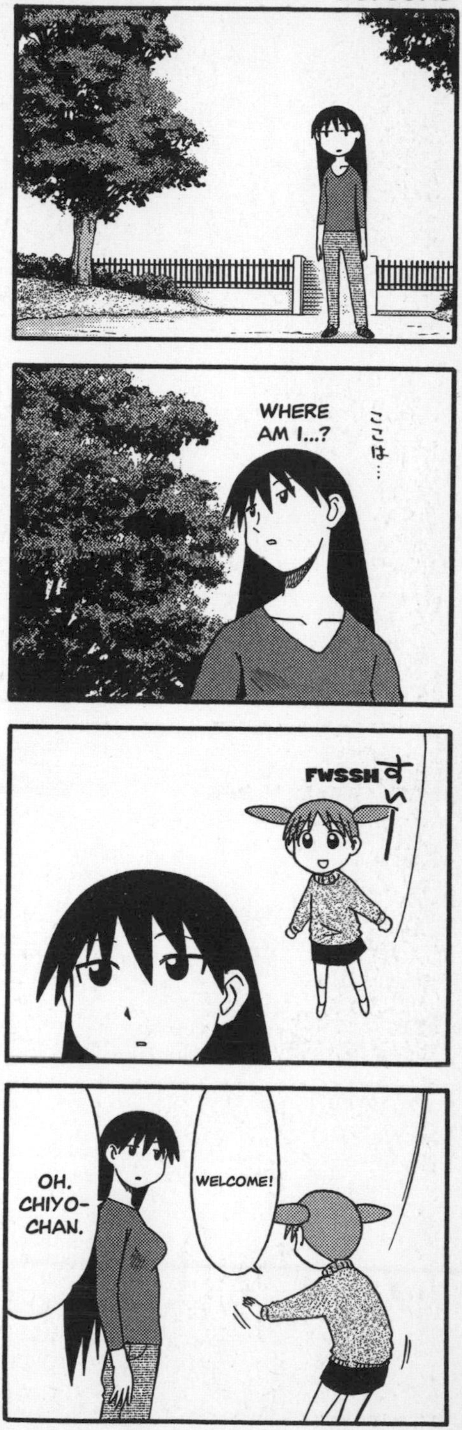
WHERE AM I...?
ここは…
FWSSH
すい～
WELCOME!
OH. CHIYO-CHAN.

WHO'S THIS?

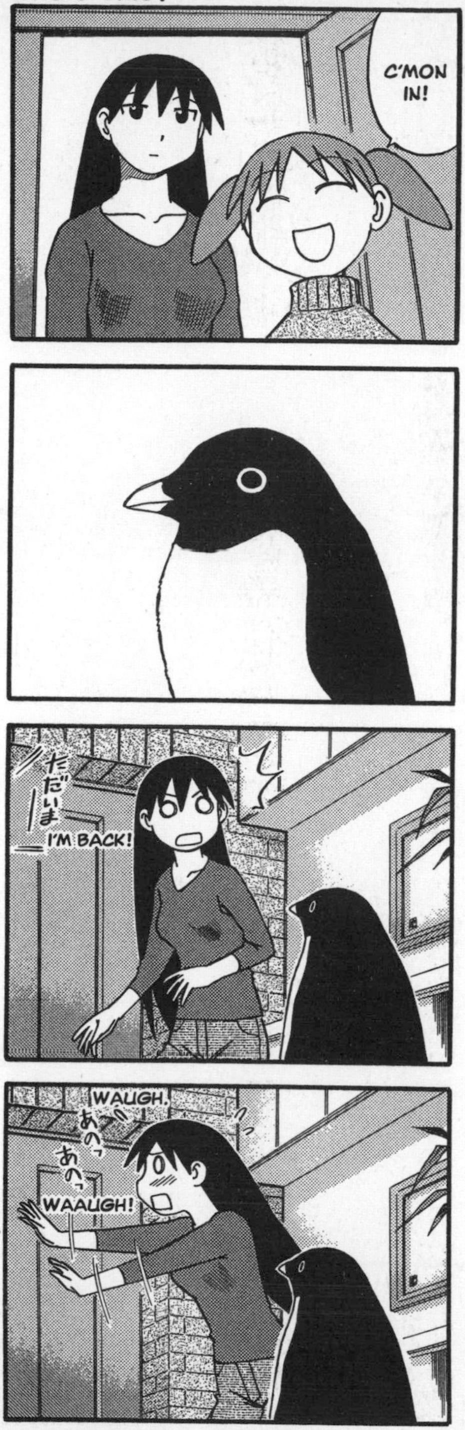
C'MON IN!
ただいま
I'M BACK!
WAUGH.
あのっ
あのっ
WAAUGH!

GOTTA CLEAN

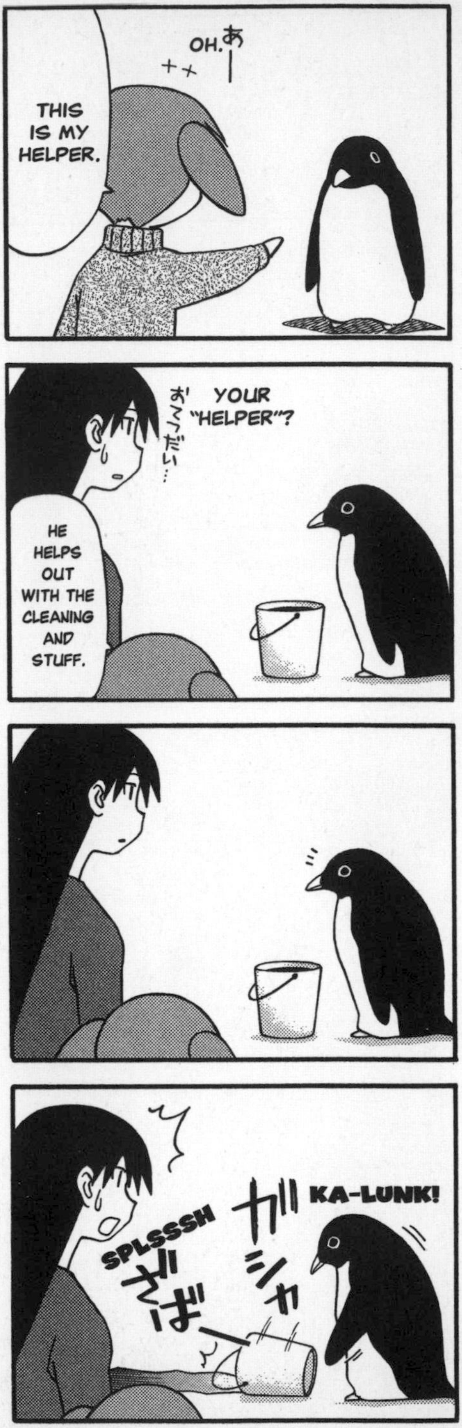
あー
OH.
THIS IS MY HELPER.
おてつだい…
YOUR "HELPER"?
HE HELPS OUT WITH THE CLEANING AND STUFF.
KA-LUNK!
ガシャ
SPLSSSH
ざばー

WHAT SHOULD I DO?

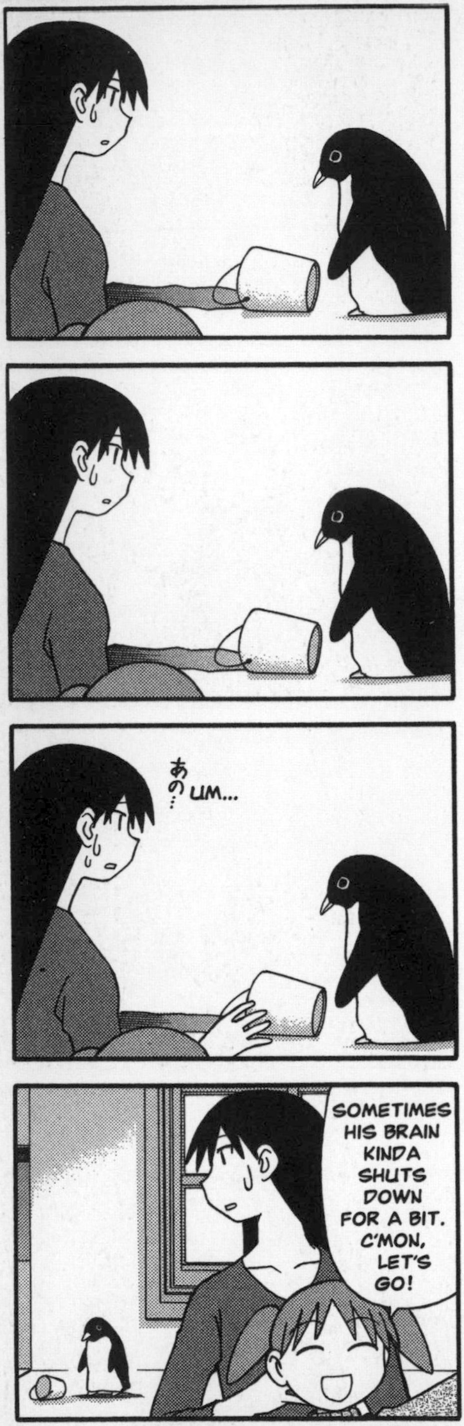
あの…
UM...
SOMETIMES HIS BRAIN KINDA SHUTS DOWN FOR A BIT. C'MON, LET'S GO!

## THE INVITATION

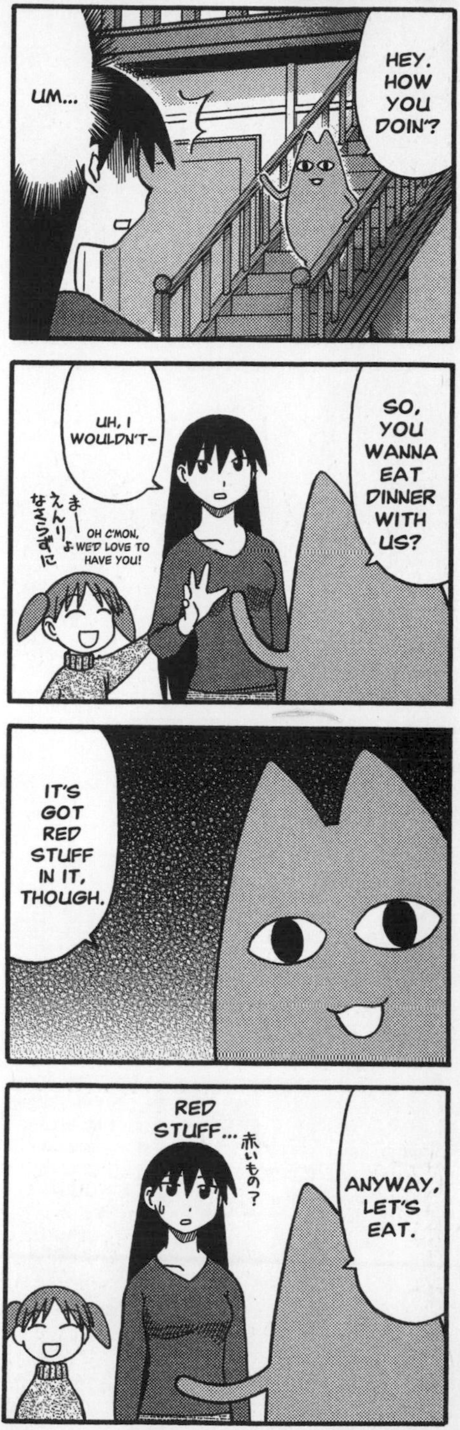
HEY. HOW YOU DOIN'?
UM...
SO, YOU WANNA EAT DINNER WITH US?
UH, I WOULDN'T–
まーえんりょなさらずに
OH C'MON, WE'D LOVE TO HAVE YOU!
IT'S GOT RED STUFF IN IT, THOUGH.
ANYWAY, LET'S EAT.
赤いもの？
RED STUFF...

## DECISIONS, DECISIONS

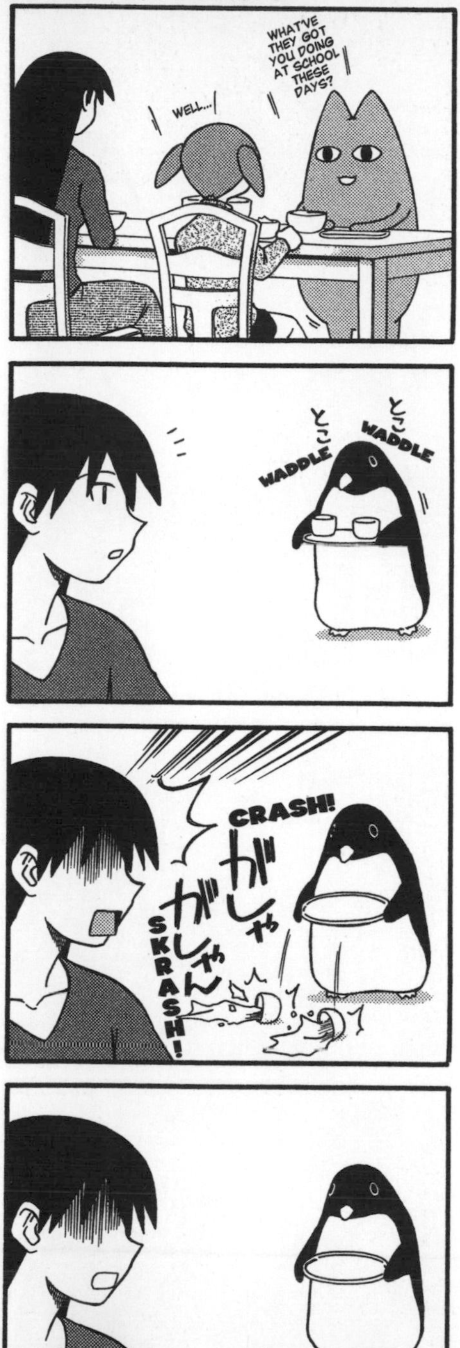
WHAT'VE THEY GOT YOU DOING AT SCHOOL THESE DAYS?
WELL...
とこ
WADDLE
とこ
WADDLE
CRASH!
がしゃ
がしゃん
SKRASH!

# RED TOMATOES

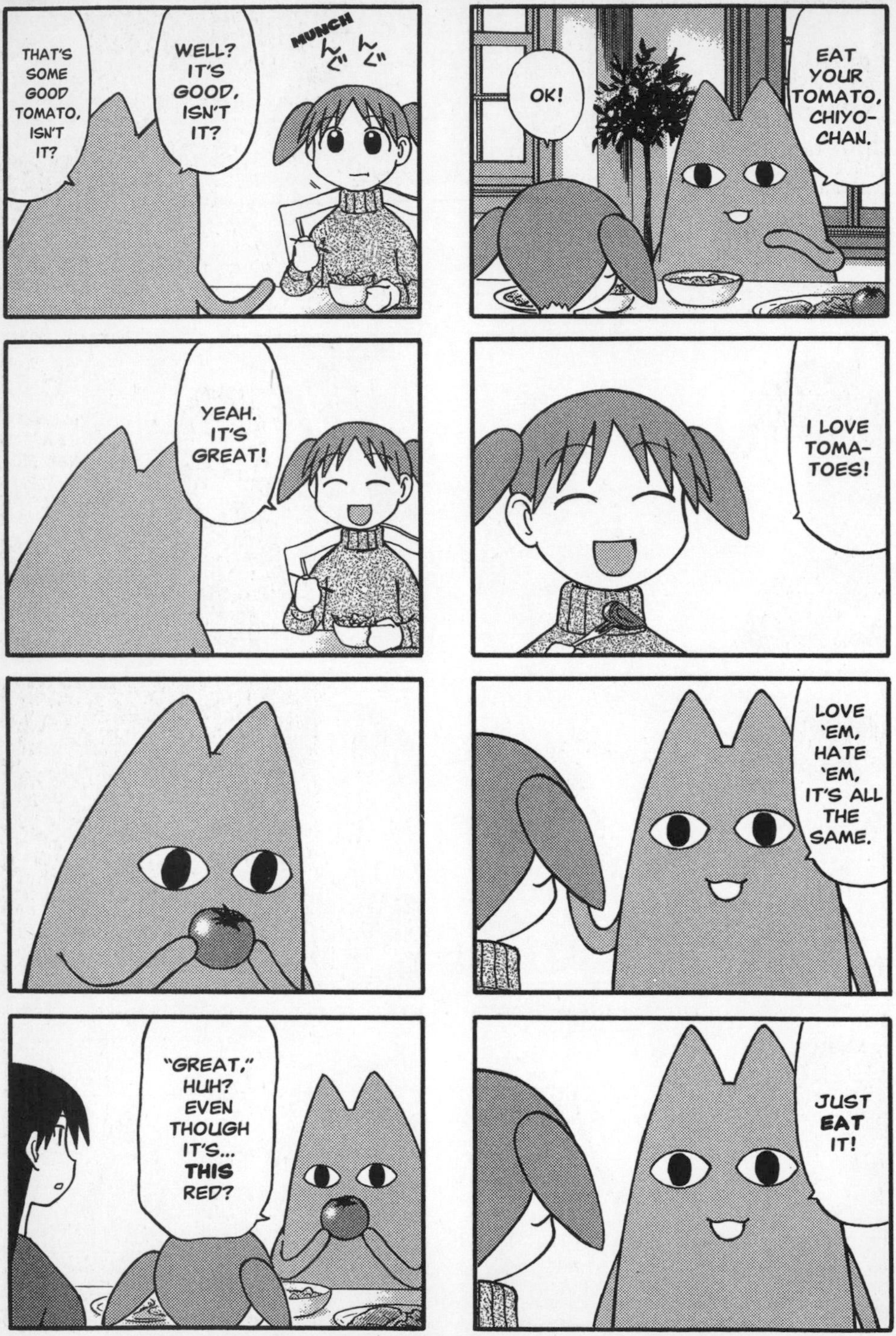
EAT YOUR TOMATO, CHIYO-CHAN.
OK!
I LOVE TOMA-TOES!
LOVE 'EM, HATE 'EM, IT'S ALL THE SAME.
JUST EAT IT!
MUNCH
んぐ んぐ
WELL? IT'S GOOD, ISN'T IT?
THAT'S SOME GOOD TOMATO, ISN'T IT?
YEAH. IT'S GREAT!
"GREAT," HUH? EVEN THOUGH IT'S... THIS RED?

MORE ADVICE

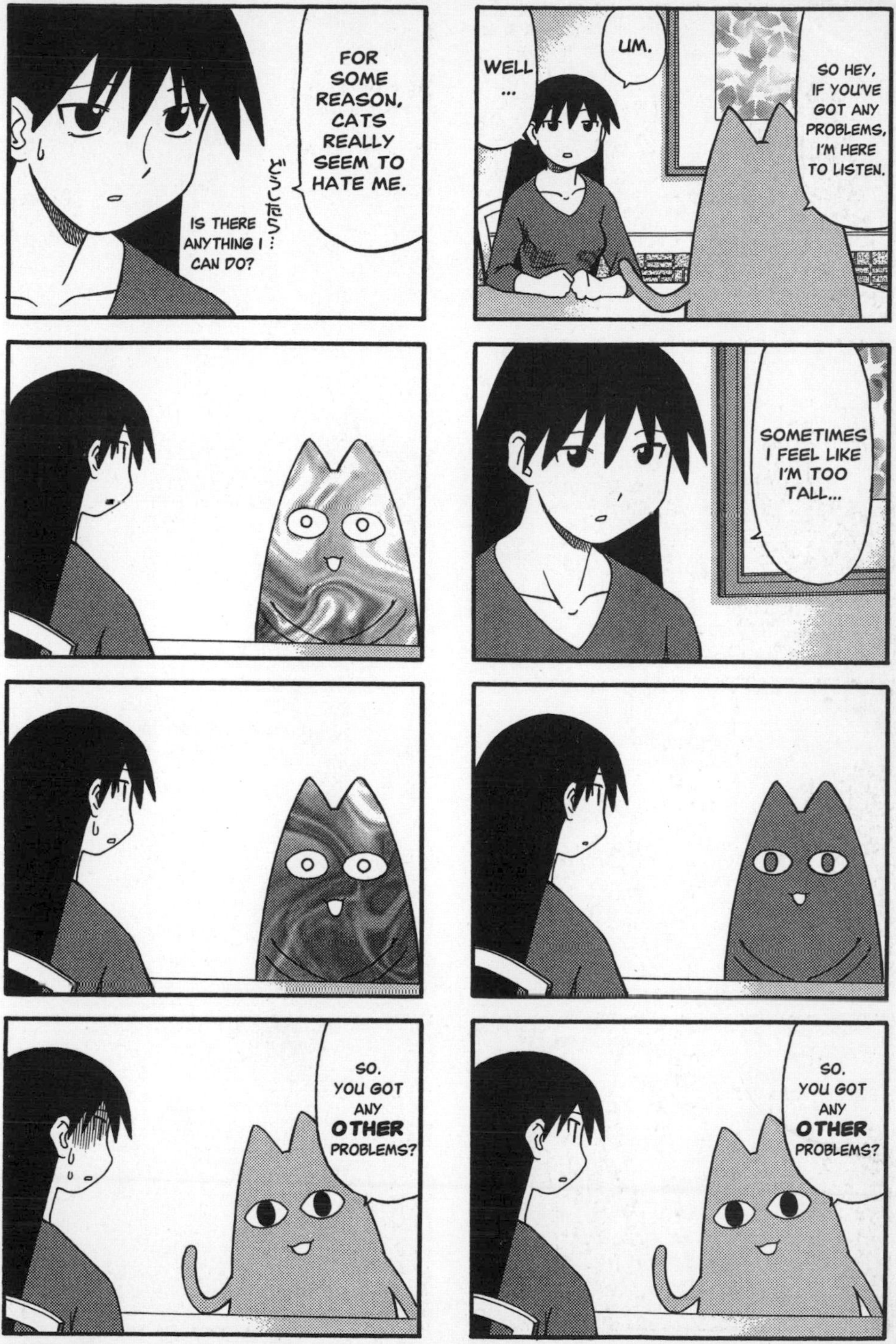
SO HEY, IF YOU'VE GOT ANY PROBLEMS, I'M HERE TO LISTEN.
UM.
WELL ...
FOR SOME REASON, CATS REALLY SEEM TO HATE ME.
どうしたら…
IS THERE ANYTHING I CAN DO?
SOMETIMES I FEEL LIKE I'M TOO TALL...
SO. YOU GOT ANY **OTHER** PROBLEMS?
SO. YOU GOT ANY **OTHER** PROBLEMS?

## FEELING

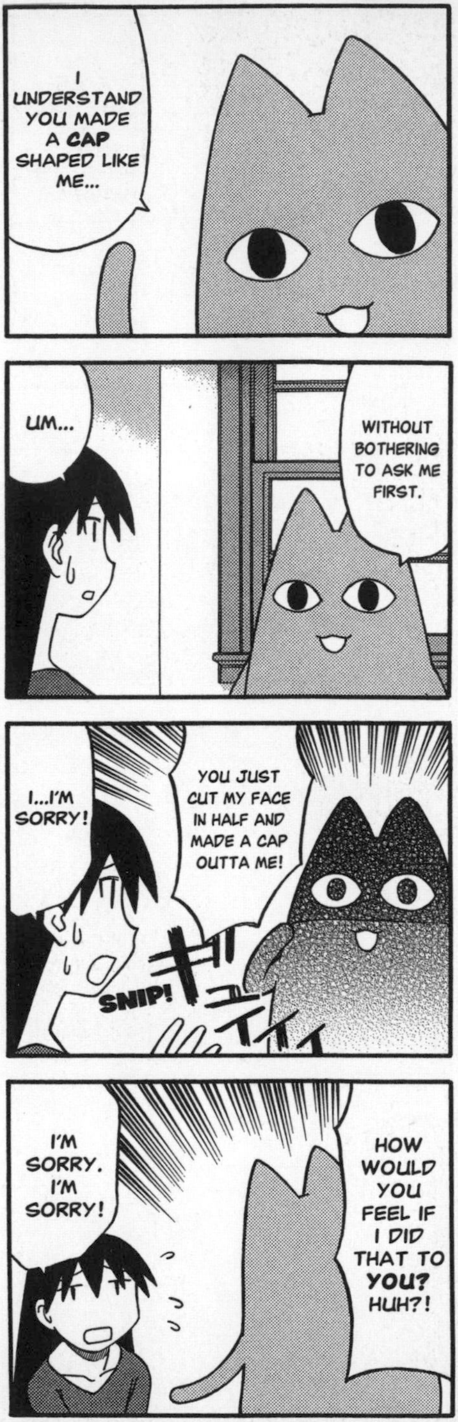
I UNDERSTAND YOU MADE A **CAP** SHAPED LIKE ME...
WITHOUT BOTHERING TO ASK ME FIRST.
UM...
YOU JUST CUT MY FACE IN HALF AND MADE A CAP OUTTA ME!
I...I'M SORRY!
ギュイイイ
SNIP!
HOW WOULD YOU FEEL IF I DID THAT TO **YOU?** HUH?!
I'M SORRY. I'M SORRY!

## WHAT WOULD HAPPEN?

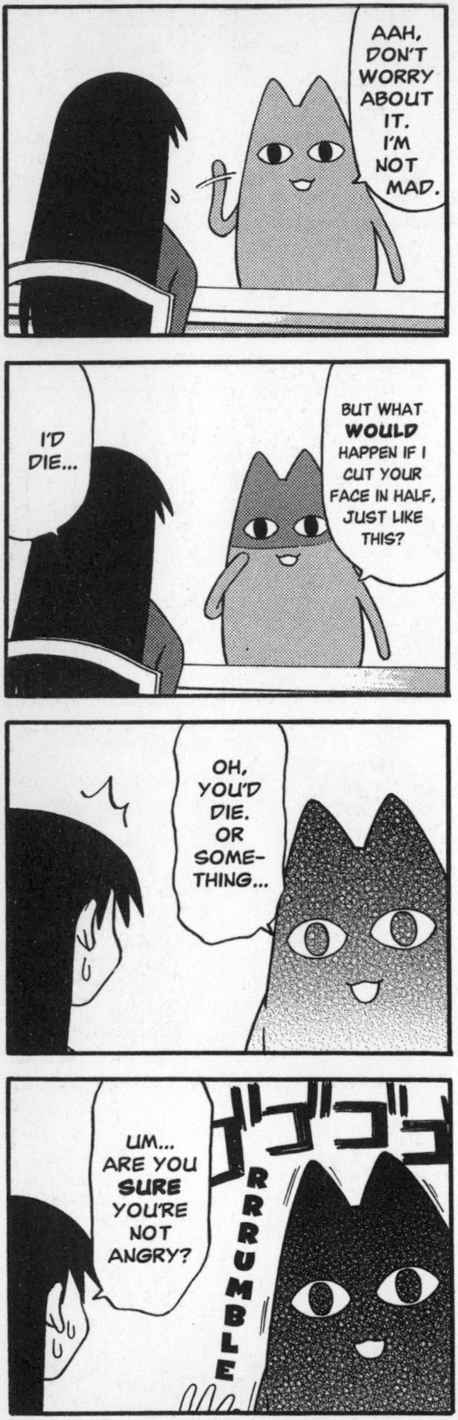
AAH, DON'T WORRY ABOUT IT. I'M NOT MAD.
BUT WHAT **WOULD** HAPPEN IF I CUT YOUR FACE IN HALF, JUST LIKE THIS?
I'D DIE...
OH, YOU'D DIE. OR SOME-THING...
ゴゴゴゴ
RRRUMBLE
UM... ARE YOU **SURE** YOU'RE NOT ANGRY?

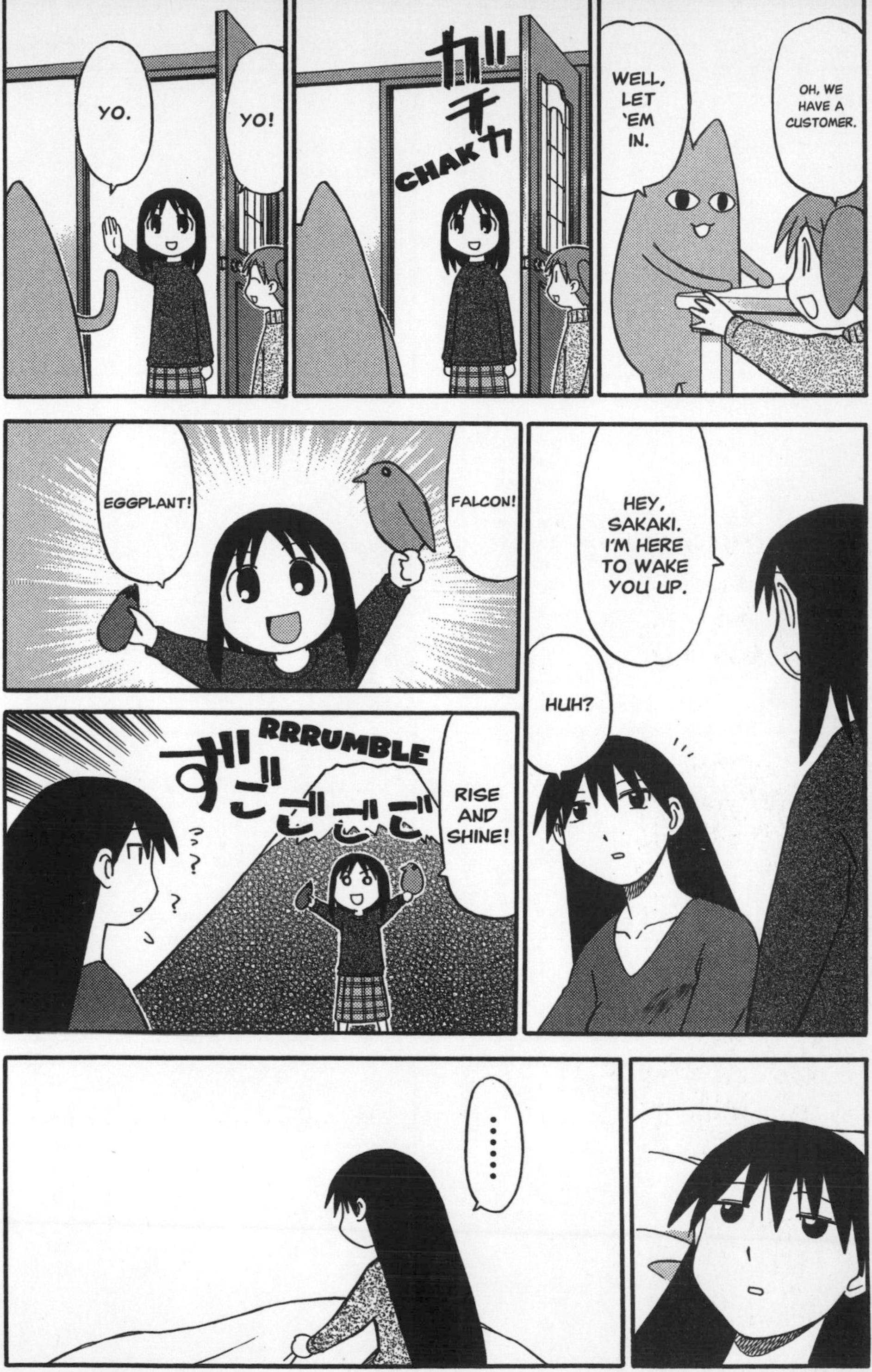

OH, WE HAVE A CUSTOMER.
WELL, LET 'EM IN.
カチャ
CHAK
YO!
YO.
HEY, SAKAKI. I'M HERE TO WAKE YOU UP.
HUH?
FALCON!
EGGPLANT!
RISE AND SHINE!
RRRUMBLE
ずごごごご
……

AZUMANGA-DAIOH

# 083

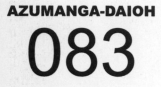

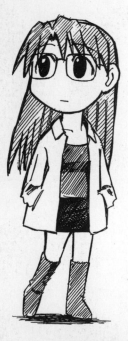

***You belong***

AZU MANGA DAIOH

JANUARY

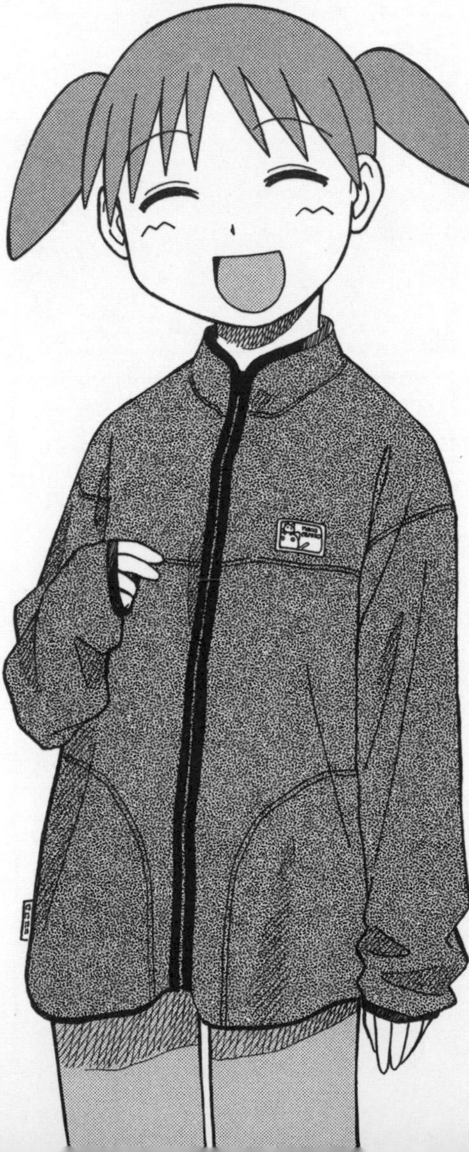

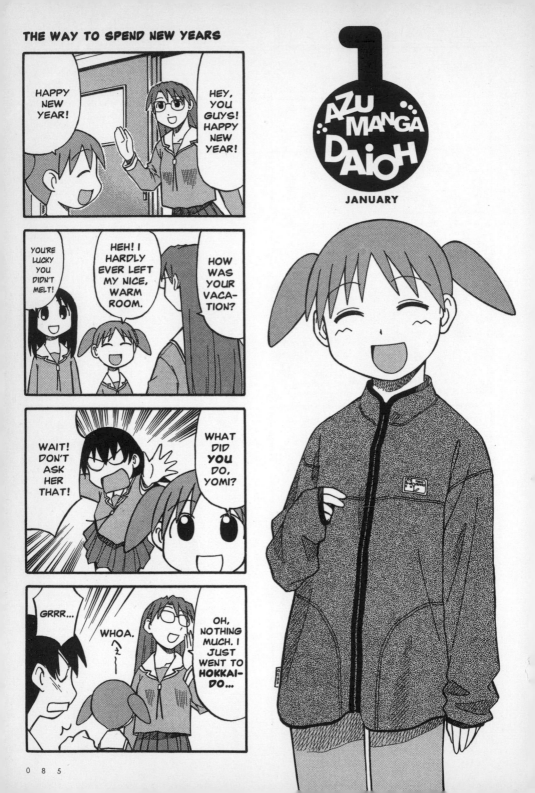

## THE WAY TO SPEND NEW YEARS

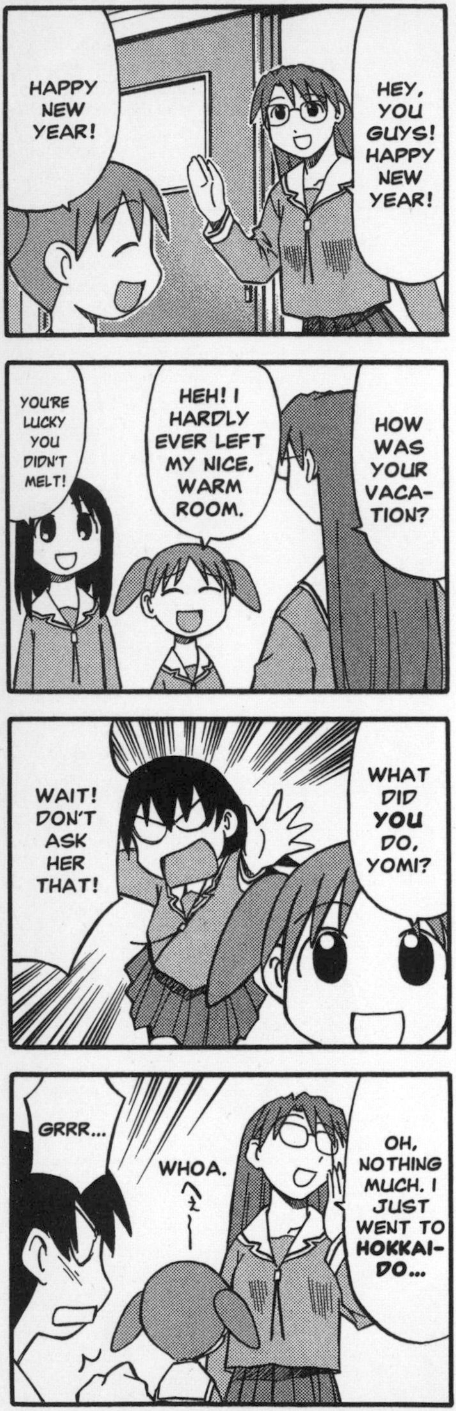
HEY, YOU GUYS! HAPPY NEW YEAR!
HAPPY NEW YEAR!
HOW WAS YOUR VACATION?
HEH! I HARDLY EVER LEFT MY NICE, WARM ROOM.
YOU'RE LUCKY YOU DIDN'T MELT!
WHAT DID YOU DO, YOMI?
WAIT! DON'T ASK HER THAT!
OH, NOTHING MUCH. I JUST WENT TO HOKKAIDO...
WHOA.
GRRR...

## HEAD IN THE CLOUDS

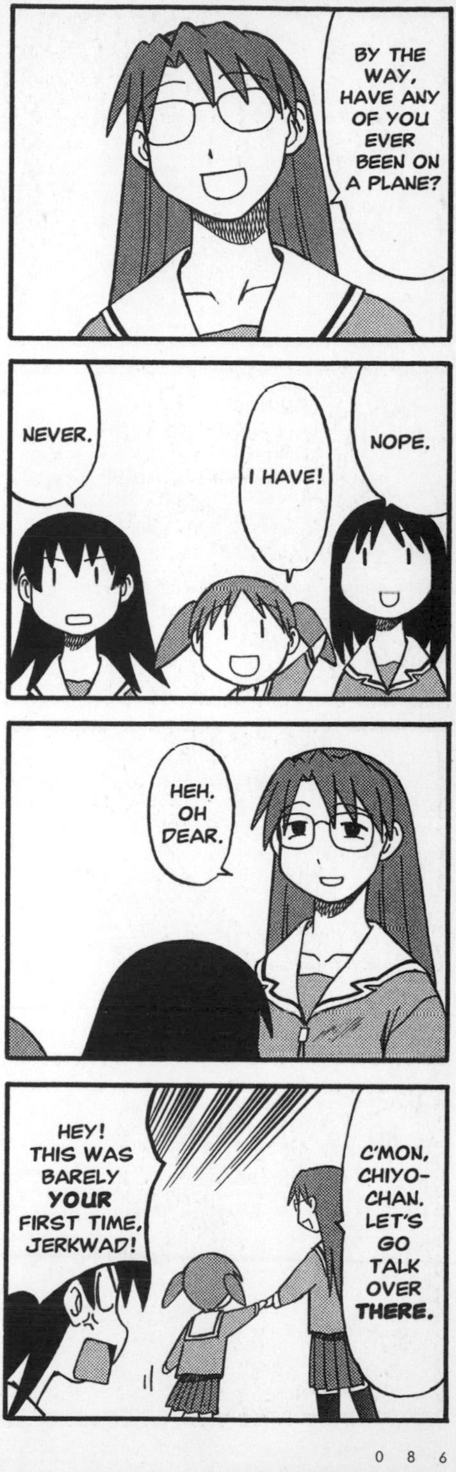
BY THE WAY, HAVE ANY OF YOU EVER BEEN ON A PLANE?
NOPE.
I HAVE!
NEVER.
HEH. OH DEAR.
C'MON, CHIYO-CHAN. LET'S GO TALK OVER THERE.
HEY! THIS WAS BARELY YOUR FIRST TIME, JERKWAD!

## THE BEARS OF HOKKAIDO

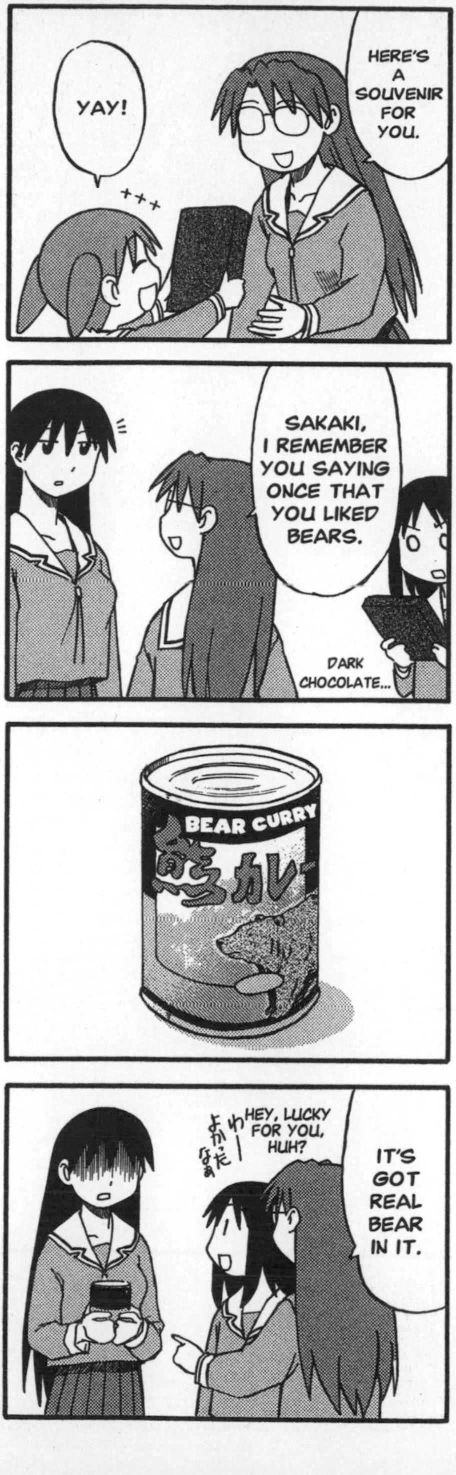
HERE'S A SOUVENIR FOR YOU.
YAY!
+++
SAKAKI, I REMEMBER YOU SAYING ONCE THAT YOU LIKED BEARS.
DARK CHOCOLATE...
BEAR CURRY
カレー
IT'S GOT REAL BEAR IN IT.
わー よかったなぁ
HEY, LUCKY FOR YOU, HUH?

## THE DIET

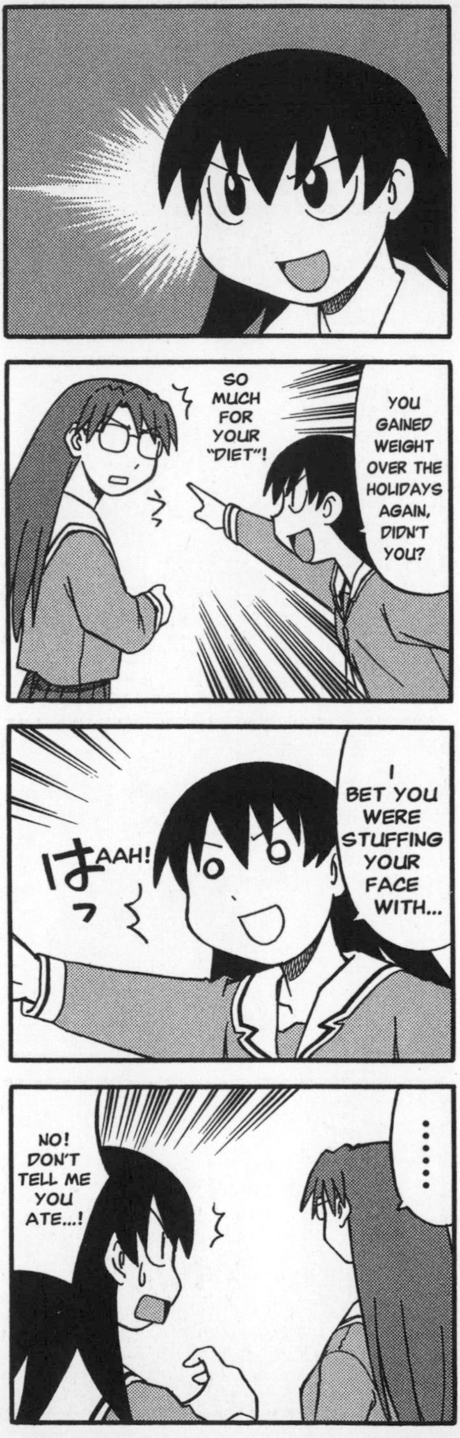
YOU GAINED WEIGHT OVER THE HOLIDAYS AGAIN, DIDN'T YOU?
SO MUCH FOR YOUR "DIET"!
I BET YOU WERE STUFFING YOUR FACE WITH...
はっ AAH!
......
NO! DON'T TELL ME YOU ATE...!

## TOO, TOO CRUEL

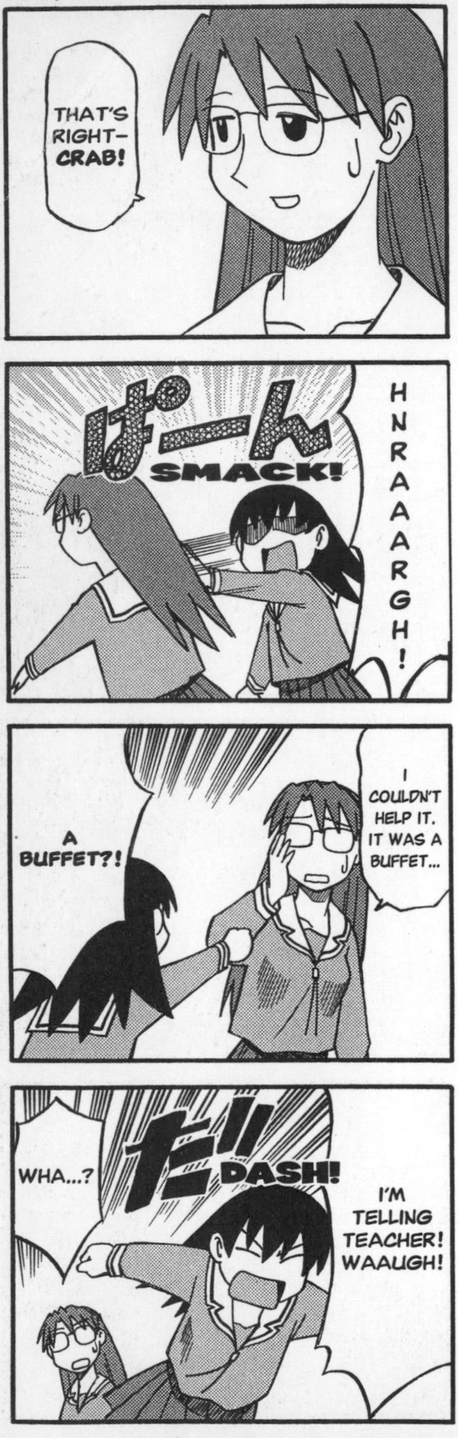
THAT'S RIGHT—CRAB!
HNRAAAARGH!
ぱーん SMACK!
I COULDN'T HELP IT. IT WAS A BUFFET...
A BUFFET?!
I'M TELLING TEACHER! WAAUGH!
だッ DASH!
WHA...?

ENTER MISS YUKARI

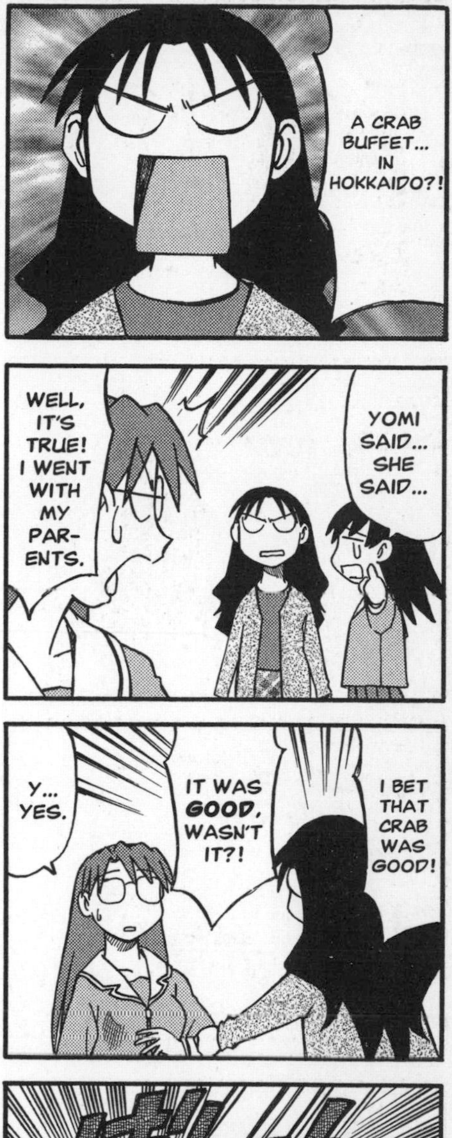
A CRAB BUFFET... IN HOKKAIDO?!
YOMI SAID... SHE SAID...
WELL, IT'S TRUE! I WENT WITH MY PAR-ENTS.
I BET THAT CRAB WAS GOOD!
IT WAS **GOOD**, WASN'T IT?!
Y... YES.
ば～ん
SMACK!

THAT WAS ALL-YOU-COULD-EAT, TOO

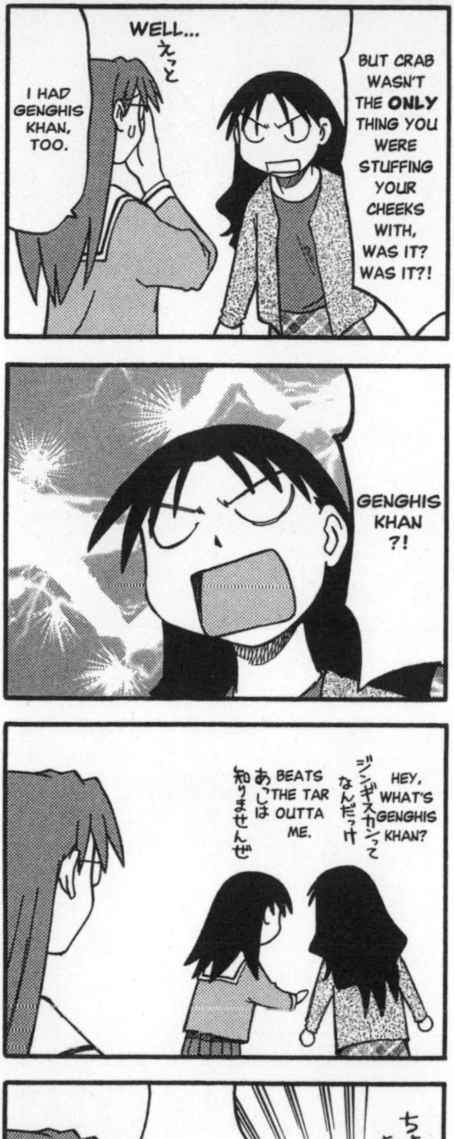
BUT CRAB WASN'T THE **ONLY** THING YOU WERE STUFFING YOUR CHEEKS WITH, WAS IT? WAS IT?!
WELL...
えっと
I HAD GENGHIS KHAN, TOO.
GENGHIS KHAN ?!
ジンギスカンってなんだっけ
HEY, WHAT'S GENGHIS KHAN?
あたしは知りませんぜ
BEATS THE TAR OUTTA ME.
ちよちゃんにきこう！
LET'S GO ASK CHIYO-CHAN.
WE'LL REMEMBER THIS!

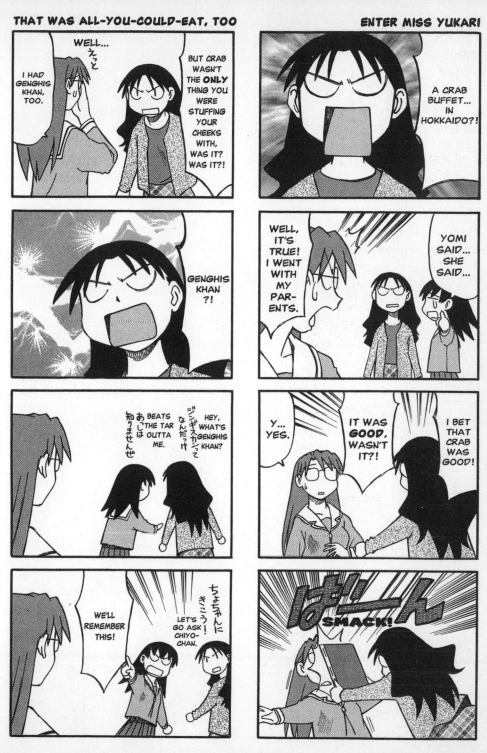

THE EXPLANATION

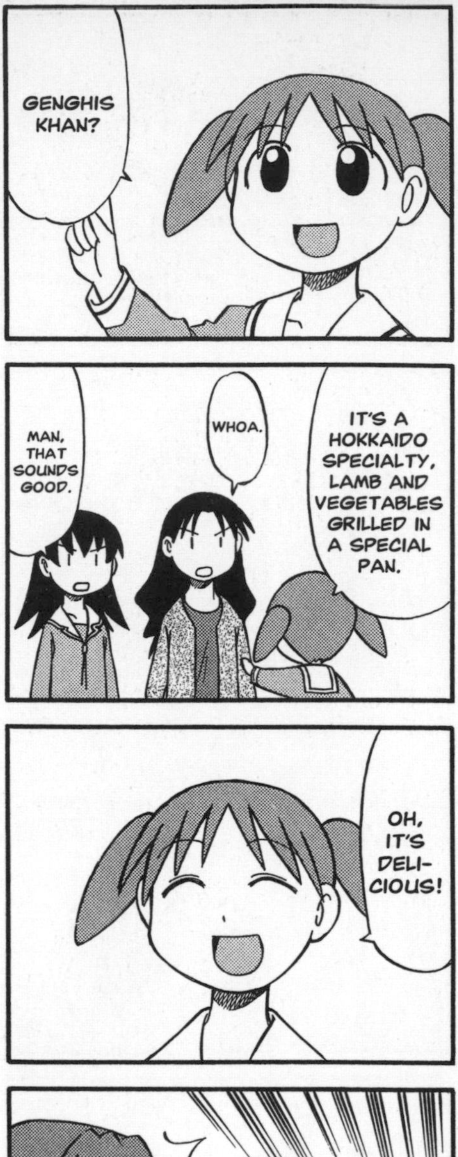
GENGHIS KHAN?
IT'S A HOKKAIDO SPECIALTY, LAMB AND VEGETABLES GRILLED IN A SPECIAL PAN.
WHOA.
MAN, THAT SOUNDS GOOD.
OH, IT'S DELICIOUS!

OW! OW!

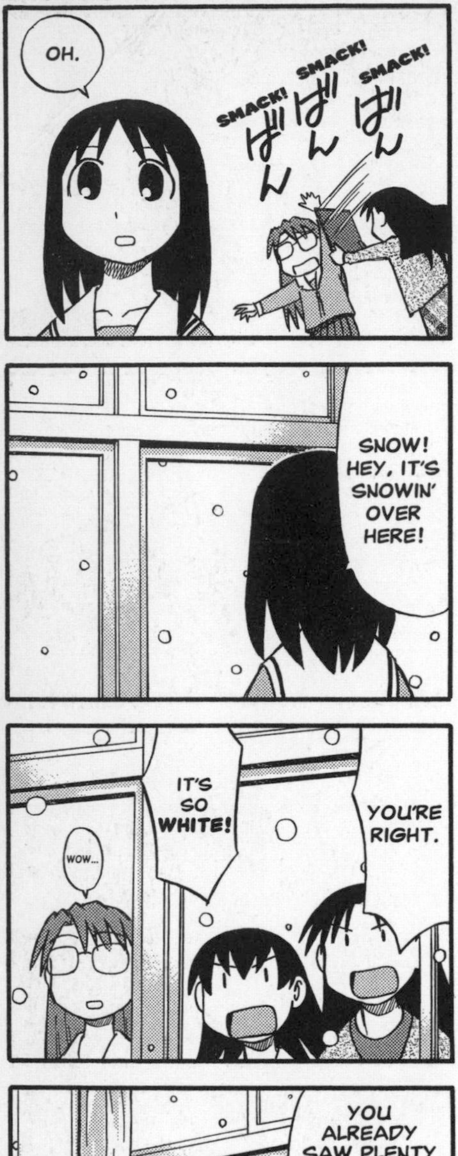
SNOW! HEY, IT'S SNOWIN' OVER HERE!
YOU'RE RIGHT.
IT'S SO WHITE!
WOW...
YOU ALREADY SAW PLENTY OF SNOW IN HOKKAIDO, DIDN'T YOU?!
ばん SMACK!
ばん SMACK!
ばん SMACK!
OH.

APPRECIATION

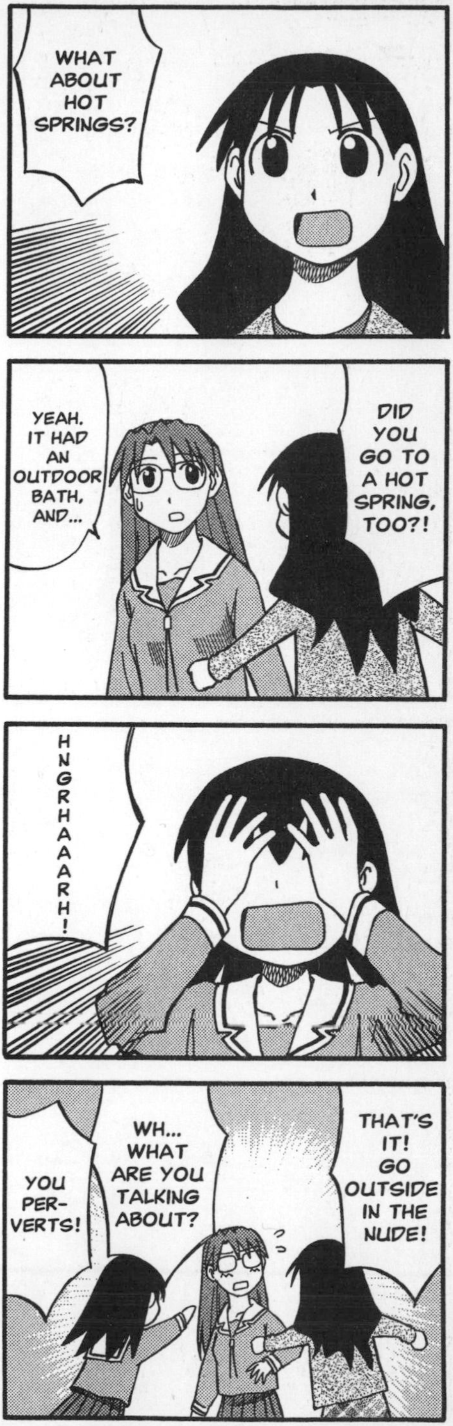
WHAT ABOUT HOT SPRINGS?
DID YOU GO TO A HOT SPRING, TOO?!
YEAH. IT HAD AN OUTDOOR BATH, AND...
HNGRHAAAARH!
THAT'S IT! GO OUTSIDE IN THE NUDE!
WH... WHAT ARE YOU TALKING ABOUT?
YOU PER-VERTS!

COLLEAGUES

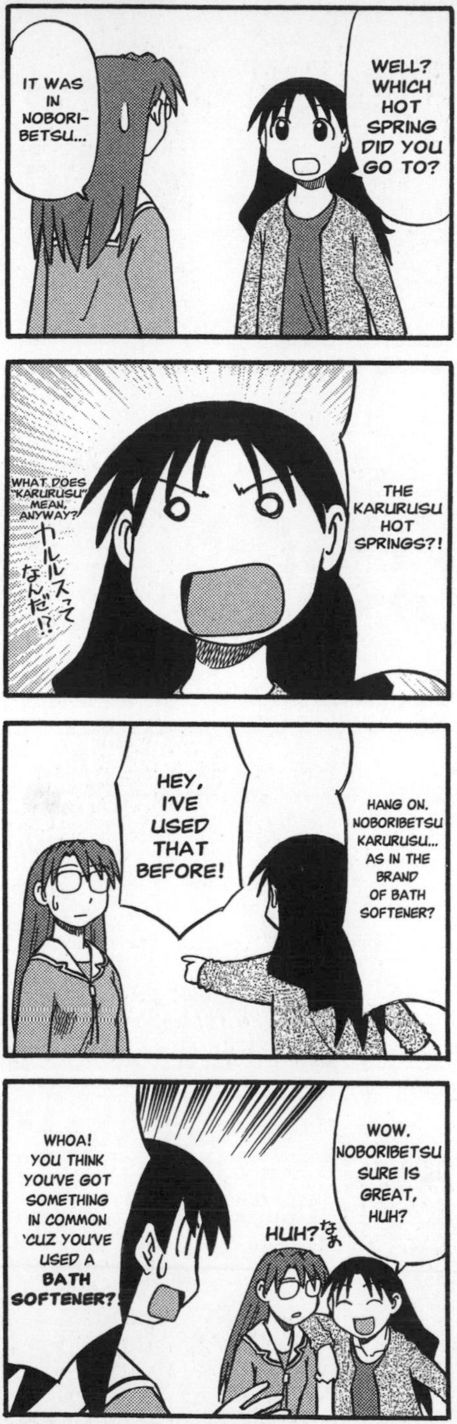
WELL? WHICH HOT SPRING DID YOU GO TO?
IT WAS IN NOBORI-BETSU...
THE KARURUSU HOT SPRINGS?!
WHAT DOES "KARURUSU" MEAN, ANYWAY?
カルルスってなんだ!?
HANG ON. NOBORIBETSU KARURUSU... AS IN THE BRAND OF BATH SOFTENER?
HEY, I'VE USED THAT BEFORE!
WOW. NOBORIBETSU SURE IS GREAT, HUH?
HUH?
WHOA! YOU THINK YOU'VE GOT SOMETHING IN COMMON 'CUZ YOU'VE USED A BATH SOFTENER?!

DANGEROUS

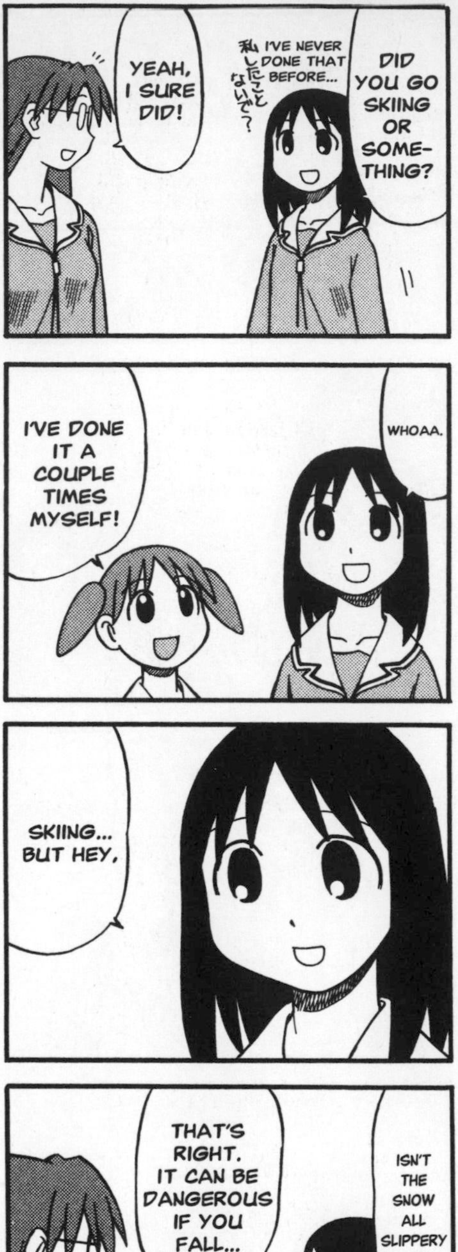
DID YOU GO SKIING OR SOMETHING?
私したことないで？
I'VE NEVER DONE THAT BEFORE...
YEAH, I SURE DID!
WHOAA.
I'VE DONE IT A COUPLE TIMES MYSELF!
SKIING... BUT HEY,
ISN'T THE SNOW ALL SLIPPERY AND STUFF?
THAT'S RIGHT. IT CAN BE DANGEROUS IF YOU FALL...

GO!

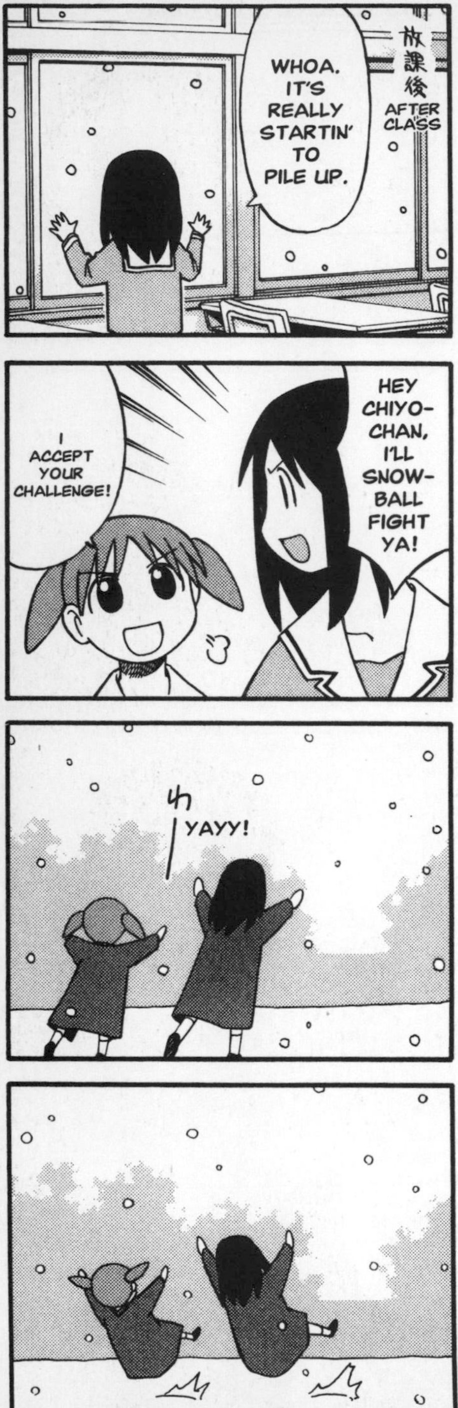
放課後
AFTER CLASS
WHOA. IT'S REALLY STARTIN' TO PILE UP.
HEY CHIYO-CHAN, I'LL SNOWBALL FIGHT YA!
I ACCEPT YOUR CHALLENGE!
YAYY!

FUN

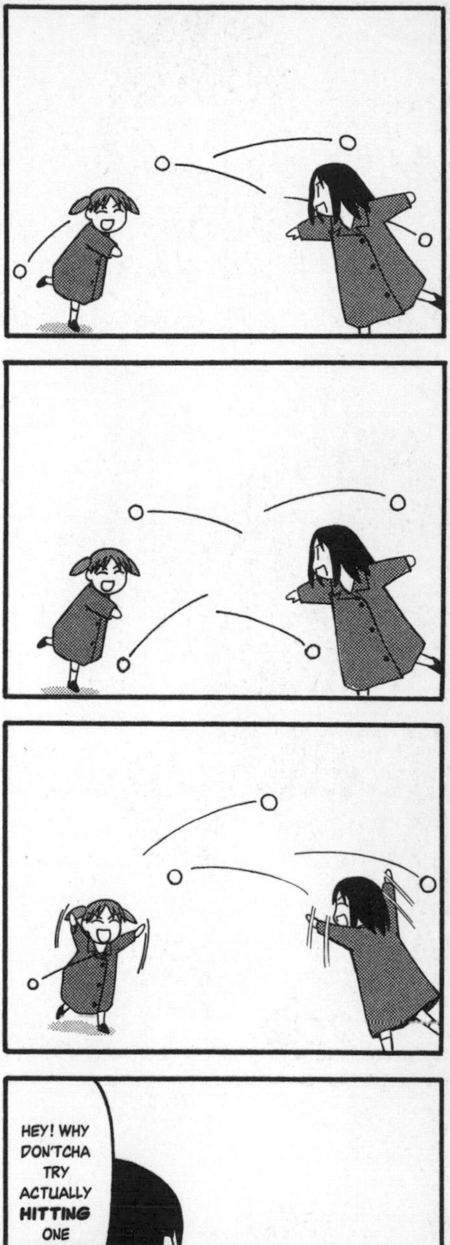
HEY! WHY DON'TCHA TRY ACTUALLY **HITTING** ONE ANOTHER?!

SHOWDOWN

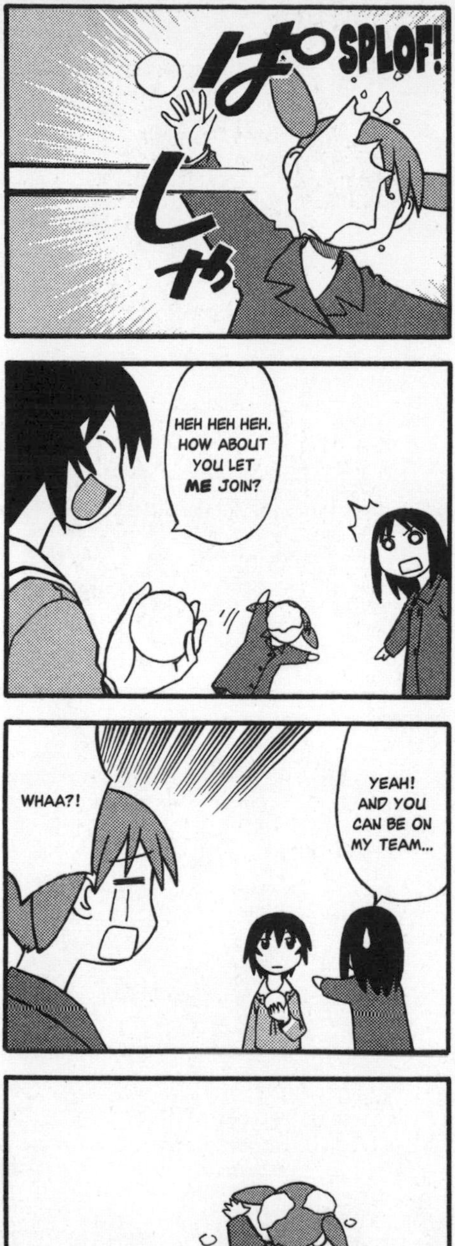
ぱしゃっ
SPLOF!
HEH HEH HEH. HOW ABOUT YOU LET **ME** JOIN?
YEAH! AND YOU CAN BE ON MY TEAM...
WHAA?!

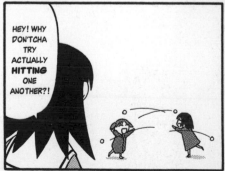

# 2

## FEBRUARY PART-1

AZU MANGA DAIOH

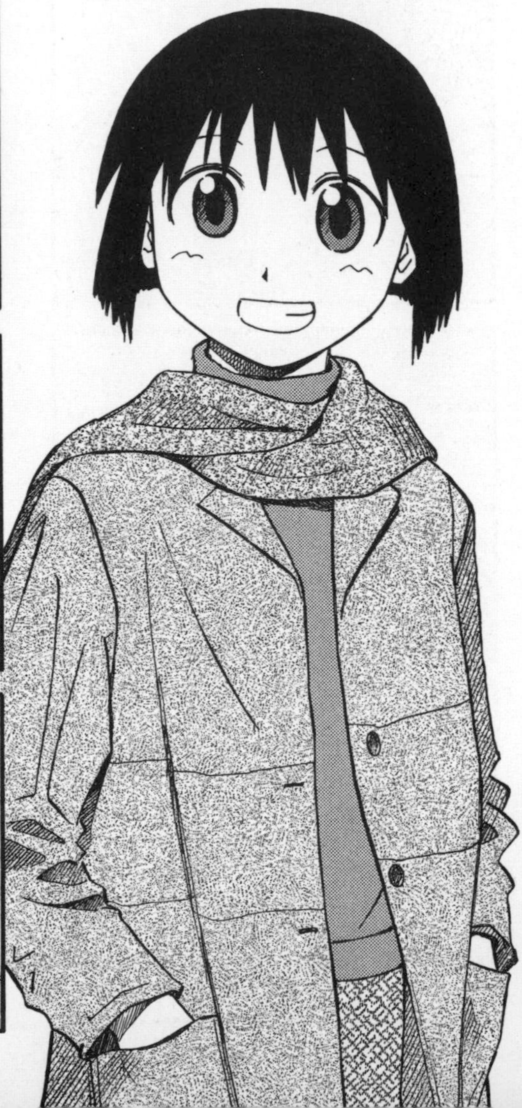

UNDER COVER

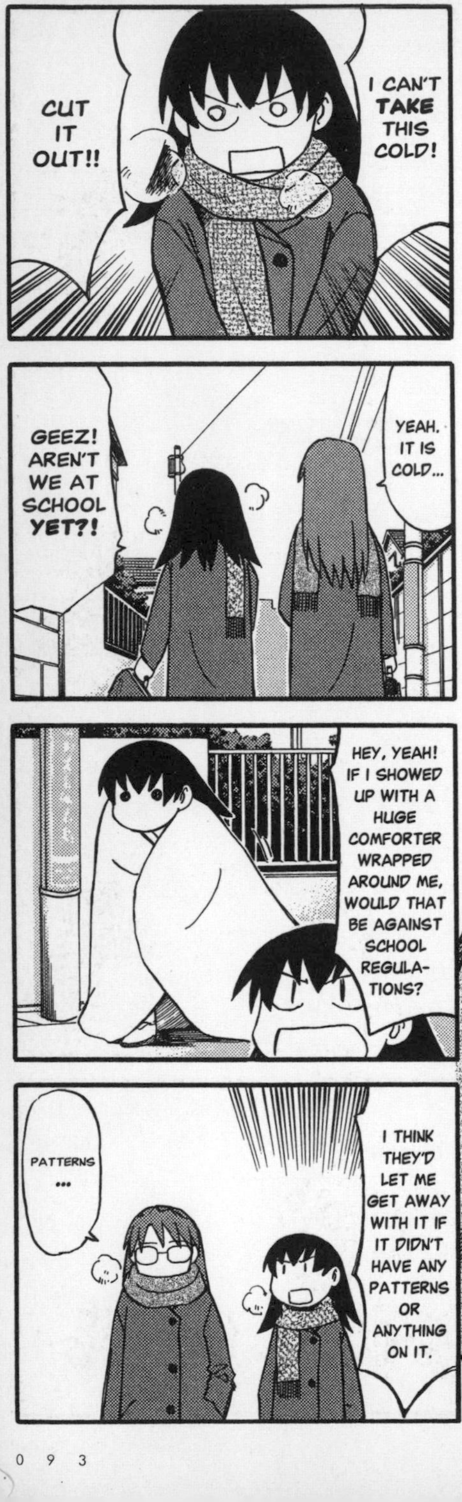
I CAN'T TAKE THIS COLD!
CUT IT OUT!!
YEAH. IT IS COLD...
GEEZ! AREN'T WE AT SCHOOL YET?!
HEY, YEAH! IF I SHOWED UP WITH A HUGE COMFORTER WRAPPED AROUND ME, WOULD THAT BE AGAINST SCHOOL REGULA-TIONS?
I THINK THEY'D LET ME GET AWAY WITH IT IF IT DIDN'T HAVE ANY PATTERNS OR ANYTHING ON IT.
PATTERNS...

THE PLAN

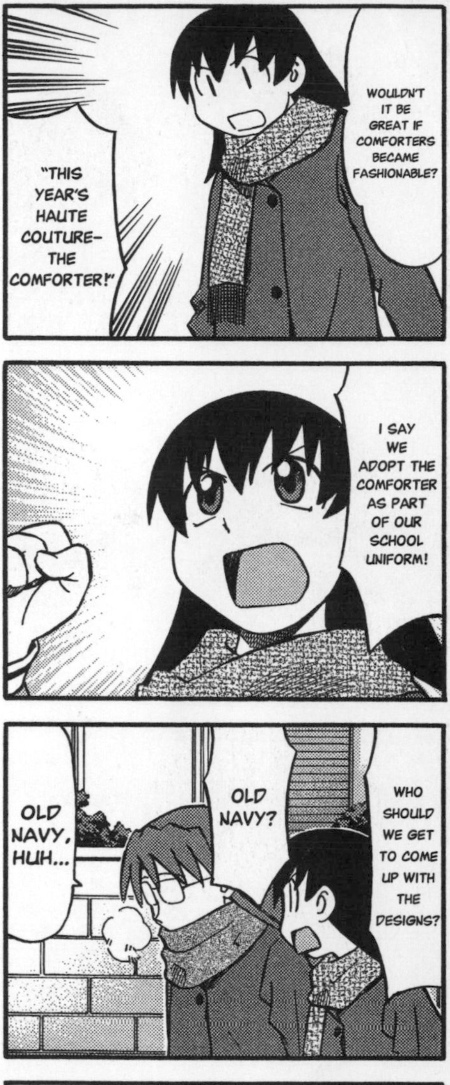

WOULDN'T IT BE GREAT IF COMFORTERS BECAME FASHIONABLE?
"THIS YEAR'S HAUTE COUTURE– THE COMFORTER!"
I SAY WE ADOPT THE COMFORTER AS PART OF OUR SCHOOL UNIFORM!
WHO SHOULD WE GET TO COME UP WITH THE DESIGNS?
OLD NAVY?
OLD NAVY, HUH...
OR TARGET, EVEN! THAT'D BE GOOD.
RIGHT? ね!?
YOU SEEM PRETTY ACTIVE FOR SOMEONE SUFFERING FROM THE COLD...


WAKE UP, KAORIN!

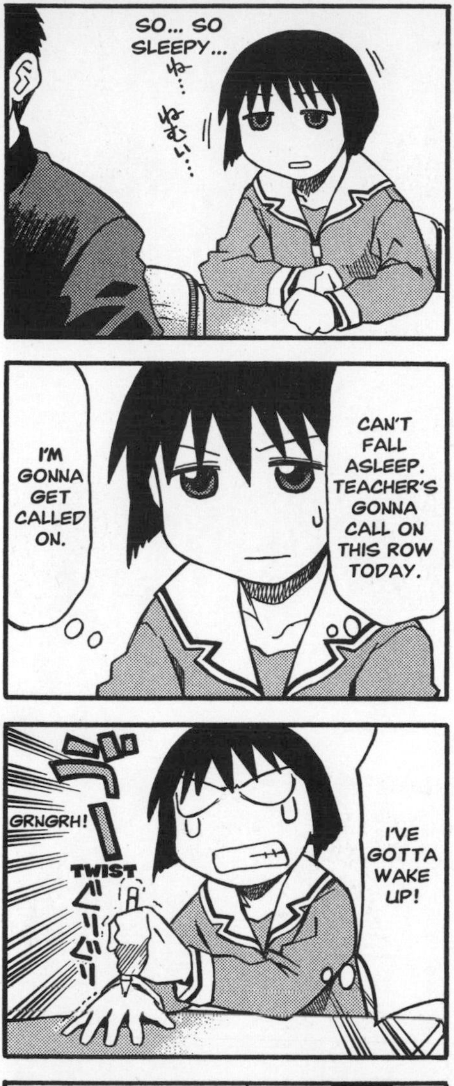

SO... SO SLEEPY...
ね… ねむい…
CAN'T FALL ASLEEP. TEACHER'S GONNA CALL ON THIS ROW TODAY.
I'M GONNA GET CALLED ON.
I'VE GOTTA WAKE UP!
ぐー
GRNGRH!
TWIST
ぐりぐり
ラーラー
HNGHH...HNGHH...
DROOP こく
DROOP こく

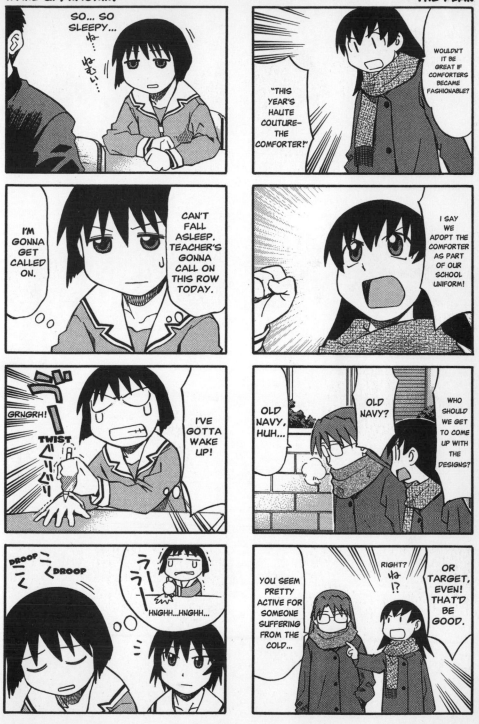

THE MECHANICAL PENCIL

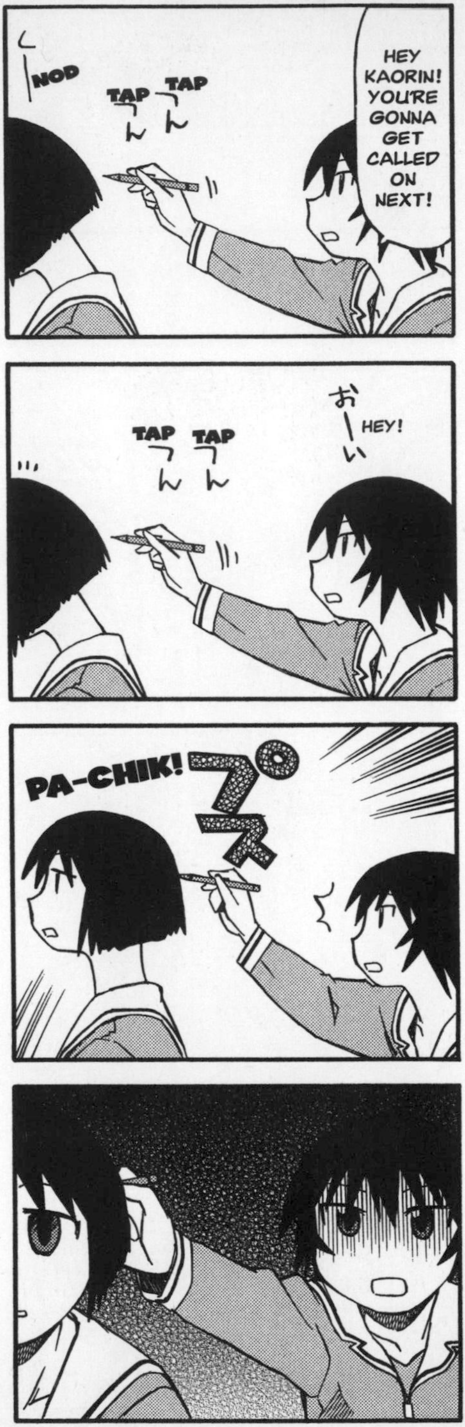

HEY KAORIN! YOU'RE GONNA GET CALLED ON NEXT!
TAP TAP
つん つん
NOD
おーい
HEY!
TAP TAP
つん つん
PA-CHIK!
プス


UH, SORRY...

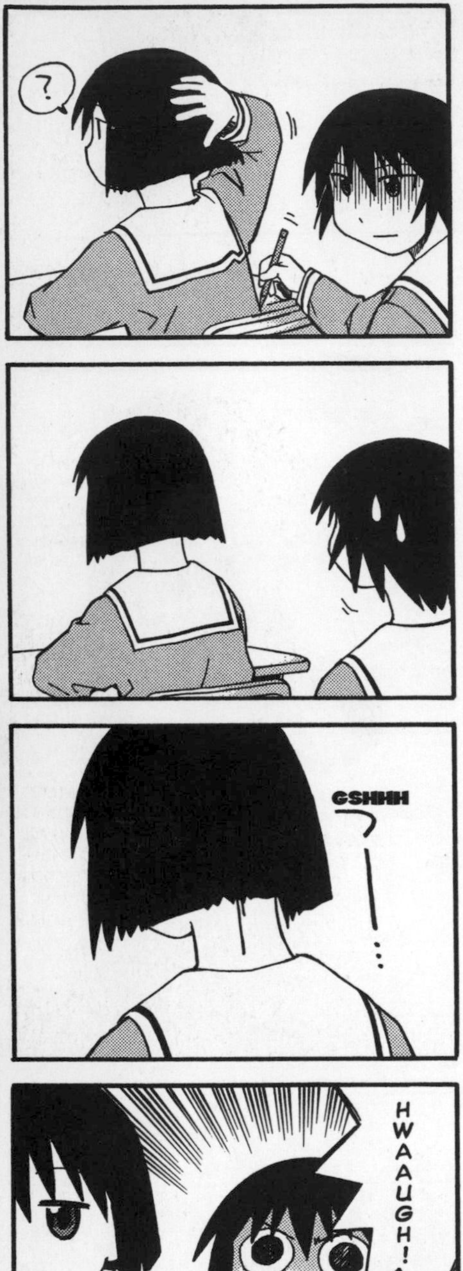

?
GSHHH
フー…
HWAAAUGH!

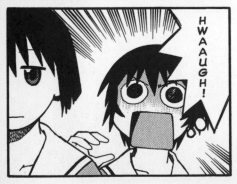

GYM SHORTS

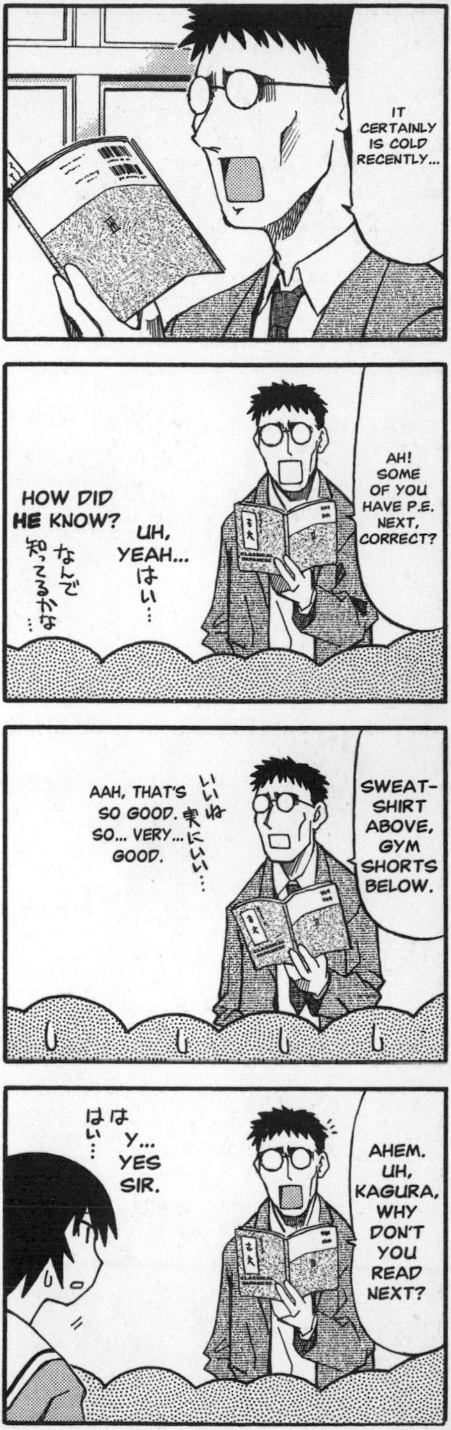
IT CERTAINLY IS COLD RECENTLY...
AH! SOME OF YOU HAVE P.E. NEXT, CORRECT?
UH, YEAH... はい…
HOW DID **HE** KNOW? なんで知ってるかな…
SWEAT-SHIRT ABOVE, GYM SHORTS BELOW.
AAH, THAT'S SO GOOD. SO... VERY... GOOD. いいね 実にいい…
AHEM. UH, KAGURA, WHY DON'T YOU READ NEXT?
Y... YES SIR. はは い…

HEART ON HIS SLEEVE

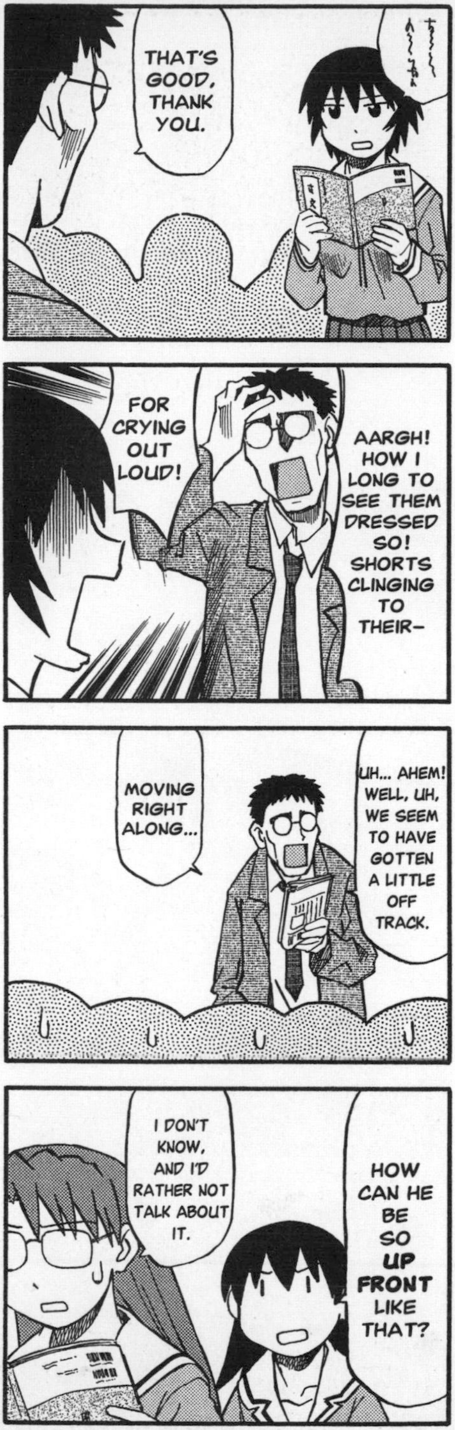
THAT'S GOOD, THANK YOU.
AARGH! HOW I LONG TO SEE THEM DRESSED SO! SHORTS CLINGING TO THEIR-
FOR CRYING OUT LOUD!
UH... AHEM! WELL, UH, WE SEEM TO HAVE GOTTEN A LITTLE OFF TRACK.
MOVING RIGHT ALONG...
HOW CAN HE BE SO **UP FRONT** LIKE THAT?
I DON'T KNOW, AND I'D RATHER NOT TALK ABOUT IT.

THE ALL-GIRLS' HIGH SCHOOL

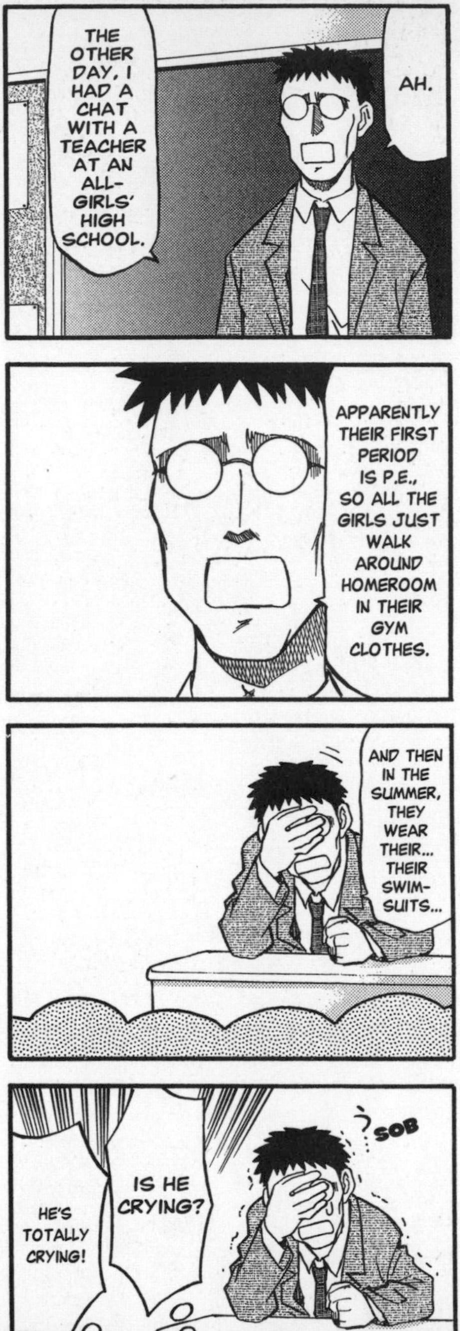

AH.
THE OTHER DAY, I HAD A CHAT WITH A TEACHER AT AN ALL-GIRLS' HIGH SCHOOL.
APPARENTLY THEIR FIRST PERIOD IS P.E., SO ALL THE GIRLS JUST WALK AROUND HOMEROOM IN THEIR GYM CLOTHES.
AND THEN IN THE SUMMER, THEY WEAR THEIR... THEIR SWIMSUITS...
SOB
IS HE CRYING?
HE'S TOTALLY CRYING!


A SENSE OF STABILITY

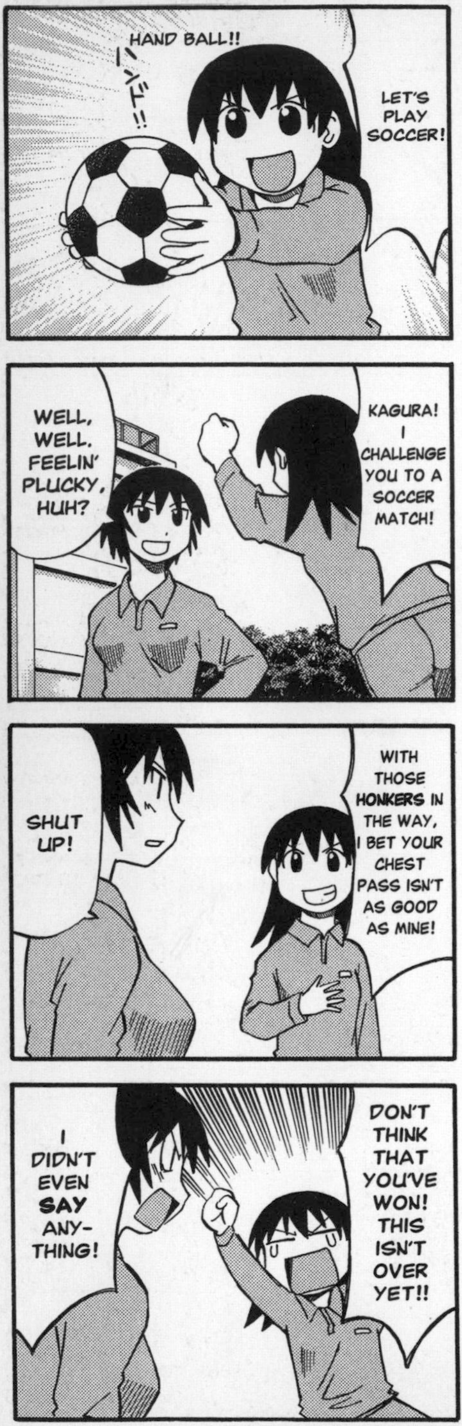

LET'S PLAY SOCCER!
HAND BALL!!
ハンド!!
KAGURA! I CHALLENGE YOU TO A SOCCER MATCH!
WELL, WELL. FEELIN' PLUCKY, HUH?
WITH THOSE HONKERS IN THE WAY, I BET YOUR CHEST PASS ISN'T AS GOOD AS MINE!
SHUT UP!
DON'T THINK THAT YOU'VE WON! THIS ISN'T OVER YET!!
I DIDN'T EVEN SAY ANYTHING!

STRAIGHT AHEAD

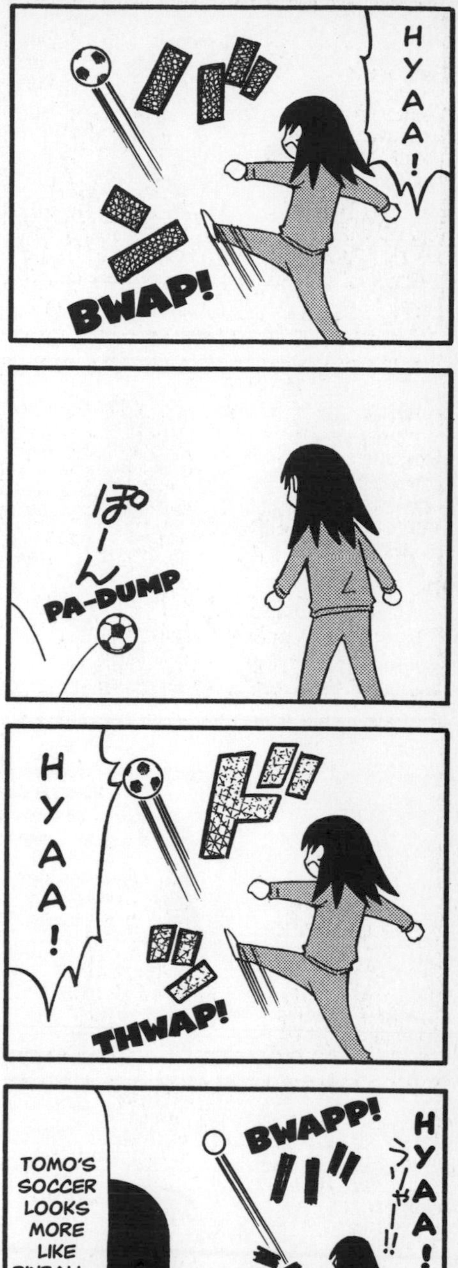
HYAA!
BWAP!
ぽーん
PA-DUMP
HYAA!
THWAP!
TOMO'S SOCCER LOOKS MORE LIKE PINBALL...
BWAPP!
HYAA!

HEADING THE BALL

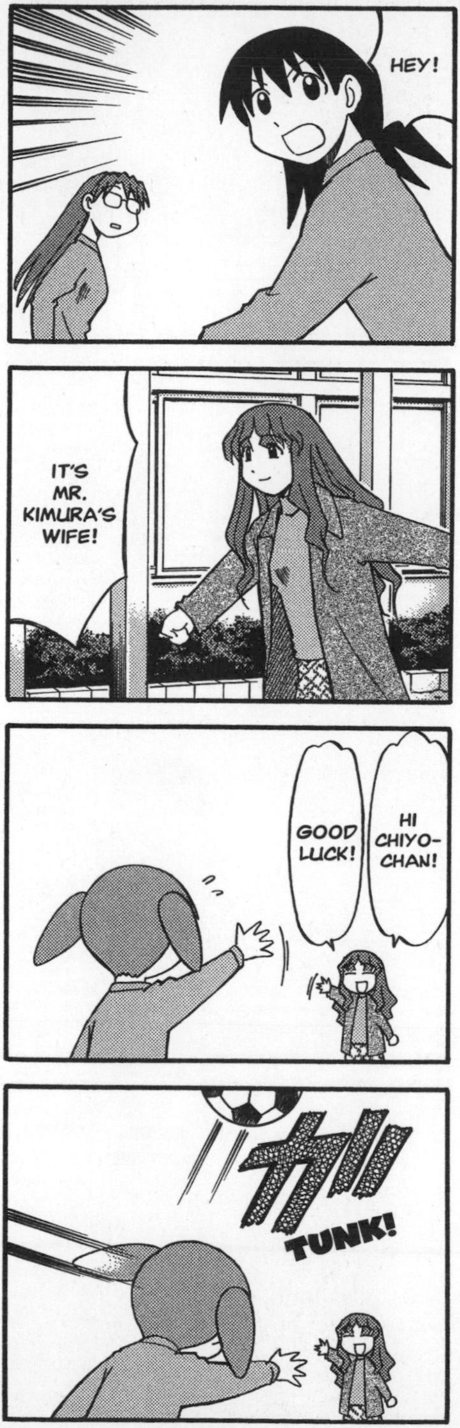
HEY!
IT'S MR. KIMURA'S WIFE!
HI CHIYO-CHAN!
GOOD LUCK!
TUNK!

## FOLLOWING THE RULES

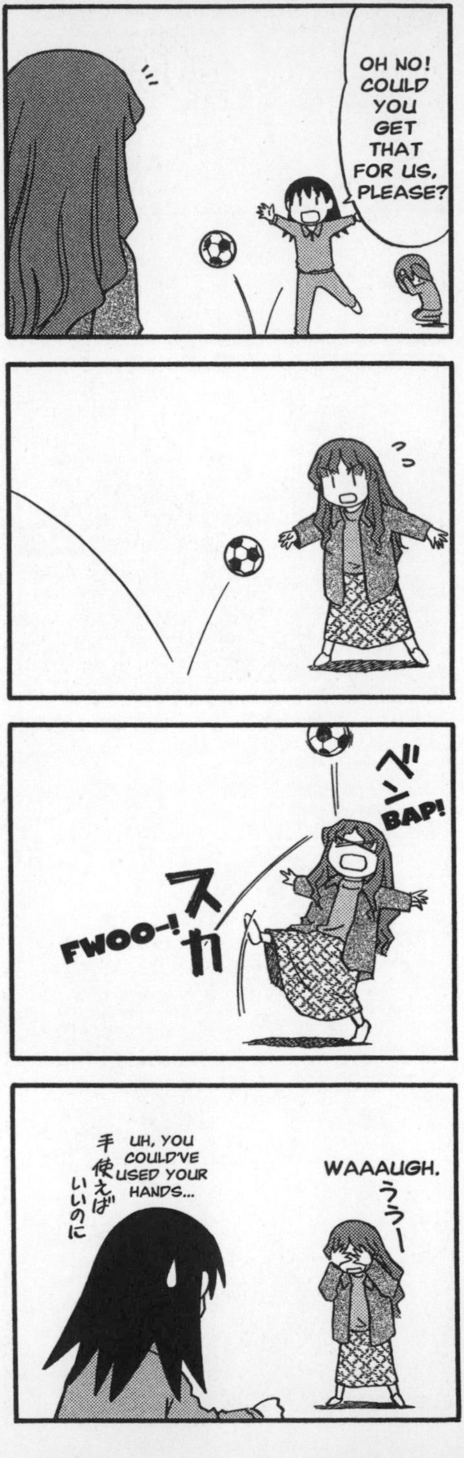
OH NO! COULD YOU GET THAT FOR US, PLEASE?
ベン
BAP!
スカ
FWOO-!
WAAAUGH.
うう~
手使えばいいのに
UH, YOU COULD'VE USED YOUR HANDS...

## SPICE IS LOVE

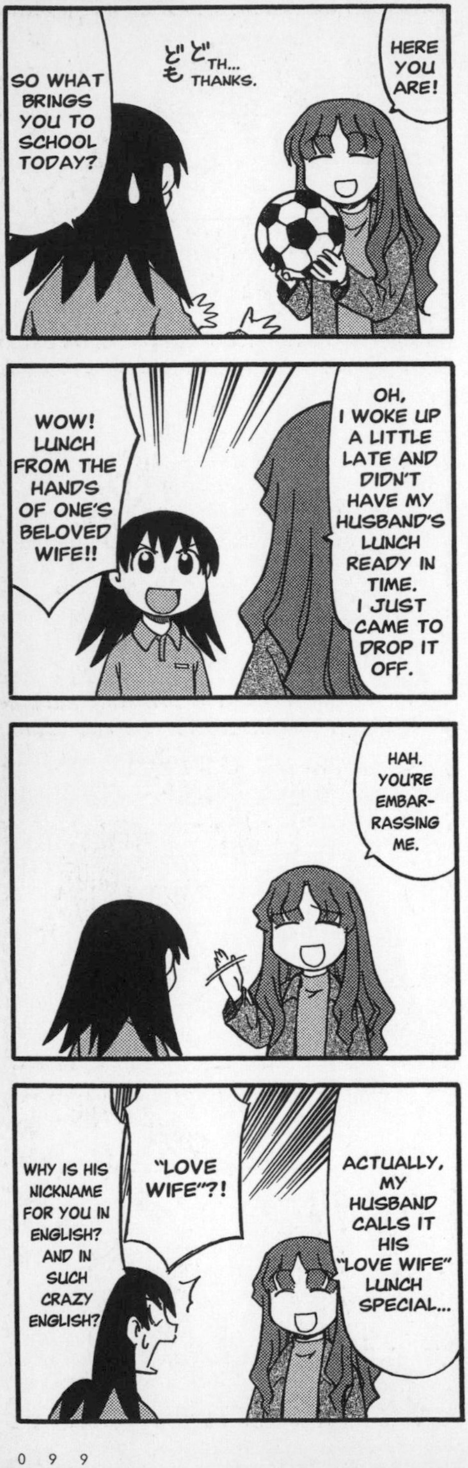
HERE YOU ARE!
どども
TH... THANKS.
SO WHAT BRINGS YOU TO SCHOOL TODAY?
OH, I WOKE UP A LITTLE LATE AND DIDN'T HAVE MY HUSBAND'S LUNCH READY IN TIME. I JUST CAME TO DROP IT OFF.
WOW! LUNCH FROM THE HANDS OF ONE'S BELOVED WIFE!!
HAH. YOU'RE EMBAR-RASSING ME.
ACTUALLY, MY HUSBAND CALLS IT HIS "LOVE WIFE" LUNCH SPECIAL...
"LOVE WIFE"?!
WHY IS HIS NICKNAME FOR YOU IN ENGLISH? AND IN SUCH CRAZY ENGLISH?

I JUST CAN'T PICK...

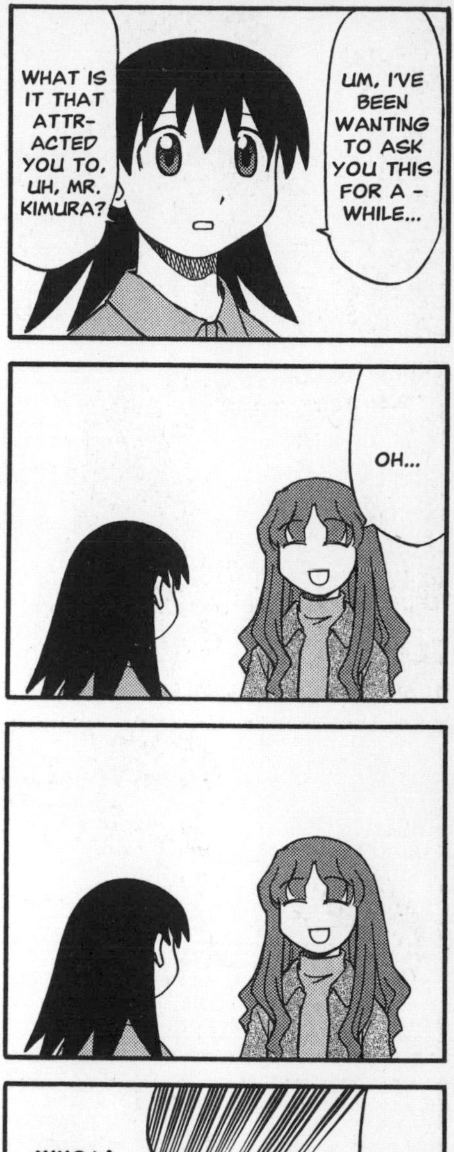
UM, I'VE BEEN WANTING TO ASK YOU THIS FOR A - WHILE...
WHAT IS IT THAT ATTR-ACTED YOU TO, UH, MR. KIMURA?
OH...
WELL, HE IS RATHER HAND-SOME...
WHOA! SOMEBODY GET THIS LADY A NEW PAIR OF EYES!

ROUND AND ROUND

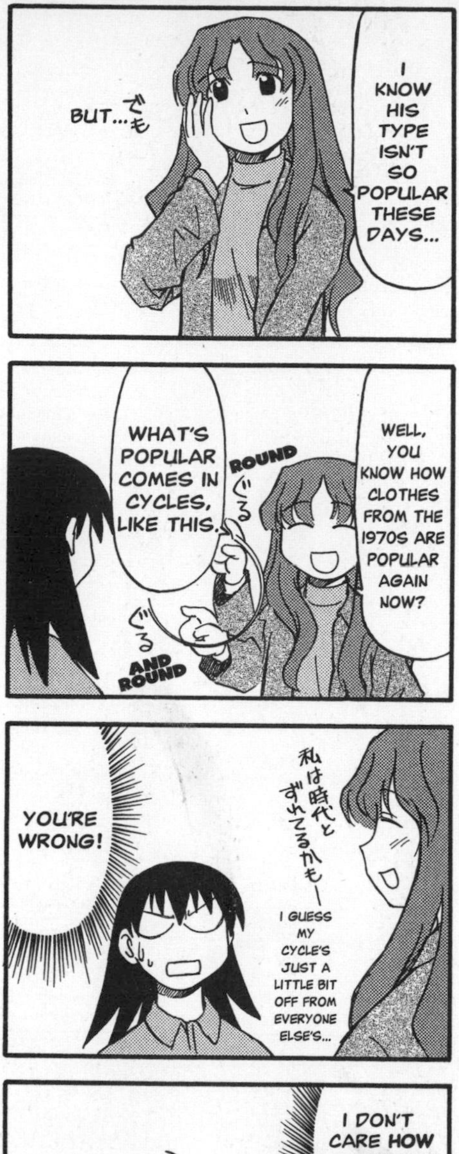
I KNOW HIS TYPE ISN'T SO POPULAR THESE DAYS...
BUT... でも
WELL, YOU KNOW HOW CLOTHES FROM THE 1970S ARE POPULAR AGAIN NOW?
ROUND ぐる
WHAT'S POPULAR COMES IN CYCLES, LIKE THIS.
ぐる AND ROUND
私は時代とずれてるかもー
I GUESS MY CYCLE'S JUST A LITTLE BIT OFF FROM EVERYONE ELSE'S...
YOU'RE WRONG!
I DON'T CARE HOW MANY TIMES THAT CYCLE TURNS– KIMURA'S NUMBER AIN'T NEVER COMING UP!
?

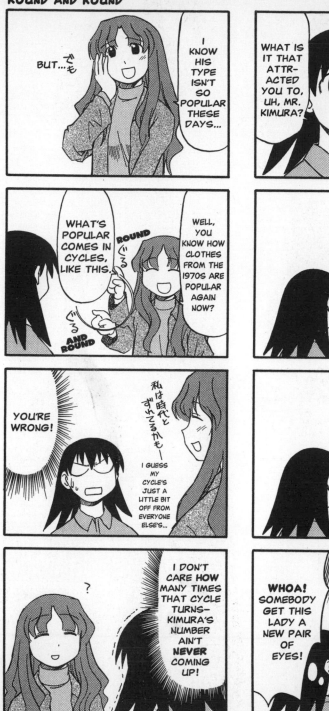

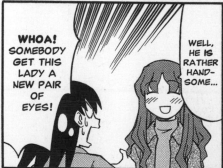

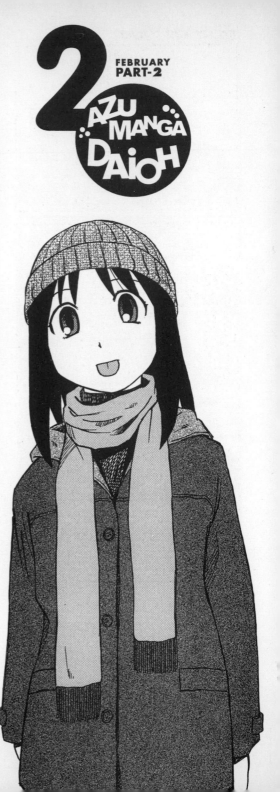

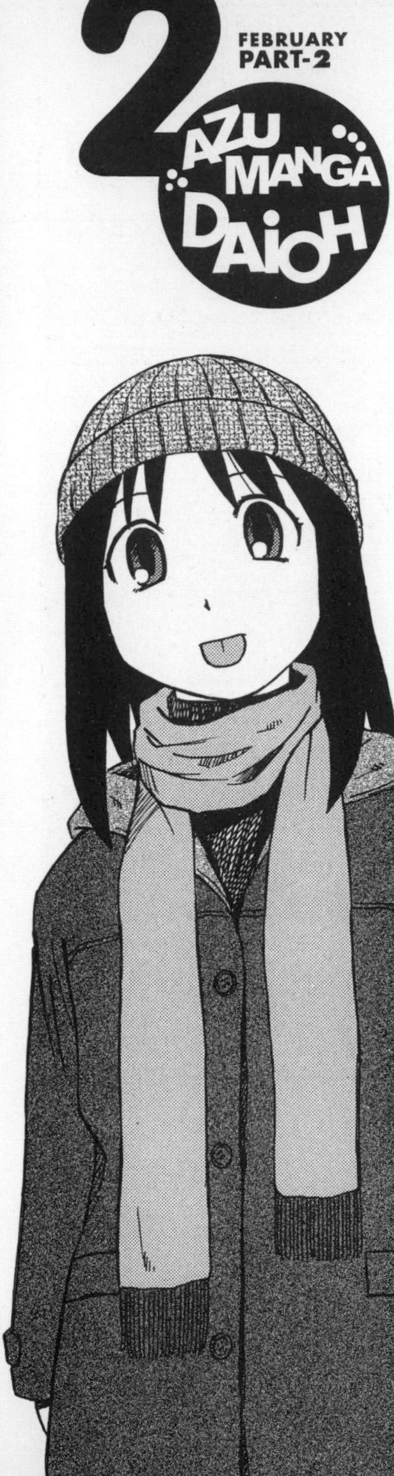
2
FEBRUARY
PART-2
AZU MANGA DAIOH

YUKARI THE GOURMET

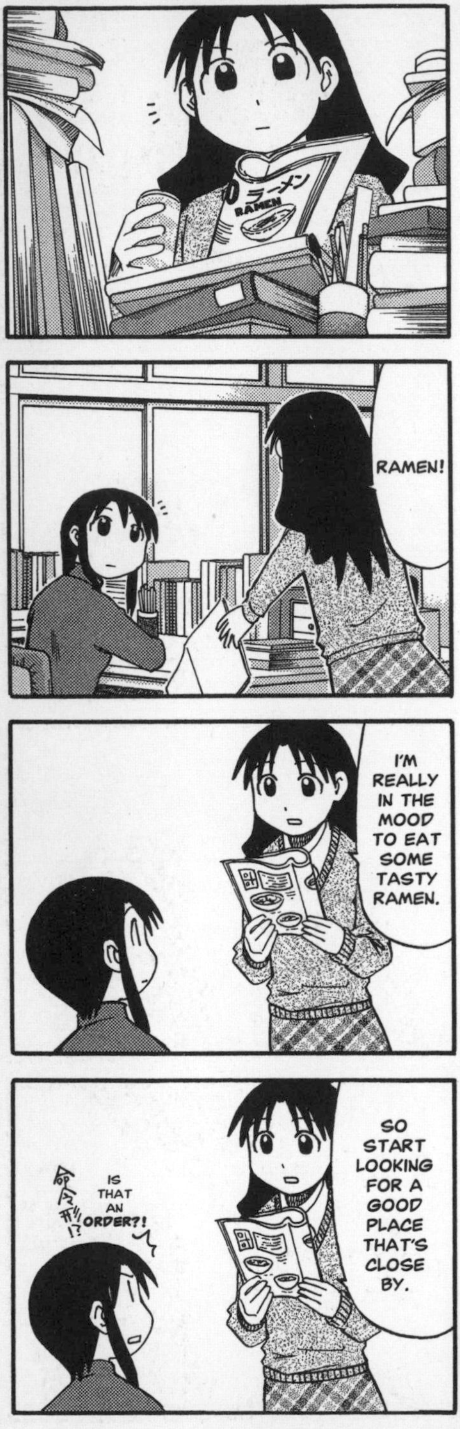
ラーメン
RAMEN
RAMEN!
I'M REALLY IN THE MOOD TO EAT SOME TASTY RAMEN.
SO START LOOKING FOR A GOOD PLACE THAT'S CLOSE BY.
IS THAT AN ORDER?!
命令形!?

WHA-?

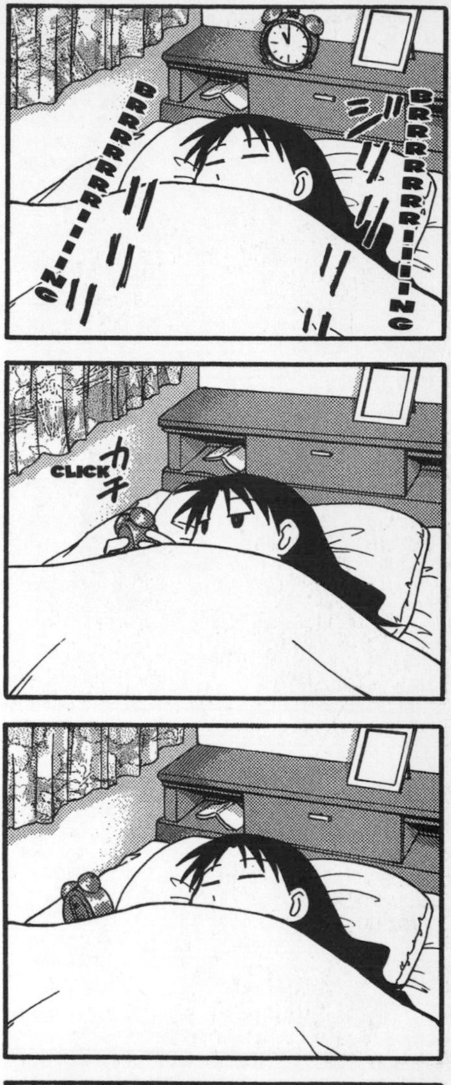
BRRRRRRIIIING
BRRRRRRIIIING
CLICK
カチ

LEAVE ME ALONE!

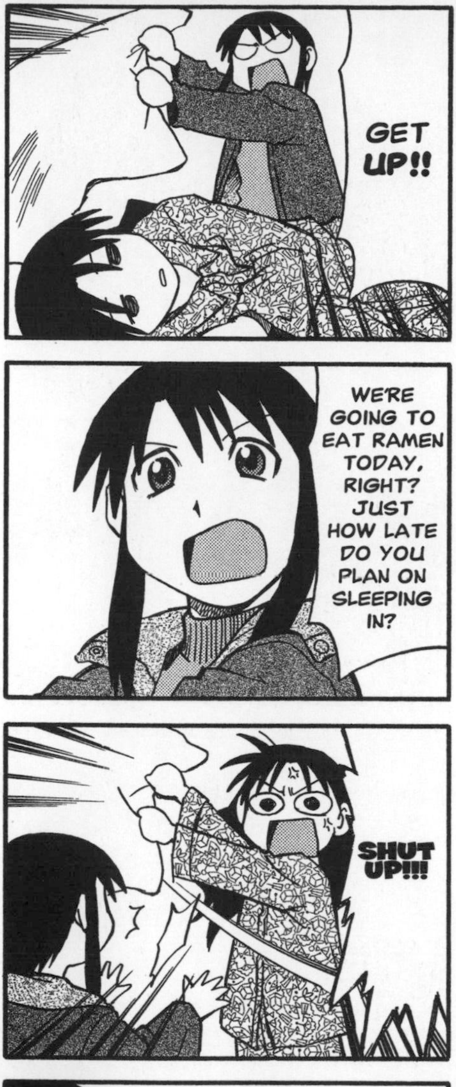
GET UP!!
WE'RE GOING TO EAT RAMEN TODAY, RIGHT? JUST HOW LATE DO YOU PLAN ON SLEEPING IN?
SHUT UP!!!
ZZZZ
もぞもぞ
な…
WHA-?

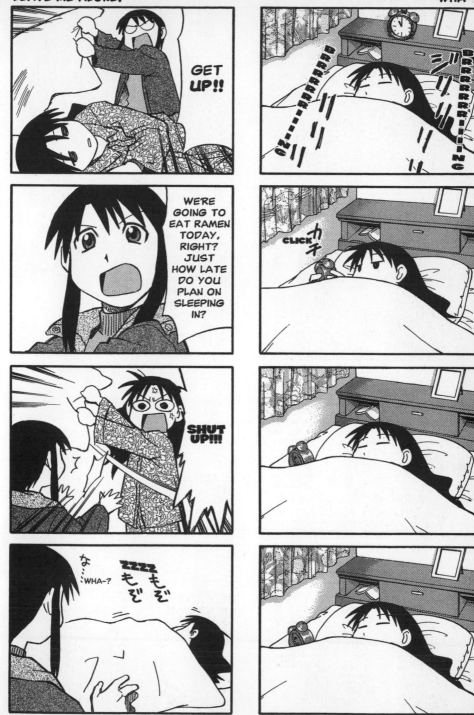

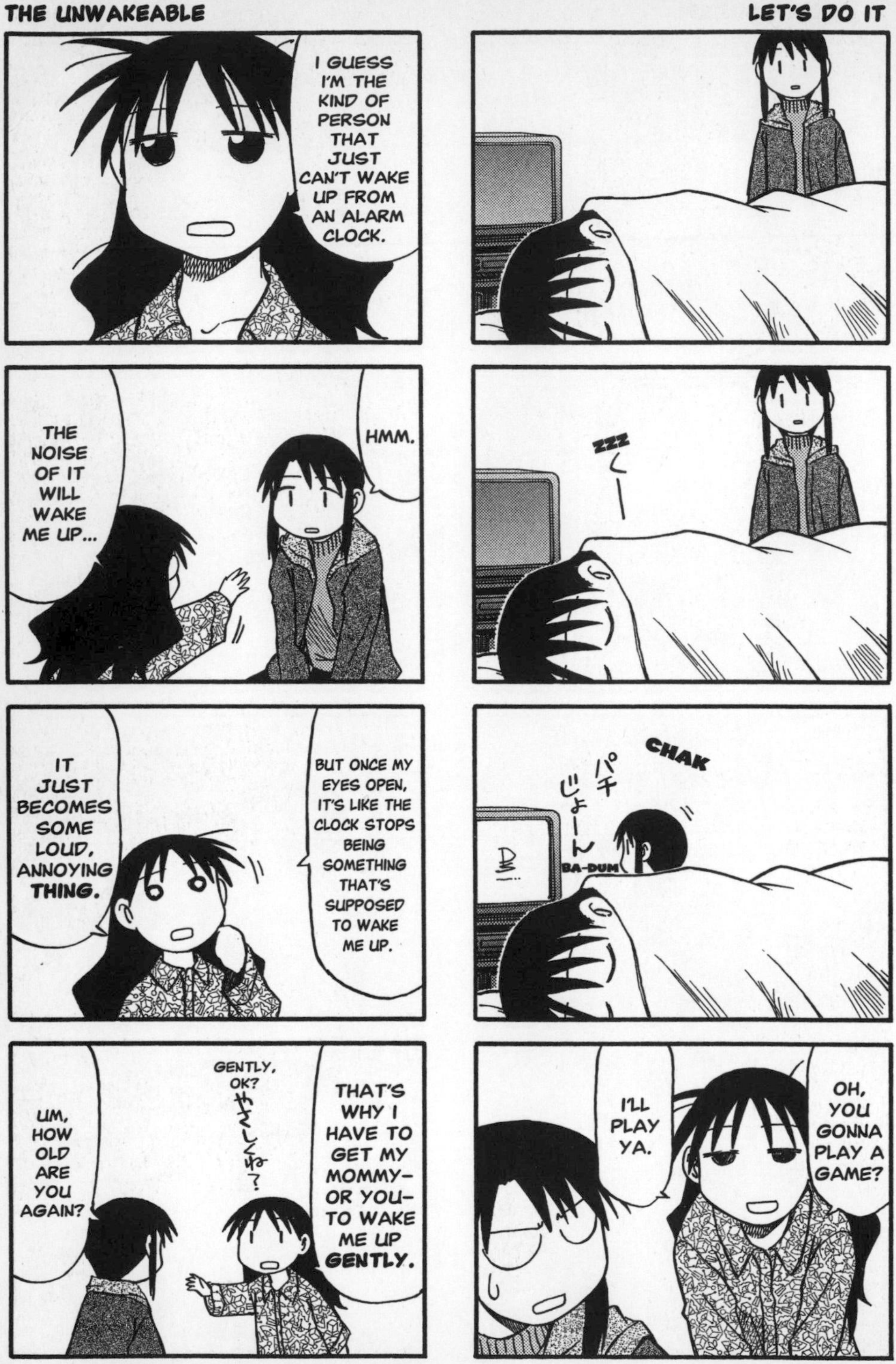
LET'S DO IT
ZZZ
くー
CHAK
パチ
じょーん
BA-DUM
OH, YOU GONNA PLAY A GAME?
I'LL PLAY YA.
THE UNWAKEABLE
I GUESS I'M THE KIND OF PERSON THAT JUST CAN'T WAKE UP FROM AN ALARM CLOCK.
HMM.
THE NOISE OF IT WILL WAKE ME UP...
BUT ONCE MY EYES OPEN, IT'S LIKE THE CLOCK STOPS BEING SOMETHING THAT'S SUPPOSED TO WAKE ME UP.
IT JUST BECOMES SOME LOUD, ANNOYING THING.
THAT'S WHY I HAVE TO GET MY MOMMY— OR YOU— TO WAKE ME UP GENTLY.
GENTLY, OK?
やさしくね?
UM, HOW OLD ARE YOU AGAIN?

MOOD

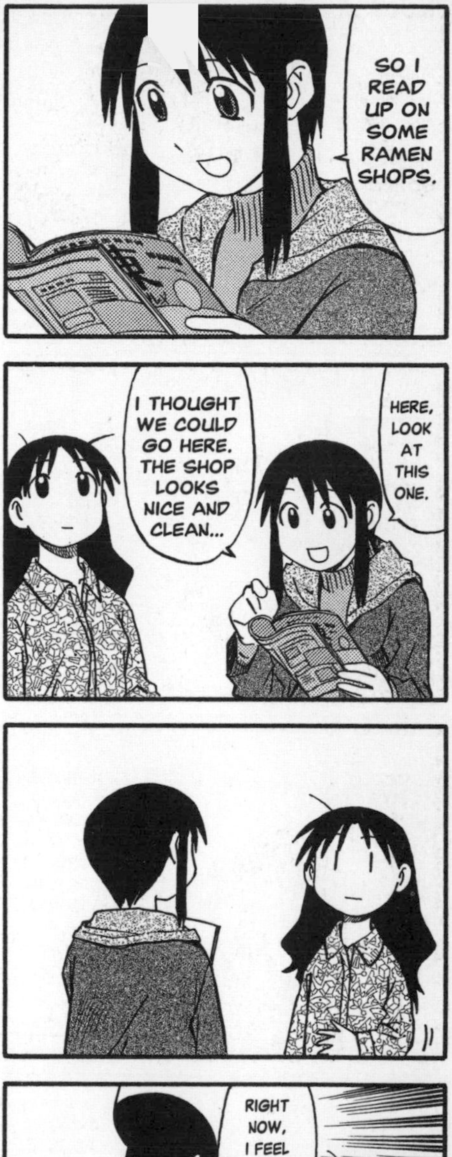
SO I READ UP ON SOME RAMEN SHOPS.
HERE, LOOK AT THIS ONE.
I THOUGHT WE COULD GO HERE. THE SHOP LOOKS NICE AND CLEAN...
RIGHT NOW, I FEEL MORE LIKE EATING SOBA.
TODAY WAS SUPPOSED TO BE RAMEN! **RAMEN!!**

FORGETFUL

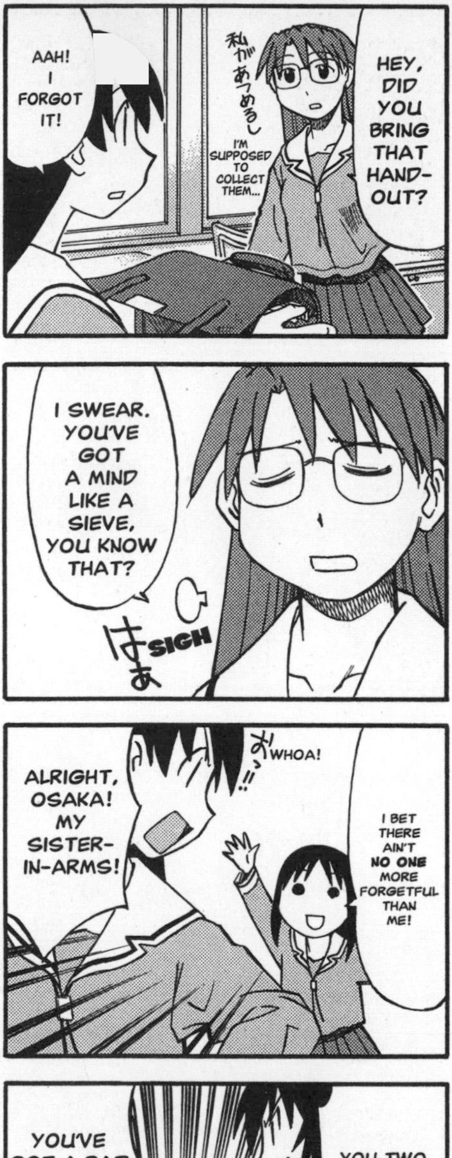
HEY, DID YOU BRING THAT HAND-OUT?
私があつめるし
I'M SUPPOSED TO COLLECT THEM...
AAH! I FORGOT IT!
I SWEAR. YOU'VE GOT A MIND LIKE A SIEVE, YOU KNOW THAT?
はぁ SIGH
I BET THERE AIN'T **NO ONE** MORE FORGETFUL THAN ME!
お!! WHOA!
ALRIGHT, OSAKA! MY SISTER-IN-ARMS!
YOU TWO MAY BE FOR-GETFUL, BUT DON'T GO FORGETTING ABOUT **ME!**
YOU'VE GOT A BAD MEMORY TOO, HUH? MARK MY WORDS—THIS SCHOOL IS IN TROUBLE!

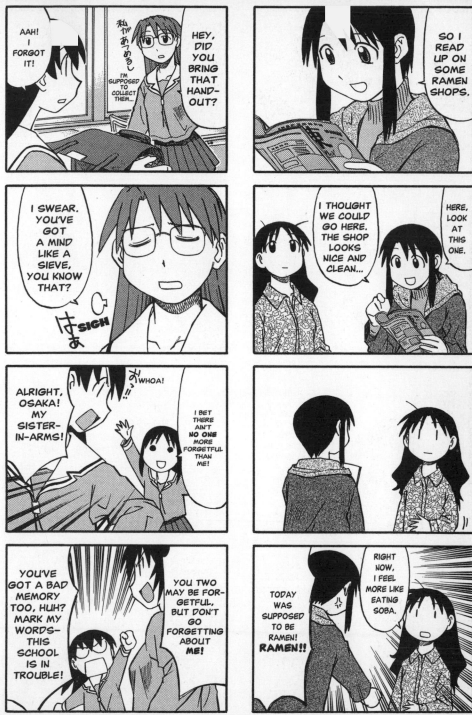

THE QUEEN

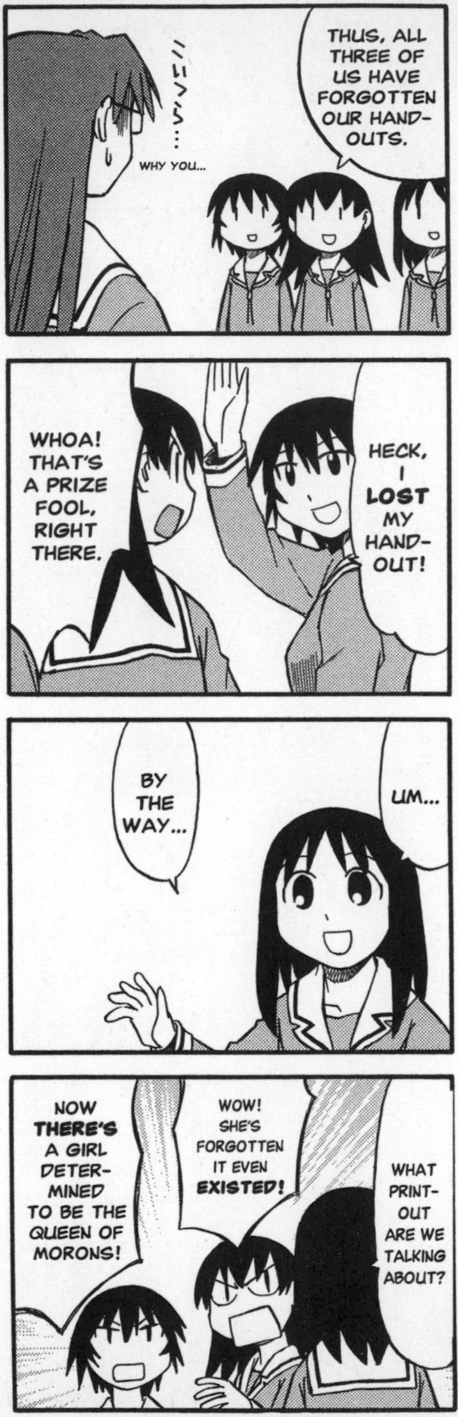
THUS, ALL THREE OF US HAVE FORGOTTEN OUR HAND-OUTS.
こいつら…
WHY YOU...
HECK, I LOST MY HAND-OUT!
WHOA! THAT'S A PRIZE FOOL, RIGHT THERE.
UM...
BY THE WAY...
WHAT PRINT-OUT ARE WE TALKING ABOUT?
WOW! SHE'S FORGOTTEN IT EVEN EXISTED!
NOW THERE'S A GIRL DETERMINED TO BE THE QUEEN OF MORONS!

A HEART AS WIDE AS...

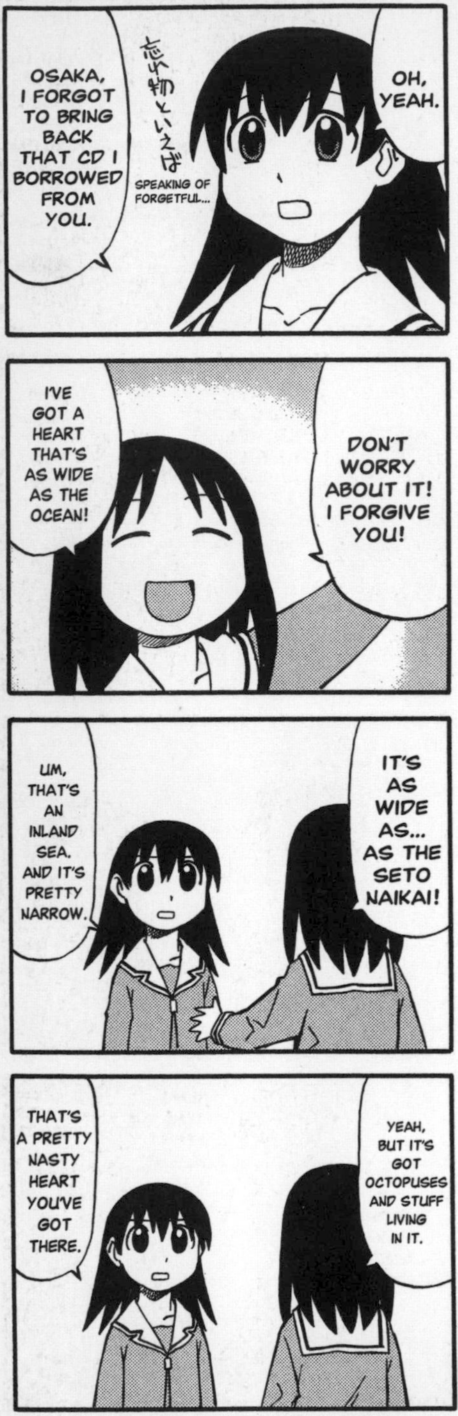
OH, YEAH.
忘れ物といえば
SPEAKING OF FORGETFUL...
OSAKA, I FORGOT TO BRING BACK THAT CD I BORROWED FROM YOU.
DON'T WORRY ABOUT IT! I FORGIVE YOU!
I'VE GOT A HEART THAT'S AS WIDE AS THE OCEAN!
IT'S AS WIDE AS... AS THE SETO NAIKAI!
UM, THAT'S AN INLAND SEA. AND IT'S PRETTY NARROW.
YEAH, BUT IT'S GOT OCTOPUSES AND STUFF LIVING IN IT.
THAT'S A PRETTY NASTY HEART YOU'VE GOT THERE.

THE QUESTION

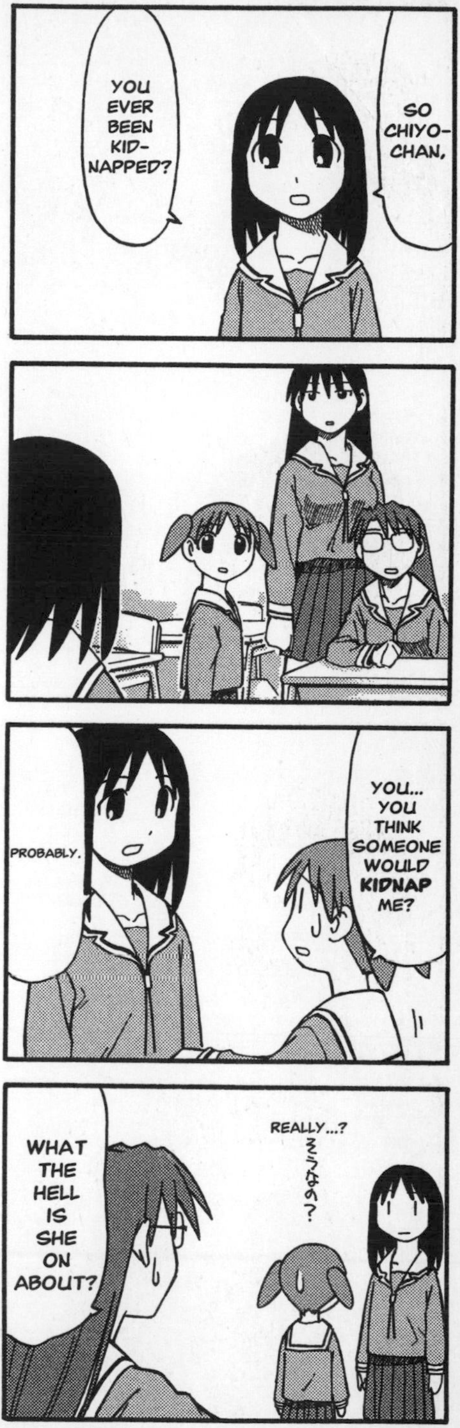
SO CHIYO-CHAN,
YOU EVER BEEN KID-NAPPED?
YOU... YOU THINK SOMEONE WOULD KIDNAP ME?
PROBABLY.
REALLY...? そうなの？
WHAT THE HELL IS SHE ON ABOUT?

CAPTURED

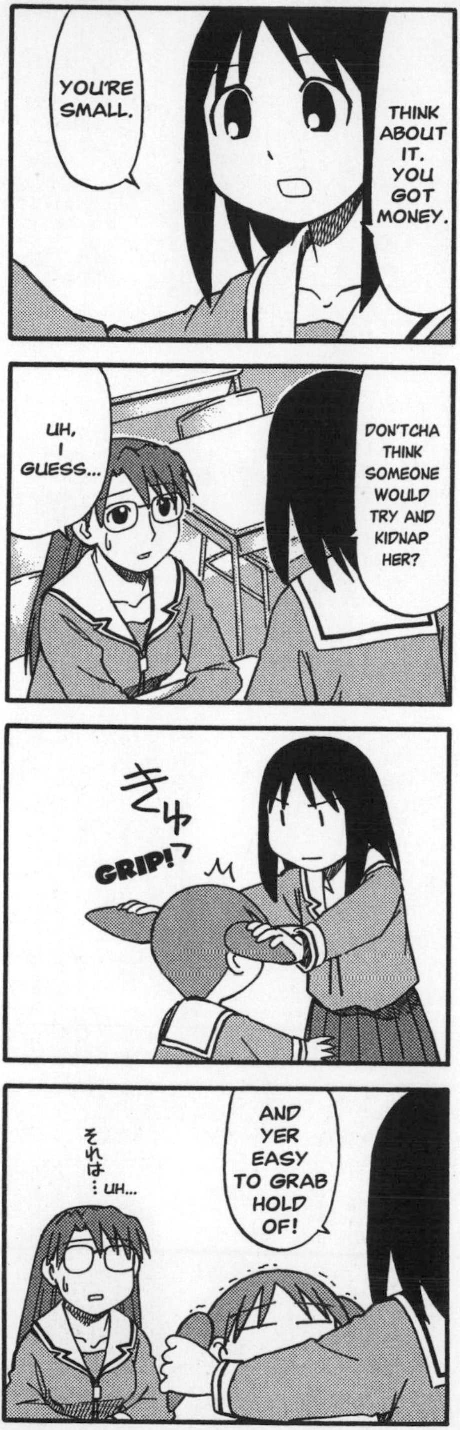
THINK ABOUT IT. YOU GOT MONEY.
YOU'RE SMALL.
DON'TCHA THINK SOMEONE WOULD TRY AND KIDNAP HER?
UH, I GUESS...
きゅ
GRIP!
AND YER EASY TO GRAB HOLD OF!
それは… UH...

## A LOYAL DOG

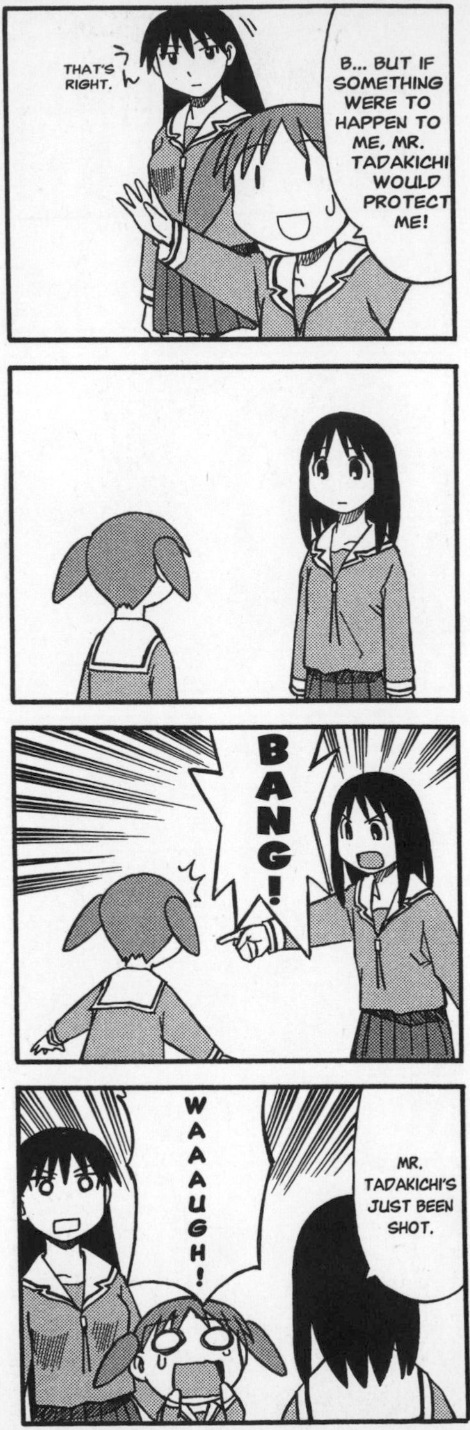
B... BUT IF SOMETHING WERE TO HAPPEN TO ME, MR. TADAKICHI WOULD PROTECT ME!
うん
THAT'S RIGHT.
BANG!
MR. TADAKICHI'S JUST BEEN SHOT.
WAAAUGH!

## CHIYO-CHAN

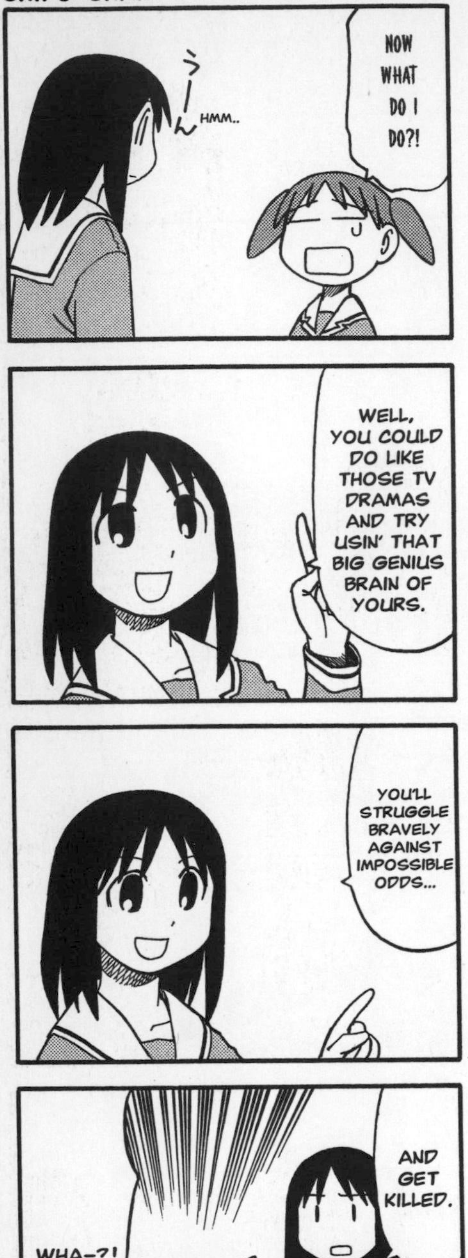
NOW WHAT DO I DO?!
うーん
HMM..
WELL, YOU COULD DO LIKE THOSE TV DRAMAS AND TRY USIN' THAT BIG GENIUS BRAIN OF YOURS.
YOU'LL STRUGGLE BRAVELY AGAINST IMPOSSIBLE ODDS...
AND GET KILLED.
WHA-?!

TO THE RESCUE

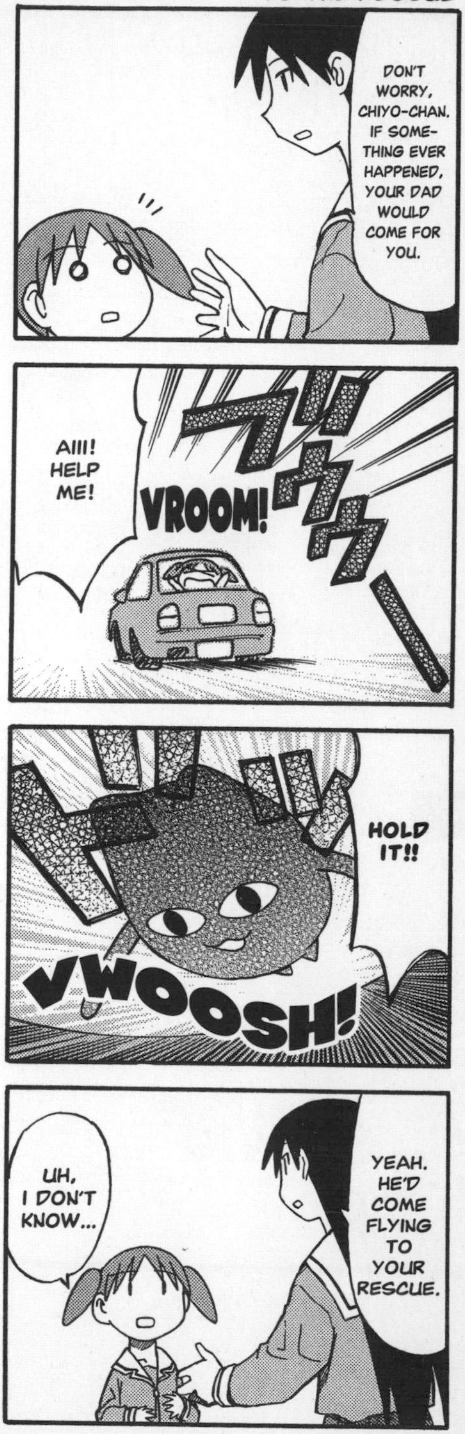
DON'T WORRY, CHIYO-CHAN. IF SOME-THING EVER HAPPENED, YOUR DAD WOULD COME FOR YOU.
AIII! HELP ME!
VROOM!
HOLD IT!!
VWOOSH!
YEAH. HE'D COME FLYING TO YOUR RESCUE.
UH, I DON'T KNOW...

FATHER!!

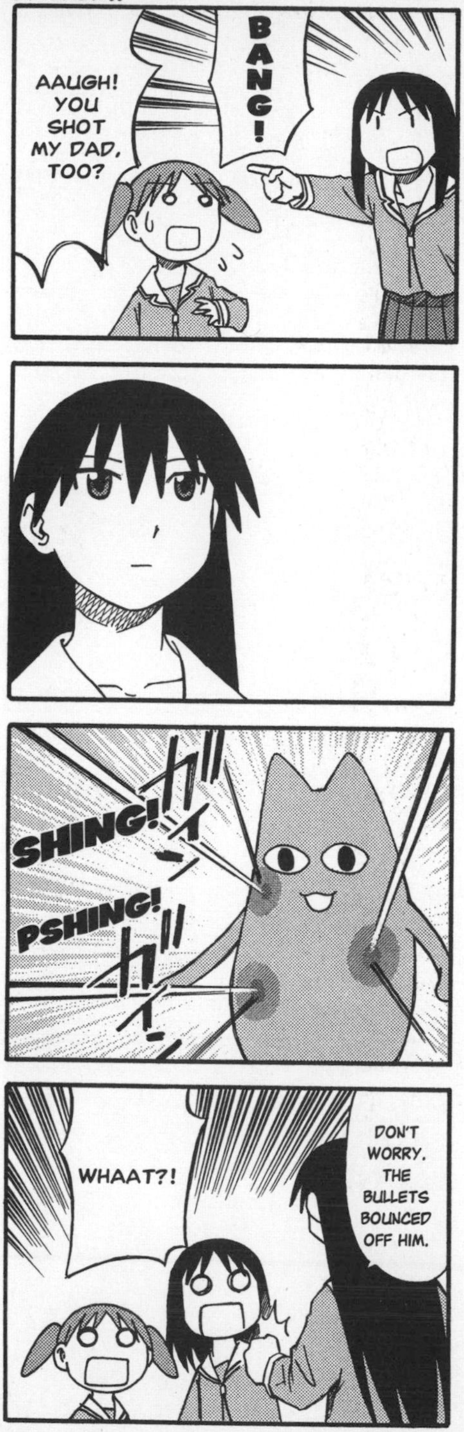
BANG!
AAUGH! YOU SHOT MY DAD, TOO?
SHING!
PSHING!
DON'T WORRY. THE BULLETS BOUNCED OFF HIM.
WHAAT?!

## AZUMANGA-DAIOH
# 109

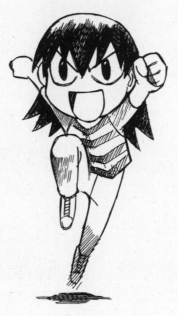

*You belong*

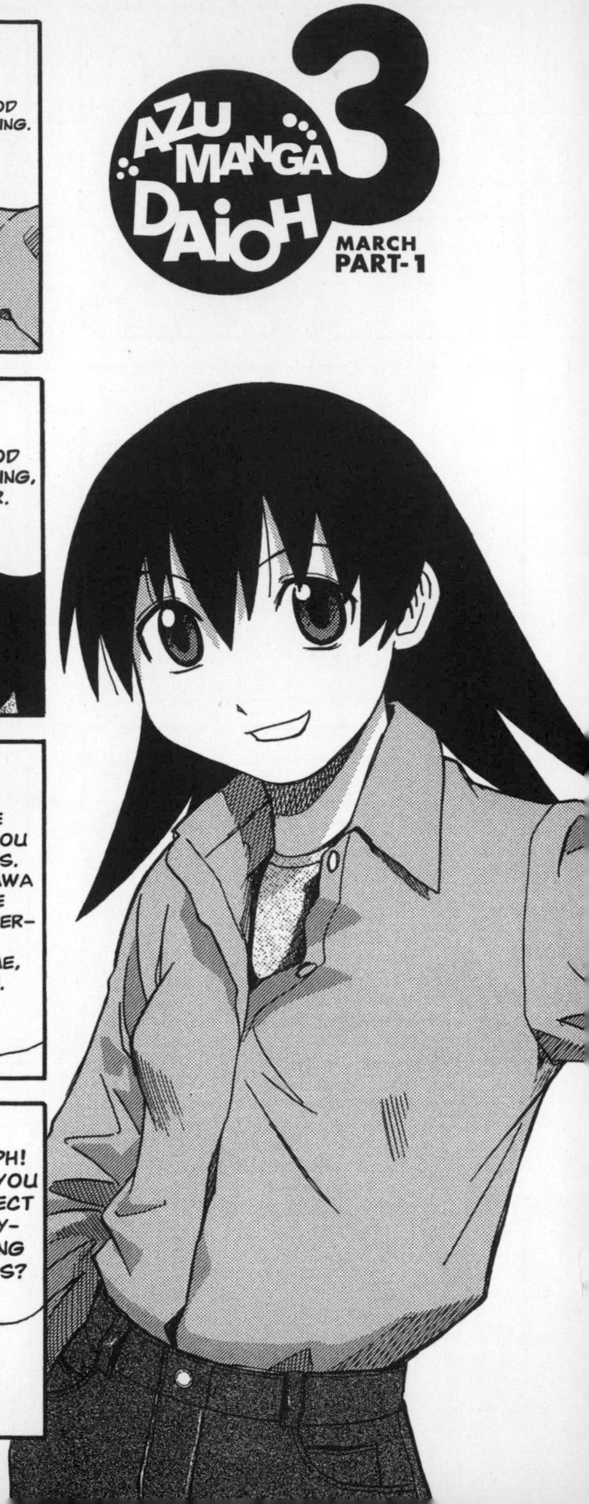

AZU MANGA DAIOH 3
MARCH PART-1


OF COURSE

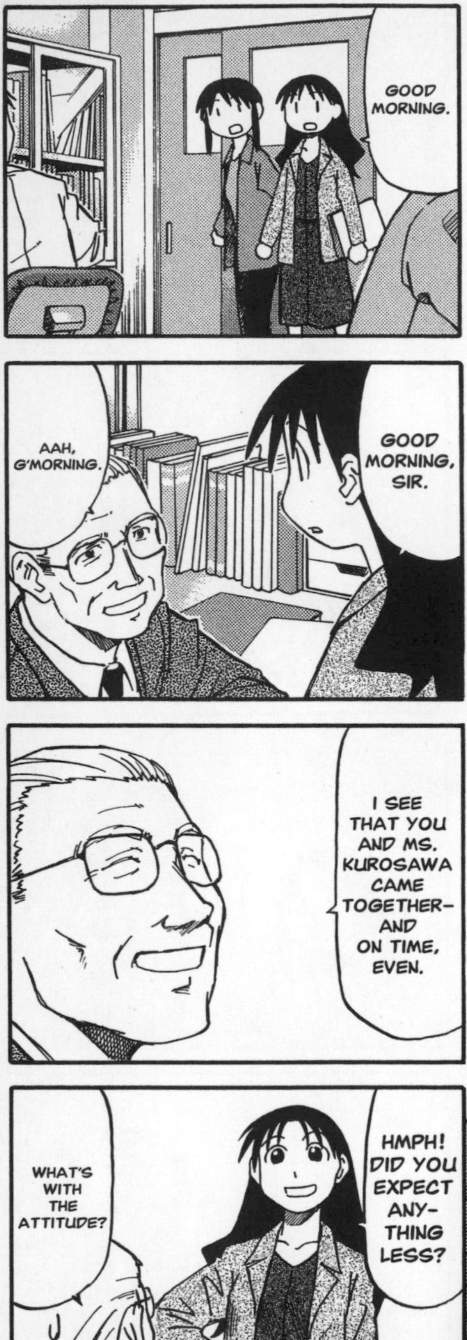

GOOD MORNING.
GOOD MORNING, SIR.
AAH, G'MORNING.
I SEE THAT YOU AND MS. KUROSAWA CAME TOGETHER– AND ON TIME, EVEN.
HMPH! DID YOU EXPECT ANY-THING LESS?
WHAT'S WITH THE ATTITUDE?

AND IN THE END...

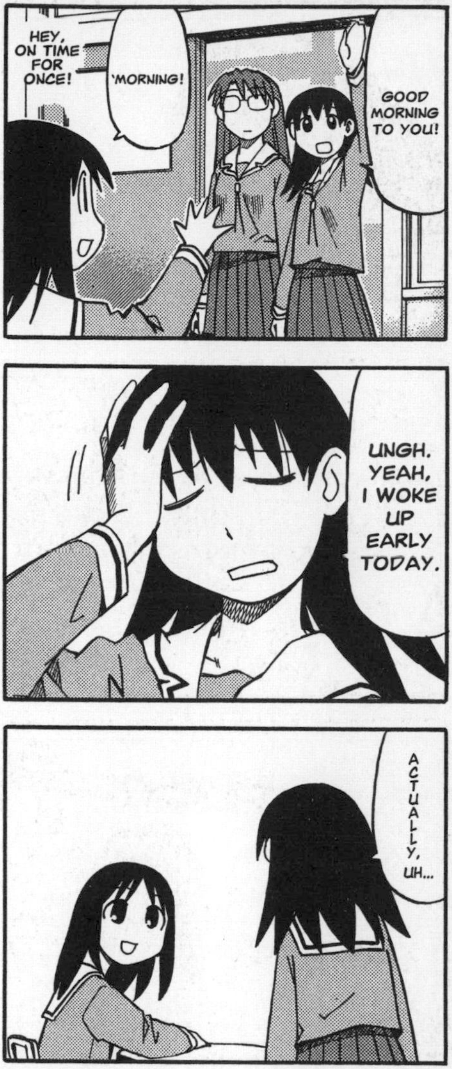
GOOD MORNING TO YOU!
'MORNING!
HEY, ON TIME FOR ONCE!
UNGH. YEAH, I WOKE UP EARLY TODAY.
ACTUALLY, UH...
I KILLED CHIYO-CHAN.

MURDER IN THE FIRST

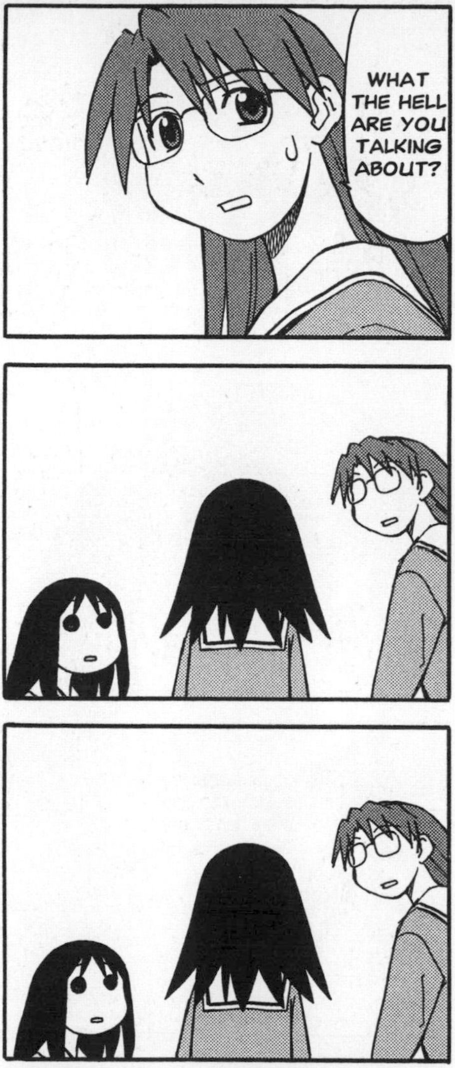
WHAT THE HELL ARE YOU TALKING ABOUT?
ARE YOU FOR REAL?!
G'MORNING!

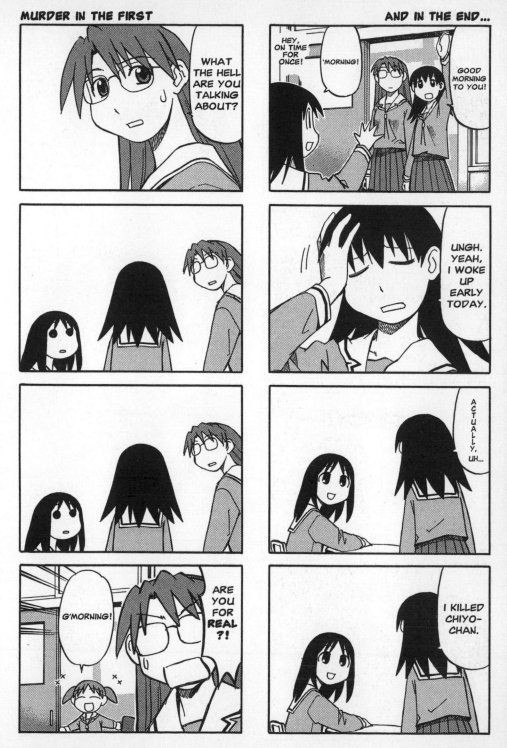

THE DEFENSE

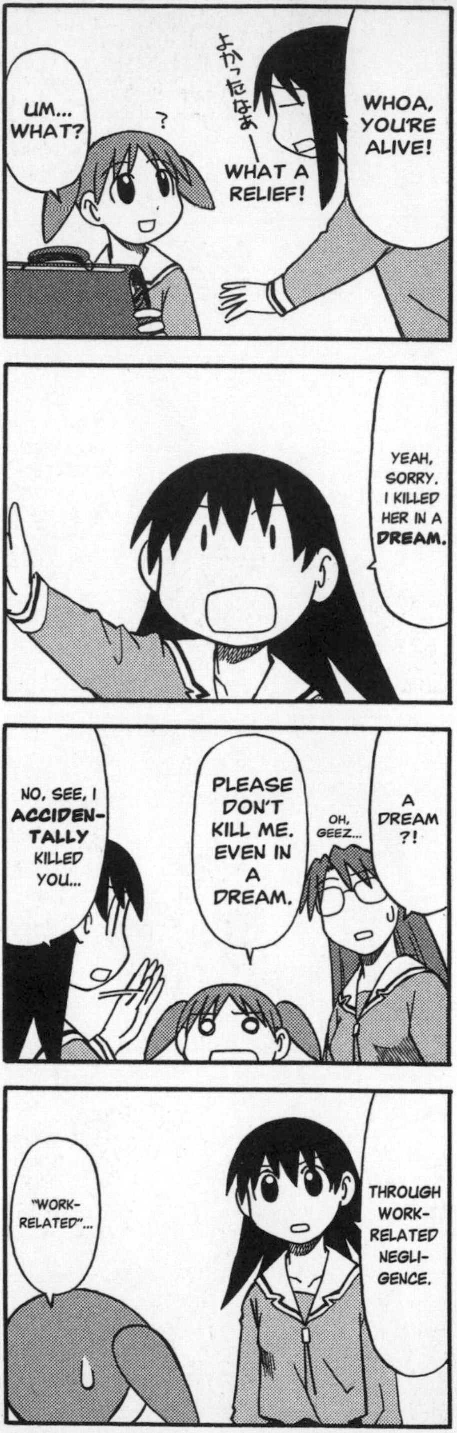
WHOA, YOU'RE ALIVE!
よかったなぁ— WHAT A RELIEF!
?
UM... WHAT?
YEAH, SORRY. I KILLED HER IN A **DREAM.**
A DREAM?!
OH, GEEZ...
PLEASE DON'T KILL ME. EVEN IN A DREAM.
NO, SEE, I **ACCIDENTALLY** KILLED YOU...
THROUGH WORK-RELATED NEGLIGENCE.
"WORK-RELATED"...

THE BUTTON

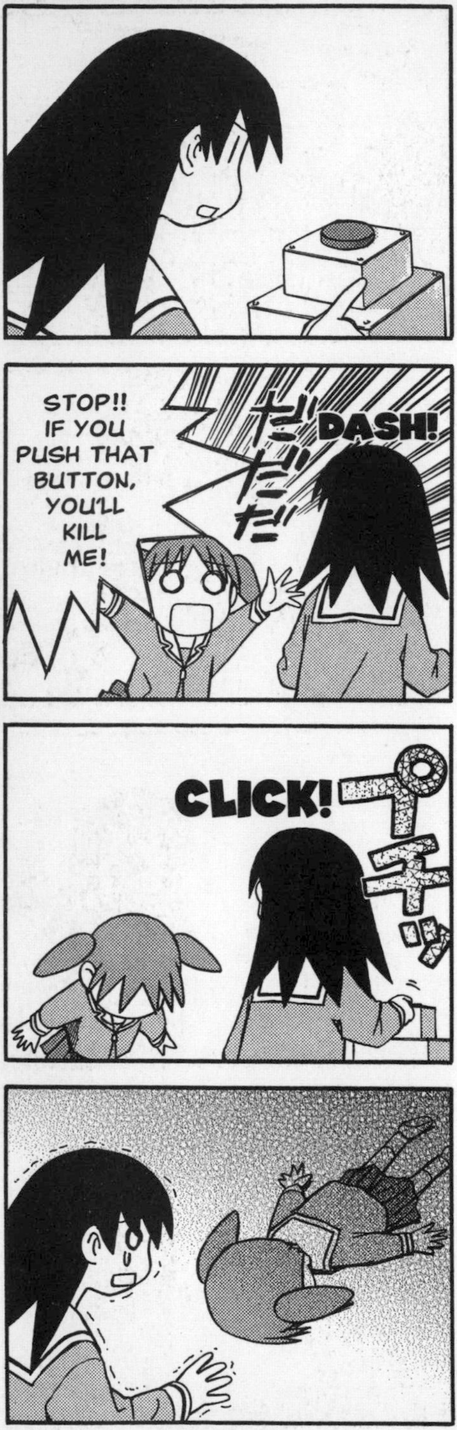
DASH!
だだだだ
STOP!! IF YOU PUSH THAT BUTTON, YOU'LL KILL ME!
プチッ
CLICK!

IT WAS A CLOSE ONE, ALRIGHT!

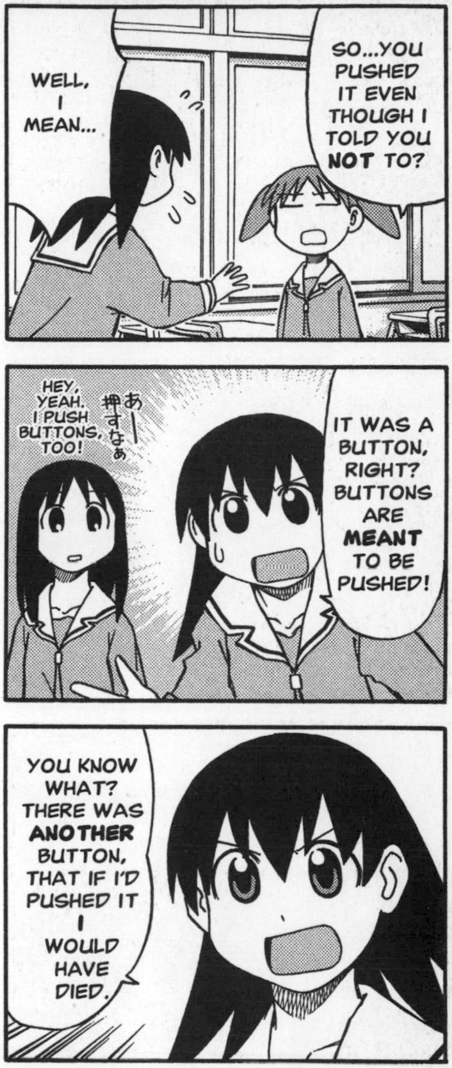
SO...YOU PUSHED IT EVEN THOUGH I TOLD YOU NOT TO?
WELL, I MEAN...
IT WAS A BUTTON, RIGHT? BUTTONS ARE MEANT TO BE PUSHED!
あー押すなぁ
HEY, YEAH. I PUSH BUTTONS, TOO!
YOU KNOW WHAT? THERE WAS ANOTHER BUTTON, THAT IF I'D PUSHED IT I WOULD HAVE DIED.
SO OF COURSE I DIDN'T PUSH IT.
ふ
HMPF.
OH, BUT YOU'LL PUSH MINE, HUH?

A BASIC KNOWLEDGE OF TERMINOLOGY

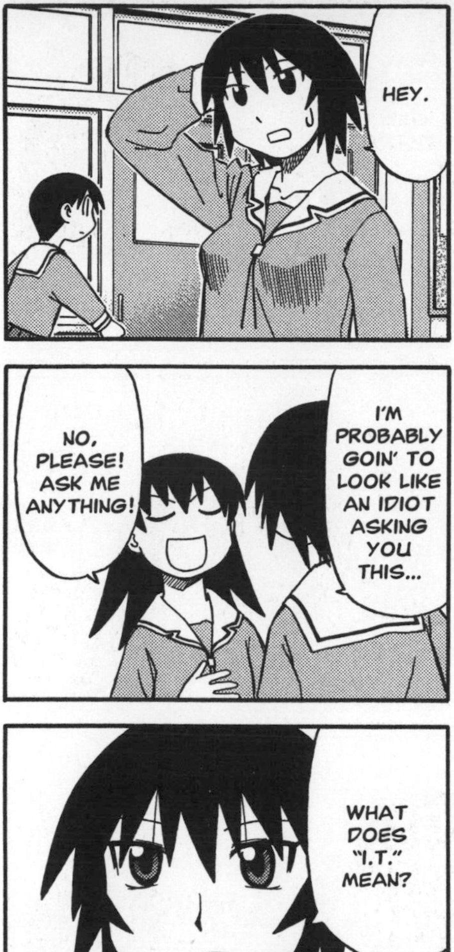
HEY.
I'M PROBABLY GOIN' TO LOOK LIKE AN IDIOT ASKING YOU THIS...
NO, PLEASE! ASK ME ANYTHING!
WHAT DOES "I.T." MEAN?
HEY, DON'T TURN AWAY FROM ME!

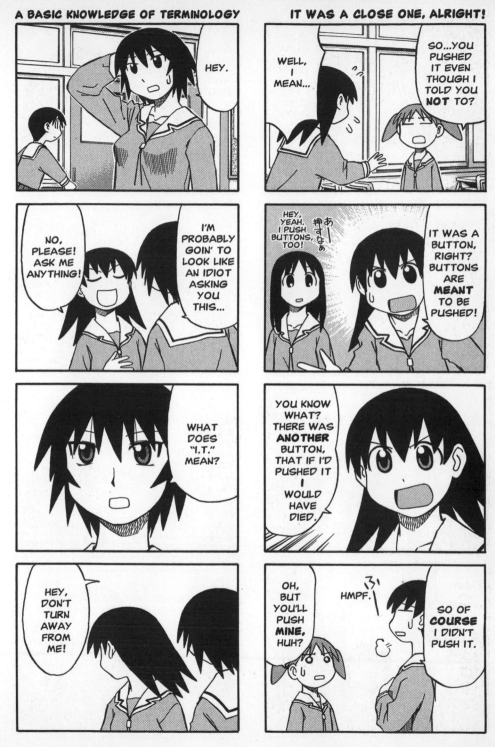

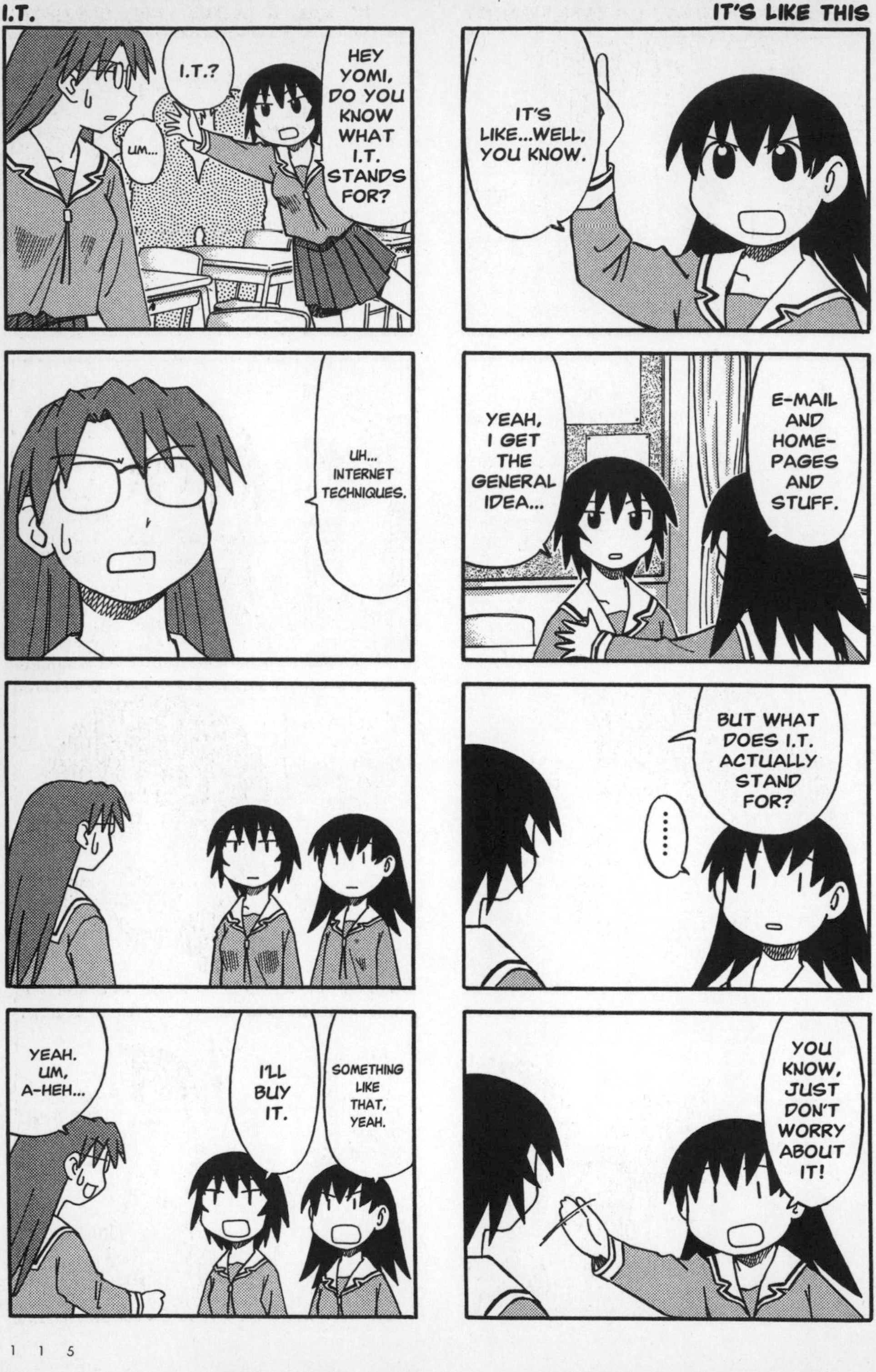
IT'S LIKE THIS
IT'S LIKE...WELL, YOU KNOW.
E-MAIL AND HOME-PAGES AND STUFF.
YEAH, I GET THE GENERAL IDEA...
BUT WHAT DOES I.T. ACTUALLY STAND FOR?
......
YOU KNOW, JUST DON'T WORRY ABOUT IT!
I.T.
HEY YOMI, DO YOU KNOW WHAT I.T. STANDS FOR?
I.T.?
UM...
UH... INTERNET TECHNIQUES.
SOMETHING LIKE THAT, YEAH.
I'LL BUY IT.
YEAH. UM, A-HEH...

THE REAL I.T.

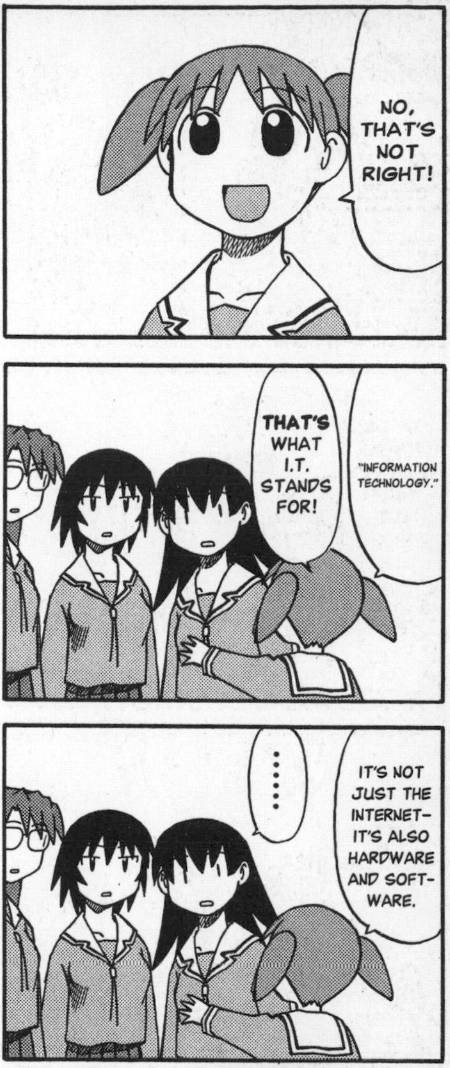
NO, THAT'S NOT RIGHT!
"INFORMATION TECHNOLOGY."
THAT'S WHAT I.T. STANDS FOR!
IT'S NOT JUST THE INTERNET– IT'S ALSO HARDWARE AND SOFT-WARE.
......
WHERE DID YOU LEARN THAT?
I...UH, I DON'T REMEMBER.

THE LAW

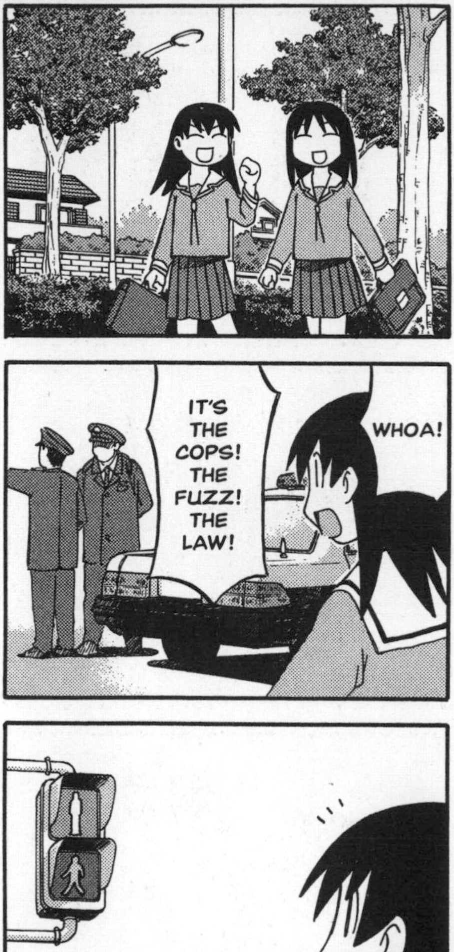
WHOA!
IT'S THE COPS! THE FUZZ! THE LAW!
信号は守らなな
GUESS WE GOTTA OBEY THAT LIGHT, HUH?
そだな
Y...YEAH...

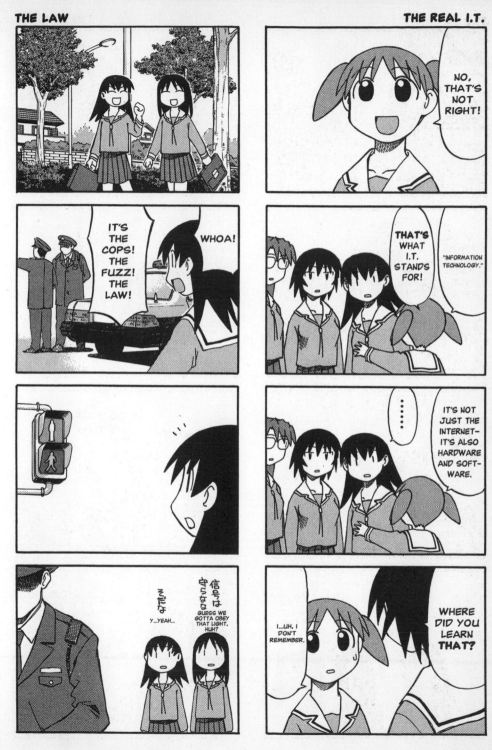

## THE APPEAL

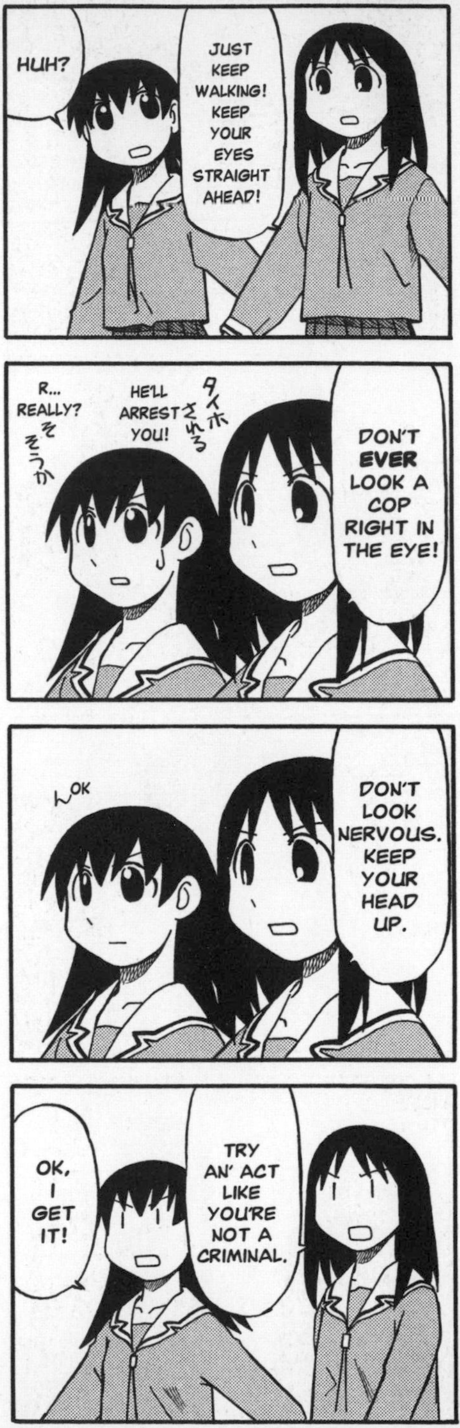
JUST KEEP WALKING! KEEP YOUR EYES STRAIGHT AHEAD!
HUH?
DON'T **EVER** LOOK A COP RIGHT IN THE EYE!
タイホされる
HE'LL ARREST YOU!
R... REALLY?
そ そうか
DON'T LOOK NERVOUS. KEEP YOUR HEAD UP.
んOK
TRY AN' ACT LIKE YOU'RE NOT A CRIMINAL.
OK, I GET IT!

## GROWTH

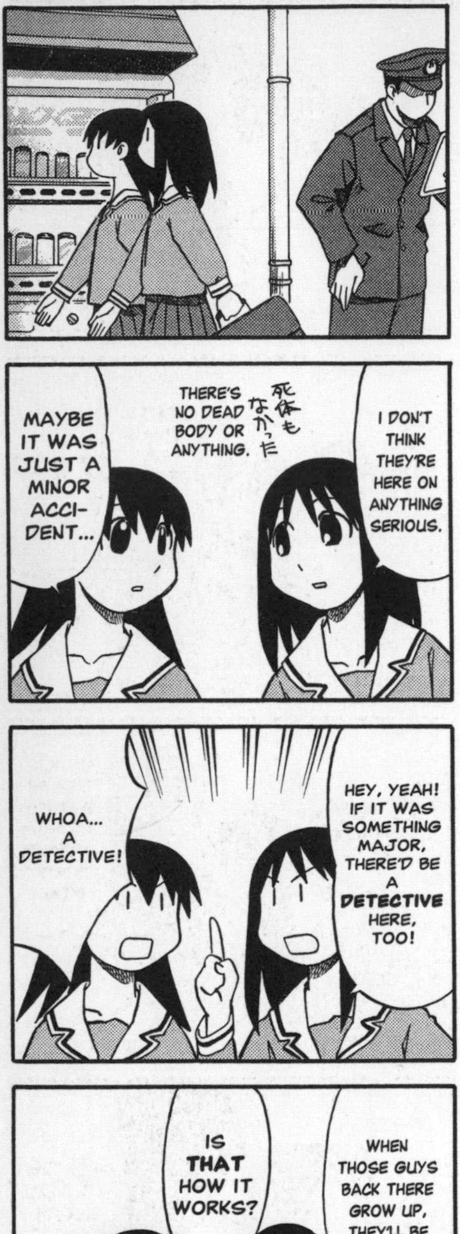
I DON'T THINK THEY'RE HERE ON ANYTHING SERIOUS.
死体もなかった
THERE'S NO DEAD BODY OR ANYTHING.
MAYBE IT WAS JUST A MINOR ACCI-DENT...
HEY, YEAH! IF IT WAS SOMETHING MAJOR, THERE'D BE A **DETECTIVE** HERE, TOO!
WHOA... A DETECTIVE!
WHEN THOSE GUYS BACK THERE GROW UP, THEY'LL BE DETECTIVES TOO.
IS **THAT** HOW IT WORKS?

MEMO

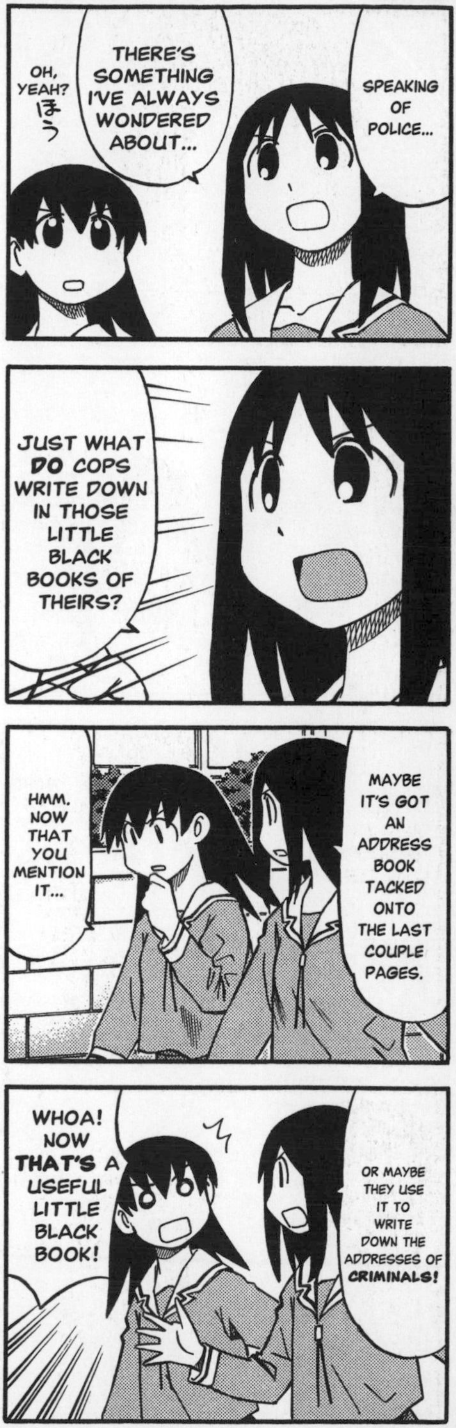
SPEAKING OF POLICE...
THERE'S SOMETHING I'VE ALWAYS WONDERED ABOUT...
OH, YEAH? ほう
JUST WHAT DO COPS WRITE DOWN IN THOSE LITTLE BLACK BOOKS OF THEIRS?
MAYBE IT'S GOT AN ADDRESS BOOK TACKED ONTO THE LAST COUPLE PAGES.
HMM. NOW THAT YOU MENTION IT...
OR MAYBE THEY USE IT TO WRITE DOWN THE ADDRESSES OF CRIMINALS!
WHOA! NOW THAT'S A USEFUL LITTLE BLACK BOOK!

REALITY

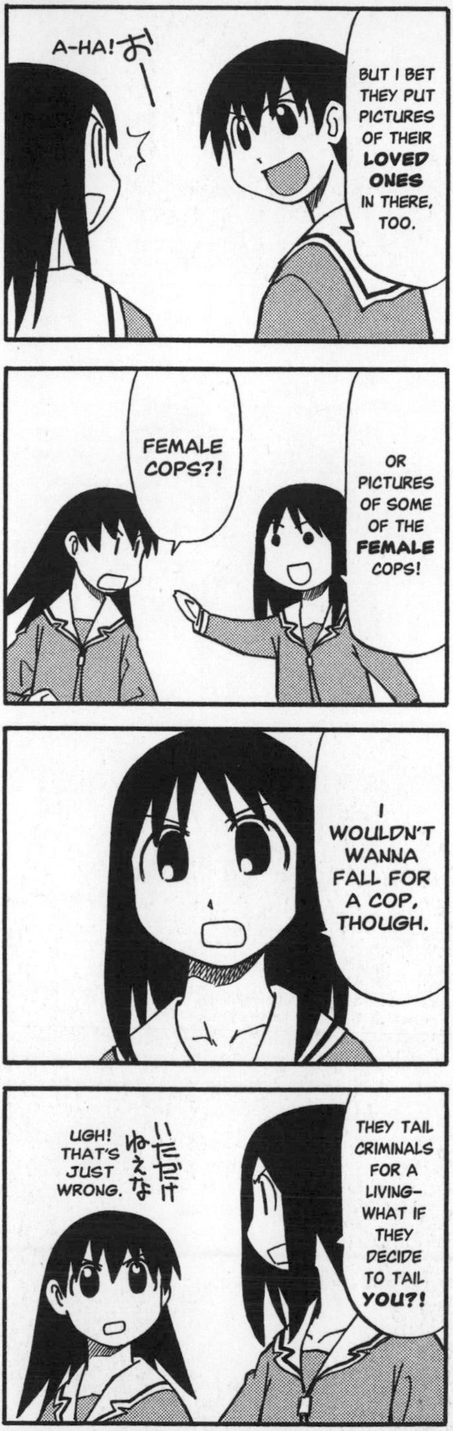
BUT I BET THEY PUT PICTURES OF THEIR LOVED ONES IN THERE, TOO.
A-HA! おー
OR PICTURES OF SOME OF THE FEMALE COPS!
FEMALE COPS?!
I WOULDN'T WANNA FALL FOR A COP, THOUGH.
THEY TAIL CRIMINALS FOR A LIVING—WHAT IF THEY DECIDE TO TAIL YOU?!
UGH! THAT'S JUST WRONG. いただけねえな

# AZUMANGA DAIOH 3

MARCH PART-2

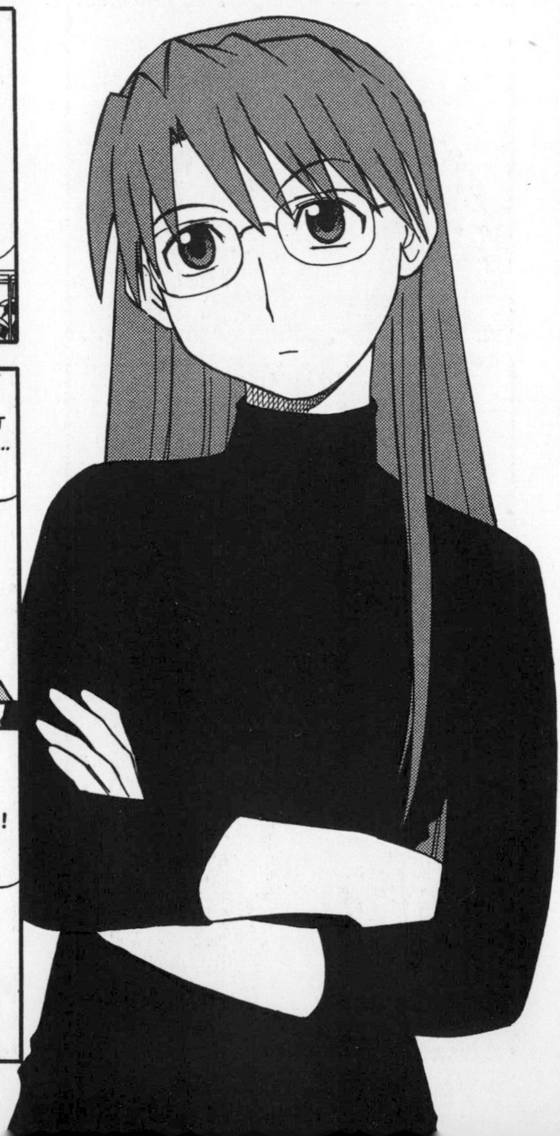

ADORATION

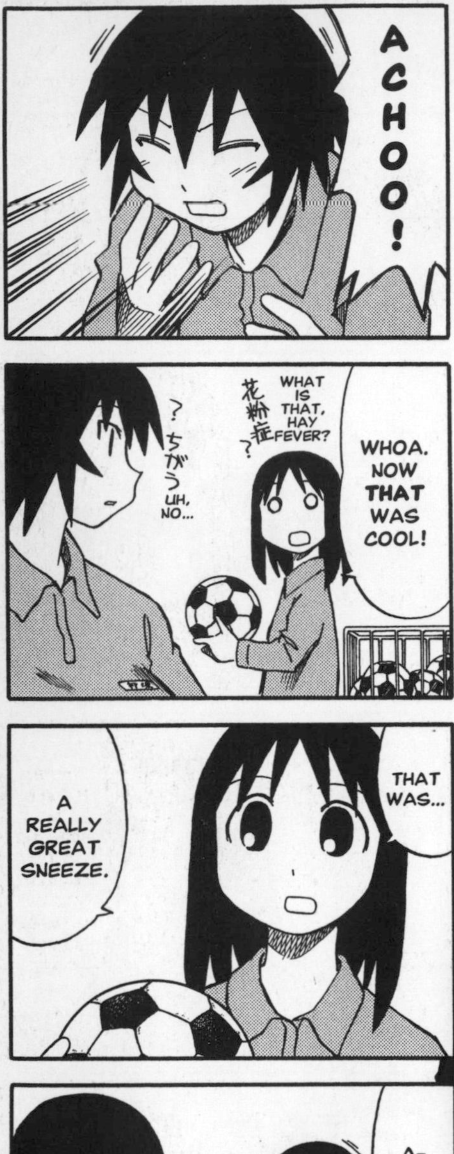
ACHOO!
WHOA. NOW THAT WAS COOL!
花粉症? WHAT IS THAT, HAY FEVER?
?ちがう UH, NO...
THAT WAS...
A REALLY GREAT SNEEZE.
A-CHOI!

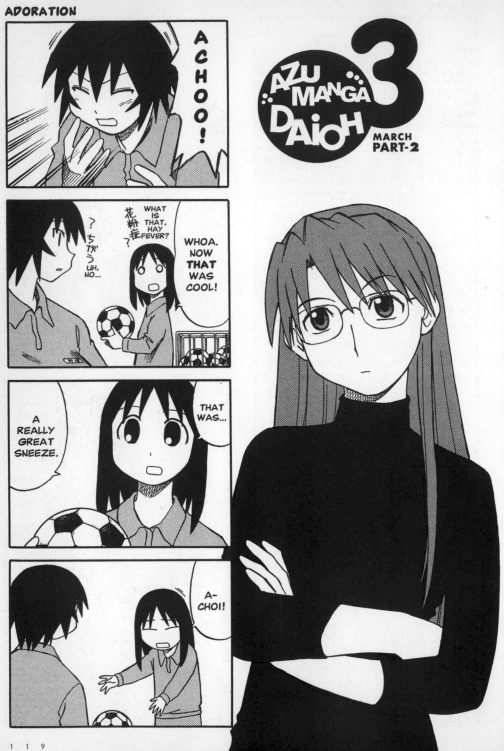

## A-CHOI!

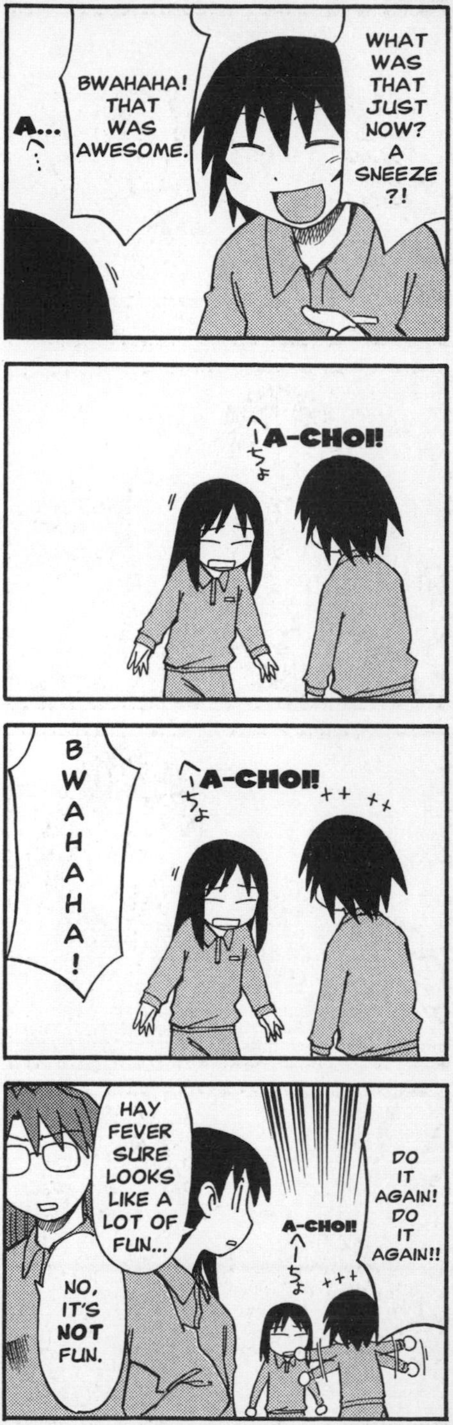
WHAT WAS THAT JUST NOW? A SNEEZE?!
BWAHAHA! THAT WAS AWESOME.
A...
A-CHOI!
A-CHOI!
BWAHAHA!
DO IT AGAIN! DO IT AGAIN!!
A-CHOI!
HAY FEVER SURE LOOKS LIKE A LOT OF FUN...
NO, IT'S **NOT** FUN.

## TO SPEAK ILL OF

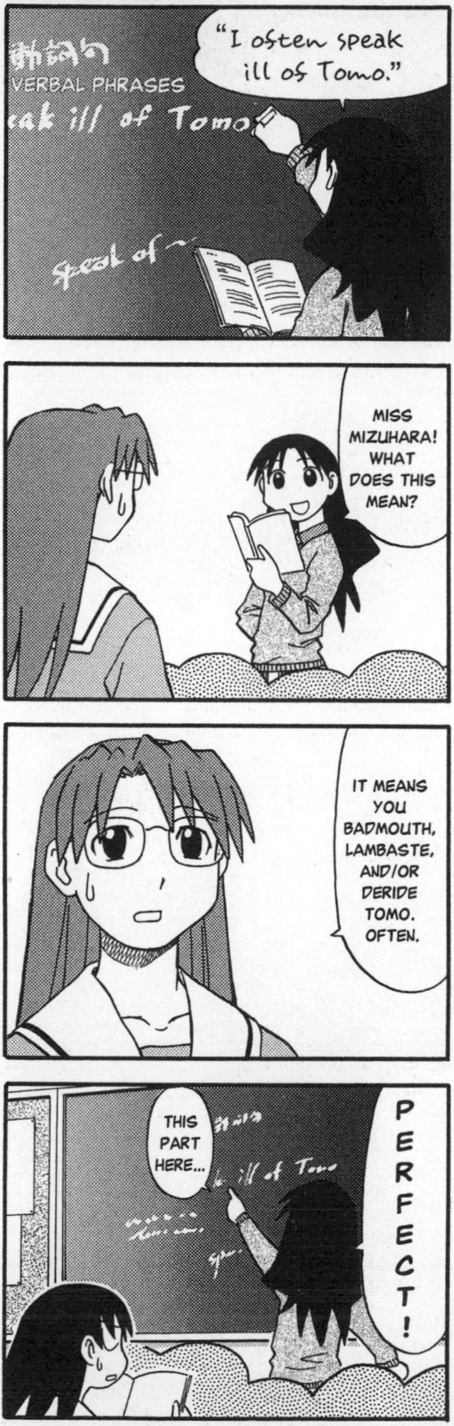
“I often speak ill of Tomo.”
動詞句
VERBAL PHRASES
eak ill of Tomo
speak of ~
MISS MIZUHARA! WHAT DOES THIS MEAN?
IT MEANS YOU BADMOUTH, LAMBASTE, AND/OR DERIDE TOMO. OFTEN.
PERFECT!
THIS PART HERE...
ill of Tomo

## INDEFINITE ARTICLES

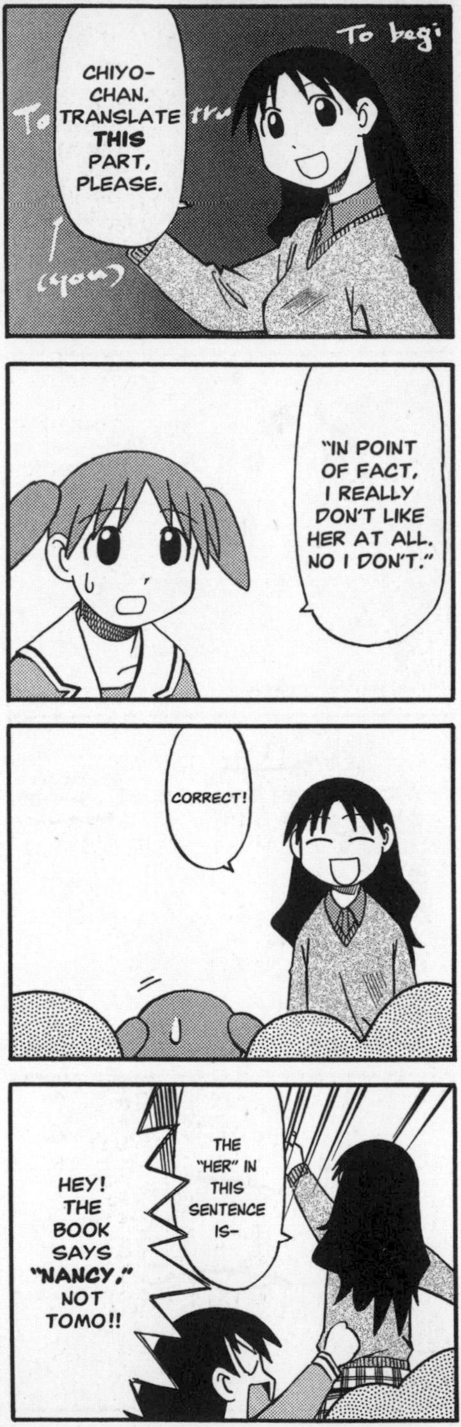

To begi
To
tru
(you)
CHIYO-CHAN. TRANSLATE **THIS** PART, PLEASE.
"IN POINT OF FACT, I REALLY DON'T LIKE HER AT ALL. NO I DON'T."
CORRECT!
THE "HER" IN THIS SENTENCE IS–
HEY! THE BOOK SAYS **"NANCY,"** NOT TOMO!!


## TYPICALLY NAIVE

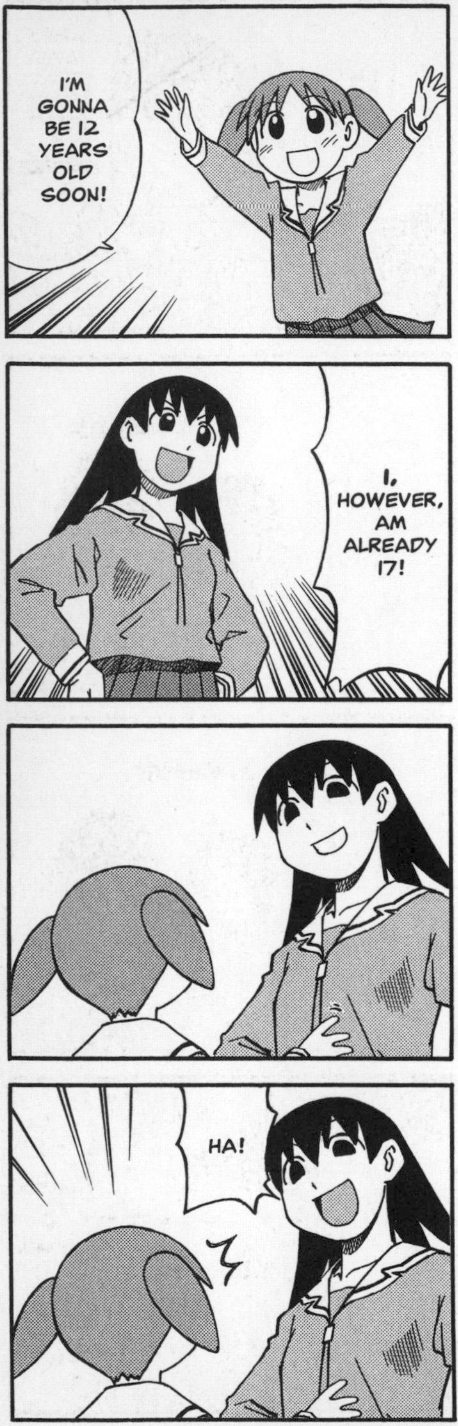

I'M GONNA BE 12 YEARS OLD SOON!
I, HOWEVER, AM ALREADY 17!
HA!

## CONGRATULATIONS

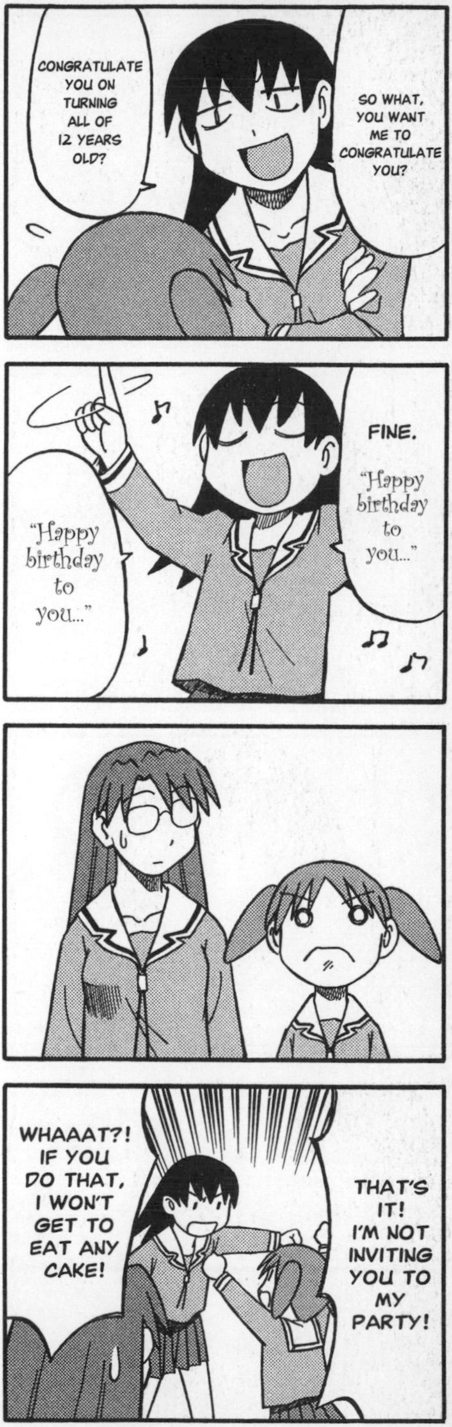
SO WHAT, YOU WANT ME TO CONGRATULATE YOU?
CONGRATULATE YOU ON TURNING ALL OF 12 YEARS OLD?
FINE. "Happy birthday to you..."
"Happy birthday to you..."
THAT'S IT! I'M NOT INVITING YOU TO MY PARTY!
WHAAAT?! IF YOU DO THAT, I WON'T GET TO EAT ANY CAKE!

## THE INVITATION

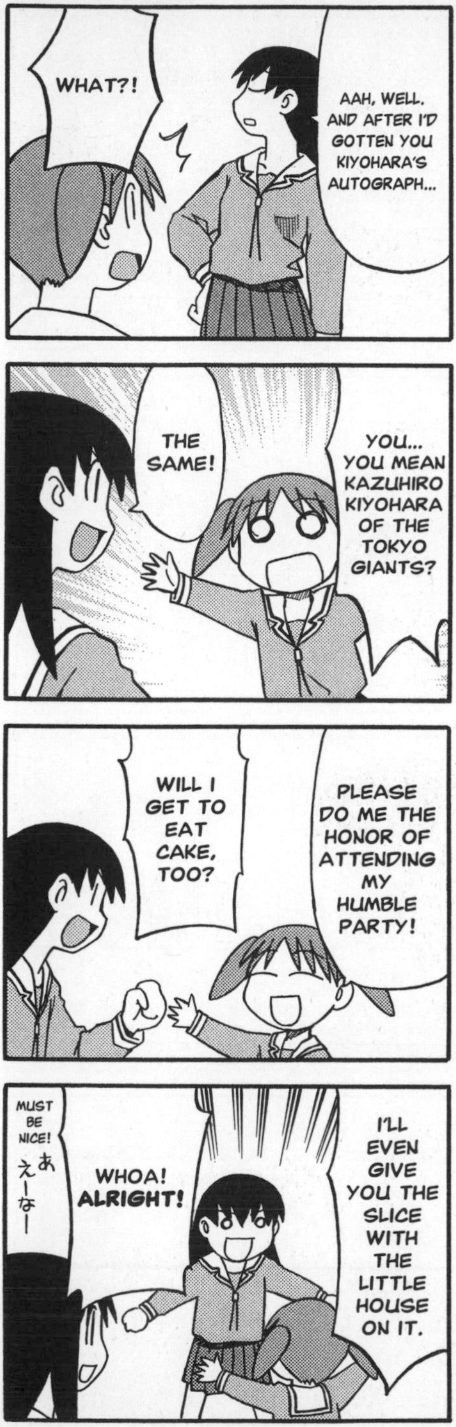
AAH, WELL. AND AFTER I'D GOTTEN YOU KIYOHARA'S AUTOGRAPH...
WHAT?!
YOU... YOU MEAN KAZUHIRO KIYOHARA OF THE TOKYO GIANTS?
THE SAME!
PLEASE DO ME THE HONOR OF ATTENDING MY HUMBLE PARTY!
WILL I GET TO EAT CAKE, TOO?
I'LL EVEN GIVE YOU THE SLICE WITH THE LITTLE HOUSE ON IT.
WHOA! ALRIGHT!
あえーなー
MUST BE NICE!

## SADNESS

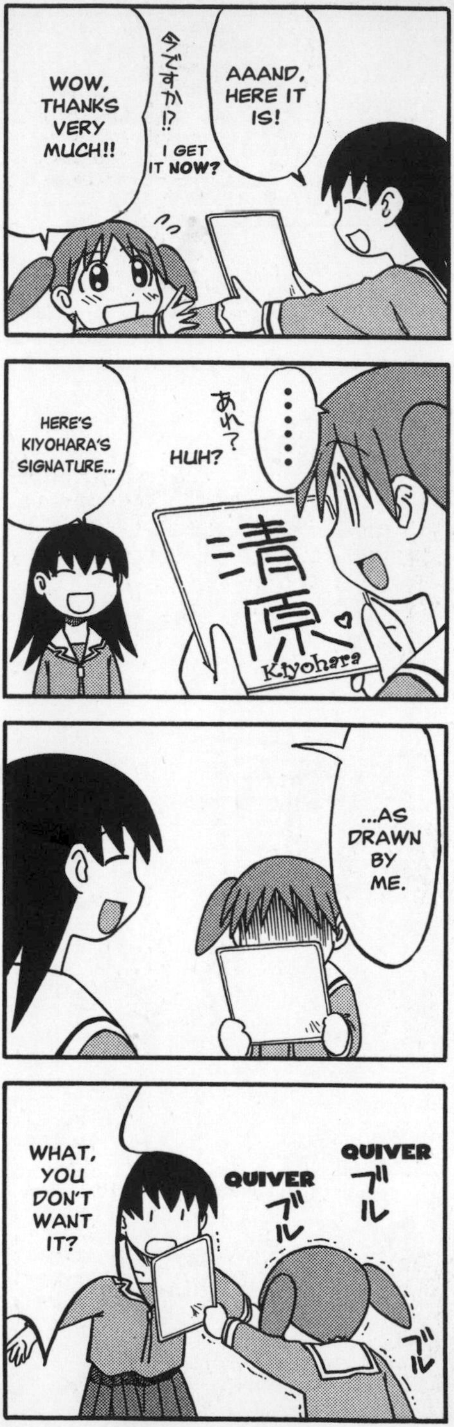
AAAND, HERE IT IS!
今ですか!?
I GET IT NOW?
WOW, THANKS VERY MUCH!!
......
あれ?
HUH?
HERE'S KIYOHARA'S SIGNATURE...
清原
Kiyohara
...AS DRAWN BY ME.
QUIVER
ブル
QUIVER
ブル
ブル
WHAT, YOU DON'T WANT IT?

## A PRESENT FIT FOR A GENIUS

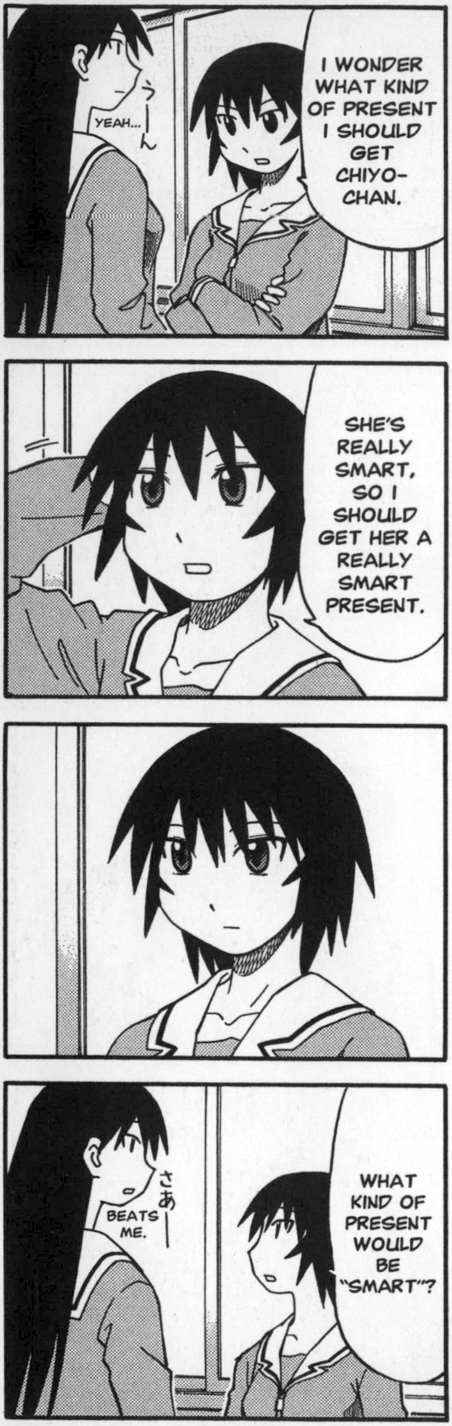
I WONDER WHAT KIND OF PRESENT I SHOULD GET CHIYO-CHAN.
うーん
YEAH...
SHE'S REALLY SMART, SO I SHOULD GET HER A REALLY SMART PRESENT.
WHAT KIND OF PRESENT WOULD BE "SMART"?
さあー
BEATS ME.

## SO CUTE, SHE CAN'T STAND IT

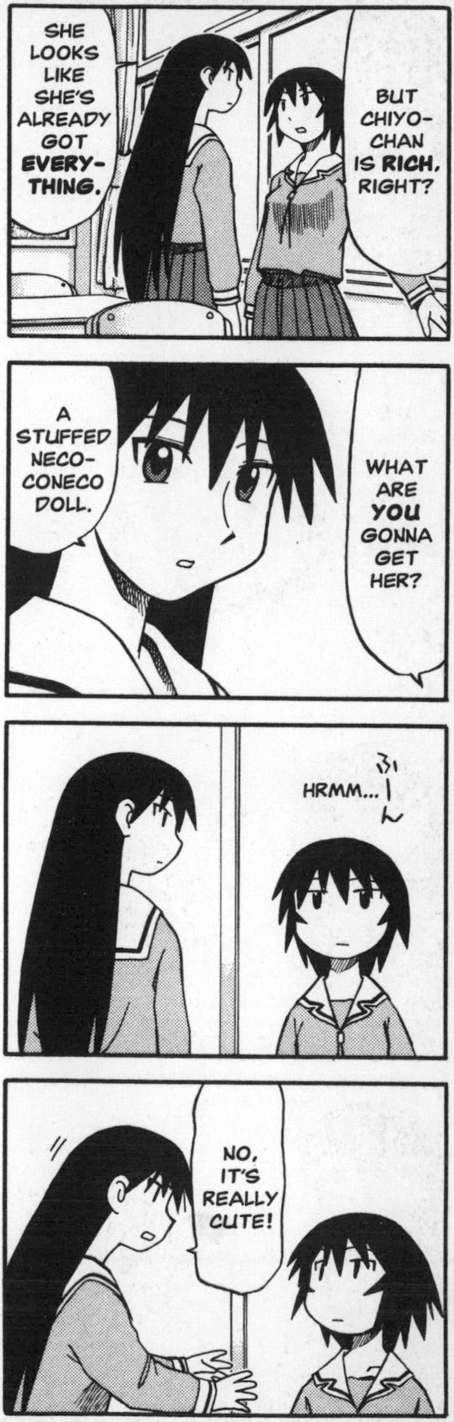
BUT CHIYO-CHAN IS RICH, RIGHT?
SHE LOOKS LIKE SHE'S ALREADY GOT EVERYTHING.
WHAT ARE YOU GONNA GET HER?
A STUFFED NECO-CONECO DOLL.
ふーん
HRMM...
NO, IT'S REALLY CUTE!

## WHEN NOT A LOT IS QUITE A BIT

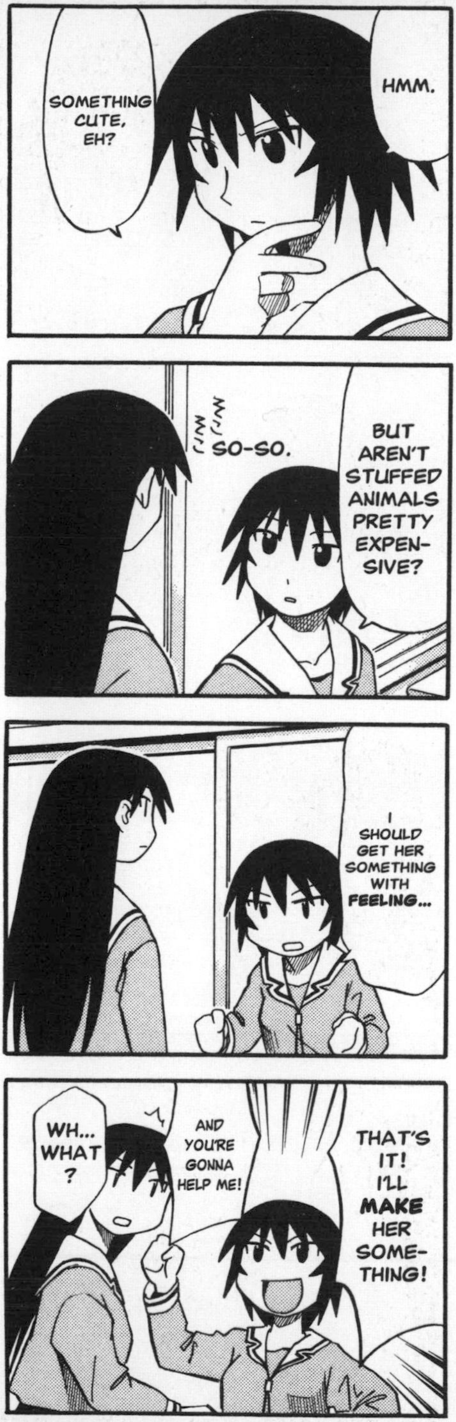
HMM.
SOMETHING CUTE, EH?
BUT AREN'T STUFFED ANIMALS PRETTY EXPENSIVE?
SO-SO.
I SHOULD GET HER SOMETHING WITH FEELING...
THAT'S IT! I'LL MAKE HER SOMETHING!
AND YOU'RE GONNA HELP ME!
WH... WHAT?

BUT I'M REALLY NO GOOD...

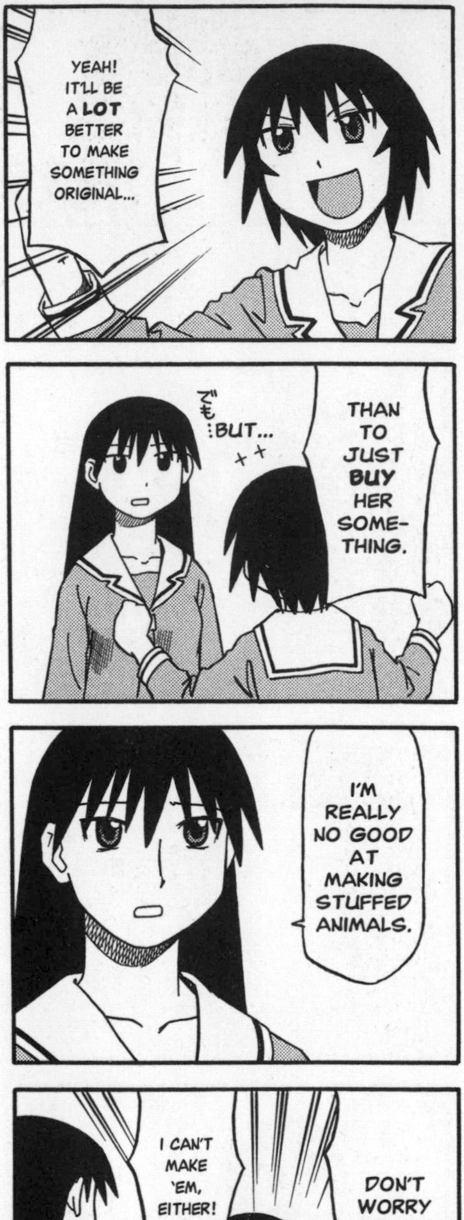
YEAH! IT'LL BE A **LOT** BETTER TO MAKE SOMETHING ORIGINAL...
THAN TO JUST **BUY** HER SOME-THING.
でも…BUT...
I'M REALLY NO GOOD AT MAKING STUFFED ANIMALS.
DON'T WORRY ABOUT IT!
I CAN'T MAKE 'EM, EITHER!

PUTTING OUR HEARTS INTO IT

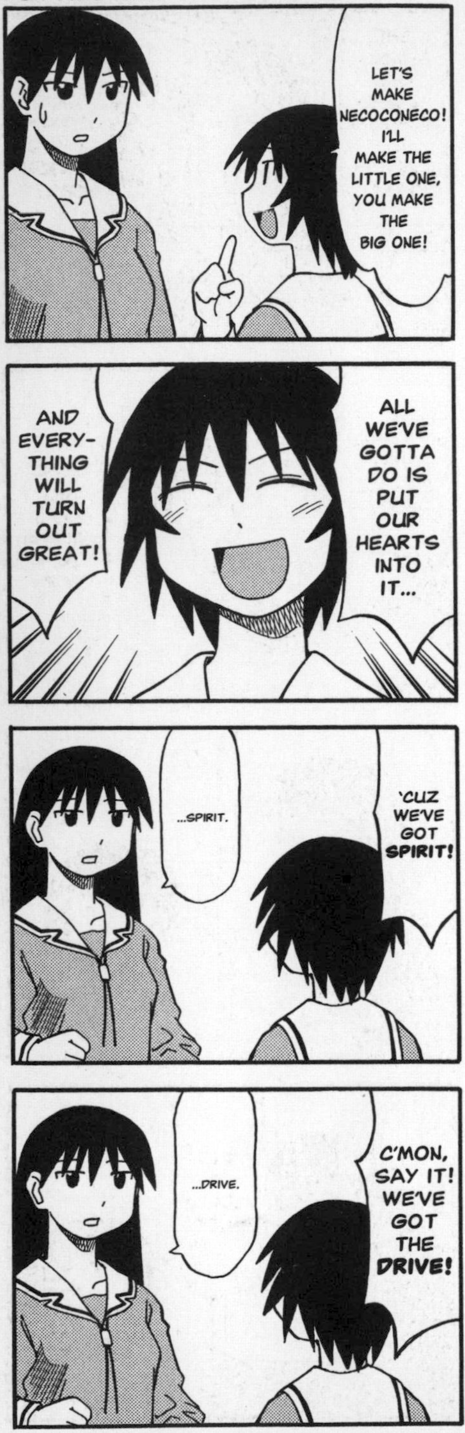
LET'S MAKE NECOCONECO! I'LL MAKE THE LITTLE ONE, YOU MAKE THE BIG ONE!
ALL WE'VE GOTTA DO IS PUT OUR HEARTS INTO IT...
AND EVERY-THING WILL TURN OUT GREAT!
'CUZ WE'VE GOT **SPIRIT!**
...SPIRIT.
C'MON, SAY IT! WE'VE GOT THE **DRIVE!**
...DRIVE.

## DRIVE AND SPIRIT

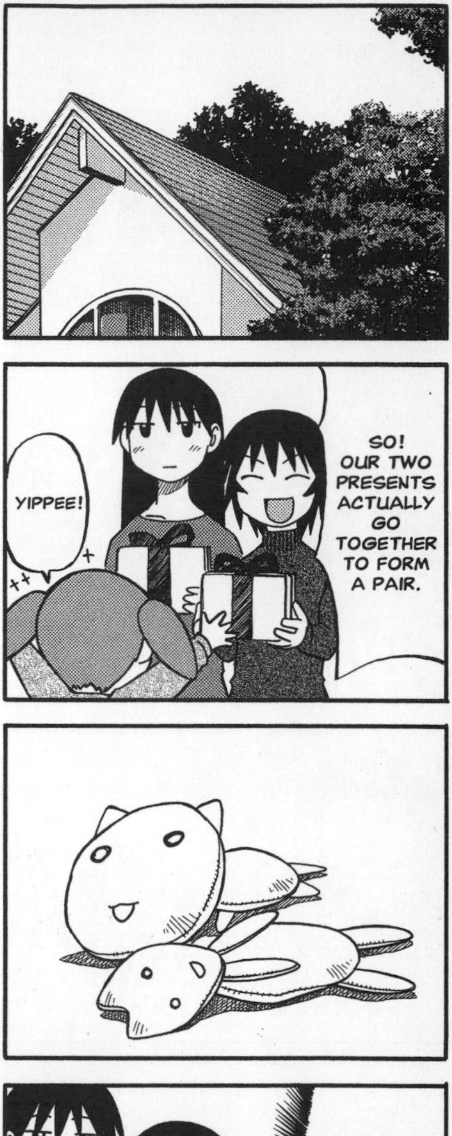
SO! OUR TWO PRESENTS ACTUALLY GO TOGETHER TO FORM A PAIR.
YIPPEE!
WH... WHAT IS IT?!

## THE FINISHING TOUCH

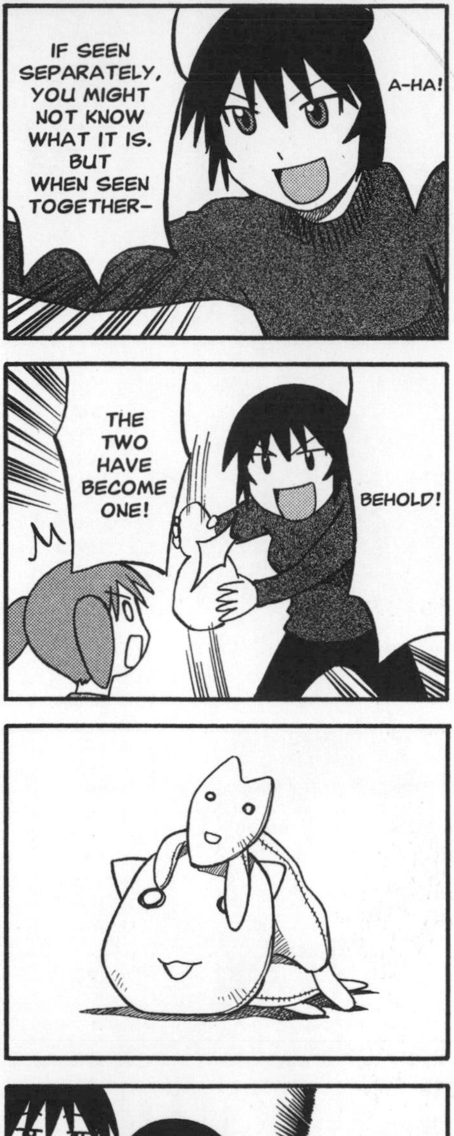
A-HA!
IF SEEN SEPARATELY, YOU MIGHT NOT KNOW WHAT IT IS. BUT WHEN SEEN TOGETHER–
BEHOLD!
THE TWO HAVE BECOME ONE!
WHAT IS IT?!

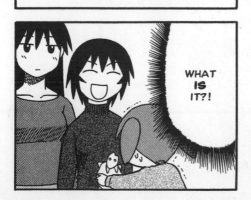

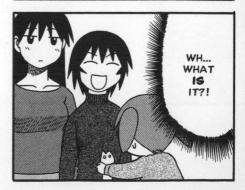

AZUMANGA-DAIOH

# 127

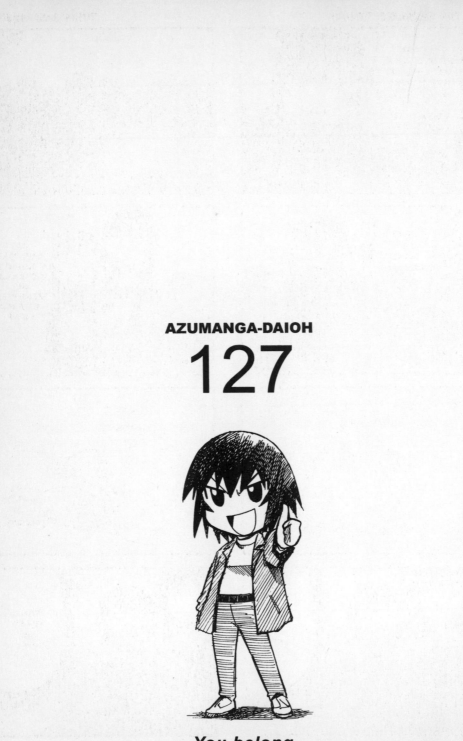

*You belong*

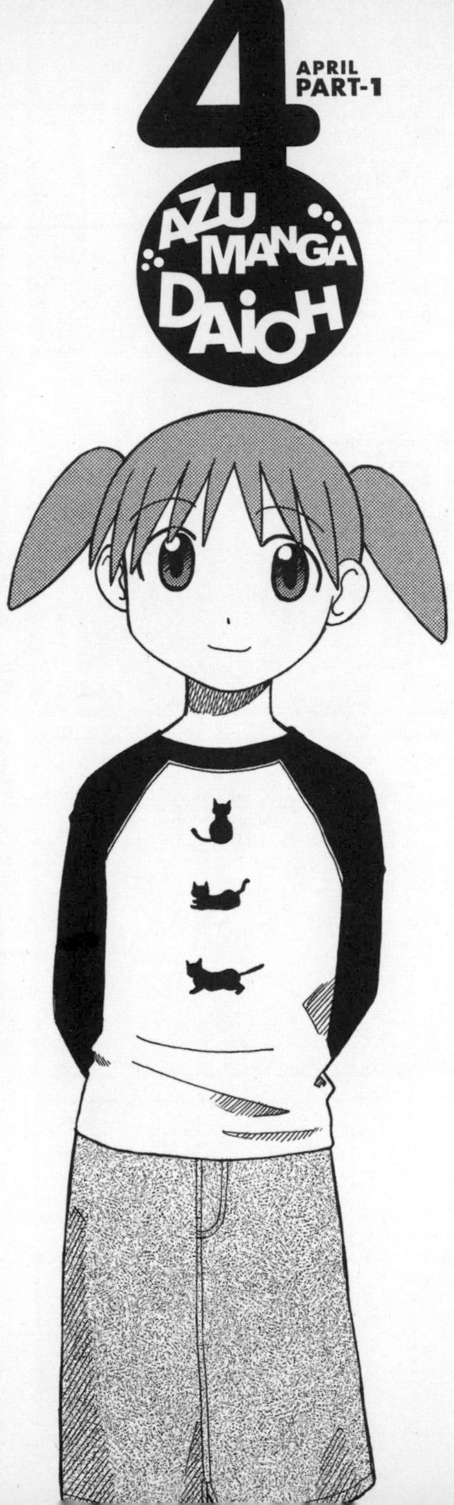
4
APRIL
PART-1
AZUMANGA DAIOH

## JUNIOR YEAR

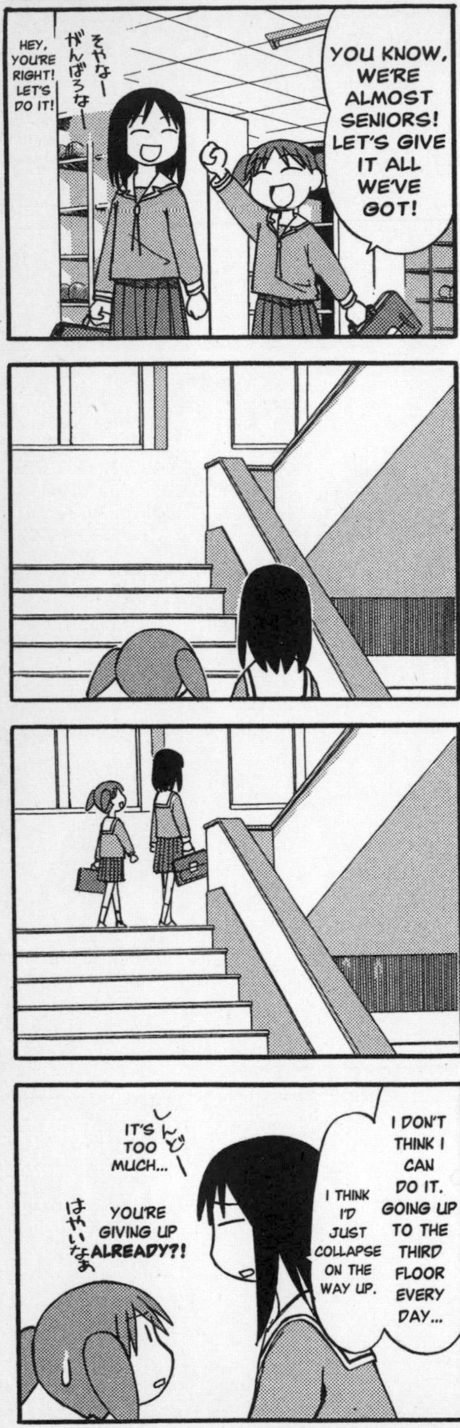
YOU KNOW, WE'RE ALMOST SENIORS! LET'S GIVE IT ALL WE'VE GOT!
そやなーがんばろなー
HEY, YOU'RE RIGHT! LET'S DO IT!
I DON'T THINK I CAN DO IT. GOING UP TO THE THIRD FLOOR EVERY DAY...
I THINK I'D JUST COLLAPSE ON THE WAY UP.
しんどー
IT'S TOO MUCH...
はやいなあ
YOU'RE GIVING UP ALREADY?!

SEPARATION

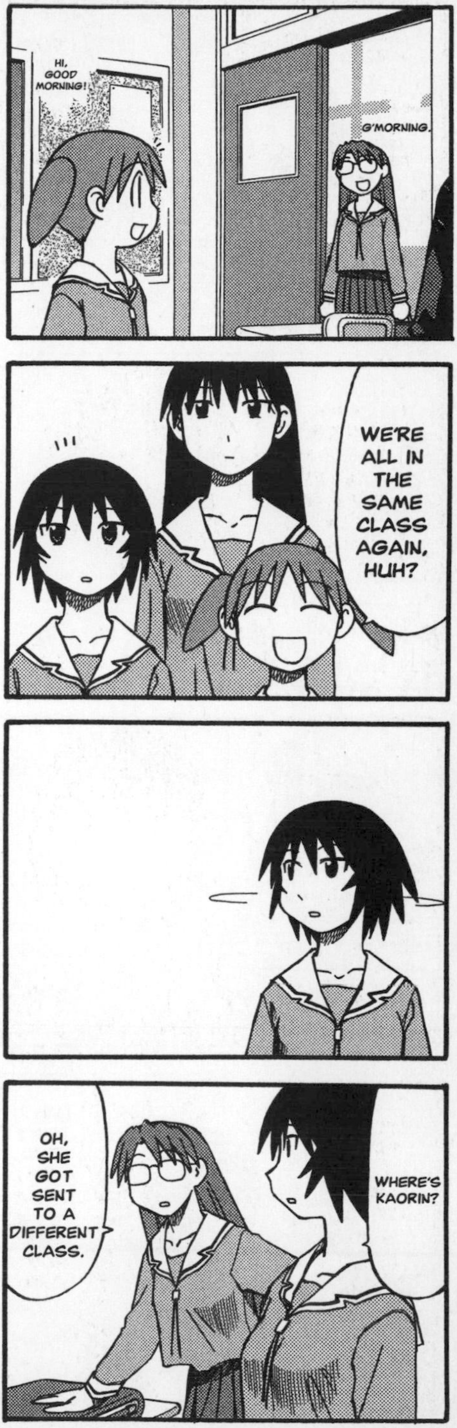
G'MORNING.
HI, GOOD MORNING!
WE'RE ALL IN THE SAME CLASS AGAIN, HUH?
WHERE'S KAORIN?
OH, SHE GOT SENT TO A DIFFERENT CLASS.

THAT THE FLOWERS MAY BLOOM IN SPRING...

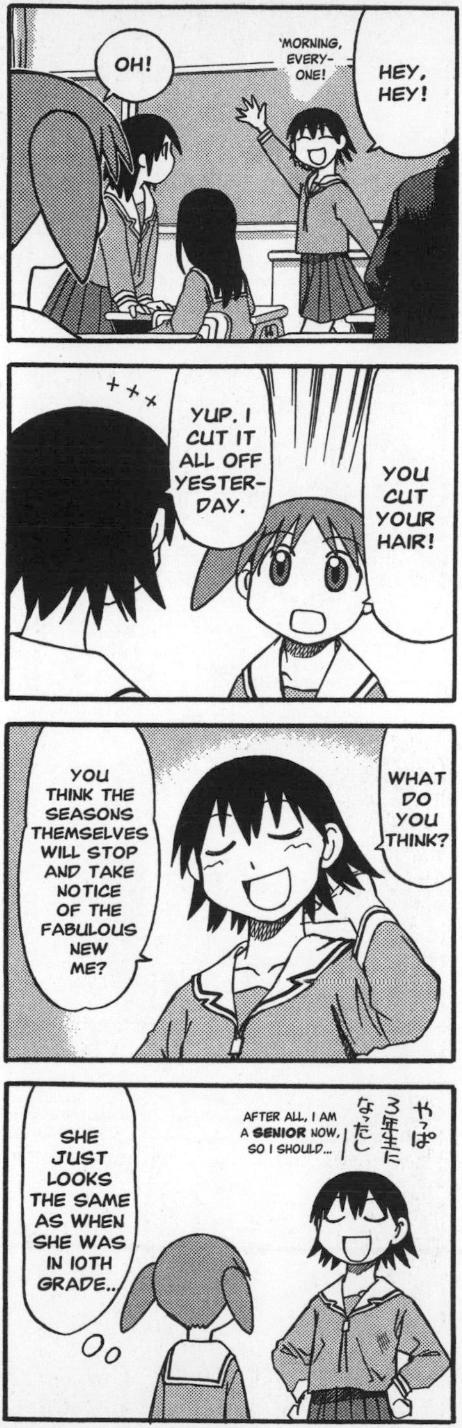
HEY, HEY!
'MORNING, EVERY-ONE!
OH!
YOU CUT YOUR HAIR!
YUP. I CUT IT ALL OFF YESTER-DAY.
WHAT DO YOU THINK?
YOU THINK THE SEASONS THEMSELVES WILL STOP AND TAKE NOTICE OF THE FABULOUS NEW ME?
やっぱ3年生になったし
AFTER ALL, I AM A SENIOR NOW, SO I SHOULD...
SHE JUST LOOKS THE SAME AS WHEN SHE WAS IN 10TH GRADE...

TO AVOID THE SHADOWS

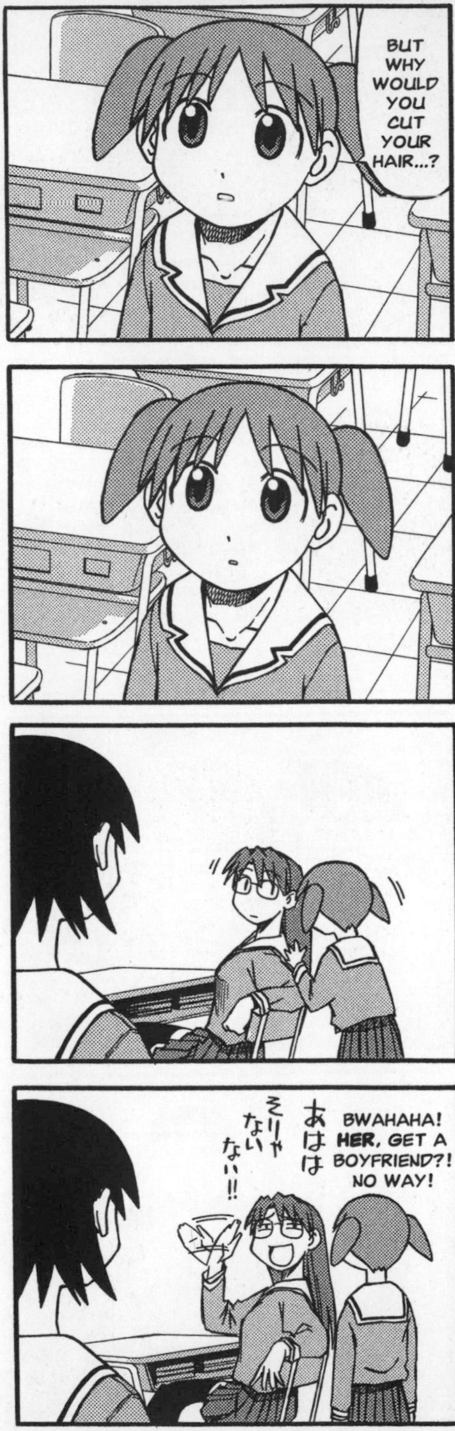
BUT WHY WOULD YOU CUT YOUR HAIR...?
BWAHAHA! HER, GET A BOYFRIEND?! NO WAY!
あはは
そりゃないない!!

A TOWER STRETCHING UP TO THE HEAVENS

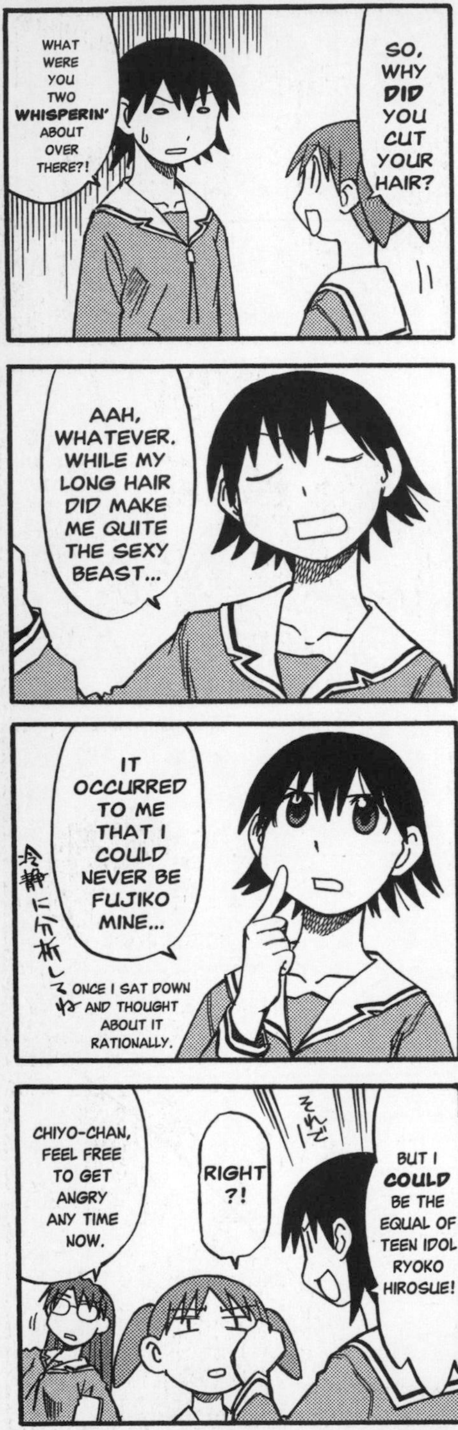
SO, WHY DID YOU CUT YOUR HAIR?
WHAT WERE YOU TWO WHISPERIN' ABOUT OVER THERE?!
AAH, WHATEVER. WHILE MY LONG HAIR DID MAKE ME QUITE THE SEXY BEAST...
IT OCCURRED TO ME THAT I COULD NEVER BE FUJIKO MINE...
冷静に分析してね
ONCE I SAT DOWN AND THOUGHT ABOUT IT RATIONALLY.
BUT I COULD BE THE EQUAL OF TEEN IDOL RYOKO HIROSUE!
それで
RIGHT?!
CHIYO-CHAN, FEEL FREE TO GET ANGRY ANY TIME NOW.

## IT'S NO PICNIC BEING A GROWNUP

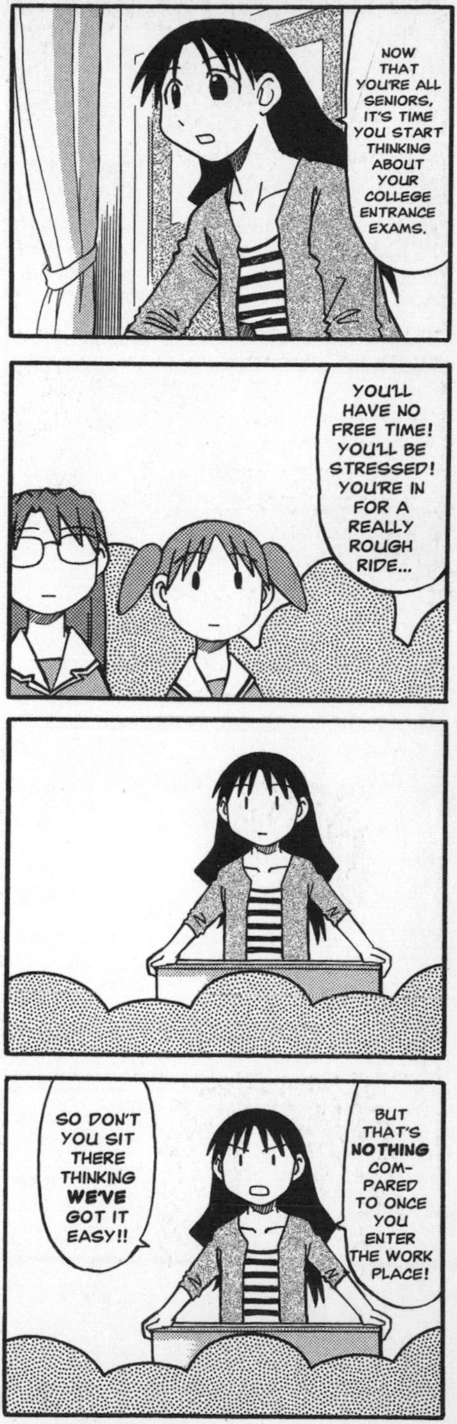
NOW THAT YOU'RE ALL SENIORS, IT'S TIME YOU START THINKING ABOUT YOUR COLLEGE ENTRANCE EXAMS.
YOU'LL HAVE NO FREE TIME! YOU'LL BE STRESSED! YOU'RE IN FOR A REALLY ROUGH RIDE...
BUT THAT'S **NOTHING** COMPARED TO ONCE YOU ENTER THE WORK PLACE!
SO DON'T YOU SIT THERE THINKING **WE'VE** GOT IT EASY!!

## DO YOU HATE US?

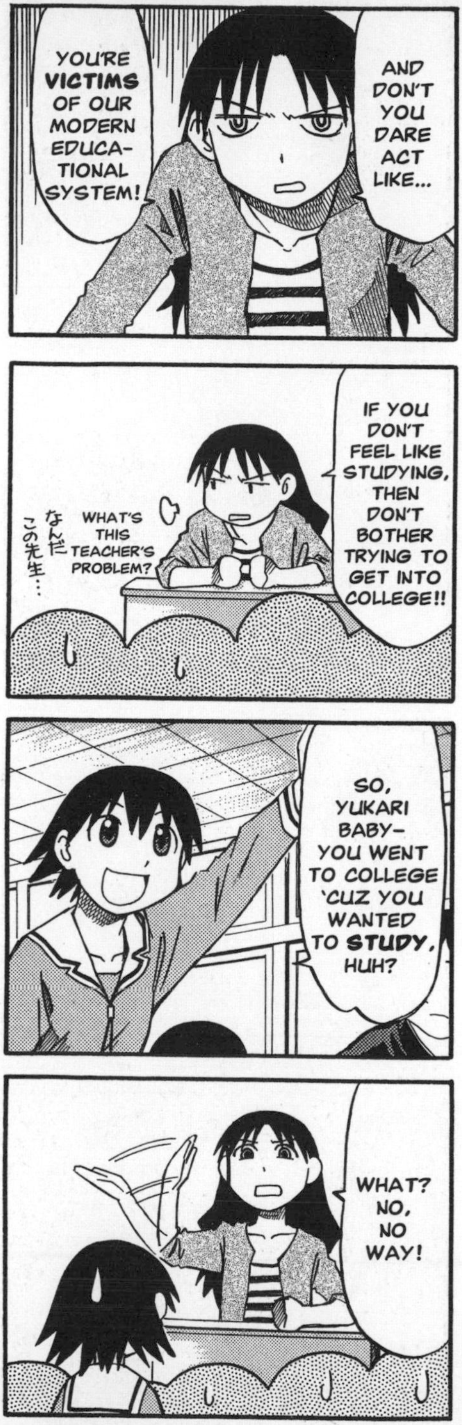
AND DON'T YOU DARE ACT LIKE...
YOU'RE **VICTIMS** OF OUR MODERN EDUCATIONAL SYSTEM!
IF YOU DON'T FEEL LIKE STUDYING, THEN DON'T BOTHER TRYING TO GET INTO COLLEGE!!
WHAT'S THIS TEACHER'S PROBLEM?
なんだこの先生…
SO, YUKARI BABY— YOU WENT TO COLLEGE 'CUZ YOU WANTED TO **STUDY**, HUH?
WHAT? NO, NO WAY!

SOMEBODY ELSE'S PROBLEM

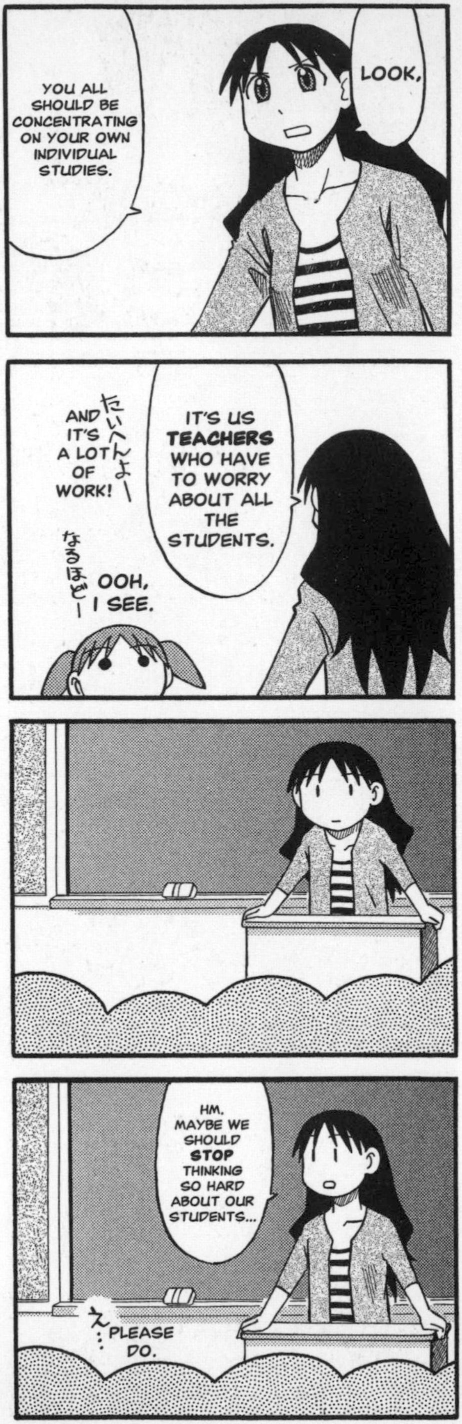
LOOK,
YOU ALL SHOULD BE CONCENTRATING ON YOUR OWN INDIVIDUAL STUDIES.
IT'S US **TEACHERS** WHO HAVE TO WORRY ABOUT ALL THE STUDENTS.
たいへんよー
AND IT'S A LOT OF WORK!
なるほどー
OOH, I SEE.
HM. MAYBE WE SHOULD **STOP** THINKING SO HARD ABOUT OUR STUDENTS...
え…
PLEASE DO.

AS THE STOMACH TURNS

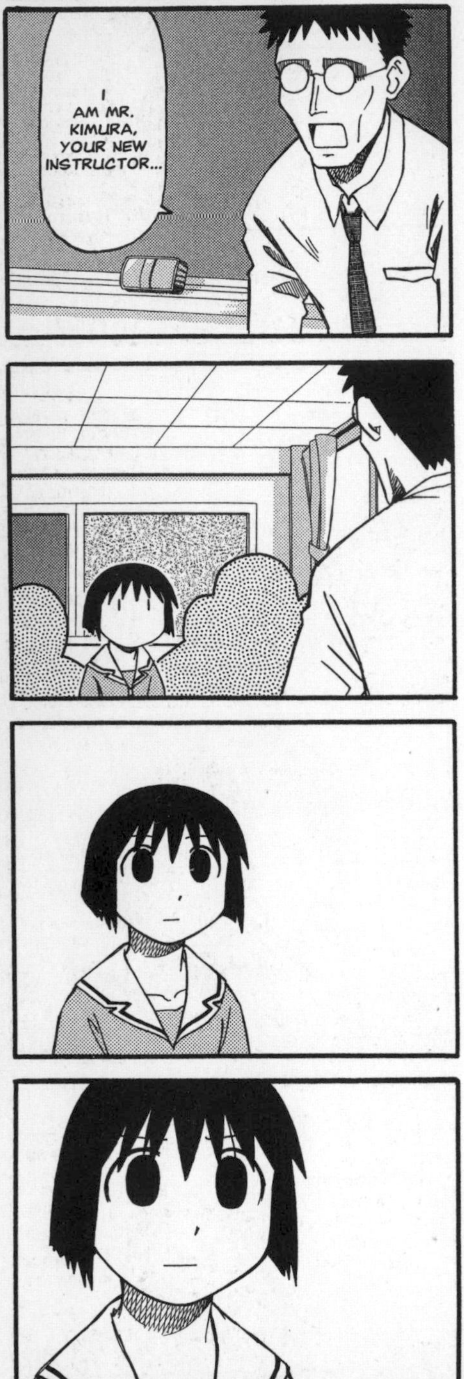
I AM MR. KIMURA, YOUR NEW INSTRUCTOR...

## IN AGREEMENT

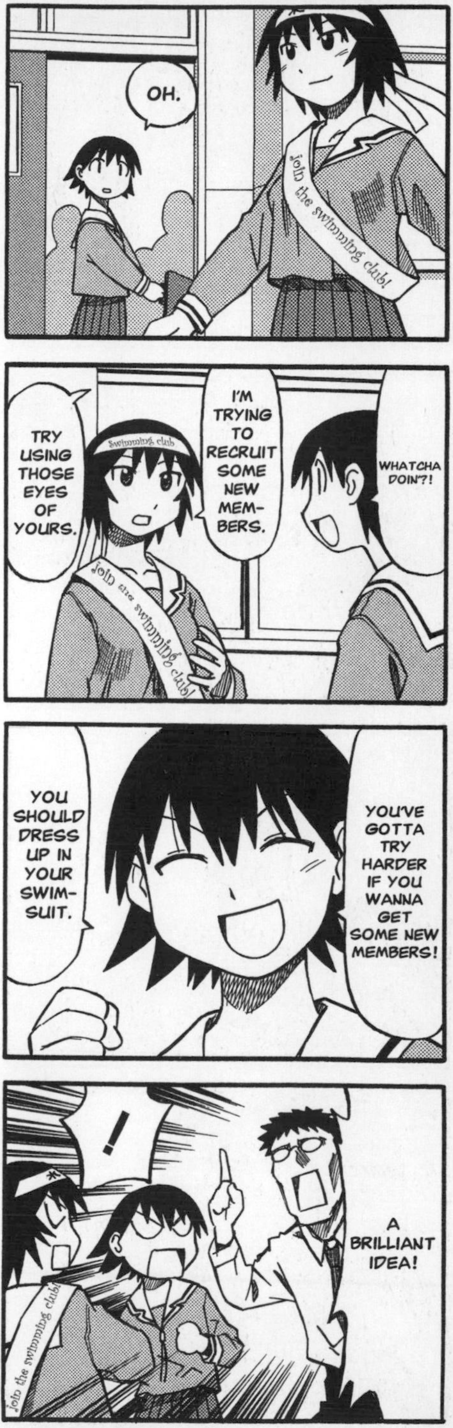
OH.
join the swimming club!
WHATCHA DOIN'?!
I'M TRYING TO RECRUIT SOME NEW MEMBERS.
TRY USING THOSE EYES OF YOURS.
swimming club
YOU'VE GOTTA TRY HARDER IF YOU WANNA GET SOME NEW MEMBERS!
YOU SHOULD DRESS UP IN YOUR SWIMSUIT.
A BRILLIANT IDEA!
!

## AN EGG THAT WILL NEVER HATCH

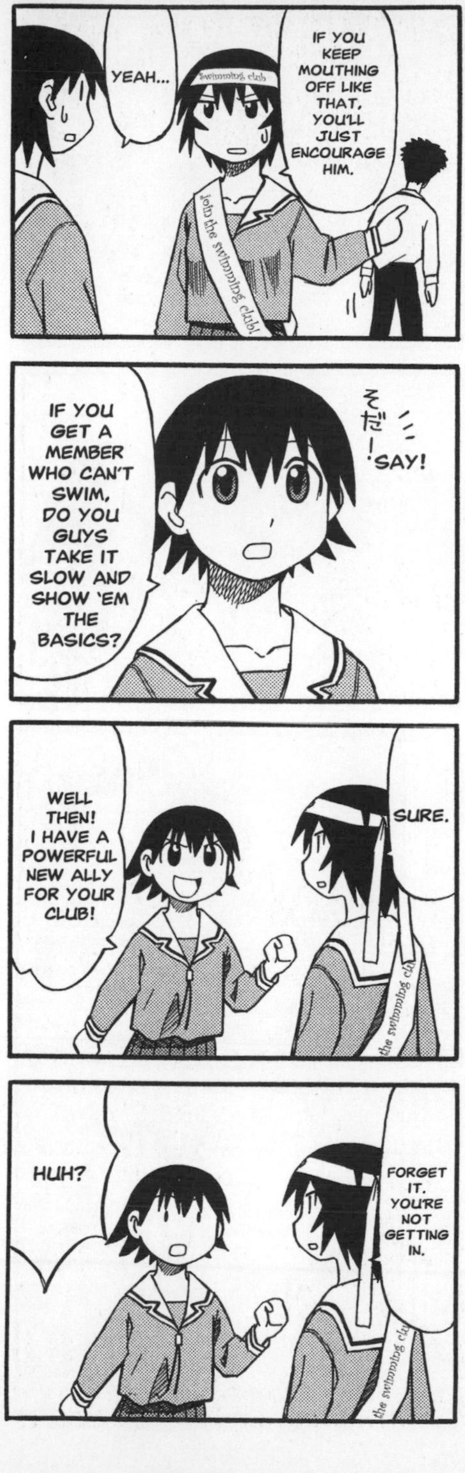
IF YOU KEEP MOUTHING OFF LIKE THAT, YOU'LL JUST ENCOURAGE HIM.
YEAH...
swimming club
join the swimming club!
そだ！
SAY!
IF YOU GET A MEMBER WHO CAN'T SWIM, DO YOU GUYS TAKE IT SLOW AND SHOW 'EM THE BASICS?
SURE.
WELL THEN! I HAVE A POWERFUL NEW ALLY FOR YOUR CLUB!
FORGET IT. YOU'RE NOT GETTING IN.
HUH?

## ELEMENTARY, JUNIOR, HIGH (SCHOOL)

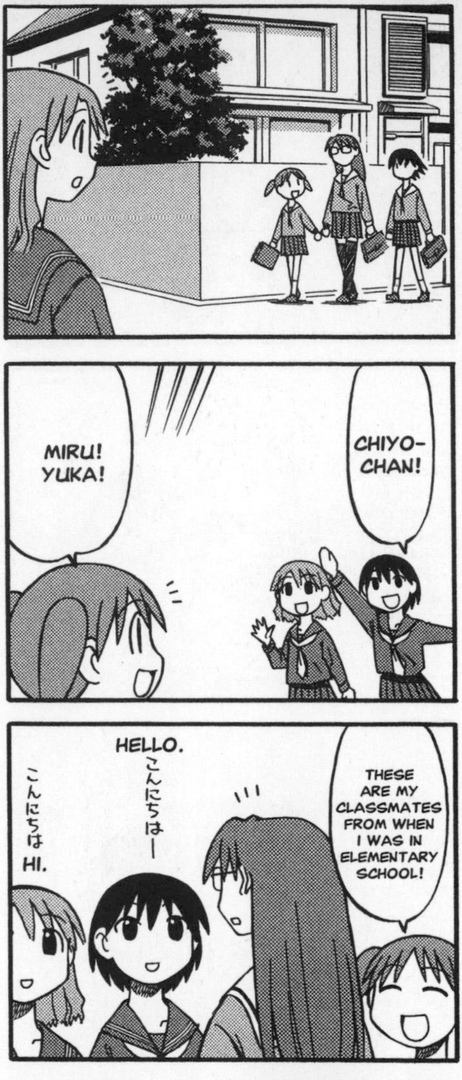
CHIYO-CHAN!
MIRU! YUKA!
THESE ARE MY CLASSMATES FROM WHEN I WAS IN ELEMENTARY SCHOOL!
HELLO. こんにちはー
こんにちは HI.
CHIYO-CHAN, YOU'RE IN JUNIOR HIGH ALREADY?
WHAT ARE YOU TALKING ABOUT? I'M IN HIGH SCHOOL!

## THE GOOD THINGS

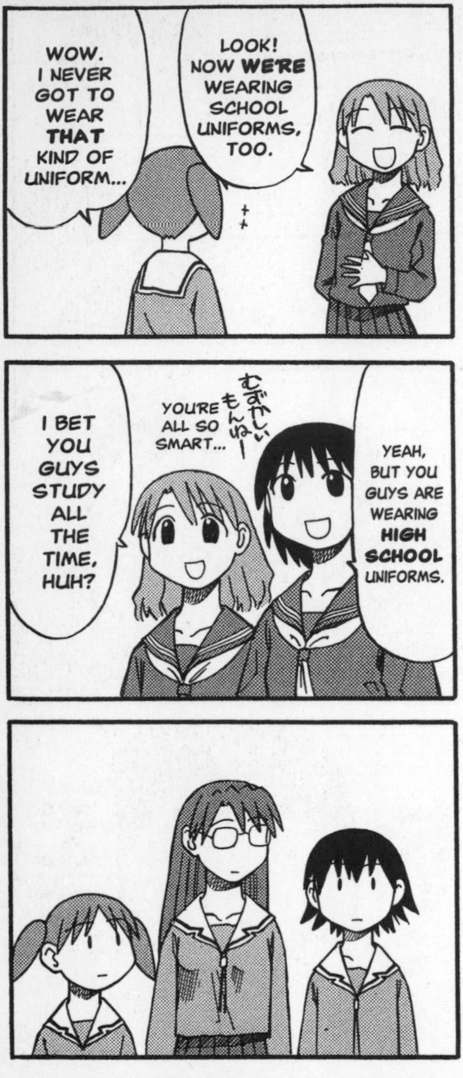
LOOK! NOW WE'RE WEARING SCHOOL UNIFORMS, TOO.
WOW. I NEVER GOT TO WEAR THAT KIND OF UNIFORM...
YEAH, BUT YOU GUYS ARE WEARING HIGH SCHOOL UNIFORMS.
むずかしいもんねー
YOU'RE ALL SO SMART...
I BET YOU GUYS STUDY ALL THE TIME, HUH?
THAT'S RIGHT.
WHAT?!

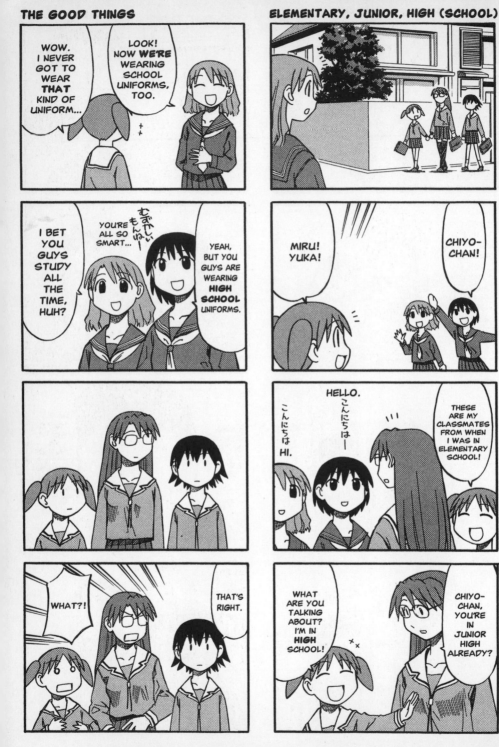

A BIRD THAT FLAPS ITS WINGS BUT CANNOT FLY

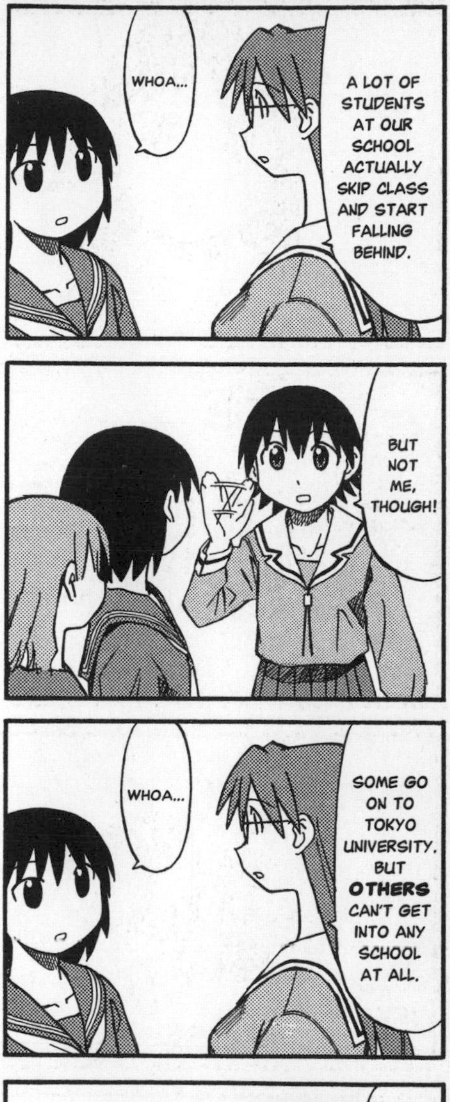
A LOT OF STUDENTS AT OUR SCHOOL ACTUALLY SKIP CLASS AND START FALLING BEHIND.
WHOA...
BUT NOT ME, THOUGH!
SOME GO ON TO TOKYO UNIVERSITY, BUT **OTHERS** CAN'T GET INTO ANY SCHOOL AT ALL.
WHOA...
BUT NOT ME, THOUGH!

HUH?

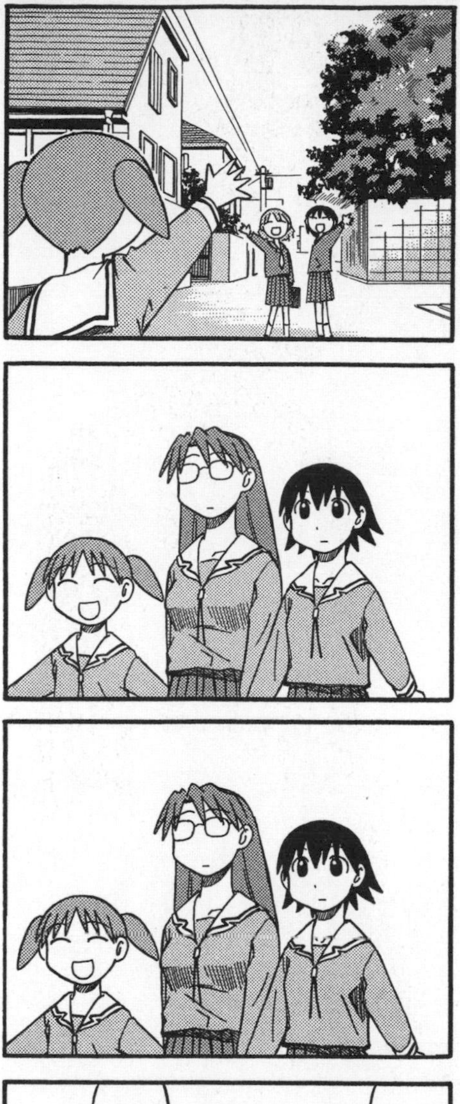
BUT NOT ME, RIGHT?
YES, **YOU!**

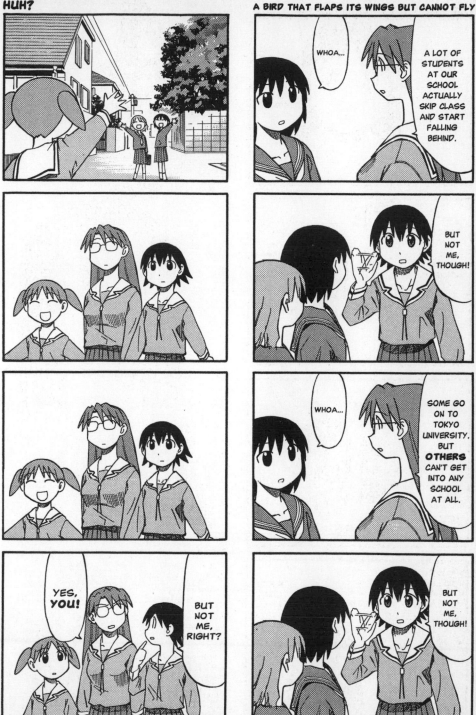

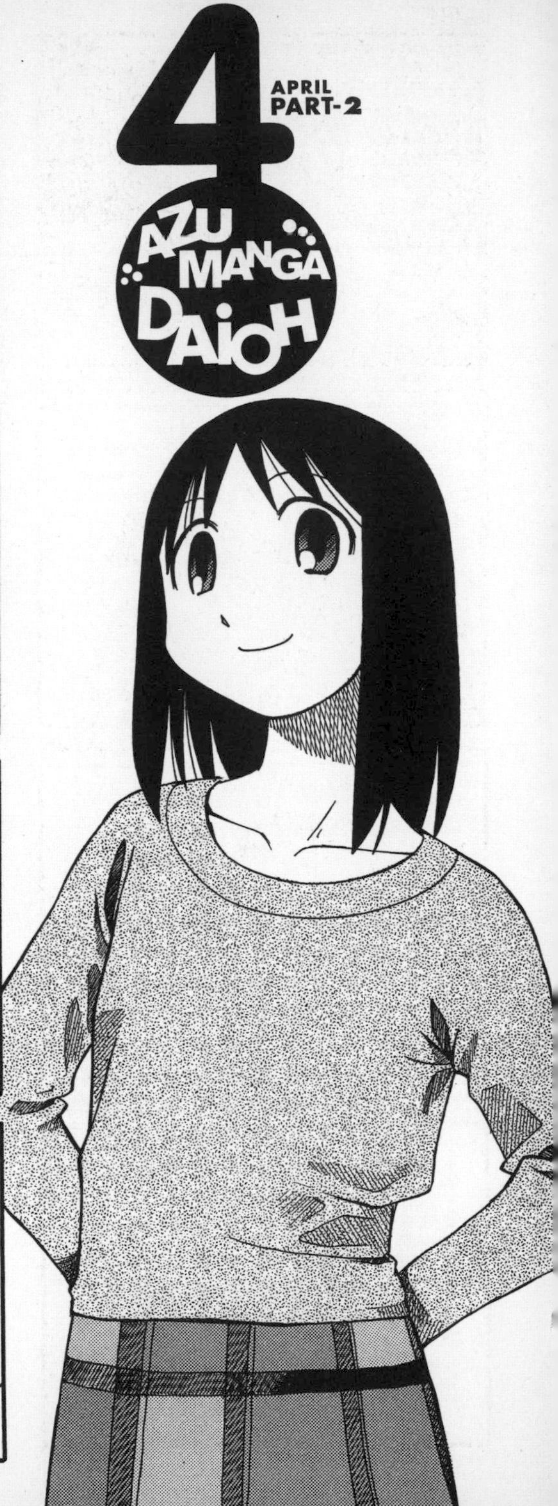
4
APRIL
PART-2
AZUMANGA DAIOH

THE HOMELESS HERMIT CRAB

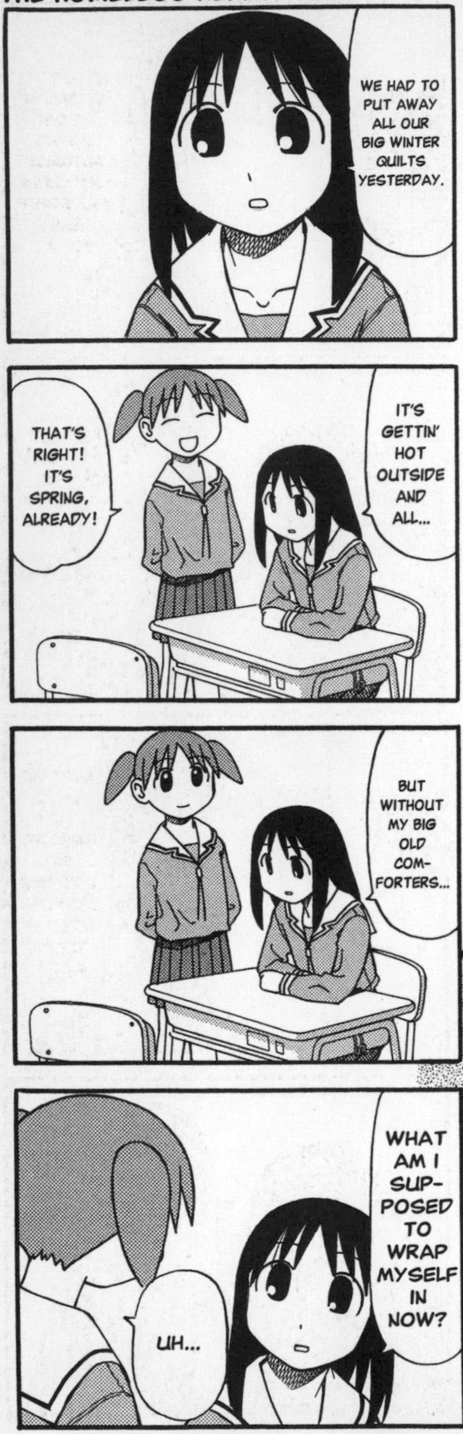
WE HAD TO PUT AWAY ALL OUR BIG WINTER QUILTS YESTERDAY.
IT'S GETTIN' HOT OUTSIDE AND ALL...
THAT'S RIGHT! IT'S SPRING, ALREADY!
BUT WITHOUT MY BIG OLD COM-FORTERS...
WHAT AM I SUP-POSED TO WRAP MYSELF IN NOW?
UH...

PORK BUNS

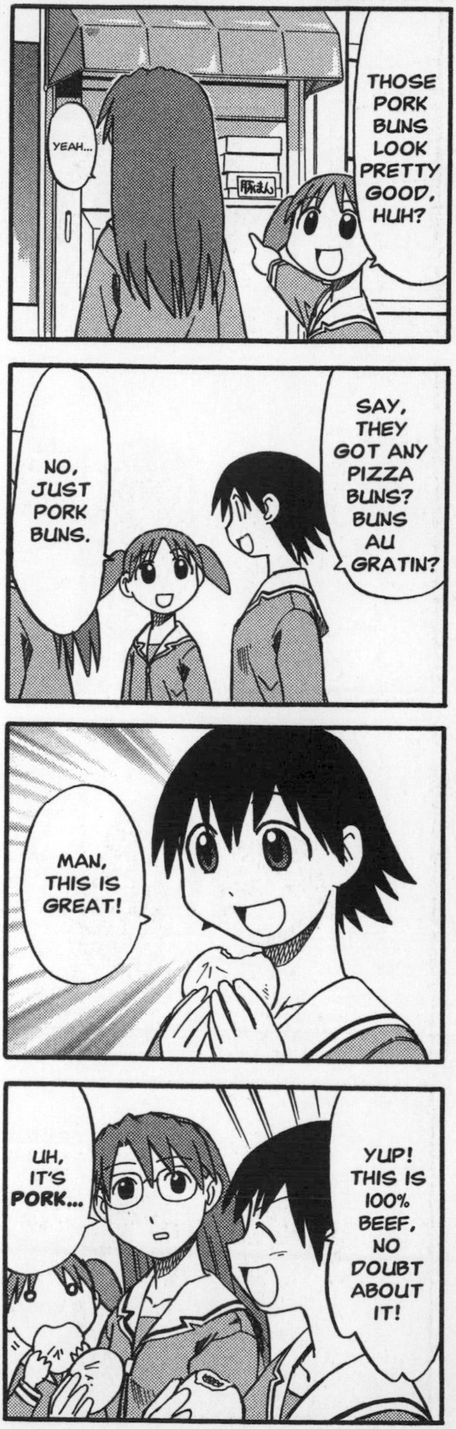
THOSE PORK BUNS LOOK PRETTY GOOD, HUH?
YEAH...
豚まん
SAY, THEY GOT ANY PIZZA BUNS? BUNS AU GRATIN?
NO, JUST PORK BUNS.
MAN, THIS IS GREAT!
YUP! THIS IS 100% BEEF, NO DOUBT ABOUT IT!
UH, IT'S **PORK**...

GOOD EATS

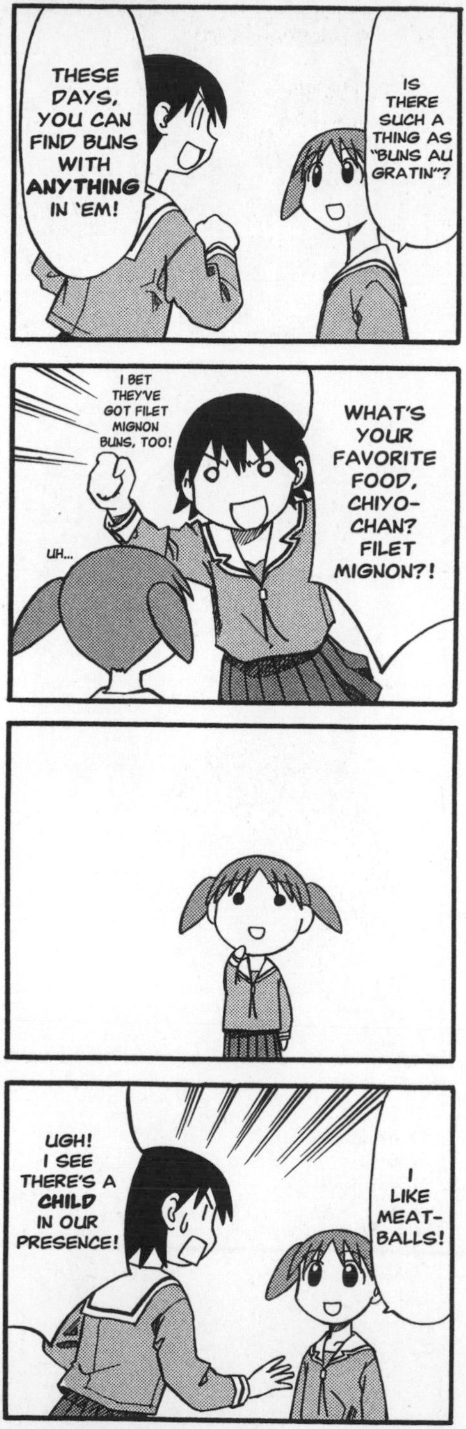
IS THERE SUCH A THING AS "BUNS AU GRATIN"?
THESE DAYS, YOU CAN FIND BUNS WITH **ANYTHING** IN 'EM!
WHAT'S YOUR FAVORITE FOOD, CHIYO-CHAN? FILET MIGNON?!
I BET THEY'VE GOT FILET MIGNON BUNS, TOO!
UH...
I LIKE MEAT-BALLS!
UGH! I SEE THERE'S A **CHILD** IN OUR PRESENCE!

MONKEY

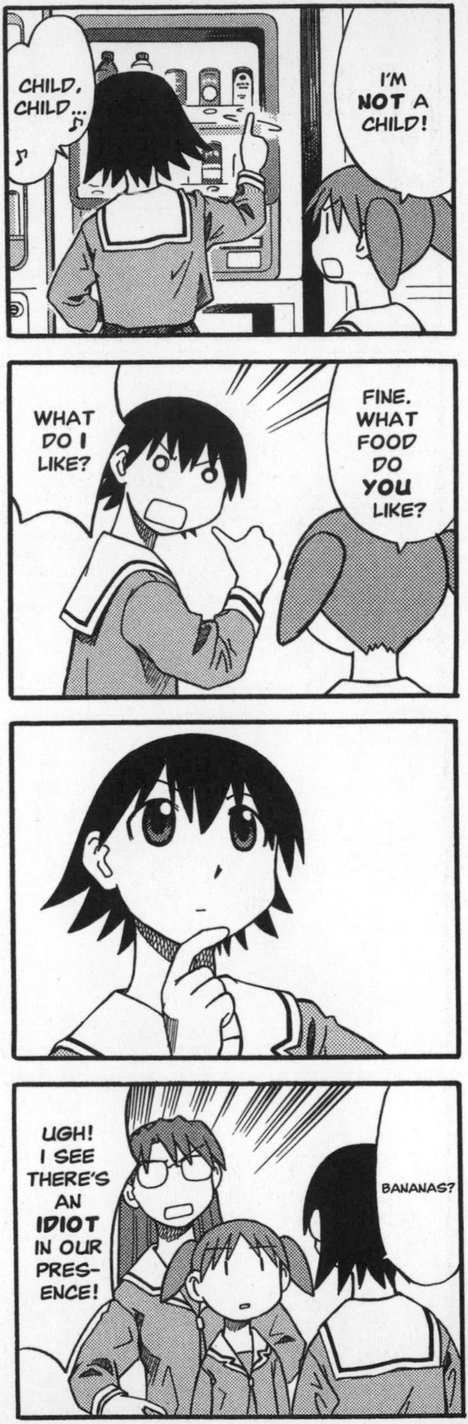
I'M NOT A CHILD!
CHILD, CHILD... ♪ ♪
FINE. WHAT FOOD DO YOU LIKE?
WHAT DO I LIKE?
BANANAS?
UGH! I SEE THERE'S AN IDIOT IN OUR PRES-ENCE!

NO GOOD

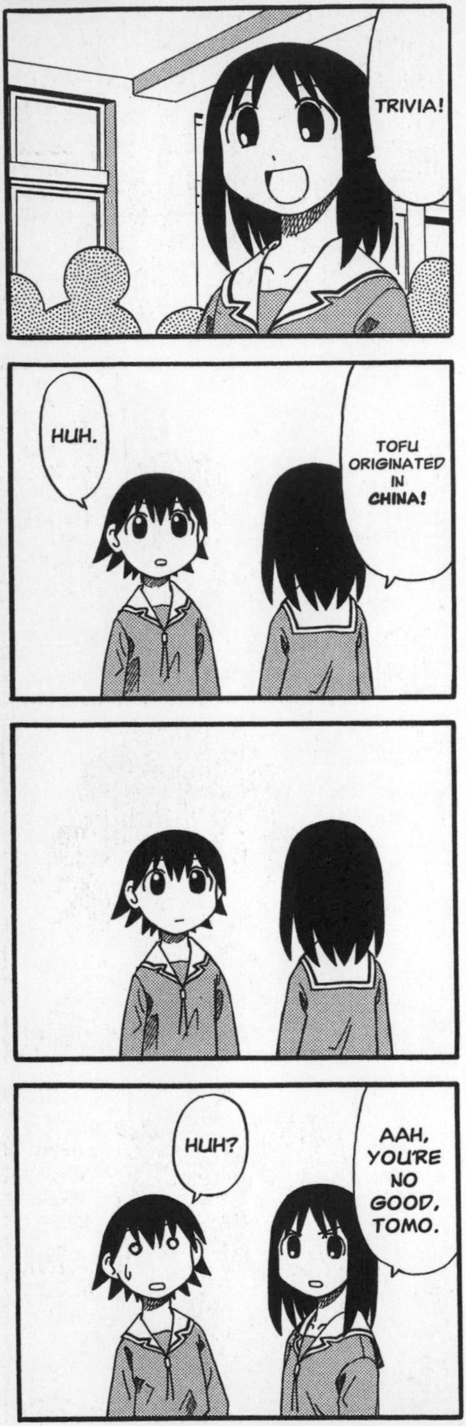
TRIVIA!
TOFU ORIGINATED IN CHINA!
HUH.
AAH, YOU'RE NO GOOD, TOMO.
HUH?

## ANTICIPATION

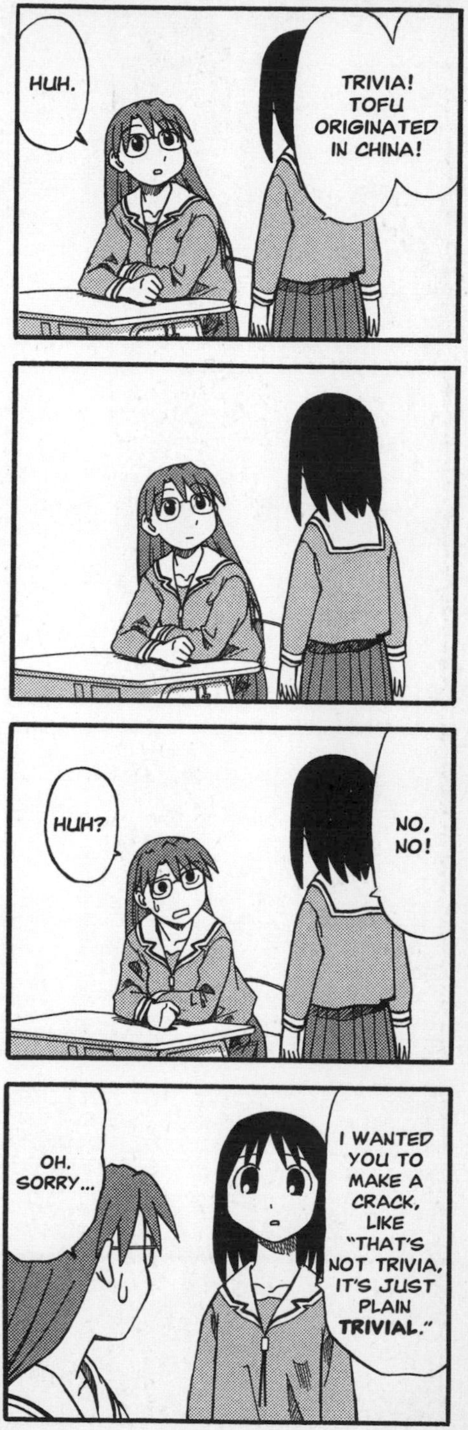
TRIVIA! TOFU ORIGINATED IN CHINA!
HUH.
NO, NO!
HUH?
I WANTED YOU TO MAKE A CRACK, LIKE "THAT'S NOT TRIVIA, IT'S JUST PLAIN **TRIVIAL**."
OH. SORRY...

## A POWERFUL IMAGINATION

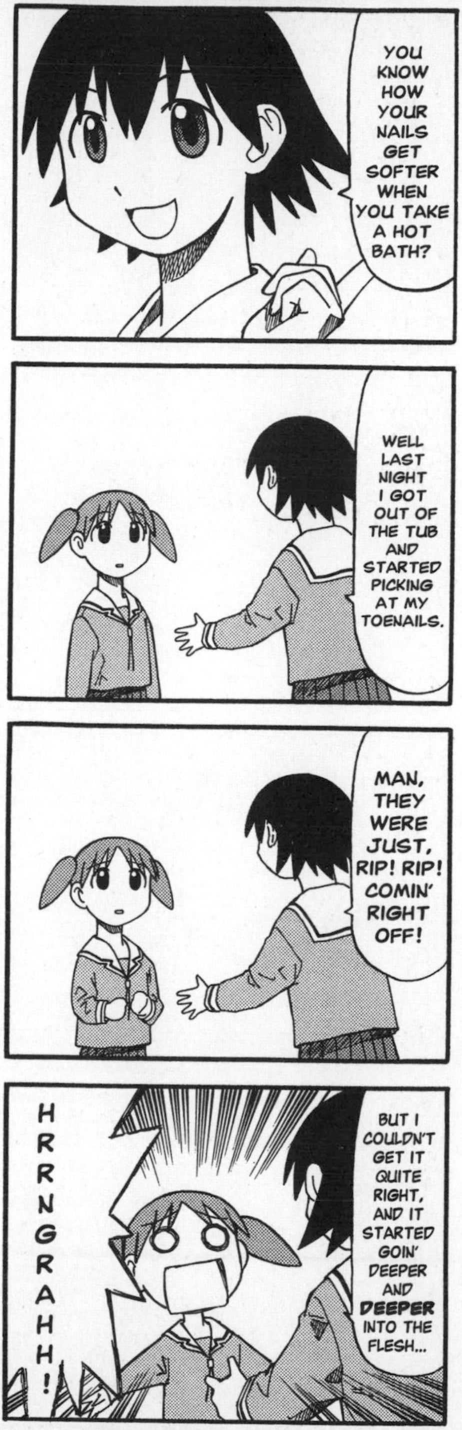
YOU KNOW HOW YOUR NAILS GET SOFTER WHEN YOU TAKE A HOT BATH?
WELL LAST NIGHT I GOT OUT OF THE TUB AND STARTED PICKING AT MY TOENAILS.
MAN, THEY WERE JUST, RIP! RIP! COMIN' RIGHT OFF!
BUT I COULDN'T GET IT QUITE RIGHT, AND IT STARTED GOIN' DEEPER AND **DEEPER** INTO THE FLESH...
HRRNGRAHH!

## THE POWER OF THE SPOKEN WORD

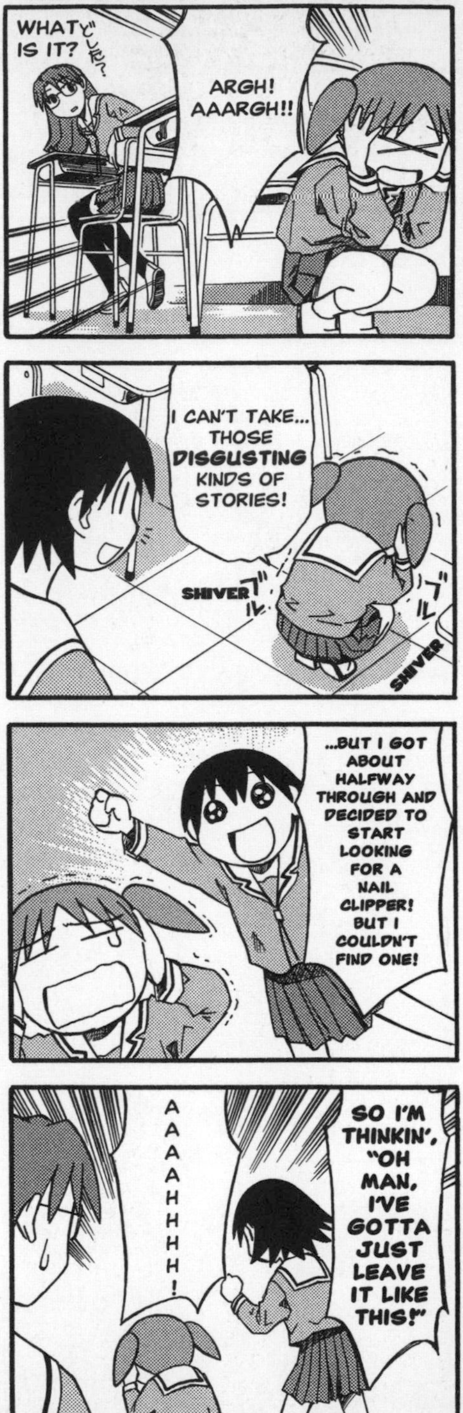
ARGH! AAAARGH!!
WHAT IS IT?
どした?
I CAN'T TAKE... THOSE DISGUSTING KINDS OF STORIES!
SHIVER
ブル
ブル
SHIVER
...BUT I GOT ABOUT HALFWAY THROUGH AND DECIDED TO START LOOKING FOR A NAIL CLIPPER! BUT I COULDN'T FIND ONE!
SO I'M THINKIN', "OH MAN, I'VE GOTTA JUST LEAVE IT LIKE THIS!"
AAAAAHHHH!

## A BAD FEELING

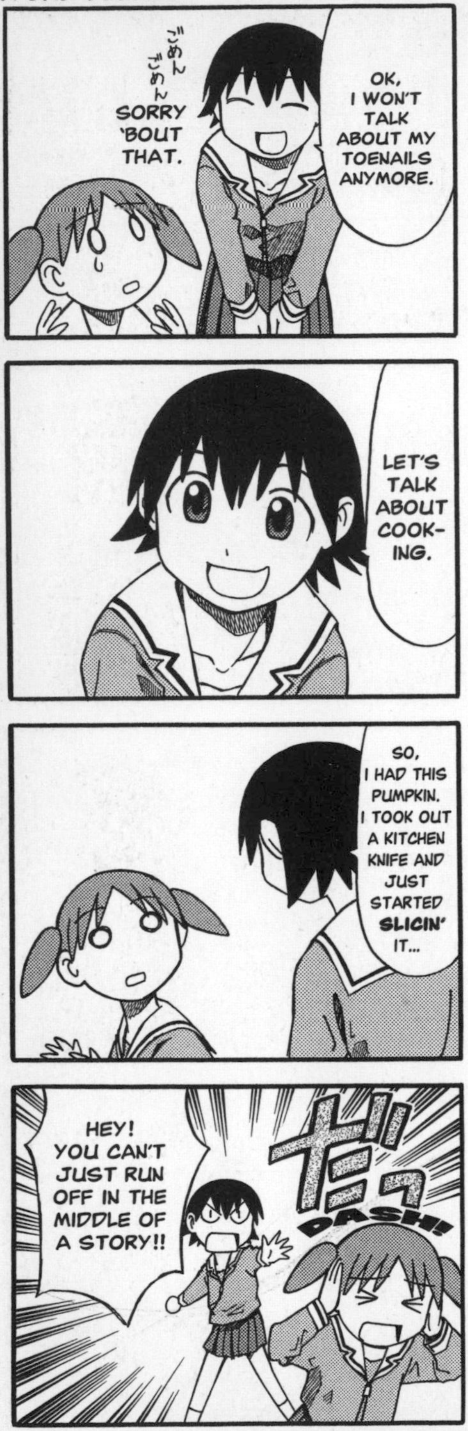
OK, I WON'T TALK ABOUT MY TOENAILS ANYMORE.
ごめん ごめん
SORRY 'BOUT THAT.
LET'S TALK ABOUT COOKING.
SO, I HAD THIS PUMPKIN. I TOOK OUT A KITCHEN KNIFE AND JUST STARTED SLICIN' IT...
だっ
DASH!
HEY! YOU CAN'T JUST RUN OFF IN THE MIDDLE OF A STORY!!

BRUISES ARE OK

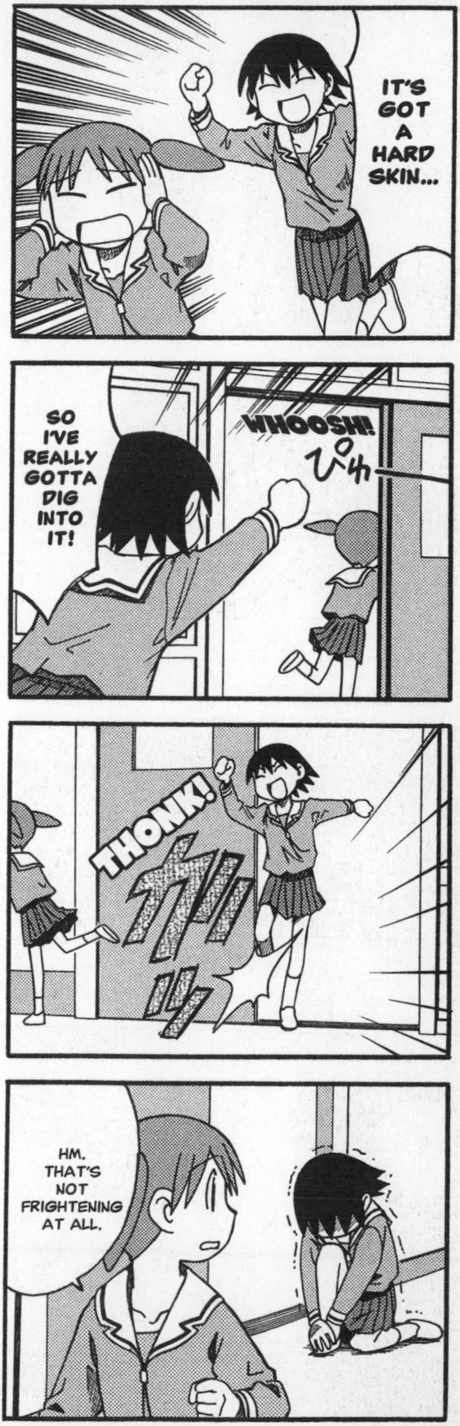
IT'S GOT A HARD SKIN...
SO I'VE REALLY GOTTA DIG INTO IT!
WHOOSH!
THONK!
HM. THAT'S NOT FRIGHTENING AT ALL.

I WAS SCARED, TOO

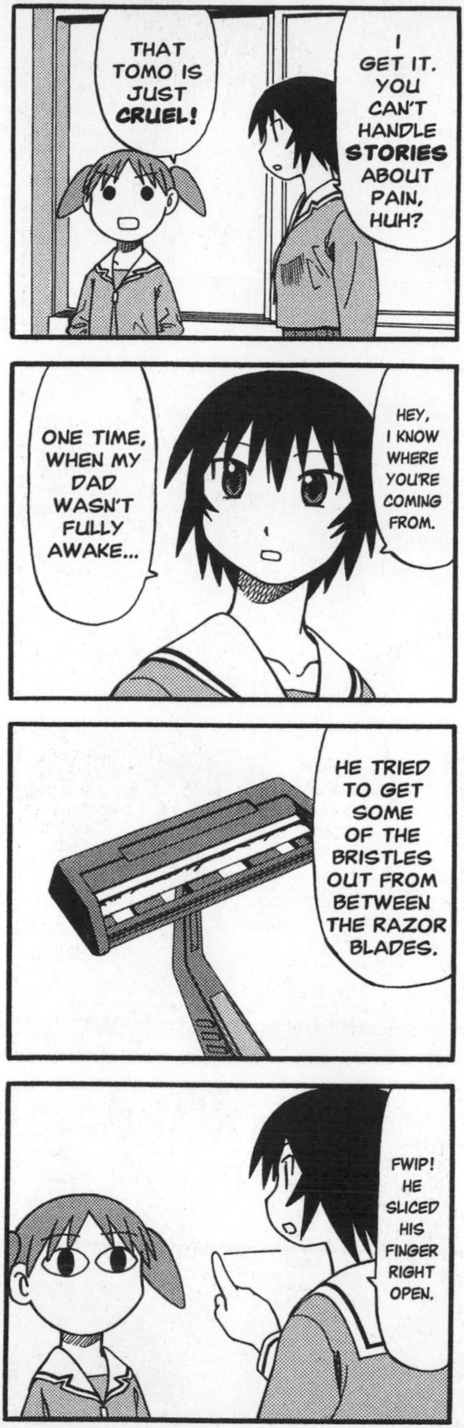
I GET IT. YOU CAN'T HANDLE STORIES ABOUT PAIN, HUH?
THAT TOMO IS JUST CRUEL!
HEY, I KNOW WHERE YOU'RE COMING FROM.
ONE TIME, WHEN MY DAD WASN'T FULLY AWAKE...
HE TRIED TO GET SOME OF THE BRISTLES OUT FROM BETWEEN THE RAZOR BLADES.
FWIP! HE SLICED HIS FINGER RIGHT OPEN.

**THE OBSTRUCTION**

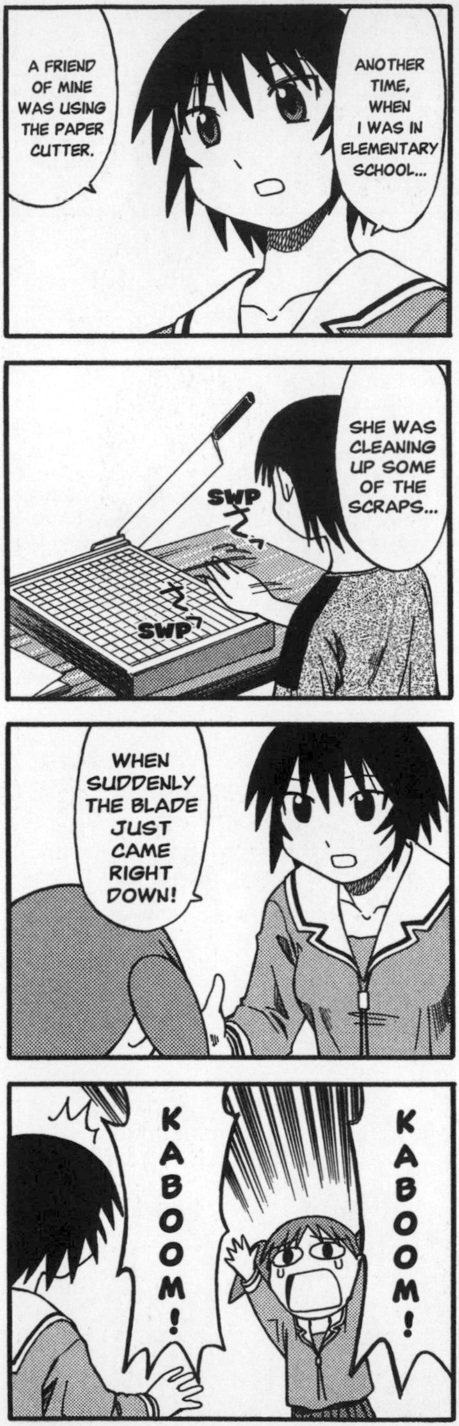
ANOTHER TIME, WHEN I WAS IN ELEMENTARY SCHOOL...
A FRIEND OF MINE WAS USING THE PAPER CUTTER.
SHE WAS CLEANING UP SOME OF THE SCRAPS...
SWP
SWP
WHEN SUDDENLY THE BLADE JUST CAME RIGHT DOWN!
KABOOM!
KABOOM!

**GET OUT OF MY HEAD!**

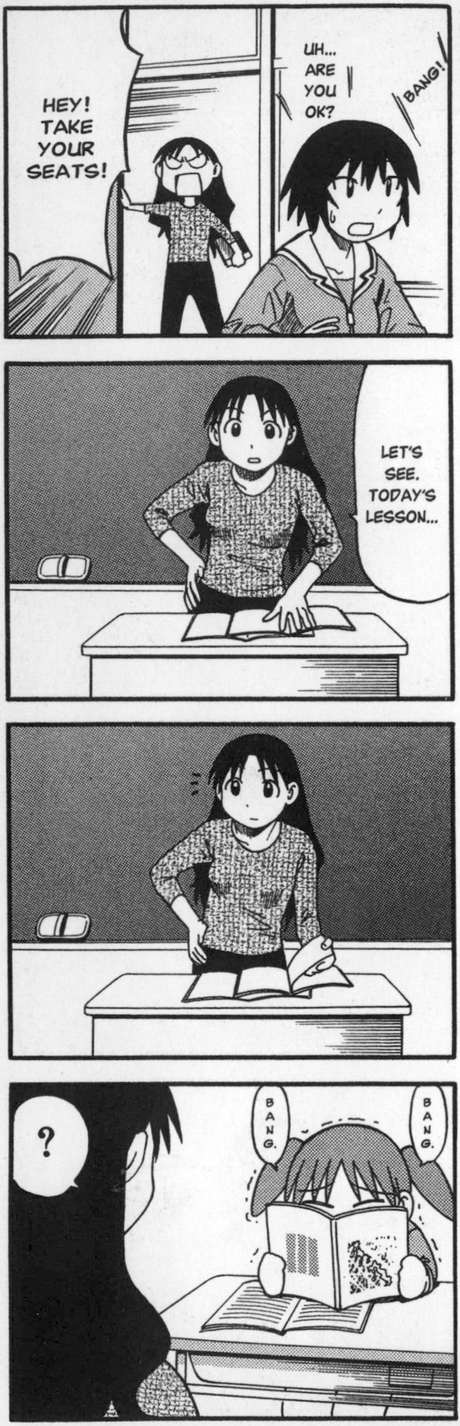
BANG!
UH... ARE YOU OK?
HEY! TAKE YOUR SEATS!
LET'S SEE. TODAY'S LESSON...
BANG.
BANG.
?

CONCENTRATION

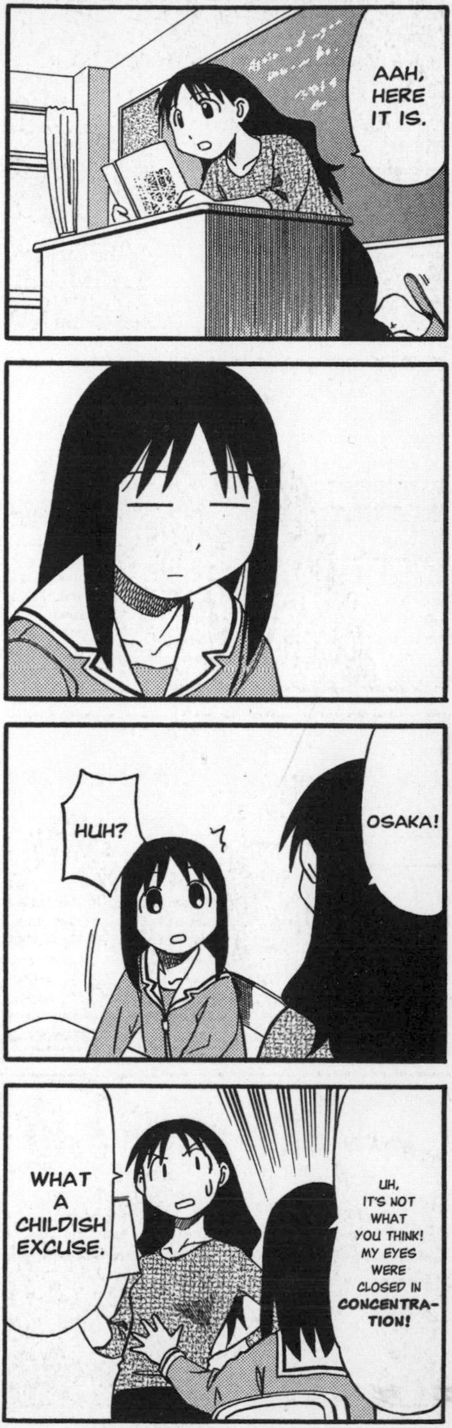

AAH, HERE IT IS.
OSAKA!
HUH?
UH, IT'S NOT WHAT YOU THINK! MY EYES WERE CLOSED IN CONCENTRATION!
WHAT A CHILDISH EXCUSE.


BELIEF

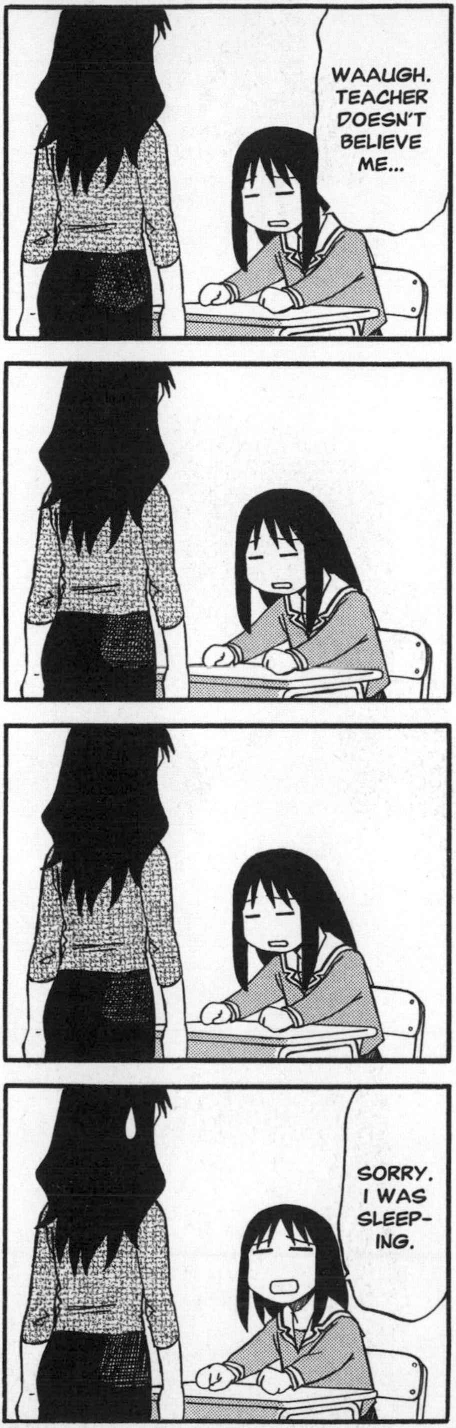

WAAUGH. TEACHER DOESN'T BELIEVE ME...
SORRY. I WAS SLEEP-ING.

# AZU MANGA DAIOH

## 5 MAY PART-1

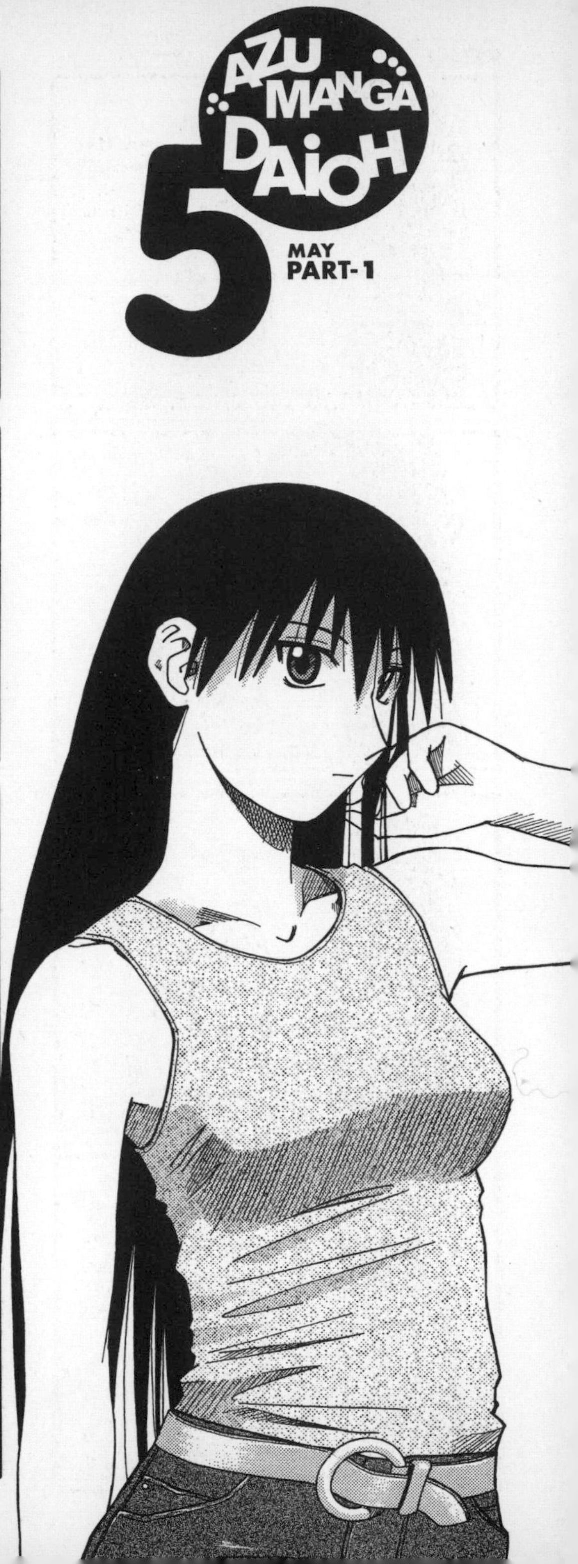

SPRING

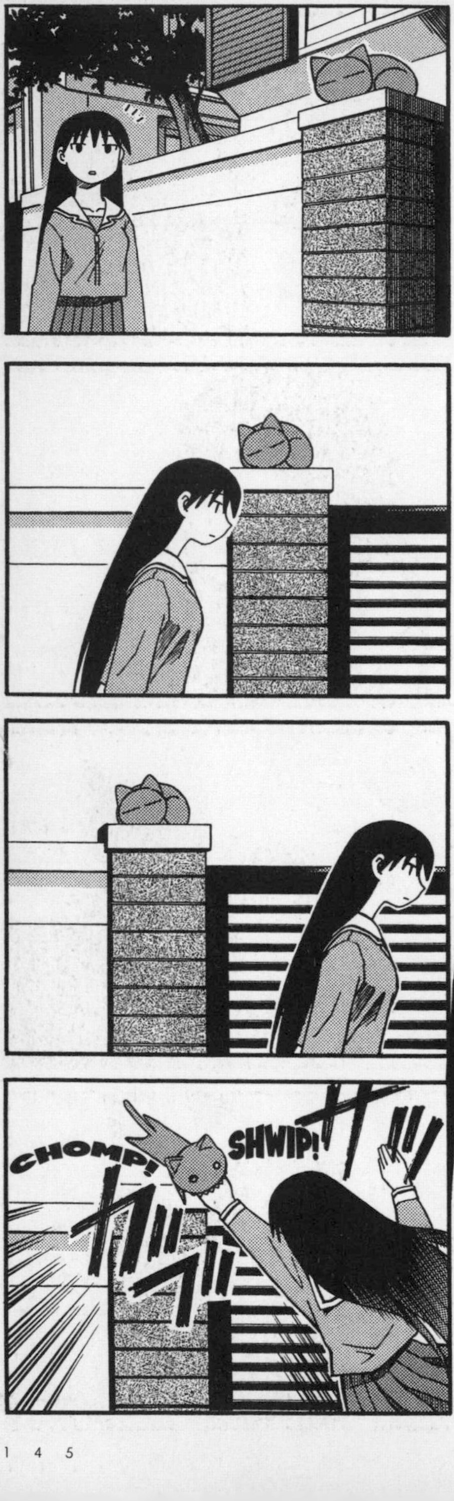
SHWIP!
CHOMP!

STOP!

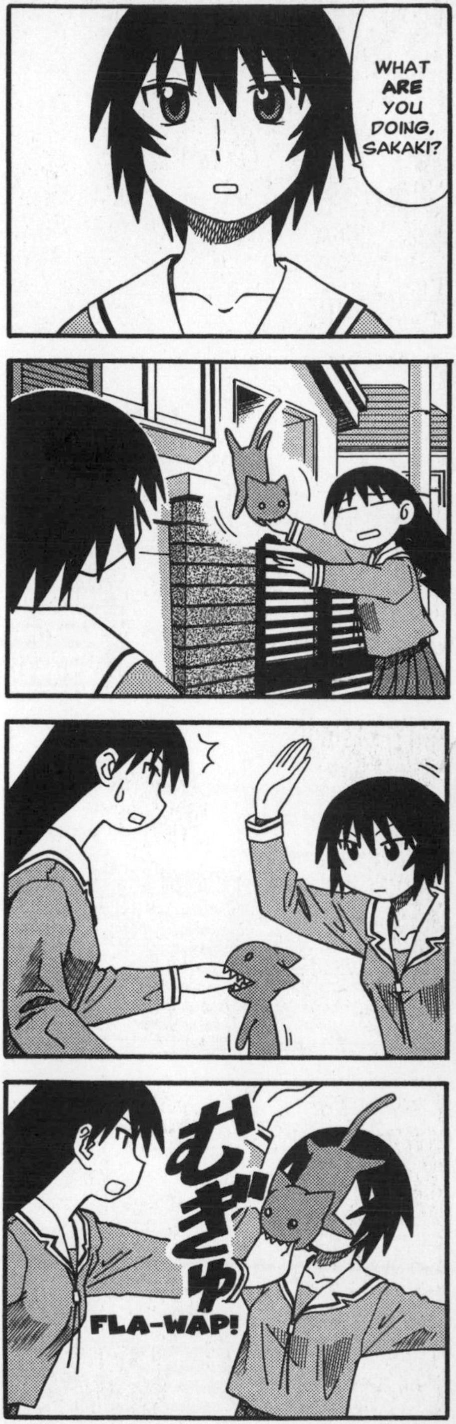
WHAT ARE YOU DOING, SAKAKI?
むぎゅ
FLA-WAP!

CATFACED

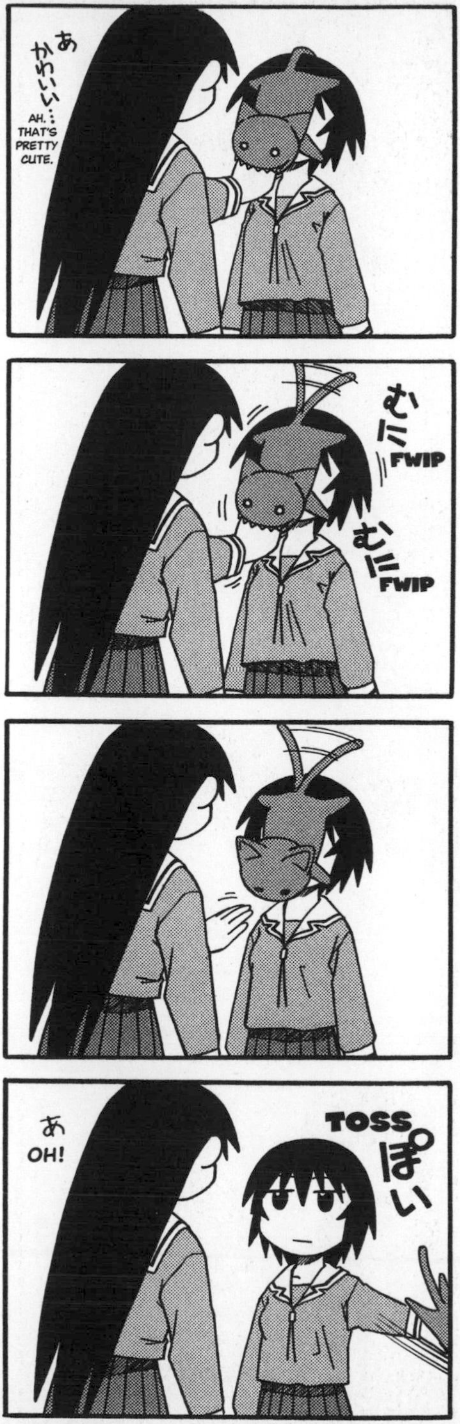
あ かわいい…
AH... THAT'S PRETTY CUTE.
むに
FWIP
むに
FWIP
あ
OH!
TOSS
ぽい

CONSIDERATE

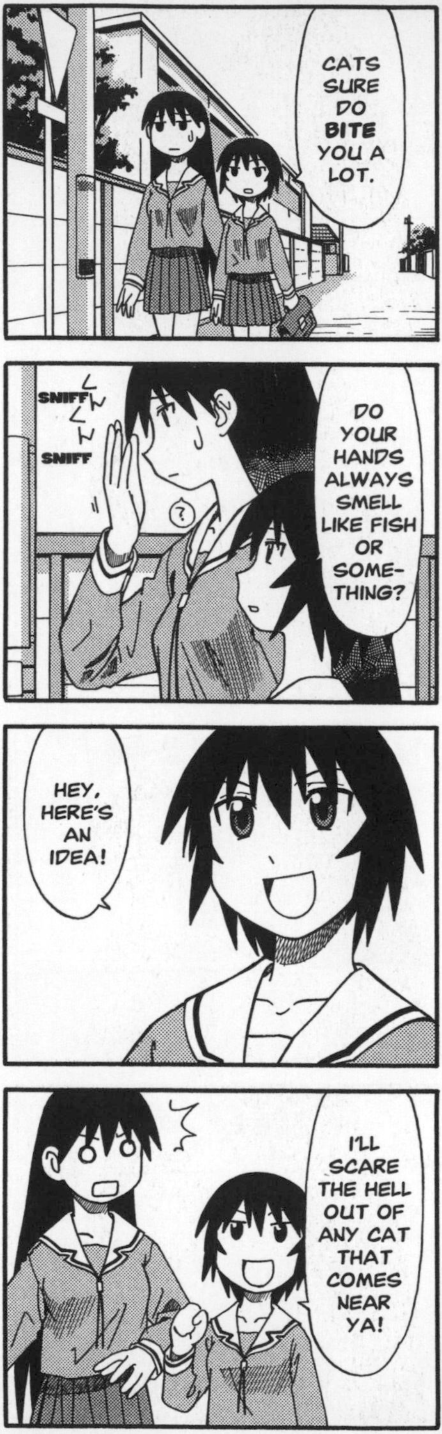
CATS SURE DO BITE YOU A LOT.
SNIFF
SNIFF
DO YOUR HANDS ALWAYS SMELL LIKE FISH OR SOMETHING?
HEY, HERE'S AN IDEA!
I'LL SCARE THE HELL OUT OF ANY CAT THAT COMES NEAR YA!

I AM KAGURA, HERE ME ROAR

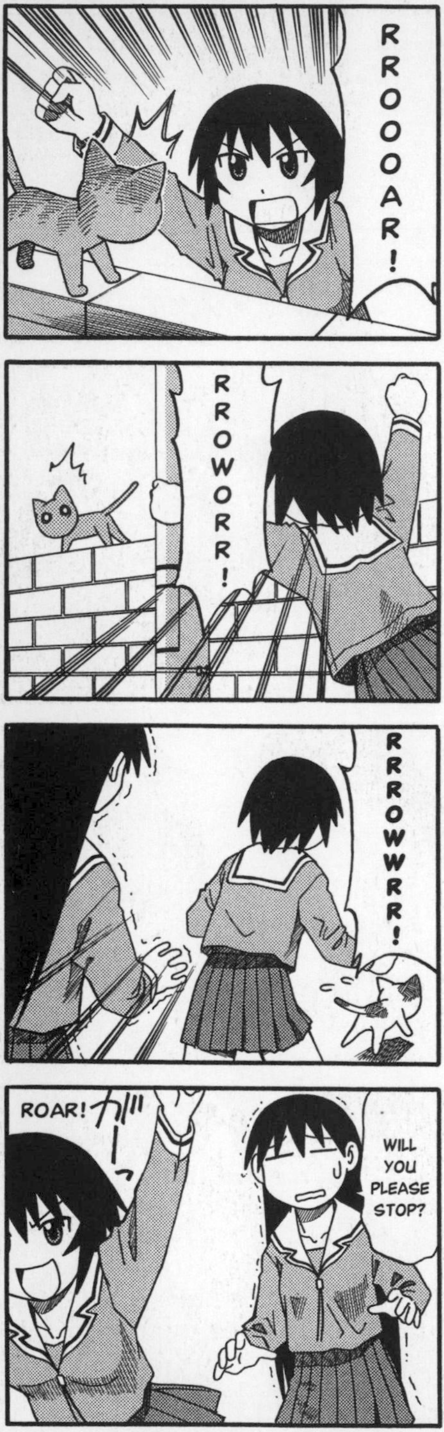
RROOOOAR!
RROWORR!
RRROWWRR!
ROAR!
WILL YOU PLEASE STOP?

EXCLUDED?

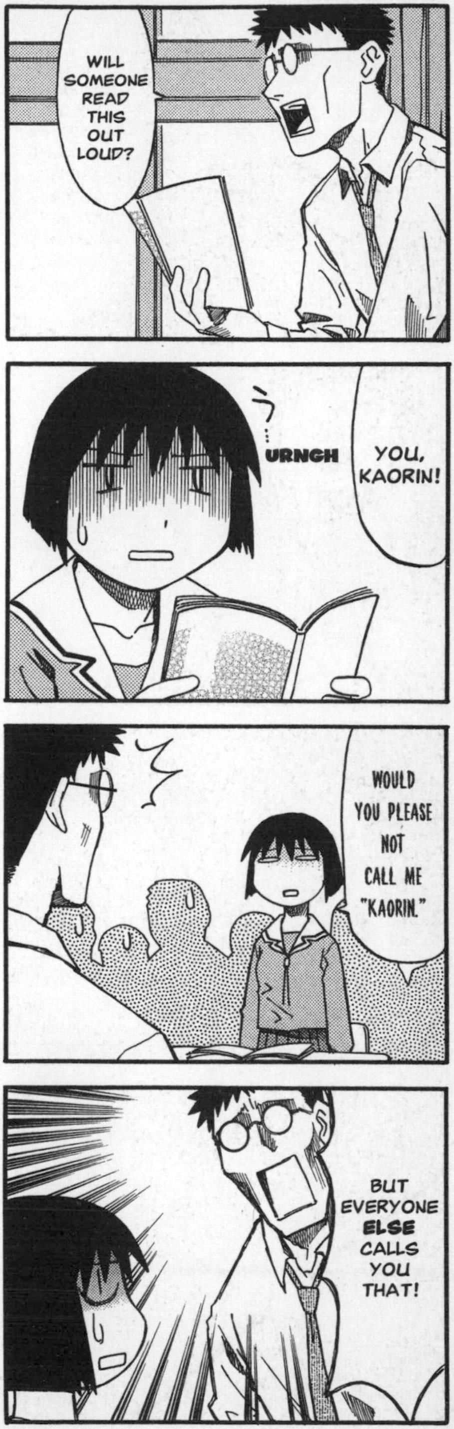
WILL SOMEONE READ THIS OUT LOUD?
YOU, KAORIN!
URNGH
WOULD YOU PLEASE NOT CALL ME "KAORIN."
BUT EVERYONE ELSE CALLS YOU THAT!

PAIR

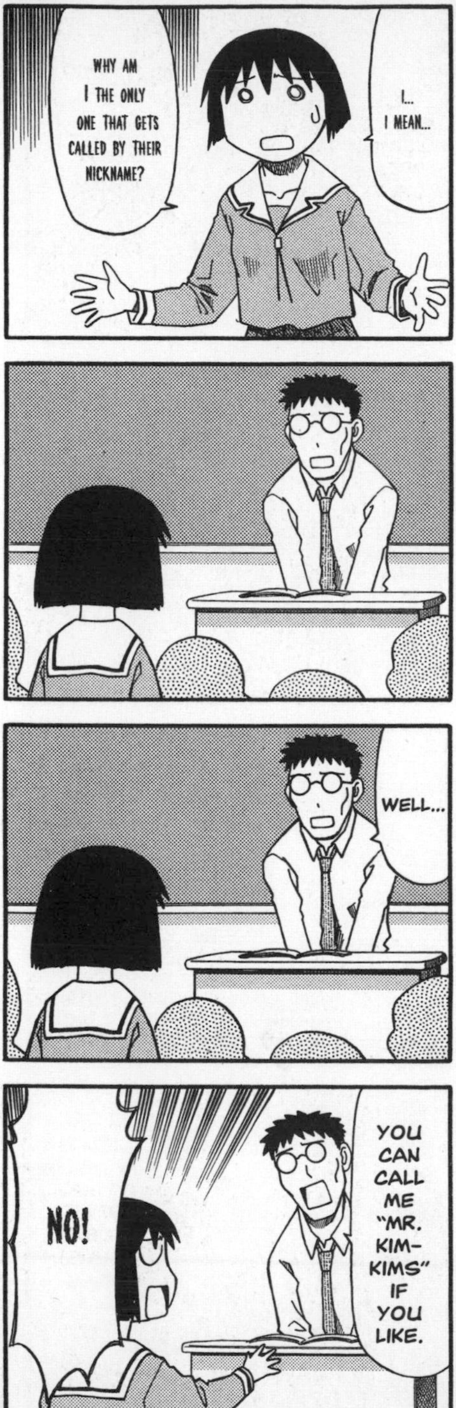
I... I MEAN...
WHY AM I THE ONLY ONE THAT GETS CALLED BY THEIR NICKNAME?
WELL...
YOU CAN CALL ME "MR. KIM-KIMS" IF YOU LIKE.
NO!

LIVE! LIVE FOR ALL YOU'RE WORTH!

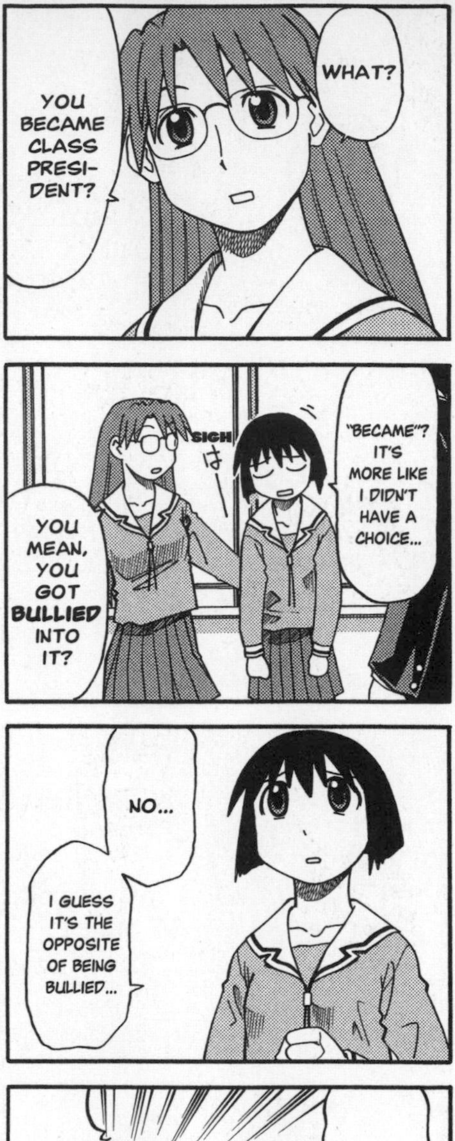
WHAT?
YOU BECAME CLASS PRESIDENT?
"BECAME"? IT'S MORE LIKE I DIDN'T HAVE A CHOICE...
SIGH
は
YOU MEAN, YOU GOT **BULLIED** INTO IT?
NO...
I GUESS IT'S THE OPPOSITE OF BEING BULLIED...
MR. KIMURA... **LIKES** ME!
うう〜
WAAUGH.
AAH! IT'S **WORSE** THAN BEING BULLIED!

FLASHBACK

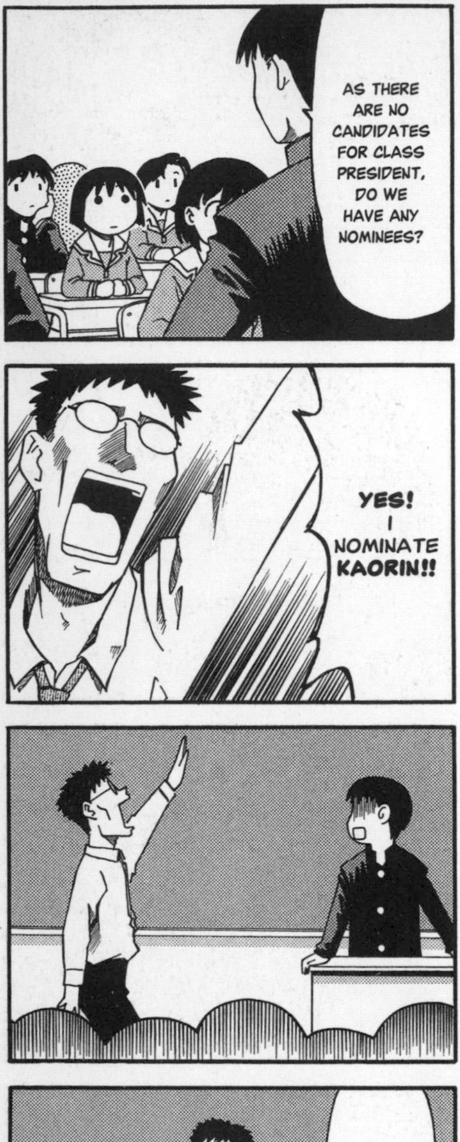
AS THERE ARE NO CANDIDATES FOR CLASS PRESIDENT, DO WE HAVE ANY NOMINEES?
**YES!** I NOMINATE **KAORIN!!**
UH... ANYONE ELSE?

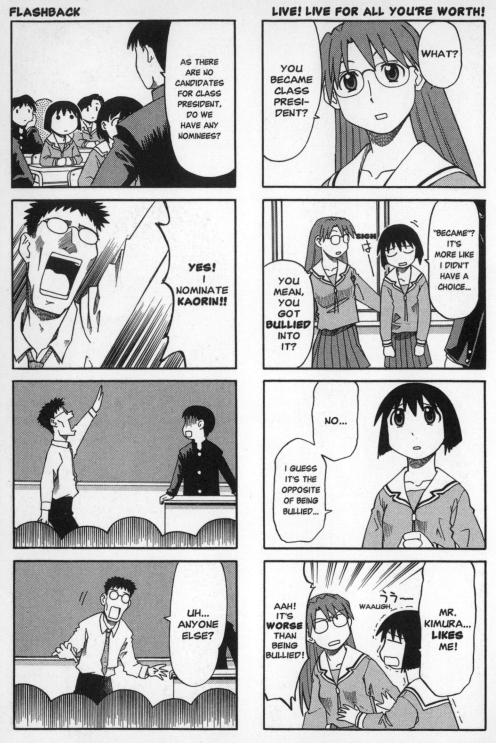

I WONDER IF IT WOULD HURT

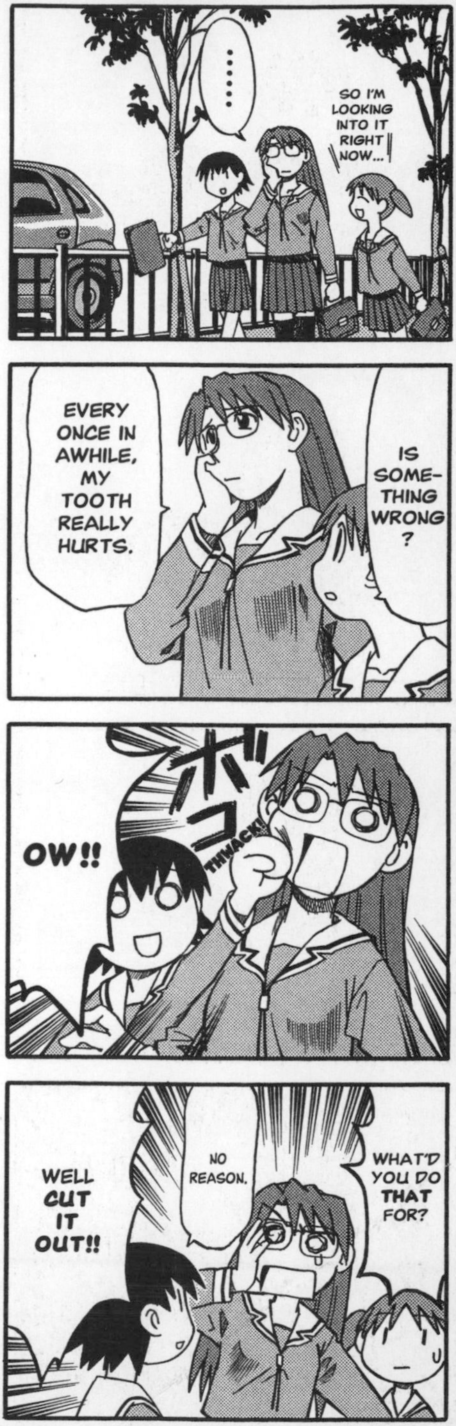
SO I'M LOOKING INTO IT RIGHT NOW...
......
IS SOMETHING WRONG?
EVERY ONCE IN AWHILE, MY TOOTH REALLY HURTS.
ボコ
THWACK!
OW!!
WHAT'D YOU DO THAT FOR?
NO REASON.
WELL CUT IT OUT!!

AN UNFORTUNATE SLIP

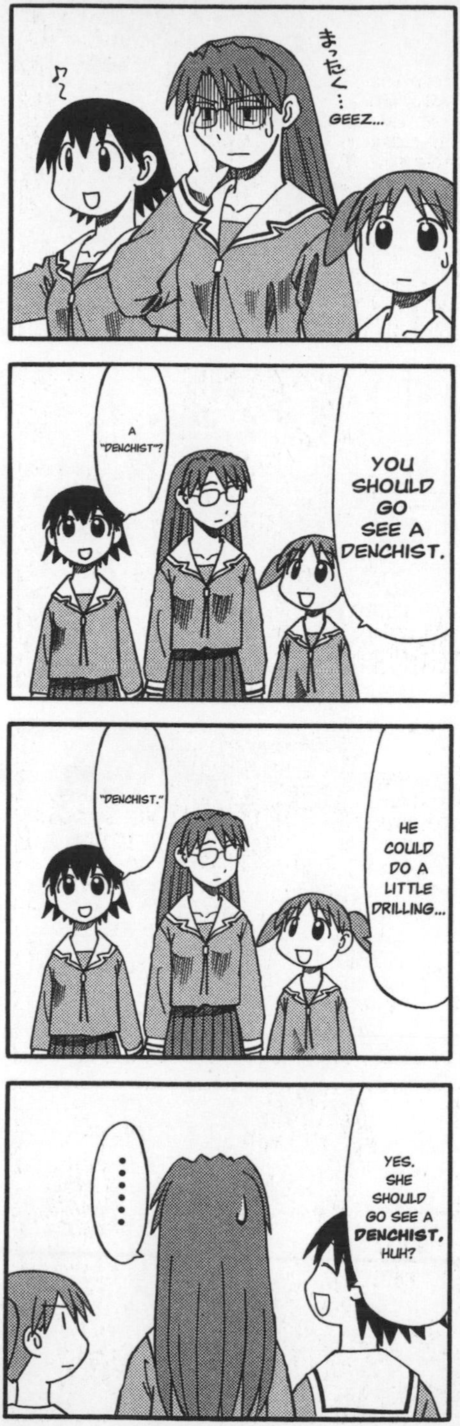
まったく…
GEEZ...
YOU SHOULD GO SEE A DENCHIST.
A "DENCHIST"?
HE COULD DO A LITTLE DRILLING...
"DENCHIST."
YES. SHE SHOULD GO SEE A DENCHIST, HUH?
......

ROLLING FOR SAFETY

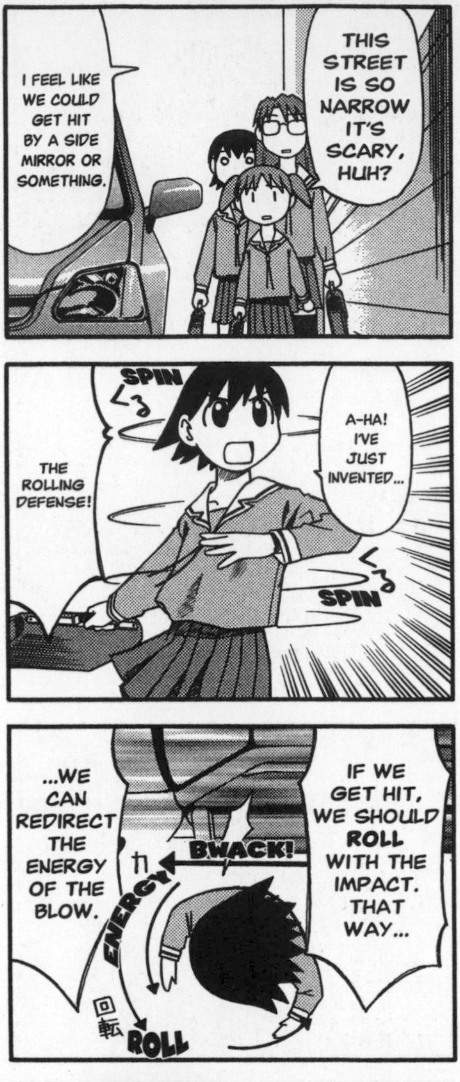
THIS STREET IS SO NARROW IT'S SCARY, HUH?
I FEEL LIKE WE COULD GET HIT BY A SIDE MIRROR OR SOMETHING.
A-HA! I'VE JUST INVENTED...
SPIN くる
THE ROLLING DEFENSE!
SPIN くる
IF WE GET HIT, WE SHOULD **ROLL** WITH THE IMPACT. THAT WAY...
BWACK!
力 ENERGY
回転 ROLL
...WE CAN REDIRECT THE ENERGY OF THE BLOW.
SPIN くる
SPIN くる

ROLLIN'

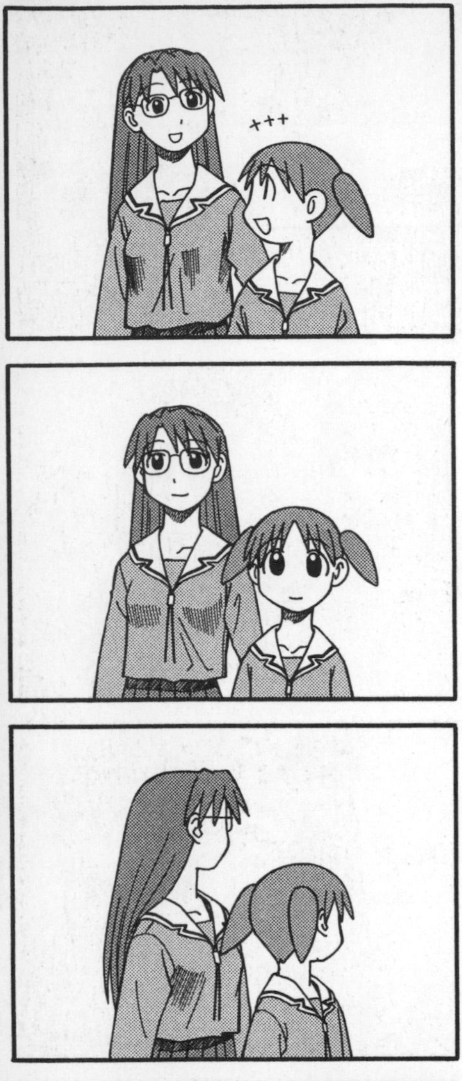
TOMO!!

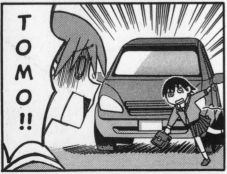

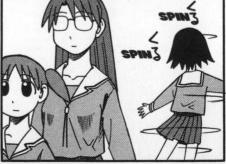

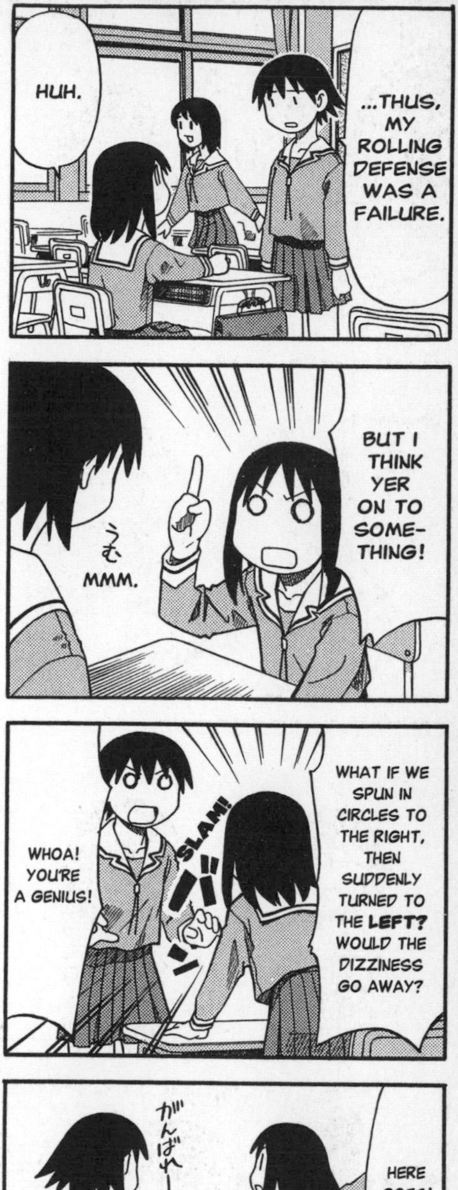
...THUS, MY ROLLING DEFENSE WAS A FAILURE.
HUH.
BUT I THINK YER ON TO SOME-THING!
うむ
MMM.
WHAT IF WE SPUN IN CIRCLES TO THE RIGHT, THEN SUDDENLY TURNED TO THE **LEFT?** WOULD THE DIZZINESS GO AWAY?
SLAM!
WHOA! YOU'RE A GENIUS!
HERE GOES!
がんばれー
DO IT!



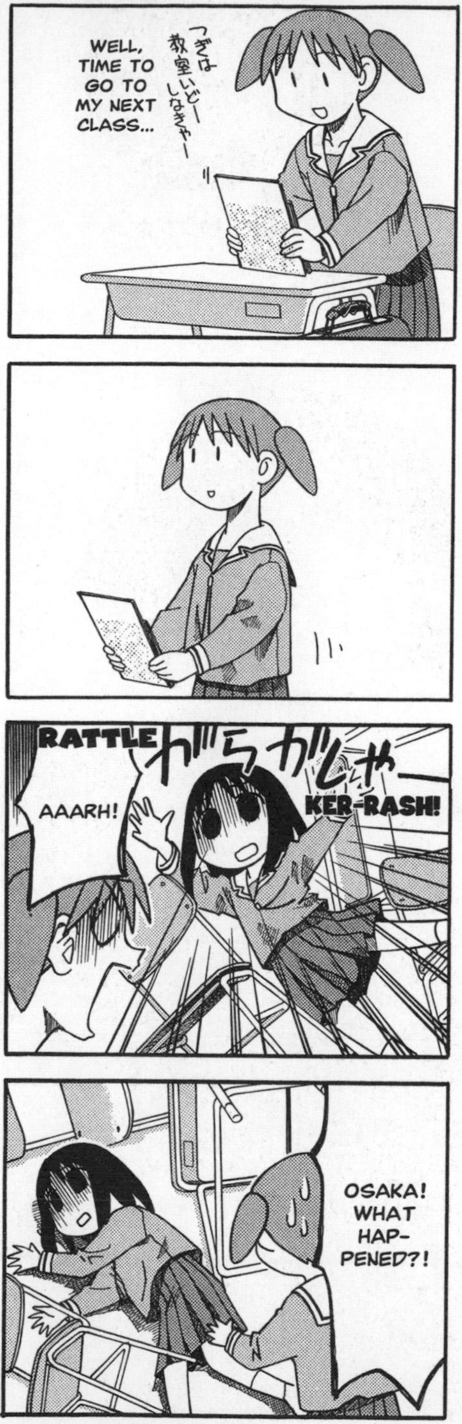
つぎは教室いどーしなきゃー
WELL, TIME TO GO TO MY NEXT CLASS...
RATTLE
KER-RASH!
AAARH!
OSAKA! WHAT HAP-PENED?!

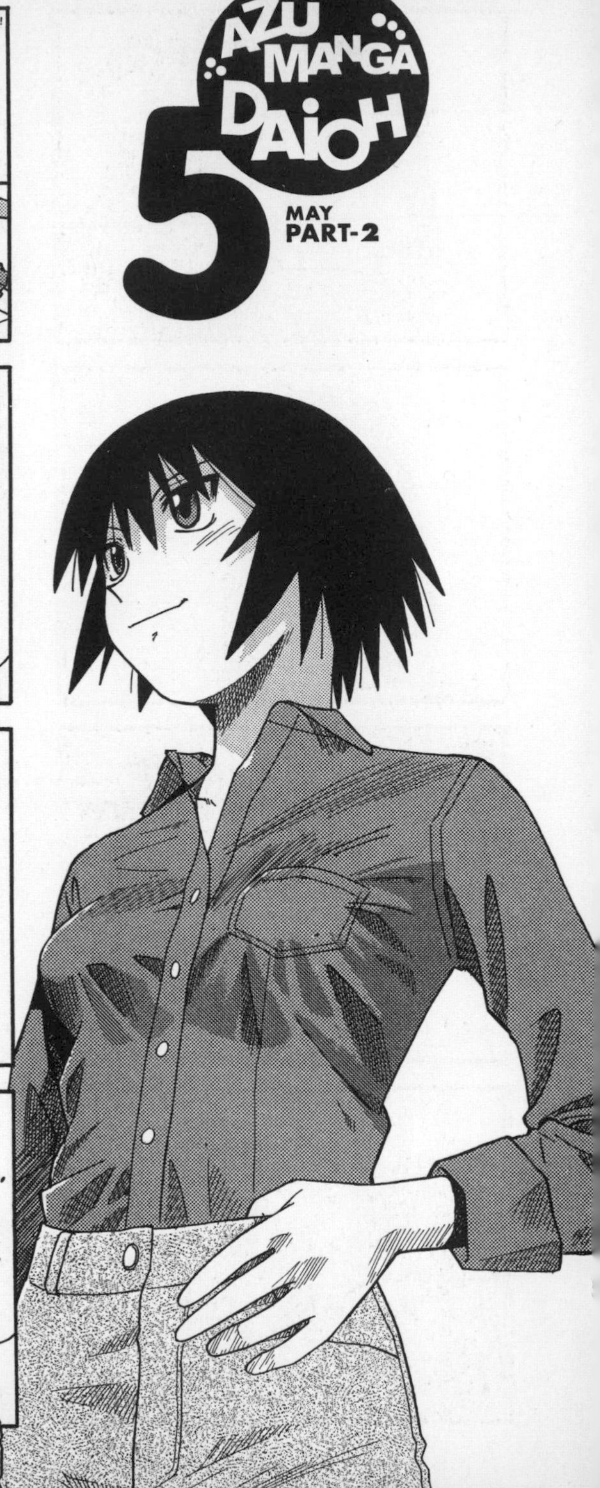
AZU MANGA DAIOH
5
MAY
PART-2

GOTCHA

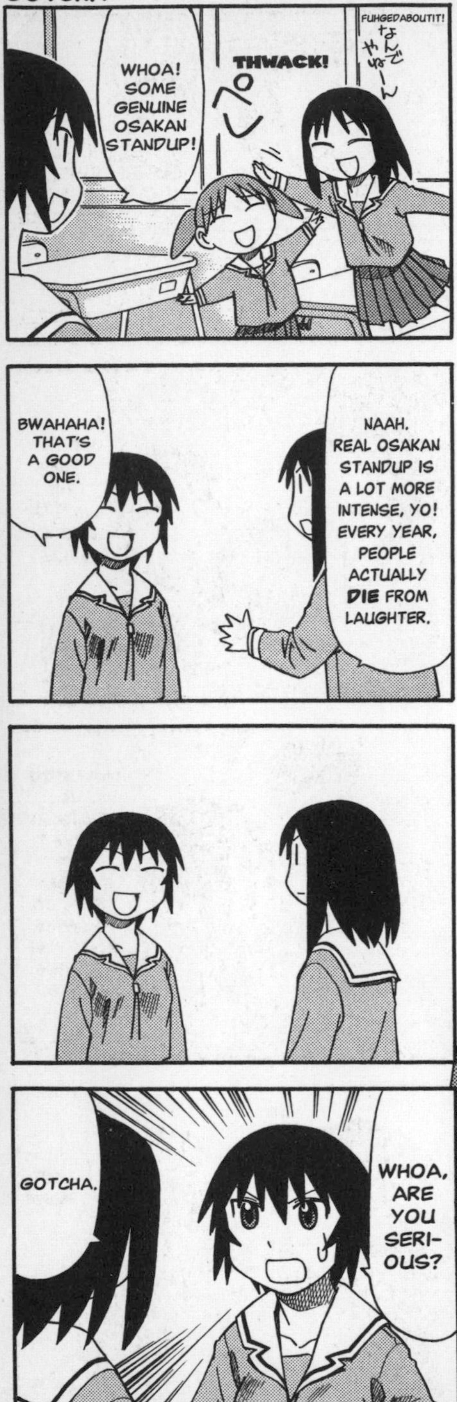
FUHGEDABOUTIT!
なんでやねーん
THWACK!
WHOA! SOME GENUINE OSAKAN STANDUP!
NAAH. REAL OSAKAN STANDUP IS A LOT MORE INTENSE, YO! EVERY YEAR, PEOPLE ACTUALLY **DIE** FROM LAUGHTER.
BWAHAHA! THAT'S A GOOD ONE.
WHOA, ARE YOU SERI-OUS?
GOTCHA.

## TODAY'S CHALLENGE

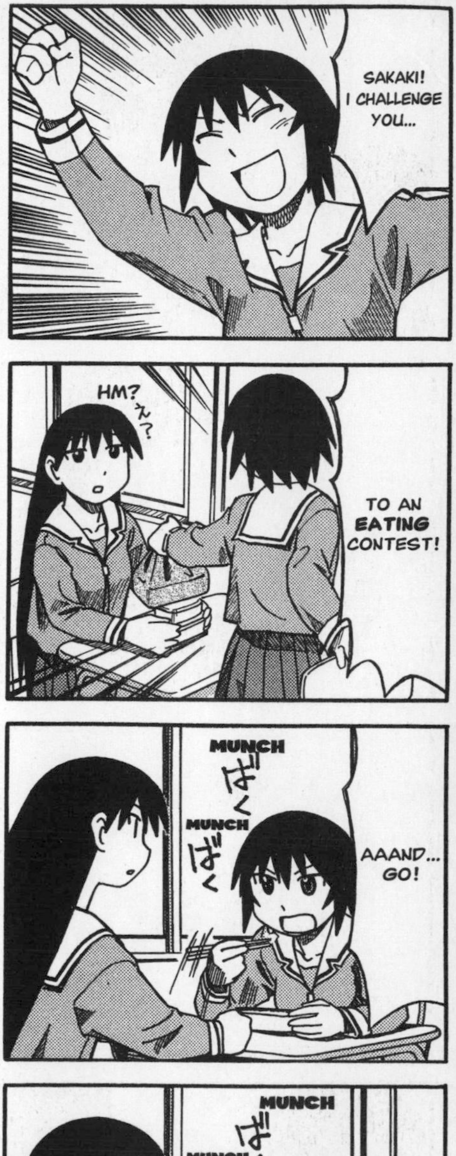
SAKAKI! I CHALLENGE YOU...
HM? え?
TO AN EATING CONTEST!
AAAND... GO!
MUNCH ばく
MUNCH ばく
MUNCH ばく
MUNCH ばく

## APPRECIATION

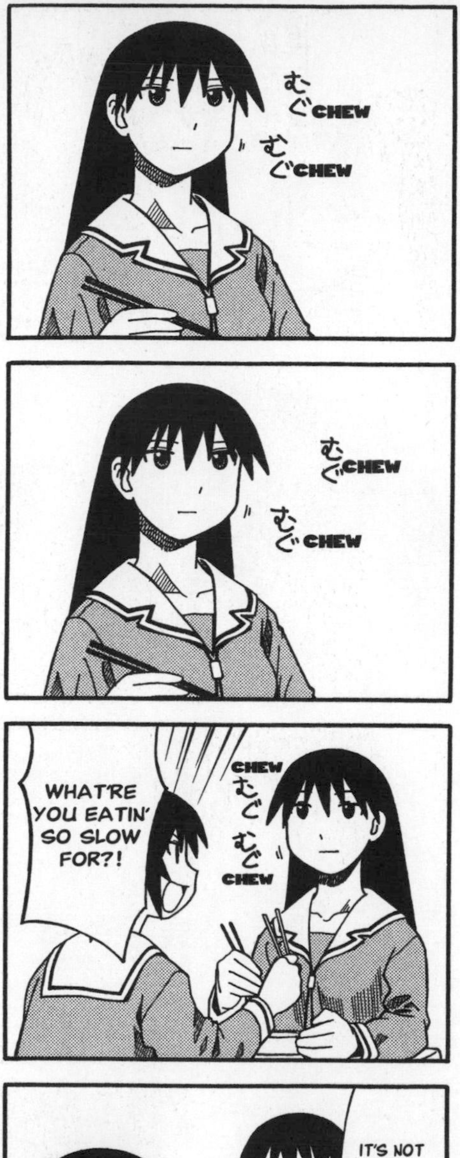
むぐ CHEW
むぐ CHEW
むぐ CHEW
むぐ CHEW
CHEW むぐ
むぐ CHEW
WHAT'RE YOU EATIN' SO SLOW FOR?!
IT'S NOT POLITE TO EAT WITHOUT PROPERLY CHEWING YOUR FOOD.

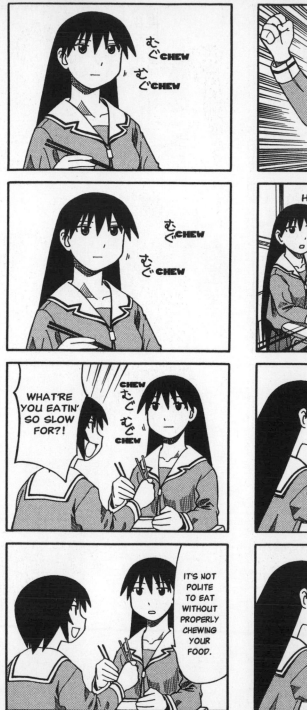

NOTE!

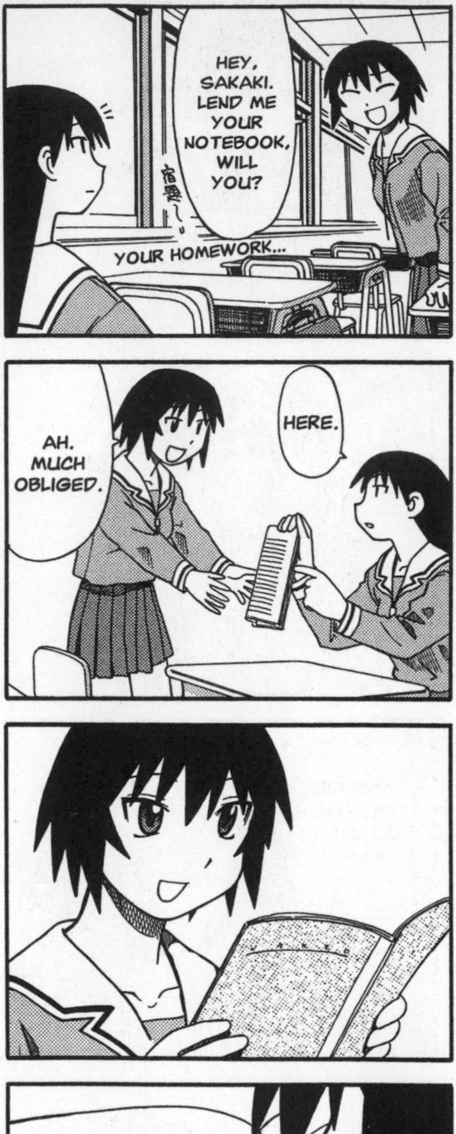
HEY, SAKAKI. LEND ME YOUR NOTEBOOK, WILL YOU?
宿題〜
YOUR HOMEWORK...
HERE.
AH. MUCH OBLIGED.
ポイント
NOTE!
チェック
CHECK!

EVOLUTION

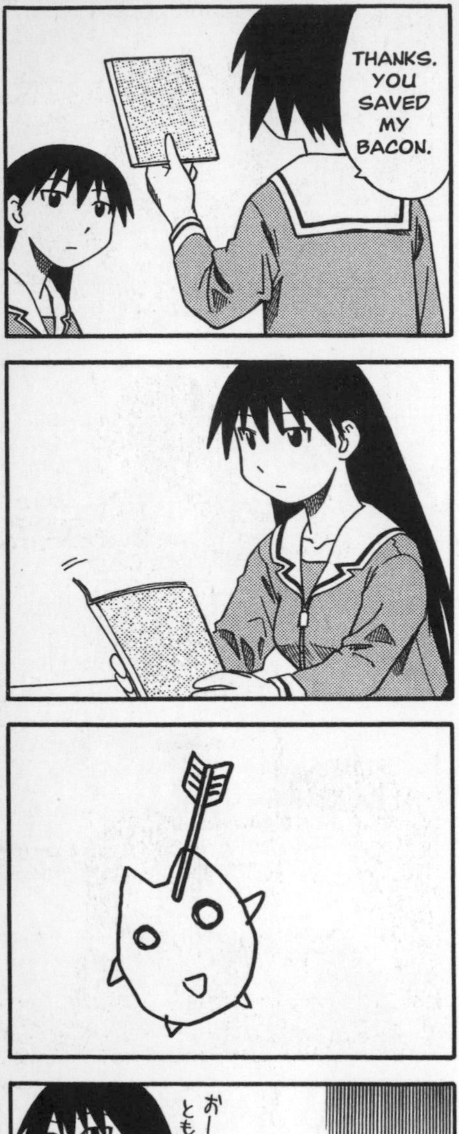
THANKS. YOU SAVED MY BACON.
おーい とも〜
HEY, TOMO!

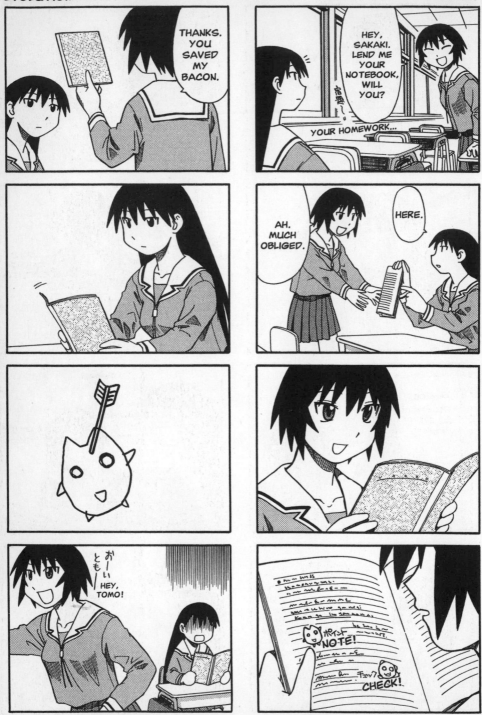

DON'T RUN AWAY!

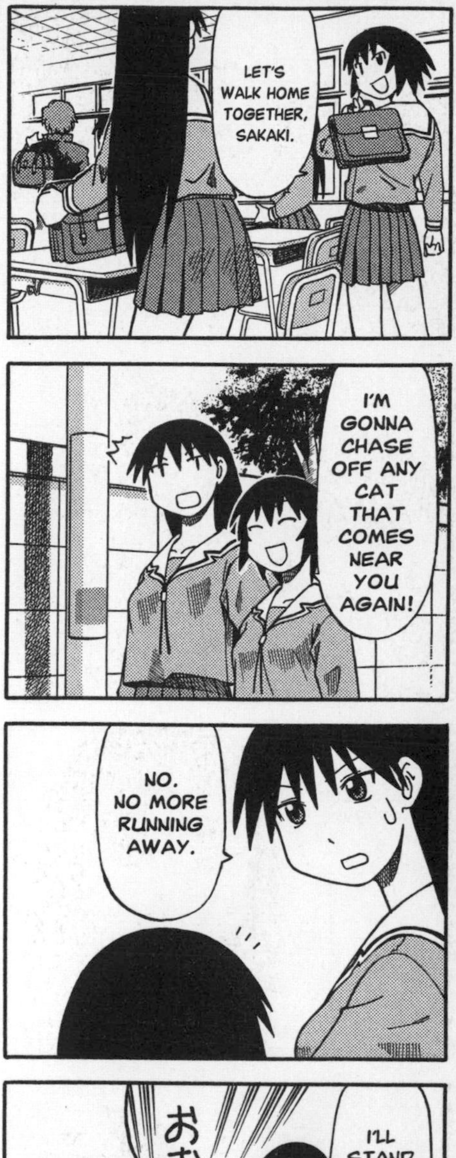
LET'S WALK HOME TOGETHER, SAKAKI.
I'M GONNA CHASE OFF ANY CAT THAT COMES NEAR YOU AGAIN!
NO. NO MORE RUNNING AWAY.
I'LL STAND UP FOR MYSELF! I WILL WIN!
おお WHOA!
THAT'S IT! THAT'S THE SPIRIT!

A CAT!

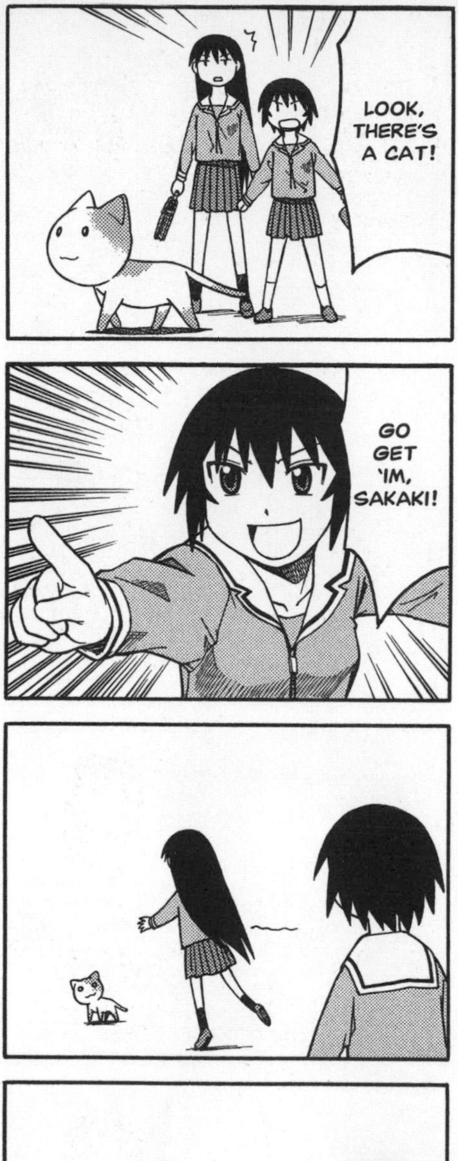
LOOK, THERE'S A CAT!
GO GET 'IM, SAKAKI!

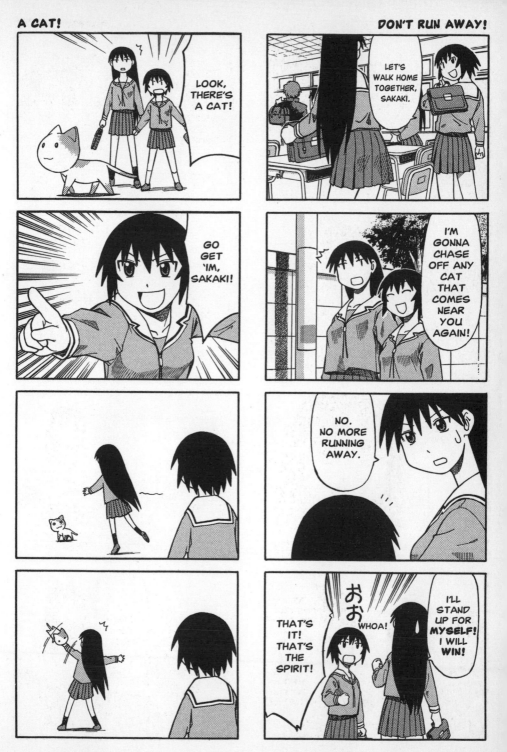

## ACCELERATION

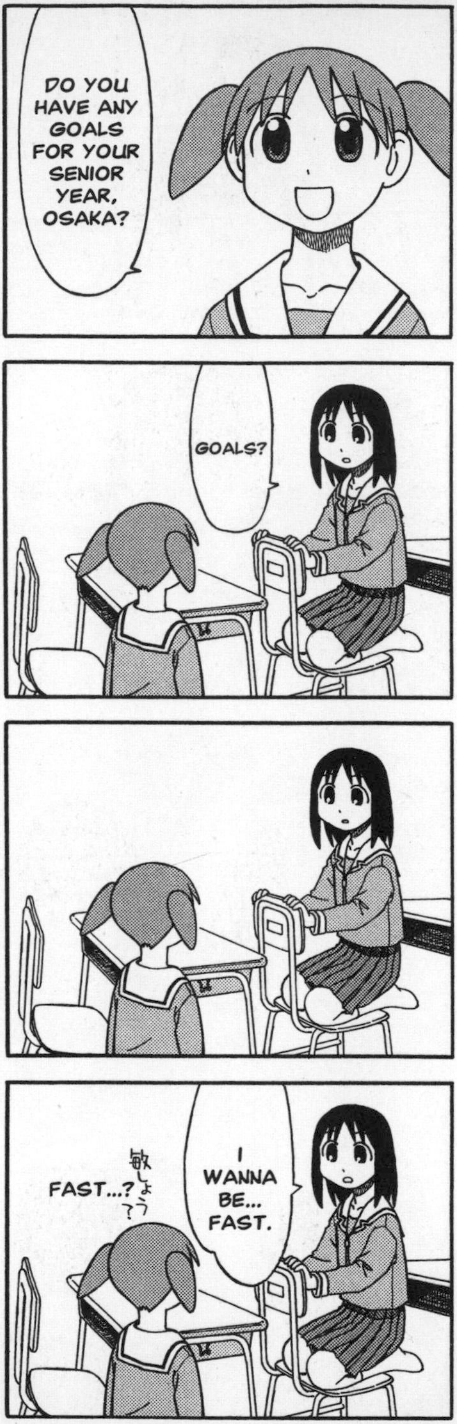

DO YOU HAVE ANY GOALS FOR YOUR SENIOR YEAR, OSAKA?
GOALS?
I WANNA BE... FAST.
FAST...?
敏しょう？


## REGRET

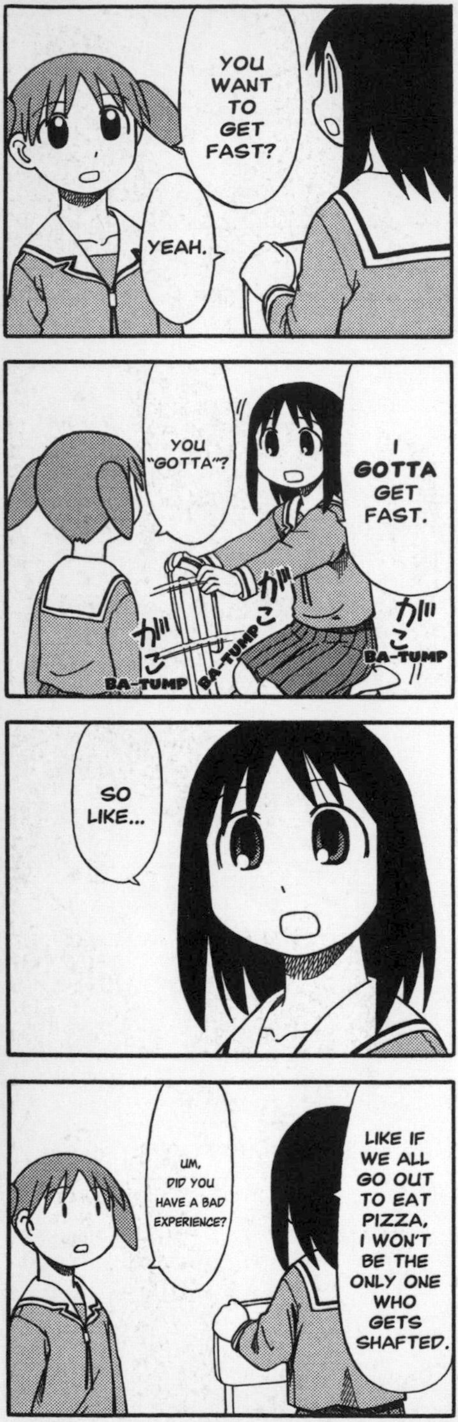

YOU WANT TO GET FAST?
YEAH.
I GOTTA GET FAST.
YOU "GOTTA"?
がこ
BA-TUMP
がこ
BA-TUMP
がこ
BA-TUMP
SO LIKE...
LIKE IF WE ALL GO OUT TO EAT PIZZA, I WON'T BE THE ONLY ONE WHO GETS SHAFTED.
UM, DID YOU HAVE A BAD EXPERIENCE?

FLYING START

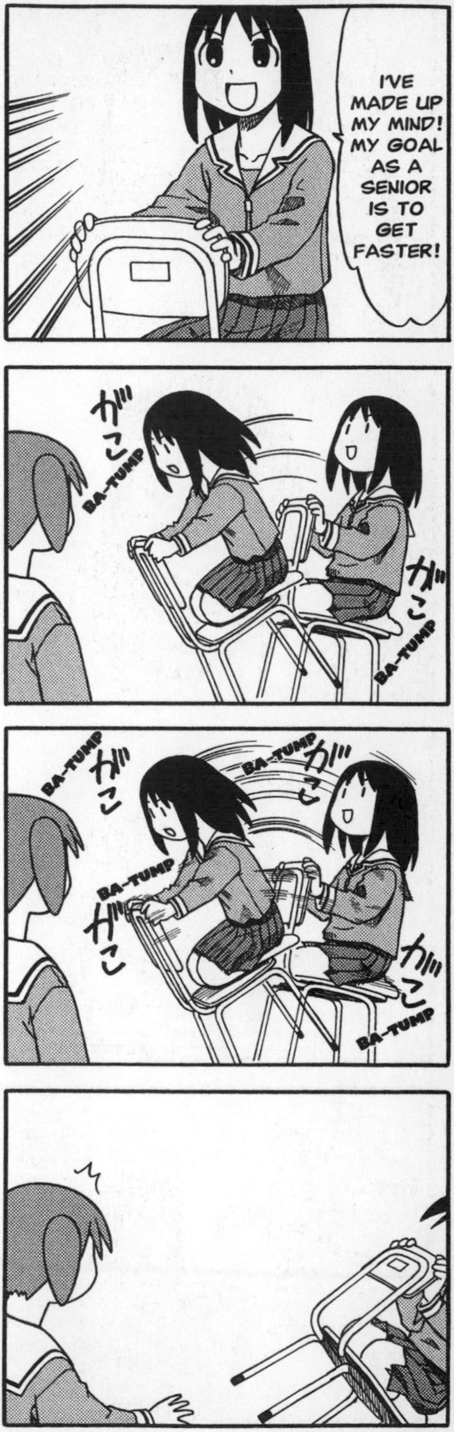
I'VE MADE UP MY MIND! MY GOAL AS A SENIOR IS TO GET FASTER!
がこ
BA-TUMP
がこ
BA-TUMP
BA-TUMP
がこ
BA-TUMP
がこ
BA-TUMP
がこ
がこ
BA-TUMP

LOOKIN' STRONG

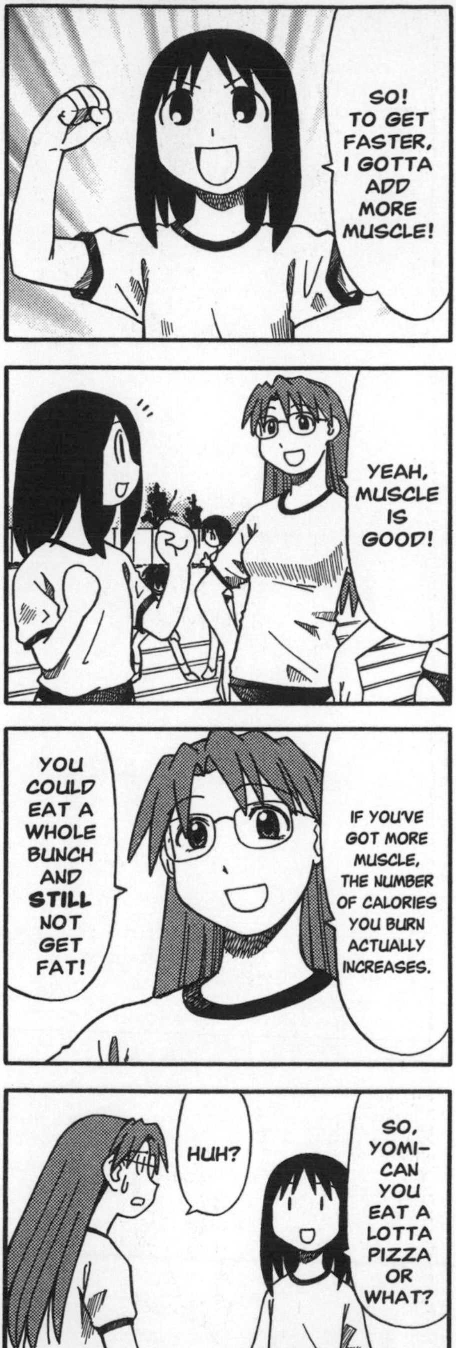
SO! TO GET FASTER, I GOTTA ADD MORE MUSCLE!
YEAH, MUSCLE IS GOOD!
IF YOU'VE GOT MORE MUSCLE, THE NUMBER OF CALORIES YOU BURN ACTUALLY INCREASES.
YOU COULD EAT A WHOLE BUNCH AND **STILL** NOT GET FAT!
SO, YOMI- CAN YOU EAT A LOTTA PIZZA OR WHAT?
HUH?

DIFFICULTY

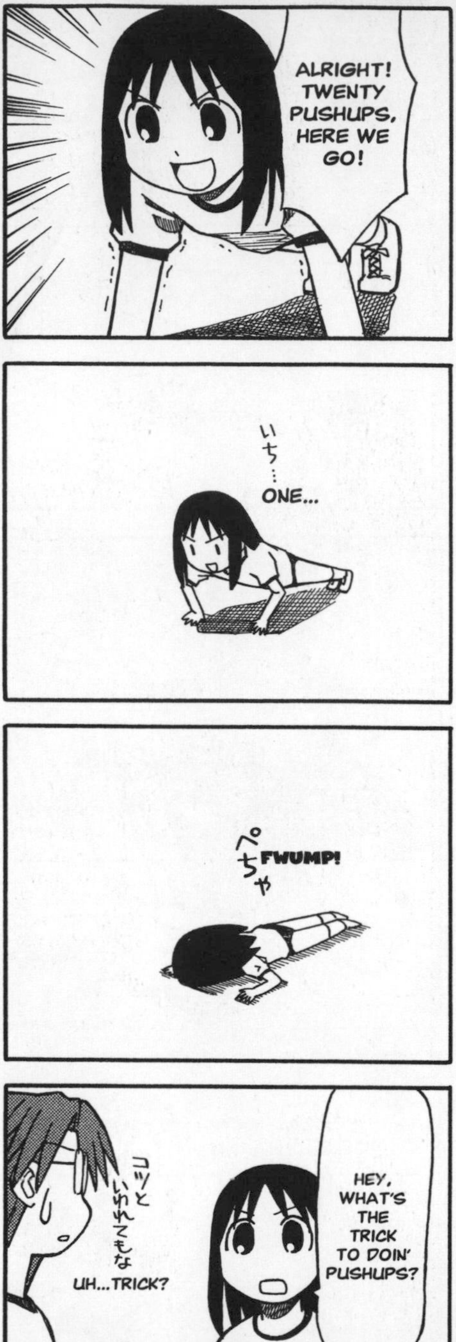
ALRIGHT! TWENTY PUSHUPS, HERE WE GO!
いち…
ONE...
ぺちゃ
FWUMP!
HEY, WHAT'S THE TRICK TO DOIN' PUSHUPS?
コツといわれてもな
UH...TRICK?

SWITCHING GEARS

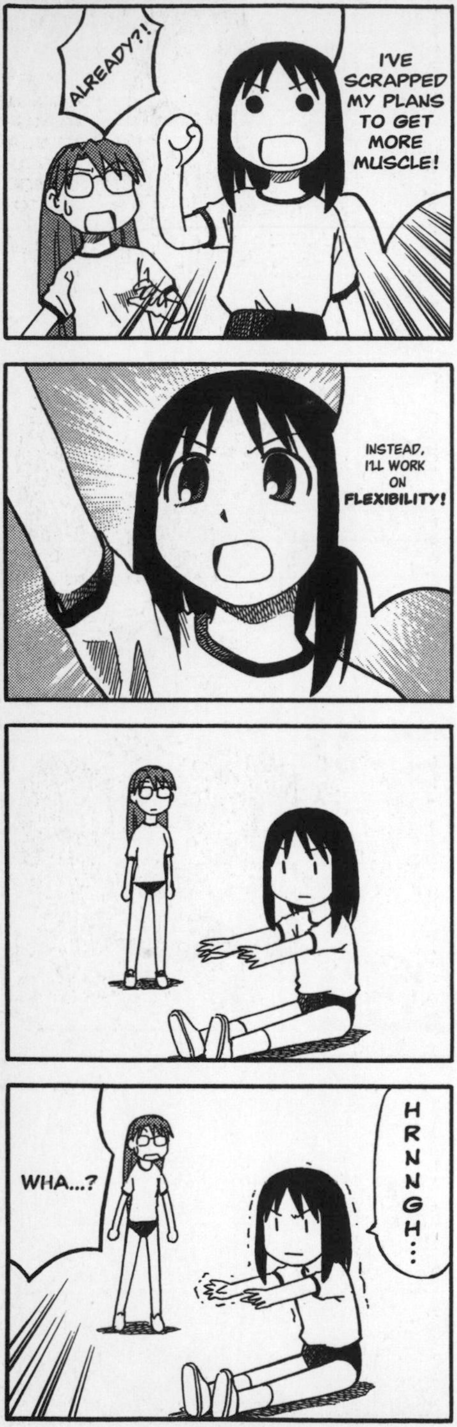
I'VE SCRAPPED MY PLANS TO GET MORE MUSCLE!
ALREADY?!
INSTEAD, I'LL WORK ON FLEXIBILITY!
HRNNGH...
WHA...?

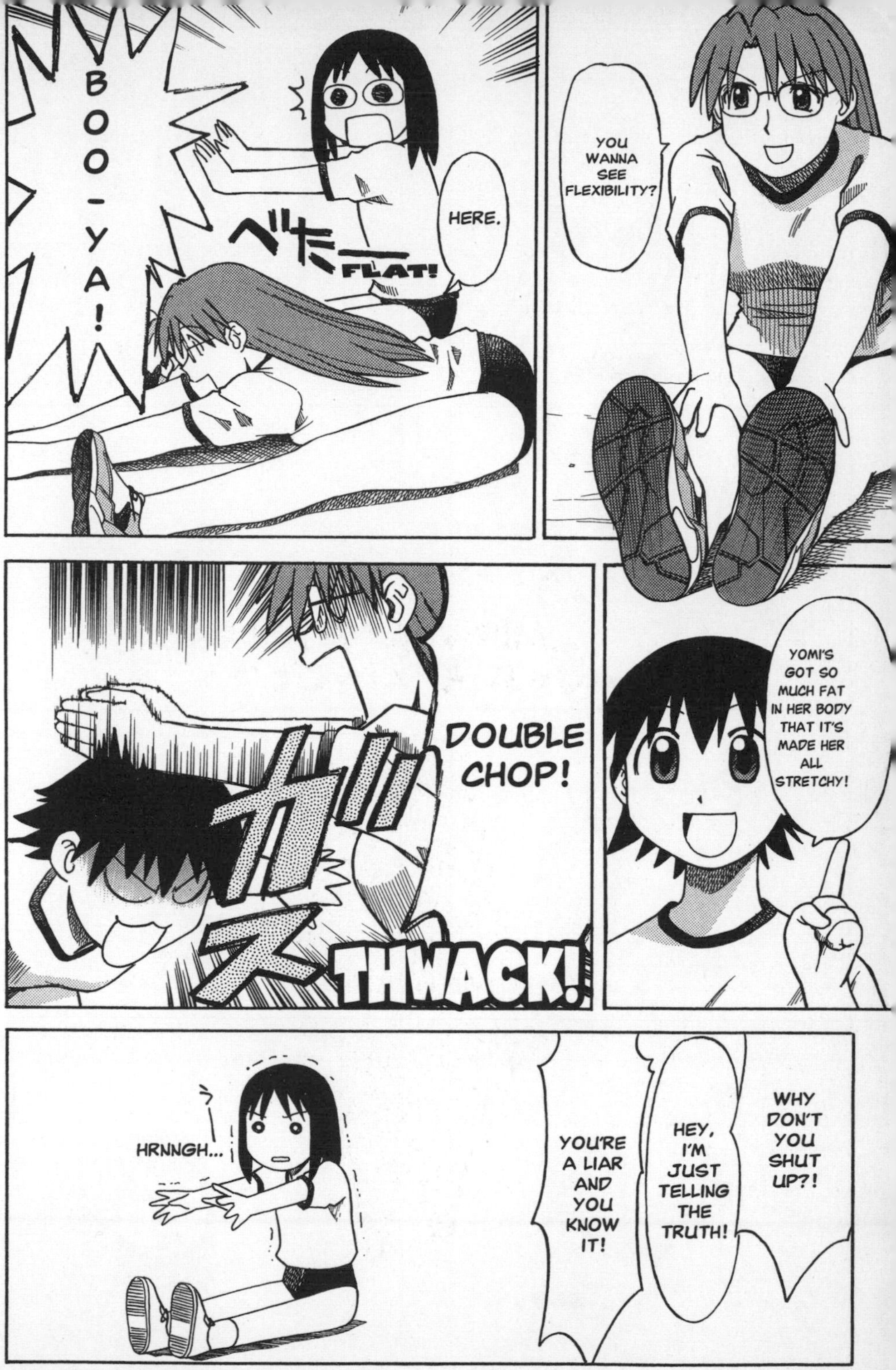
YOU WANNA SEE FLEXIBILITY?
HERE.
べたー
FLAT!
BOO-YA!
YOMI'S GOT SO MUCH FAT IN HER BODY THAT IT'S MADE HER ALL STRETCHY!
DOUBLE CHOP!
ガス
THWACK!
WHY DON'T YOU SHUT UP?!
HEY, I'M JUST TELLING THE TRUTH!
YOU'RE A LIAR AND YOU KNOW IT!
HRNNGH...

...AND THAT'S ALL.
じゃあ、そういうことで。

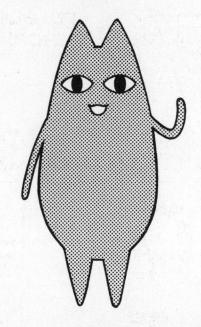

# Azumanga Daioh Volume Three

© KIYOHIKO AZUMA 2001
First published in 2001 by MEDIA WORKS, Inc., Tokyo, Japan.

English translation rights arranged with MEDIA WORKS, Inc.

Translator  JAVIER LOPEZ
ADV Manga Translation Staff  KAY BERTRAND, AMY FORSYTH, BRENDAN FRAYNE, and EIKO McGREGOR
Print Production Manager/Art Studio Manager  LISA PUCKETT
Graphic Design  WINDI MARTIN, SHANNON RASBERRY
Logo Design  FUMIKO CHINO
Graphic Artists  JORGE ALVARADO, RYAN MASON, WINDI MARTIN, KRISTINA MILESKI, GEORGE REYNOLDS
International Coordinators  TORU IWAKAMI, ATSUSHI KANBAYASHI

Publishing Editor  SUSAN ITIN
Assistant Editor  MARGARET SCHAROLD
Editorial Assistant  VARSHA BHUCHAR
Proofreader  SHERIDAN JACOBS
Traffic Coordinator  MARSHA ARNOLD

President, C.E.O. & Publisher  JOHN LEDFORD

Email: editor@adv-manga.com
www.adv-manga.com
www.advfilms.com

For sales and distribution inquiries please call 1.800.282.7202

 is a division of A.D. Vision, Inc.
10114 W. Sam Houston Parkway, Suite 200, Houston, Texas 77099

ISBN: 1-4139-0030-5

First printing, February 2004
10 9 8 7 6 5 4 3 2
Printed in Canada

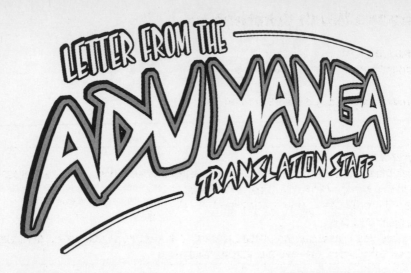

# LETTER FROM THE ADV MANGA TRANSLATION STAFF

Dear Reader,

On behalf of the ADV Manga translation team, thank you for purchasing an ADV book. We are enthusiastic and committed to our work, and strive to carry our enthusiasm over into the book you hold in your hands.

Our goal is to retain the true spirit of the original Japanese book. While great care has been taken to render a true and accurate translation, some cultural or readability issues may require a line to be adapted for greater accessibility to our readers. At times, manga titles that include culturally-specific concepts will feature a "Translator's Notes" section, which explains noteworthy references to the original text.

We hope our commitment to a faithful translation is evident in every ADV book you purchase.

Sincerely,

**Javier Lopez,**
Lead Translator

**Eiko McGregor**

**Kay Bertrand**

**Brendan Frayne**

**Amy Forsyth**

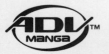

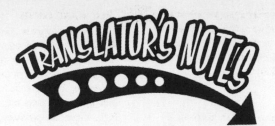

# TRANSLATOR'S NOTES

## Azumanga Daioh Vol 03

 **PG. 39** **What's the story, morning glory?**

In the original Japanese, "Good Morning Musume!" Morning Musume is a girl-pop band that's quite popular in Japan. For more about the band, see their official website: **http://www.morningmusumeonline.com/**

**PG. 41-2** **Nurikabe and Karakasa**

Monsters from Japanese folklore are pretty different from their Western counterparts, and range from the horrific to the just plain weird. Nurikabe is an invisible wall that enjoys blocking the paths of would-be travelers. In its visible form, it appears as a wall with limbs. Karakasa looks like a one-eyed, one-legged parasol, which explains why Osaka was hopping while trying to carry her tray.

**PG. 65** **Be not late for thine own class**

In the Japanese, this was originally *shiwasu*, which actually means the end of the year. The word is made up of the second character in "teacher" and the character meaning "to run." Thus, Kimura thought it was the height of hilarity that a teacher would actually be running at this time of year.

**PG. 67** **What Year will it be?**

This is referring to the Chinese zodiac, which is commonly referenced in Japan at the start of the New Year, or in asking when someone was born.

**PG. 82** **Hawks, eggplants and Mt. Fuji**

In Japan, New Year's dreams of hawks, eggplants or Mt. Fuji (or a combination of the three) are said to bring good luck for the rest of the year.

**PG. 6** **Numbnuts**

The word used in the Japanese was *bonkura*, a term that originated from a form of gambling popular in the Edo period. Two dice were placed inside a bowl called a *bon*. The *bon* would be shaken and people would place bets on whether the numbers on the two dice would equal an odd or even number. The winnings would then be divvied up by the referee, who was called a *chubon*. If the *chubon* couldn't quickly and accurately do the necessary math, he was called *bon ni kurai*, or "Dim when it comes to the *bon*." *Bon ni kurai* corrupted into simply *bonkura*, and today it refers to someone who isn't the sharpest tack in the box.

Kagura used the term *bonkuras*, an English-influenced pluralization of the word. "Numbnuts" was chosen not only for its closeness to the modern meaning of *bonkura*, but because it ends in "s" (which, as we saw, was instrumental in having it refer to both Tomo and Osaka).

**PG. 7** **Ultra-Osaka**

Osaka's mask is of the perennial Japanese superhero Ultraman. For more on this long-running series, see the excellent site Absolute Ultraman! at www.waynebrain.com/ultra/

**PG. 22** **Ham and bacon**

The original Japanese read, "So, they're as different as curry and *hayashi rice*?" Japanese curry is more like spiced gravy with vegetables, and quite different from what you'll find at genuine Indian restaurants (which is in no way meant deprecatingly—it's rockingly delicious). *Hayashi* ("hashed") rice is quite similar to Japanese curry, hence Sakaki's confusion.

PG. 85 **Nice warm room**

In the original Japanese, Chiyo-chan stated that she did nothing but lounge around under the *kotatsu*. A *kotatsu* is a table set low to the ground that has a heating element built into the underside. A heavy comforter is then draped over it, and one stays warm by sticking one's legs under the *kotatsu* and pulling the comforter to the waist or neck. The *kotatsu* is a mainstay of Japanese homes because of the lack of central air and heating.

PG. 86-9 **Crabs, bears and Genghis Khan**

Hokkaido, Japan's northernmost (and coldest) island, is famous for a variety of foods. One of these is crab, and all-you-can eat crab buffets are a big tourist draw. For more on the foods of Hokkaido, see the Sapporo Koiki-ken Kumiai homepage (in English) here: **http://www.kouiki.chuo.sapporo.jp/foreign-language/english/002_living/living_04.html**

**p/s –** "Bear curry" is real. The drawing in the comic is an accurate depiction of the label.

PG. 91 **Karurusu**

An actual hot spring in Noboribetsu, Hokkaido. The radium-rich waters are like those of the famed Karlovy Vary spa in the Czech Republic, from which the name "Karurusu" is said to have come.

PG. 93 **No patterns**

Japanese schools have rigidly enforced dress codes, one of which is that any additional clothes worn over one's school uniform must be solid colors, free from patterns.

PG. 94 **Old Navy and Target**

The original Japanese referenced UNIQLO (a Japanese clothing company that, while actively operating in the UK, may or may not be familiar to our English-language audience at large) and Mujirushi Ryohin, a company that produces a wide variety of goods at low prices (the name means "brand-nameless goods"). Old Navy and Target were chosen as substitutes for name recognition as well as similarity in store atmosphere (though, truthfully speaking, Mujirushi Ryohin feels more like a Bed, Bath and Beyond).

This substitution of names is no way meant to disrespect either UNIQLO or Mujirushi Ryohin. I've spent quite a bit of time in both stores, and if you're ever in Japan, I highly recommend that you stop by and do a little shopping.

PG. 101 **Ramen**

If your only exposure to this dish has been the instant variety then you don't know what you're missing. Ramen is an incredibly tasty dish that is big business in Japan—famous restaurants will have customers lined up around the block, waiting for over an hour to sit down and have a bowl of those hot, delicious noodles. For a glimpse of the breadth and appeal of ramen, **www.worldramen.net** is an absolute must-visit.

PG. 104 **Soba**

Another kind of Japanese noodle dish. See the "Noodle Variations" section of worldramen.net for more.

PG. 121 **(1) Fujiko Mine**

The incredibly busty Fujiko appears in the popular ***Lupin the 3rd*** anime series (from creator Monkey Punch). Tomo mentioned in Volume 2 how she thought Fujiko possessed the ultimate female form, and that all she (Tomo) lacked to replicate that form was the chest.

**(2) Ryoko Hirosue**

Though she has been active in the entertainment industry since 1994, it was around 1999 that this teen model suddenly leapt to superstardom, appearing in numerous commercials and television dramas. She also appeared in the well-received ***Poppoya*** ("Railroad Man") alongside the legendary Ken Takakura. Ryoko's official homepage (in Japanese) is: **www.ryoko-hirosue.org/**

**(3) HER, get a boyfriend?!**

While in the West we may associate a haircut with the turning of some new leaf, in Japan there is the idea that a girl will get a haircut if she's been dumped by her boyfriend. The joke was changed slightly to make it more culturally accessible.

### PG. 134 Whatcha doin'?!

The original Japanese read something like, "What are you supposed to be? A barker?" If you've spent any time in Japan (or Mexico, for that matter) then you're well accustomed to the barkers—the people that stand outside their places of employment and call out to passersby, urging them to come in. For some reason, Tomo (who's admittedly something of a *bonkura*) thought that Kagura was off to do some barking. The line was changed not only for space considerations, but for the fact that some may not be familiar with what a "barker" is.

### PG. 136 Tokyo University

Often referred to as "Japan's Harvard," this university is considered *the* most prestigious school in the country.

### PG. 137 (1) The homeless hermit crab

This is a direct translation of the original Japanese, which is a play on the words *yadonashi* (homeless) and *yadogari* (hermit crab). It was kept as-is because the idea of a hermit crab (which is distinguished by its large shell) being without a home (the aforementioned shell) was pretty amusing.

### (2) Big winter quilts

This, too, was originally *kotatsu* (see note for p. 85). In both instances, the change was because not everyone may be familiar with the venerable *kotatsu*.

### PG. 138 Filet mignon buns

In the original Japanese, Tomo asked Chiyo-chan if she liked *fukahire* (shark's fin). While chances are high that you've heard of shark's fin soup, the image of that dish probably fails to convey the way that *fukahire* is considered to be a delicacy—and an expensive one at that. In Japan, shark's fin can range from tens to hundreds of dollars for a single dish.

### PG. 139 Tofu originated in China

In the Japanese, Osaka stated, "Edamame are actually soybeans!" Edamame are the salted "green beans" served as a snack at Japanese pubs and some sushi restaurants. This was changed because not all of our readers may be familiar with edamame. In Japan, however, it is common knowledge that they *are* soybeans—thus, "Tofu is originally from China" was chosen as a similar bit of knowledge that should be commonly known by any Japanese native.

### PG. 140 That's not trivia, it's just plain trivial

In the Japanese, Osaka announced *Mame-chishiki!* (rendered as "Trivia!") before launching into her soybean anecdote. *Mame-chishiki* refers to a piece of information, with *chishiki* meaning "information" and *mame* literally meaning "bean." Thus, Osaka wanted someone to slap her with a zinger like "That's not *mame-chishiki* (a piece of information), it's *mame* no *chishiki* (information about beans).

### PG. 148 Kaorin and Mr. Kim-kims

"Kaorin" isn't a name—it's a nickname. That word-final "n" is a diminutive that implies cuteness and closeness. In the Japanese, Mr. Kimura said that Kaorin could call him "Kimurin," which doesn't have quite the same punch in English. Hence, "Mr. Kim-kims."

### PG. 152 Genuine Osakan standup

This is referring to *manzai*, a form of two-man standup strongly associated with Western Japan in general and Osaka (the city) in particular. "Fuhgedaboutit!" in Japanese is *nandeyanen*, a dialectical phrase that means simply "Why?" but has such a comedic (and belittling) sound that it is often used as a punchline.

### PG. 152 Pizza

This was changed from Korean barbecue, as not everyone may be familiar with the concept. Basically everyone pitches in for a tray of sliced meat that they grab with their chopsticks and fry up on a heated grill. Obviously the faster you cook and eat, the more meat you can devour. This is the same basic concept of everyone pitching in for a pizza and the slower eaters getting an unequal share of the slices.

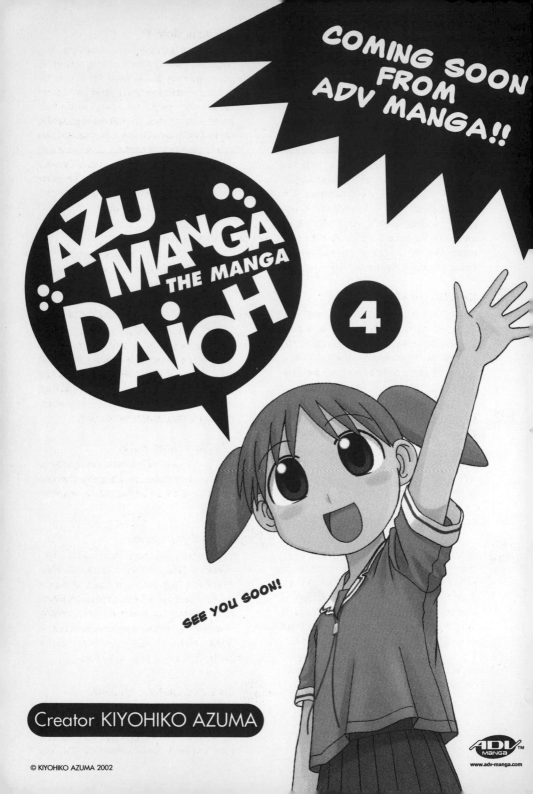

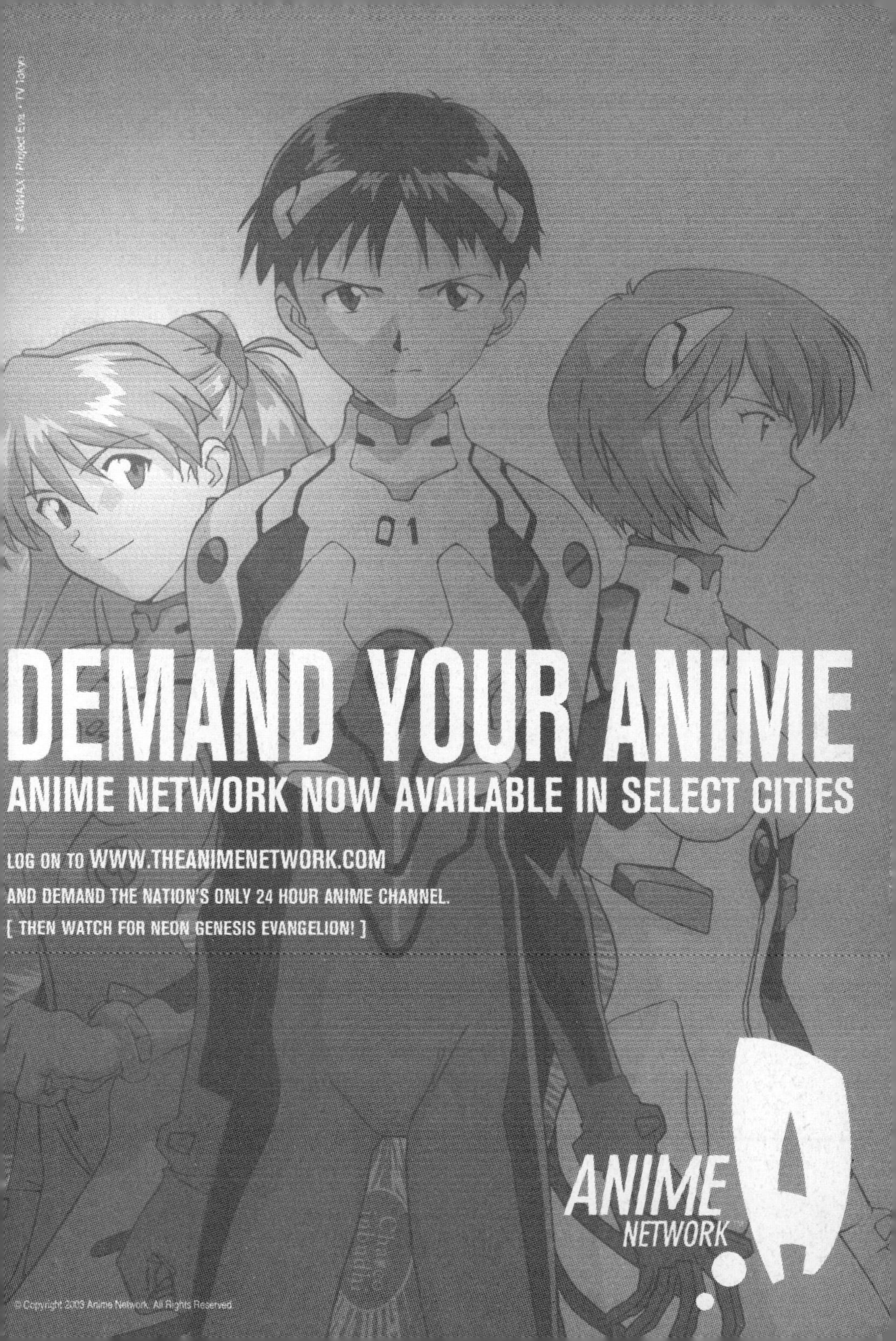
DEMAND YOUR ANIME
ANIME NETWORK NOW AVAILABLE IN SELECT CITIES
LOG ON TO WWW.THEANIMENETWORK.COM
AND DEMAND THE NATION'S ONLY 24 HOUR ANIME CHANNEL.
[ THEN WATCH FOR NEON GENESIS EVANGELION! ]
ANIME NETWORK
© GAINAX · Project Eva. · TV Tokyo
© Copyright 2003 Anime Network. All Rights Reserved.

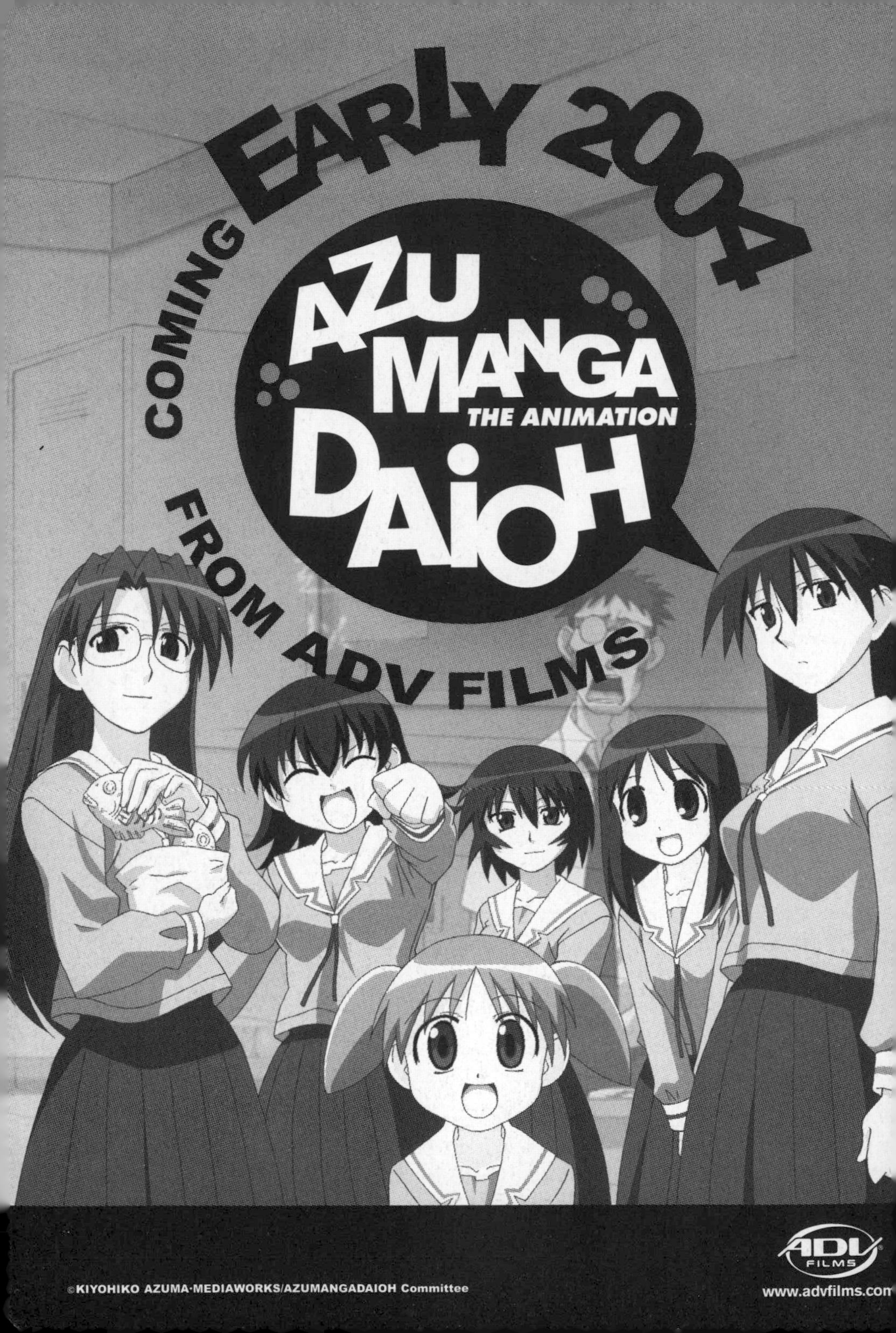
COMING EARLY 2004
AZU MANGA DAIOH
THE ANIMATION
FROM ADV FILMS
ADV FILMS
©KIYOHIKO AZUMA·MEDIAWORKS/AZUMANGADAIOH Committee
www.advfilms.com

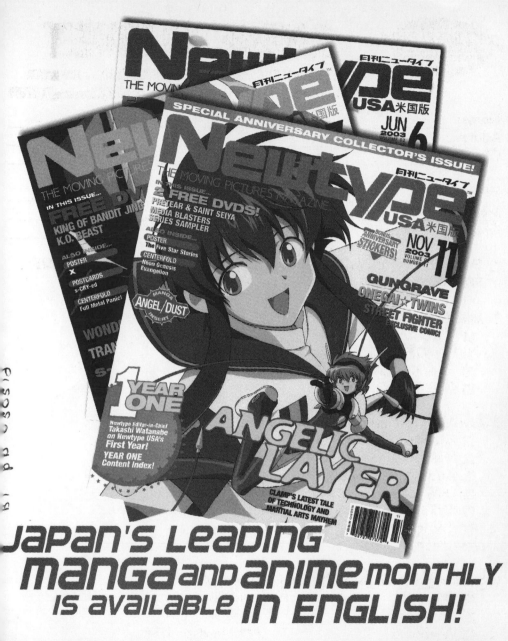

# JaPaN's LeaDING
# maNGa aND aNime mONTHLY
# IS aVaILaBLE IN ENGLISH!

**Packed with exclusive insider information, features and reviews, plus a manga insert, free DVDs, posters, postcards and much, much more! Available at bookstores, specialty shops and newsstands everywhere, or subscribe online today for huge savings off the cover price!**

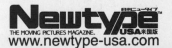

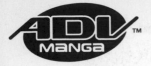

# A IM- I :V Y

**PLEASE MAIL THE COMPLETED FORM TO:** EDITOR – ADV MANGA
℅ A.D. Vision, Inc. 10114 W. Sam Houston Pkwy., Suite 200 Houston, TX 77099

Name: _____

Address: _____

City: State: Zip: _____

E-Mail: _____

Male ☐ Female ☐     Age: _____

Cable Provider: _____

☐ **CHECK HERE IF YOU WOULD LIKE TO RECEIVE OTHER INFORMATION OR FUTURE OFFERS FROM ADV.**

**1. Annual Household Income** (*Check only one*)
- ☐ Under $25,000
- ☐ $25,000 to $50,000
- ☐ $50,000 to $75,000
- ☐ Over $75,000

**2. How do you hear about new Anime releases?** (*Check all that apply*)
- ☐ Browsing in Store
- ☐ Internet Reviews
- ☐ Anime News Websites
- ☐ Direct Email Campaigns
- ☐ Online forums (message boards and chat rooms)
- ☐ Carrier pigeon
- ☐ Other:_____
- ☐ Magazine Ad
- ☐ Online Advertising
- ☐ Conventions
- ☐ TV Advertising

**3. Which magazines do you read?** (*Check all that apply*)
- ☐ Wizard
- ☐ SPIN
- ☐ Animerica
- ☐ Rolling Stone
- ☐ Maxim
- ☐ DC Comics
- ☐ URB
- ☐ Polygon
- ☐ Original Play Station Magazine
- ☐ Entertainment Weekly
- ☐ YRB
- ☐ EGM
- ☐ Newtype USA
- ☐ SciFi
- ☐ Starlog
- ☐ Wired
- ☐ Vice
- ☐ BPM
- ☐ I hate reading
- ☐ Other:

**4. Would you subscribe to digital cable if you could get** ~~a 24 hour/7 day a week~~ **anime channel (like the Anime Network)?**
- ☐ Yes
- ☐ No

**5. Would you like to see the Anime Network in** ~~your area?~~
- ☐ Yes
- ☐ No

**6. Would you pay $6.99/month for the Anime Network?**
- ☐ Yes
- ☐ No

**7. What genre of manga and anime would you like to see from ADV?**
(*Check all that apply*)
- ☐ adventure
- ☐ romance
- ☐ detective
- ☐ fighting
- ☐ horror
- ☐ sci-fi/fantasy
- ☐ sports

**8. How many manga titles have you purchased in the last year?**
- ☐ none
- ☐ 1-4
- ☐ 5-10
- ☐ 11+

**9. Where do you make your manga purchases?** (*Check all that apply*)
- ☐ comic store
- ☐ bookstore
- ☐ newsstand
- ☐ online
- ☐ other: _____
- ☐ department store
- ☐ grocery store
- ☐ video store
- ☐ video game store

**10. What's your favorite anime-related website?**
- ☐ advfilms.com
- ☐ anipike.com
- ☐ rightstuf.com
- ☐ animenewsservice.com
- ☐ animenewsnetwork.com
- ☐ animeondvd.com
- ☐ animenation.com
- ☐ animeonline.net
- ☐ planetanime.com
- ☐ other: _____

*All information provided will be used for internal purposes only. We promise not to sell or otherwise divulge your information.*